LONE STAR AND DOUBLE EAGLE

Civil War Letters of a German-Texas Family

Minetta Altgelt Goyne

LIBRARY OF CONGRESS CATALOGING IN PUBLICATION DATA

Goyne, Minetta Altgelt,   1924-
    Lone star and double eagle.

    Bibliography: p.
    Includes index.
    1. United States—History—Civil War,
1861-1865—Personal narratives—Confederate
side. 2. Coreth family. 3. Texas—History—
Civil War, 1861-1865—Biography. 4. German
Americans—Texans. I. Title.
E605.G667.   973,7'82   82-5491
ISBN 0-912646-68-3   AACR2

Contents

List of Photographs

Acknowledgements

Concerned that the Coreth correspondence from the Civil War period find its way to those most likely to value it, my mother late in life acted on my suggestion that she give to her nephew the letters that constitute the heart of this volume. Some years later my cousin thoughtfully gave them to me, along with other family memorabilia. Thus Franz Ernst Coreth is foremost among those I wish to thank for having enabled me to experience the deciphering, translating, and clarifying of these keepsakes, which I herewith make public.

Others providing personal memories and treasures were older cousins—Rudolph C. Coreth, Hedwig Love, and Esther Riske in particular—and my sister, Jeanette Altgelt. Two cousins of the Austrian line—Dr. Anna Coreth, renowned archivist in Vienna, and Maximilian A. Coreth, now residing in Richmond, Virginia—most generously placed their intimate knowledge of their homeland and of the family's early history at my disposal more than once.

To list here the names of all who gave me useful suggestions along the way would be impossible. Of special assistance were Fred Oheim and Oscar Haas of New Braunfels, both now deceased, and Irene Nuhn, the County Clerk of Comal County, all of whom led me to indispensable source material. Dr. and Mrs. Sam Woolvin, present owners of the Kapp farm at Sisterdale, were most hospitable on several occasions. Paul Freier and R. W. Shook, well acquainted with the Lavaca-Matagorda Bay area, aided me in solving some tantalizing riddles. A good friend, Durel Reid, lent me specialized reference material from his professional library. Also Elizabeth Runge of Galveston cordially eliminated some areas of confusion.

For thirty-five years of enlightened counsel and unfailing encouragement, no less in this undertaking than in all matters of importance, I am indebted to my husband, Prof. A. V. Goyne, Jr.

These and all others who have helped me to persevere I thank most profusely, hoping that *Lone Star and Double Eagle* rewards their patience and kindness.

In loving memory of
two Coreth descendants,
my parents:

Agnes Antonie Coreth Altgelt
(1884-1962)
and
Max Axel Altgelt
(1882-1944)

Preface

"Happy families are all alike," Tolstoy wrote; "every unhappy family is unhappy in its own way." *Lone Star and Double Eagle* concentrates upon a strongly bonded family during a period of separation that is necessarily preserved in much greater detail than their happier moments spent in one another's company. Being based to a large extent on letters that surely were never intended for the eyes of anyone outside the family and an intimate circle of friends, it also gives a more spontaneous view than most journals offer.

These letters, preserved for more than eleven decades, are the record of years during which the Ernst Coreth family began really to enter into the affairs of its new homeland. No wish to magnify the importance of these people, no intent to dramatize their fate motivated the accompanying study, for much of what the Coreths experienced other immigrants experienced also. Not every family, however, included such faithful and articulate correspondents as Ernst and Rudolf Coreth.

Of the Coreth descendants few can now either decipher the various scripts or perceive the linguistic and stylistic contrasts among the correspondents. A dwindling handful can still dredge up childhood recollections of often-repeated stories that illuminate some of the puzzles residing in the more intimate allusions. At last there remains only one with the experience, the library resources, the inclination, and—most essential of all—the time to transform a boxful of crumbling and faded papers into a coherent account.

The combined life spans of Ernst Coreth and his son Rudolf essentially covered the entire nineteenth century. Inextricably woven into the fabric of these two lives are the strands of the receding frontier in Texas and the changing balance of power between Austria and Prussia. Political unrest and economic stagnation on the Continent stimulated the emigration of many Germans to Texas, where their descendants still retain some vestiges of a distinctive culture. For some German immigrants, the rise of Prussia was an inducement to leave America after the fall of the Confederacy and return to Germany to live. The Austrian Coreths cast their lot with Texas.

Rudolf Coreth, the principal correspondent, in many ways exemplified traits we consider as typically Victorian: the energetic approach to life, the concern with home and family, the voracious appetite, the occasional prudishness. It may at first seem irrelevant to point out that his life did in fact almost exactly coincide with the limits of the Victorian Age. When Rudolf was not quite two months old, Victoria, already the monarch, was crowned. The death of the Prince Consort, causing a major shift in the spirit of the reign, occurred just one month after Rudolf's entry into the Confederate army. When Rudolf died, Victoria's son Edward VII, a man almost Rudolf's age, had at last succeeded to the throne of England but was still awaiting coronation.

It has been suggested more than once, however, that the *Verein zum Schutze deutscher Einwanderer in Texas* (Society for the Protection of German Immigrants in Texas), under whose aegis the Coreths and over 7,000 other Germans came to Texas, was organized under the tacit patronage of Queen Victoria's England. No hard evidence to support this contention has yet been found, but it is startling nevertheless to discover that Prince Solms, the first Commissioner General the Society appointed to govern the colony, was not only an intimate of Prince Albert, but also was the stepson of Victoria's uncle, the Duke of Cumberland, fifth son of George III, whom Salic law made ruler of Hanover in Victoria's stead. Furthermore, Prince von Leiningen, Victoria's half-brother, and other members of his family were among the leading lights of the organization and thus in part responsible for the largest German colonization effort affecting Texas. There is ample evidence that Prince Solms's early departure from the colony resulted largely from his recognition that the imminent annexation of the Republic of Texas by the United States spelled the end of a truly German colony in Texas.

Surprisingly little firsthand information is readily available to help us understand the feelings, thoughts, and activities of the immigrants in the Confederacy, especially those in the Trans-Mississippi South. The numerous Union sympathizers and the occasional fire-eating Confederates among the German Texans usually called attention to themselves by their stances. Some died fighting; some, while trying to get out of the country. Some were terrorized while attempting to live peaceably among people with different political views. The "silent majority" were loyal to Texas, whatever misgivings they may have had about its seceding from the Union. The Coreths evidently belonged to this group and are, therefore, to a degree representative, though many individualizing details make their story the more interesting.

Facts and identifications are supplied when necessary or useful. Whenever feasible, German terms and phrases from the letters are included in brackets in order to convey to some readers a bit of the special flavor of the original that translation necessarily dilutes. Contrasts between the kinds of language used by the various correspondents will be obvious to readers who bring to the book some acquaintance with German regional speech, including that which is peculiar to Texas Germans.

No letters written by Rudolf after 1865 have come to light, but on the basis of what we have, he was weak in the mechanics of writing and spelling. The Coreths first came to America when Rudolf was eight, and whatever education he may have had during the following four years must have been erratic since the family returned to Austria when he was ten and did not settle permanently in Texas until he was twelve. His spelling reveals far more Upper German coloration than that of any other Coreth represented by letters except the mother, who wrote and apparently spoke like a rural Tyrolean of limited education. Rudolf wavers between spelling phonetically as his ear dictated and over-correcting when in doubt.

His father, Ernst, a cultivated but evidently not profoundly educated nobleman, used essentially standard New High German interspersed with an occasional term from one of several other languages and, less frequently, from his Austrian dialect. That he also spoke with Upper German coloration is safe to assume, because he occasionally spells a loan word the way he must have pronounced it or thought it ought to look, as does Rudolf. The only other orthographic distinctions in his letters are those now obsolete but then standard.

It is unlikely that Ernst Coreth was his children's only teacher, as family tradition insists. The 1850 census for New Braunfels lists Agnes (the oldest child) as a student living in town at the home of Phillip Meckel, laborer. Ernst Coreth's letter of 17 February 1867 shows that he encouraged his son Franz to study English with several other young men under a tutor in town shortly after the war. Serving as a member of the Board of Examiners of Comal County School Teachers in 1858 along with George Kendall and Alex Rossy (both prominent in the history of the county), Coreth surely would not have insisted upon private tutoring for his children exclusively. The mention of several teachers in later letters suggests that Ernst Coreth did not merely help select the county's teachers, but also received them in his home and became their friend in several instances. That the father used a somewhat different form of script from that employed by his children and his wife, all of whom used the pointed Gothic script, is additional evidence that he was not the children's only teacher.

While Rudolf dated almost all his letters, Ernst Coreth's often bear no date or only an incomplete one. Ernst usually completely filled all lines of his letters both during and immediately after the war, probably to conserve paper since later letters have the complimentary close and salutation on a separate line each and there is logical paragraphing. Rudolf paragraphed only when the subject changed very drastically or when he continued after an interruption. Whereas his father's letters are on essentially uniform paper of reasonably good quality, Rudolf's are on a wide variety of types of stationery ranging from very good to extremely poor and including some pages obviously torn from a ledger. This variety helps in the arrangement of undated letters or those bearing an incomplete date. An additional aid is the abrupt change of spelling from *Aeltern* to *Eltern* in the almost consistent salutation *Liebe Aeltern/Eltern und Geschwister* (Dear parents and siblings).

Although the letters written by Rudolf are too contiguous to allow for an earlier culling process, the same, unfortunately, cannot be said of Ernst Coreth's letters. Some of these Rudolf probably discarded before he began to realize what they would later mean to him. Others must have been lost, either before or after he received them. He, after all, was not at a fixed address and at times was probably at a location unknown even to his company commanders with any degree of certainty. That such a large number of these letters was preserved together for so long is attributable to the circumstance that Ottilie, youngest of the family, moved with her husband Hermann Altgelt to the family home about the time of her mother's death, later inheriting the farm from Rudolf, who had purchased it from his brothers and sisters. Ottilie thus came into possession of and saved essentially all the existing letters written to Rudolf and to the parents.

That translating and editing these letters should have become my project is an almost equally strange happenstance. Ottilie Coreth was my paternal grandmother, and Franz Alcad Coreth, my maternal grandfather. By far the youngest of my parents' children, I had the privilege of growing up bilingual in a German-speaking community, an asset shared by few Texans of my generation, born as we were so shortly after World War I. This circumstance helped to determine my major fields of study at the University of Texas at Austin just before and during World War II, where one of my teachers was Rudolph L. Biesele, a family friend, whose doctoral dissertation is still the definitive work on the Germans of Texas. The Biesele study ends with the beginning of the Civil War.

My master's degree thesis, a set of original short stories about life in a Texas German community between the two world wars, was supervised by Mody C. Boatright, who made me aware of folklore as literature. When, much later after having earned the Ph.D. degree in Germanic Languages, I came into possession of these letters, I recognized that here was the stuff of a story with a symmetry often lacking in consciously constructed works. What was more compelling was the developing sense of having known these people—the family and their friends—as few of us are allowed to become acquainted with those from whom we are separated by two or more generations.

Perhaps the most startling aspect of this intimacy was the degree to which I came to appreciate Agnes Erler Coreth, the mother of the family, whose presence and influence are pervasive and speak eloquently for the noble qualities of this simple, modest woman. Her background and education cannot have prepared her for such drastic adjustments as she was forced to make when her husband, even less suited than she for life on the frontier, succumbed to the lure of the West. Without her steadfast, practical, and constantly busy hands, this might have been a far sadder story.

From Tyrol to Texas

It is 3 October 1846, a few months after the United States has annexed Texas. The *Georg,* with 136 passengers aboard, has landed at Galveston, the principal port of the new state. Captain Moril's ship has been fortunate in escaping severe damage from the season's storms that have wrecked or even sunk some other vessels in the Gulf of Mexico during the month. The exhausting voyage has lasted almost two months, and everyone is eager to set foot on land once more. Many of the passengers are entering the country under the auspices of the Society for the Protection of German Immigrants in Texas. Among them, first on the ship's list, is a family that is not German actually, but has given its residence as Hallein, Austria. The head of the family, Ernst, Count Coreth zu Coredo, is accompanied by his wife Agnes and five young children.[1]

On the docks excited men greet the voyagers, urging them not to continue by way of the route suggested by the Society: westward by schooner to Carlshafen farther down the coast where the Society has set up stop-over facilities for new arrivals, then by wagon to New Braunfels, the main German settlement founded by the Society less than two years earlier. Agents for Henri Castro's rival colony of Alsatians and Swiss that is floundering west of San Antonio, these agitators probably exaggerate, but do not entirely falsify, what the immigrants will encounter if they go by way of Carlshafen. The route inland they describe as marked by the corpses of Germans who have sickened and died along the way. In point of fact, just as the *Georg* was leaving Antwerp, newspapers in Bremen began to publish letters written by the Society's own Carlshafen agent, desperate about the apparent indifference of the Society's officers in Europe to the deteriorating conditions in Texas.

The unusually heavy rains of the season have made the road to New Braunfels even more difficult to travel than usual and, to complicate matters further, the United States army has outbid the settlers for teamsters who ordinarily would transport households and families northward, but instead are taking soldiers and their supplies to the scene of the war that has broken out with Mexico. Some of the newcomers, impatient to reach the land and houses for which they have contracted, have tried to escape the epidemic that is raging in Carlshafen, but those fortunate enough to survive the trip to New Braunfels have introduced the sickness there. To make matters even worse, the illness has been misdiagnosed and consequently improperly treated.

Though hundreds of immigrants have been delayed at points along the coast, all land and houses worth mentioning have already been assigned in New Braunfels, and thus settlers now arriving are being directed to Fredericksburg, an additional eighty miles inland, spreading the illness with them. To be sure, Fredericksburg is much nearer the Fisher-Miller grant, the ultimate objective of the Society's settlers, but it is far from civilization and a frequent target of Indian raiders. As a result, some enterprising Germans are clustering in tiny rural communities on the left bank of the Guadalupe River opposite New Braunfels and Comaltown, its neighbor. Many of these late settlers are highly cultivated people, among them some of the area's most progressive farmers and most politically active citizens.[2] The new arrivals also hear rumors that the Society, or *Mainzer Adelsverein,* as it is generally called, is incapable of filling its obligations to settlers and creditors alike.

None of Ernst Coreth's extensive reading in German accounts of American life can possibly have been an adequate cushion for the shock induced by these revelations. A cultivated man, he makes contact with some of the prominent Germans in Galveston, people with whom he will maintain friendly ties for the rest of his life. Following their advice, he arranges passage for his family on one of the small steamers going regularly up the Buffalo Bayou to Houston. As he looks with wonder at the magnolias along the bayou, his thoughts may well be very troubled.

By the time he reached Houston, Ernst Coreth had surely learned that there were no vacant houses available there and that the best hotel, the former capitol now converted into quarters for the increasing number of immigrants, was scarcely what he would consider suitable.[3] His best hope, perhaps, was to find shelter for his family in one of the houses belonging to Henry F. Fisher, an official with whom immigrants regularly dealt. It was to Fisher and Burchard Miller (both Germans with anglicized names) that the land now designated as the Society's had originally been granted. In any case, there was no time to lose, because Coreth's pregnant wife was rapidly reaching term.

When the family was safely settled in Houston, Ernst Coreth investigated the possibility of investing there. As security on a note, he took three and a half lots of a centrally-located block between the so-called "Long Row" of mercantile establishments and the former capitol. For another $500 he received 12% annual interest and became mortgagee of almost 3,000 acres of fertile land: two tracts of one-third league each, situated on the Cypress Bayou nearly thirty miles to the northwest on an established road.[4] Was Ernst Coreth investing or speculating? Can he have thought of becoming a planter with an outlet for his produce in central Houston? Would settlers or slaves have worked the land, since the oldest of his four sons was not yet ten? These ideas pique one's curiosity but unfortunately lead to nothing concrete.

Of 29 October 1846, however, we do have definite information. On that day the first American Coreth was born, and the next day he was baptized Franz Alcad Traugott Coreth. The priest, James Fitzgerald, was Irish; the sponsor, Belgian.[5] The name Franz was that of many a male ancestor. *Traugott* means "Trust in God," a sentiment that the family must often have felt at this period. The sponsor, one Jean Alcad Rochette, was a stonemason the family had come to respect while they crossed the ocean together.[6]

It would be useful to this story to know for certain why Ernst Coreth emigrated, but one may state with certainty that he was not typical of the 7,380 settlers brought over during 1844, 1845, and 1846 by the Society.[7] At forty-three he was relatively old to be starting a new life in such unfamiliar surroundings. Even among the comparatively few titled emigrants, the rank of count was quite high. Austrians constituted an almost invisible minority, and those claiming to be Tyrolean like Coreth and his wife were still rarer. From the acquisitions and investments he is known to have made during the early months of his residence in Texas, he must be judged to have been fairly affluent.

Of the people coming over on the *Georg* with the Coreths, only one other family and no unmarried passengers appear as the Coreths do on both the 1850 census for New Braunfels and in the records of Ss. Peter and Paul (Catholic) Church there. Most settlers arriving in the German settlements at the time went on to Fredericksburg, especially the Catholics, and the Coreths were historically Catholic. Ernst Coreth's only sister and one of his two half-sisters were abbesses, and among the many clerics in the family one had been Bishop of Trieste in the late sixteenth century.[8]

Although Ernst Coreth was certainly breaking family tradition in some ways by emigrating, he evidently had no intention of totally renouncing his past. Had he not named his new son Franz, as traditional a name as the family could offer? It had been the name of Ernst Coreth's father and also of his maternal grandfather, Francis Dillon, a native of Dublin who had germanized his name to Franz after coming to serve the Empress Maria Theresa, who found the Irish lieutenant colonel so faithful a servant that she awarded him a baronetcy.

Antonia Dillon, Ernst Coreth's mother, later the Countess Coreth twice over, had been born in Hungary. A childless widow when she married Franz Joseph Coreth, Antonia became a mother for the first time 2 December 1803 with the birth of Ernst Ignaz Franz Seraph Camill, Graf (Count) von Coreth zu Coredo, Frei- und Elder Herr zu Starkenberg. On the child's first birthday, Bonaparte crowned himself Emperor Napoleon I of France. On his second birthday, his father, a captain of cavalry and guard, fell victim to a French canister shot at the Battle of Austerlitz, which also effectively signalled the demise of the Holy Roman Empire.[9]

Family tradition has it that Franz Joseph Coreth need not have gone to war against Napoleon because he was already thirty-five years old and the father of two small children. He had served earlier, but the Emperor, it is said, persuaded him to re-enter the army during the crisis. Coreth, a native of Innsbruck and thus a Tyrolean, might perhaps have insisted upon immunity under the terms of the *Landlibell* of 1511, which granted all Tyrolean adult males the right to serve in the army but made them responsible only for the protection of their own province, exempting them from service outside its boundaries. Since, after 1800, the Austrian army was undergoing great changes in organization, gradually moving

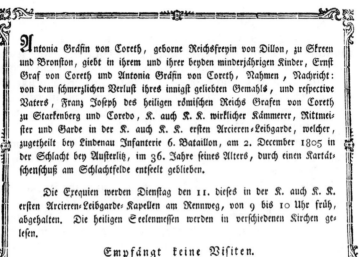

Antonia Gräfin von Coreth, geborne Reichsfreyin von Dillon, zu Skreen und Bronston, giebt in ihrem und ihrer beyden minderjährigen Kinder, Ernst Graf von Coreth und Antonia Gräfin von Coreth, Nahmen, Nachricht: von dem schmerzlichen Verlust ihres innigst geliebten Gemahls, und respective Vaters, Franz Joseph des heiligen römischen Reichs Grafen von Coreth zu Starkenberg und Coredo, K. auch K. K. wirklicher Kämmerer, Rittmeister und Garde in der K. auch K. K. ersten Arcieren-Leibgarde, welcher, zugetheilt bey Lindenau Infanterie 6. Bataillon, am 2. December 1805 in der Schlacht bey Austerlitz, im 36. Jahre seines Alters, durch einen Kartätschenschuß am Schlachtfelde entseelt geblieben.

Die Exequien werden Dienstag den 11. dieses in der K. auch K. K. ersten Arcieren-Leibgardes Kapellen am Rennweg, von 9 bis 10 Uhr früh, abgehalten. Die heiligen Seelenmessen werden in verschiedenen Kirchen gelesen.

Empfängt keine Visiten.

Death notice of Franz Joseph Coreth

from voluntary enlistments toward a system of conscription, Coreth presumably rejoined the army because his sovereign's empire was at a critical point and suitable commanders were in short supply.[10] It was a fatal choice, in any case.

Until the age of two, Franz Joseph Coreth had borne the ancestral title of Freiherr (Baron), but in 1772, his grandfather and great-uncle were made Counts Coreth. Apart from his uncles, little Ernst Coreth was the first Coreth to be born to the higher title. The last quarter century of his life he lived without it, and it applied to none of his sons after they became American citizens.

By birth Ernst Coreth was Viennese, but in later years it was Innsbruck, the ancestral home of his father's family, that was especially dear to his heart. That city would have seemed a possible refuge for Antonia Coreth and her children when the French were about to besiege the Austrian capital in November of 1805. During the siege it would have been difficult to make the trip, if not impossible; after the Treaty of Pressburg that followed upon defeat at Austerlitz, Tyrol and Vorarlberg, the westernmost provinces, were isolated from the remainder of the empire, which was deprived of Salzburg and the Italian territories, too.[11] At Innsbruck lived little Ernst's grandmother, the Countess Leopoldine Coreth, who in her youth had been a lady-in-waiting to Marie Antoinette.[12]

After the death of her eldest son Franz, the Countess Leopoldine Coreth had two sons remaining. Of these, the elder became progenitor of the Italian or Salorno line of the family, the last member of which owns the family castle at Coredo (the original form of the family name now pronounced *kór-ret*) in the South Tyrol, a part of Italy since World War I. Some eighteen months after Austerlitz, the younger of the brothers, Kaspar, almost ten years Antonio Dillon Coreth's junior, married his twice-widowed sister-in-law, thus becoming step-father to his nephew Ernst and niece Antonie. In 1807 Antonia and her husband moved to her estate at Grasnitz (Styria), from which the Austrian line of Counts Coreth takes its name.[13] A month before his seventh birthday Ernst was enrolled in the Theresianum, the elite military academy in Vienna, where he remained for the next nine and a half years. At least part of the time between 1807 and 1810 Ernst and his sister spent in the Grasnitz household. Judging from the prevailing custom, Ernst was probably turned over to tutors about 1812.

Ernst Coreth's background scarcely seems likely to have produced a republican, but the provincial charter of A.D. 1342, it has been said, makes the Tyrolians the first democrats since the ancient Greeks.[14] It is quite likely that, as Leopoldine Coreth's life came to a close in 1808 and her estate was being settled, Tyrol was often the focus of the family's thoughts, even if they were not there. In 1809 this area attracted far wider attention when the Tyrolean patriot Andreas Hofer led the struggle of his people to shed themselves of Bavarian rule and restored Innsbruck to the apparently grateful Austrian emperor. All year long, in a political game punctuated by demonstrations and parades, the city was tossed back and forth between Bavarian, French, and Austrian control. Perhaps often left in the care of family retainers, Ernst Coreth may have been influenced by the fervor of their patriotism, for—though clearly too young to understand the subtleties of their politics—he was at an impressionable age.

The year 1809 also marks the beginning of Klemens Metternich's repressive domination of Austrian affairs, a tenure that was to last for thirty-nine years. Within this era falls the "Biedermeier," a way of life reflective of the spirit of the time: energetic outbursts ending repeatedly in melancholy resignation as the authorities thwarted every attempt to improve conditions. Characteristic of the period was a determined cheerfulness and a retreat from public into family life. So pervasive was this spirit that even within the imperial family itself there was a true Biedermeier man, one who was a model for the many Austrians who admired and loved him. There is reason to think that Ernst Coreth may have been one such, and it is even conceivable he may have had personal contact with "Herr Johann," as the thirteenth child of Leopold II was known.

Leopold's enlightened reign, ending in 1792 just before the French Revolution, had been the last hope for liberal government in Austria under the Hapsburgs. Cast in his father's mold, Johann was much influenced by the ideas of Rousseau and Romanticism. Particularly, he felt a bond with the Swiss and preferred to spend much of his time in close contact with the worshipful burghers and peasantry of Tyrol, living simply and wearing the traditional hunter's gray like ordinary men. At crucial junctures he exerted an influence upon his emperor brother, but in the abortive popular uprising of the Alpine League of April 1813 the Tyroleans and southern Germans gladly followed Johann. When, not long afterward, Johann was suspected of involvement in a plot to assassinate Metternich, the emperor forbade Johann to enter Tyrol for twenty years. Soon after he was permitted to leave Vienna once more, he turned his attention to Styria, where he applied his extensive knowledge and energies to the advancement of technology. For many years Johann lived, chastely it is said, with Anna ("Nani") Plochl, the very religious daughter of a postmaster, until in 1829 he gained imperial permission to marry her and she was made Countess of Merano. Not until shortly before Johann's death in 1859 was his close association with the outlawed Freemasons proved.[15]

Ernst Coreth's youthful actions indicate that he, too, tried to escape some of the bonds of his social class. In an autobiographical account which he gave his children, he told of how he had been sent to military school because that was the decree of the emperor, who had agreed to educate him when persuading Franz Joseph Coreth to re-enter the army. Like many another real and fictive cadet in German stories, he had chafed under the discipline and had run away at the first opportunity. Soon out of resources but unwilling to go back, he enlisted for a two-year stint in the army—the Hungarian army, as one granddaughter recalled having been told—as a private under the assumed name of Ernst Win(c)kler.

As an officer Ernst Coreth saw active army service for ten years and five months and for an additional eleven months held reserve status while awaiting his honorable discharge. On 1 January 1832, he was severed as a First Lieutenant from the First Uhlan Corps of the Imperial-Royal Duke of Sachse-Coburg. Ernst Coreth, thus, was in the service of the family that in 1819 produced the future consort of Queen Victoria. His discharge papers describe him as Catholic, born in Lower Austria, from Vienna, and planning to return to that city. Probably as a result of his untimely departure from the academy years earlier, his age is given erroneously as thirty, whereas all other extant records would make twenty-eight the correct age.[16]

For historians, 1832 is the year in which Napoleon's only legitimate offspring, the Duke of Reichstadt, died and the Archduke Ferdinand Maximilian, future Emperor of Mexico, was born. To literary scholars the growing political awareness among Hapsburg subjects is illustrated by the growing popularity of the satirist Nestroy's works in the Viennese theater at the expense of the gentler Raimund. Beyond Austria's borders, it is thought of as the end of the Romantic period, since both Goethe and Sir Walter Scott died in the course of the year. Far more relevant to the subject at hand are two equally contrasting writers, Austrians who told of personal experiences in North America during the second quarter of the nineteenth century.

Originally from Bohemia, Karl Postl, an ordained priest who had left holy orders, generally used the pen name Charles Sealsfield. The first of his books (published in Stuttgart in 1827) deals with life at the Austrian court as he had witnessed it, but most of his other works concern his adopted land, the United States, and in two instances Texas, which he visited. Sealsfield's stories, like various other German works appearing after 1820, are known to have encouraged emigration to the New World. The writings of the Hungarian nobleman and Austrian poet known as Nikolaus Lenau can only have discouraged those contemplating resettlement in the United States. Actually a Count Niembsch, Lenau remains the archetypal European for whom America does not live up to its reputation as the land of unlimited opportunity. Nikolaus Lenau and Ernst Coreth, essentially of the same age and class and with many experiences in common, could easily have become acquainted in their youth, but, fortunately for Coreth, their later lives diverged more and more. Lenau's visit in America occurred just as Ernst Coreth was becoming a civilian.

Five days after Ernst Coreth's army discharge, his mother was widowed for the third time. This circumstance, probably anticipated, may have occasioned his leaving the service. Particularly if an inheritance was involved, Kaspar Coreth's death must have sharpened Ernst's consciousness of how different were his prospects from those of his younger half-brother Rudolph. Five months after Kaspar died, his son married and within just ten more months became first the father of a daughter, then immediately a widower. How natural that Antonia and Rudolph should have been drawn closer together by common grief and mutual dependency, and how likely that Ernst for these reasons should seek to establish familial ties elsewhere.

Exactly when Ernst Coreth became engaged his descendants do not know, but one great-grandchild recalls hearing that many years later in Texas he relegated to flames a picture of a noblewoman once his fiancée after identifying it for his grown sons. Why the noble marriage did not take place remains a mystery hinted at even in his obituary.[17] Soon after the death of his sister-in-law, Ernst was married at Hallein to Agnes Erler, a nineteen-year-old Tyrolean girl of far simpler family. When Ernst died, they had been together for almost half a century and had watched ten of their children become adults on the frontier.

The first of these children, born 1835, was named Agnes Antonia after her mother and her Irish grandmother, who lived only a few months longer. That year the Austrian crown passed to the intellectually weak Ferdinand, who lacked almost every capability when even a strong ruler would have had difficulty assuaging the impatience of the upper circles for a real voice in public affairs. In the imperial family itself there was disunity about the most pressing problems: agrarian reform, industrial development, labor relations, provincial authority, and peasant liberation. What may have most profoundly disquieted the Coreths was an action that disrupted the lives of former neighbors of Agnes Erler Coreth's family—the banishment to Prussia in 1837 of some 500 Protestants from the Ziller Valley.[18]

The growing family of Ernst Coreth lived first at Schloß Friedberg (Volders near Innsbruck) with Coreth relatives. The second Coreth child and first son, Carl, was born at Schloß Kahlsperg (Oberalm near Hallein) south of Salzburg (16 January 1837), as were Rudolf (7 May 1838), Amalia (22 June 1841), Franziska (10 June 1843), and Johann (19 February 1845)—six children in a period of less than ten years![19]

Two items of public interest shortly before Johann's birth cannot have entirely escaped the attention of so avid a reader as Ernst Coreth. The first was the publication of a treatise, *Austria and Its Future,* composed by Baron Viktor von Andrian-Werburg and various provincial legislators, which attempted to define the problems that confronted the nation. The other was the formation of the Society for the Protection of German Immigrants in Texas, whose membership included men Coreth knew by reputation and in some cases probably personally and which may have seemed to offer a possible solution for a family expanding so rapidly in a land of diminishing hopes. The death of the fifth Coreth child, Franziska (26 November 1844?), may have made emigration the more attractive. Among the family keepsakes is a tattered picture of the family taking leave of the little grave beside the chapel at which the family worshipped. The white and black watercolor and ink painting on brown paper was probably done from memory at a later date, possibly by one of the older children, since Ernst Coreth's known sketches are on much better paper and show a far more mature technique. In any case, on 8 August 1846 Ernst Coreth signed one of the customary emigration contracts of the Society at Antwerp, and a week later he, his wife, who was already in her seventh month of pregnancy, and their five children were under way.[20]

Watercolor and ink drawing of Ernst Coreth family at church near Oberalm in 1846-47

The pre-unification German lands, distinct in many ways, had markedly differing attitudes toward emigration. Some sanctioned it officially as a remedy for over-population and related ills. Others confiscated the emigrant's property or the income derived from it. Elsewhere, to encourage persons to emigrate was deemed the act of a traitor and was punishable by prison terms that might last as long as eight years. Bavaria permitted emigration reluctantly and only after formal applications had been approved by designated officials of the government. Once the employment of Hessians had ceased to interest the British, law-abiding Prussians experienced difficulty in getting permission to emigrate except in a single instance, when some left with the actual aid and encouragement of their government in 1848.[21]

The Austrian government's early policy of preventing emigration to the American colonies had grown even more restrictive after 1783, when Joseph II had become deeply offended that two members of a scientific expedition sent to America to fetch plants and animals for the garden and menagerie of the imperial palace of Schönbrunn preferred to settle permanently in the United States instead of returning home. Well into the nineteenth century, Austria, while not preventing emigration entirely, continued to discourage it, especially from among its better educated and more substantial populace.[22]

From the time of the American Revolution, throughout the Napoleonic period, and until well after the Congress of Vienna, which gave discontented Europeans hope of disposing of their property at acceptable prices again, European emigration to the United States was not substantial. On the average, the scale doubled annually for Germans emigrating to the United States after 1845 until it reached a peak for the pre-unification period in 1854. The *coup d'état* of Louis Napoleon on 2 December 1851 (coincidentally Ernst Coreth's forty-eighth birthday) caused many Europeans to despair of ever enjoying liberty and democracy at home. Over the years some Germans had come to Texas, where by 1845, it is said, they numbered 20,000, well over 13% of the total population.[23] Earlier, most Germans had preferred settling where summers were somewhat cooler and the population denser.

The first attempt to bring large numbers of Germans to Texas that met with any real success was that of the Society for the Protection of German Immigrants in Texas (*Verein zum Schutze deutscher Einwanderer in Texas* or, simply, *Adelsverein*) that first met at Biberich in 1842 and organized formally at Mainz in March of 1844. After its first meeting the group of noblemen sent emissaries to Texas and, these having returned to report, then appointed Prince Carl von Solms-Braunfels the first commissioner general. From its beginnings the venture was plagued with problems of authority, responsibility, and judgement.

The first colonists arrived at Galveston 23 November 1844 only to find that the enormous grant the Society had acquired from Henry F. Fisher and Burchard Miller was not only inaccessible but unsuitable for settlement at the time. The nearest borders of the grant lay 100 miles beyond Austin, the only settlement of consequence. The nature of the land, much of which was not to prove arable, remained a mystery to almost everyone but the hostile Indians who claimed the uncharted area as their hunting grounds. Far exceeding the entire amount for which the organization was capitalized was the huge cost of the mandatory surveying, normally borne by the grantee but in this case the responsibility of the Society. These were only the most obvious drawbacks of the grant lands.

In a series of quick maneuvers, some quite ill-advised, Prince Solms did manage to find a beautiful spot for locating the Society's first real settlement—near the springs called "Las fontanas," about thirty miles north of San Antonio and fronting on the road leading to Nacogdoches. The tract lay on either side of Comal Creek and extended to the Guadalupe River along the northeast, therefore including the entire length of the Comal River and its source. To the north and west lay wooded hills that Prince Solms likened to those of the Black Forest.

The first contingent of immigrants arrived at the confluence of the Comal and the Guadalupe on Good Friday, 21 March 1845; this became the site of New Braunfels. On 28 April, whether because there was no German flag or because Solms was an officer in the service of Austria, the imperial Austrian colors were hoisted at the primitive hilltop fort (the Sophienburg, named for the Prince's fiancée), while at the market place there flew the banner of the moribund Republic of Texas.

Solms departed, ostensibly because he wished to get back to his fiancée, in May. He had waited to make sure that his successor, Baron Otfried Hans von Meusebach, was on the way from New Orleans to New Braunfels, but hardly longer. At the settlement late that month Meusebach found the Society's ledgers so shocking that he immediately rushed to Galveston to intercept the Prince before the latter sailed. For many months to come the new commissioner general was occupied with determining the extent of the problems that the consultation with the Prince had brought to light, reassuring creditors, and hiding his alarm— and sometimes himself—from the settlers. These absences cost Meusebach the confidence of some settlers, who questioned his motives and management, but few can doubt his daring in having undertaken at this critical time a second way station nearer the grant, the town of Fredericksburg, founded on 8 May 1846. New Braunfels became the seat of Comal County, and Fredericksburg, of Gillespie County, both units carved from the Bexar District.

On the last day of 1846, while Meusebach, who had just returned to New Braunfels after a long absence, was entertaining Henry F. Fisher, a mob of colonists threatened the commissioner general with lynching. Meusebach survived the threat and, in part because of his reddish beard and sometimes dramatic ways, became almost legendary among Texas Germans and certain Indians over the years ahead. To the Coreths, who arrived in New Braunfels during December of 1846, shortly before the insurrection, he was to become an intimate.[24]

By what route did the Coreth family get to New Braunfels from Houston? Probably by the usual one that led from San Felipe to Industry, on to Cummins Creek and thence to LaGrange or Bastrop, and from there to their destination. However, there were a few possible variations. Did they go in a train with other settlers, in ox-drawn wagons or, the faster way, in wagons hitched to horses? Oxen were cheaper but slower and needed English commands. Also they tended to wander away when unhitched and often refused to move when bidden. But horses were inclined to get stuck in the ubiquitous mud, and the trip was full enough of hazards and frustrations with its many streams to ferry or ford. We can be sure, after reading contemporary accounts, that the trip took about three weeks. The family got to New Braunfels three days too late for Ernst Coreth's birthday on 2 December, normally an occasion for celebrating, but if just this once it had to be neglected, surely Christmas that year was all the more special.

On 22 January 1847 Ernst Coreth and Henry F. Fisher signed a contract that entitled Coreth to 320 acres of the grant lands, the amount set aside for every married man coming to Texas through arrangements with the Society.[25] This acreage actually represented only half a married man's usual portion. From the beginning, the Society had stipulated its claim to the other half for expenses incurred on the settler's behalf. In 1854 the State of Texas decided that heads of families among the Society's settlers were entitled to the entire 640 acres and single males seventeen years of age or older, to half that amount. Only then did any of them come into their full rights in connection with the Fisher-Miller lands. By then the Society under the several names it used during its history had ceased to function, and Meusebach, daring once more, had long since made a treaty with the Indians (2 March 1847) that led to the westward spread of the white man's civilization in Texas.[26]

For Coreth's activities in 1847 we have some testimony from Viktor Bracht, a New Braunfels merchant and Texas booster. On 20 February 1847 he wrote to a friend:

> I have just learned that Rahn, the butcher, sold for $3000. cash the few acres he bought at New Braunfels at the time of the Prince for thirty-dollars—which seemed an extravagant price at the time—together with improvements valued at $200. Baron von Meusebach sold to Count Coreth of Tirol [sic] a hundred and eighty acres, two miles from town, with improvements (valued about five hundred dollars) for two thousand dollars.[27]

A little later (13 March) he comments, apparently to the same correspondent:

> You are mistaken if you think that there is no luxury here. Women pay more attention to dress and finery in San Antonio than they do in New York, and in the large cities of Europe. We have balls and soirees. A fashionable ball will be given here [New Braunfels] on the twenty-first of this month in the large home of Baron von Wedemeyer, at which Count Coreth and family will attend.[28]

It is possible that the whole Coreth family attended, despite the ages of the children, for in New Braunfels even now very young children do sometimes participate at German dance halls, occasionally with adult partners. But Bracht's report of the Coreth purchase of land was apparently both premature and inaccurate. Probably Coreth took all or some of the land as security for a loan to Meusebach, who surely needed money for his expedition to the Indians, and the family lived on a part of the land (later known as "the old farm") before actually receiving title. Officially the 280-acre tract on Comal Creek belonged to Baron Meusebach (now simply John O. Meusebach) until late 1847, when for $3,266 Coreth bought it with improvements listed in the deed as:

> one large dwelling frame house with galleries one and half storey high, two out houses or cedar log cabins, one well walled up in wood with rope and bucket, two ploughs, one harrow, some other farming utensils, garden seeds, ploughed lands, ditches and fences.[29]

The more recently acquired part of the tract, where the Coreths lived from that point forward, was known as *"die Weiher-farm"* ("the weir farm"; *der Weiher*=the fish pond), because of a large, deep, spring-fed pond that still exists today.

By the late spring of 1848 Coreth had accumulated additional, smaller parcels of land in Texas, including town lots in New Braunfels proper. Any doubt about Coreth's intention to put down roots in Texas should certainly be removed by a testimonial appearing in the German *Galveston Zeitung* of 7 June 1848. Signed by thirty-one men, it urged others to come to New Braunfels. It praised the climate as temperate and healthful; made light of the threat from Indians, saying they had never attacked a German settlement or farm; stated that property and life were no more secure in Germany than here; and described the lands, soil, crops, and cattle as of superior quality and favorable price. It requested that all the editors of Germany publish the information in their newspapers and list the signatories.[30] Among the names was "Ernst Graf Coreth from Tyrol," who by then had transferred the Houston note, possibly for passage money, for he and his family were on their way back to Europe.

Obviously it was not from dissatisfaction that Ernst Coreth left Texas in the late spring of 1848, but probably because the newspapers had brought reports that revolutions had begun in France, Germany, Hungary, Bohemia, and, by 13 March, in Vienna, where students with friends in high places forced Metternich to resign. It has been impossible to confirm or to refute that Coreth went home to participate in the uprisings, or even that he was ever in communication with the revolutionaries. It is known, however, that he intended to be in direct contact with an old comrade-at-arms, Count Colloredo, in Prague, a prominent member of the Society with intimate contacts at the Viennese court.[31] By late November of 1848 the Coreth family was housed at Schloß Aschach, where a daughter Marie was born, almost in the shadow of their former residence outside Innsbruck. Beyond this, essentially nothing is known about the family's stay in Europe between 1848 and 1850.[32]

On Ernst Coreth's forty-fifth birthday (2 December 1848), Franz Joseph, who was to reign over the Austrian (and Austro-Hungarian) Empire until 1916, replaced his abdicating uncle on the throne. The revered Archduke Johann became first the emperor's representative in Vienna, then the chosen administrator of the constitutional assembly at Frankfurt. Almost the only worthwhile result of the convention was the expansion of the trade alliance *(Zollverein)* to include virtually all the German states—except Austria. No one knows whether at any point the Coreths wavered about returning to America. On 13 June 1850 they arrived at Galveston via Hamburg on the bark *Colonist* under the command of a master named Jergensen. On the ship's list the head of the family is simply "Ernst Coreth, merchant from Texas."[33] No longer did the anticipated appearance of Count Coreth at a ball create a stir as it had early in 1847. Henceforth, rightly or wrongly, many of his fellow-settlers looked on him as a "forty-eighter." Actually he found himself in the situation of being neither a "gray" (basically conservative early settler) nor a "green" (liberal, intellectual late arrival) in the parlance of some American Germans. Once more he did not fit any stereotypical mold. But when they reached New Braunfels in 1850, the Coreths could feel that they were really coming home, for friends and a homestead awaited them after their two-year absence.

In the Coreths' home there had lived while they were away a group of intellectual Germans whose hope of founding a communistic settlement on the frontier had failed. One of several ventures attempted as civilization penetrated beyond Fredericksburg in the wake of Meusebach's treaty with the Indians, Bettina (named for the feminist author Bettina Brentano von Arnim) had been abandoned by late summer of 1848. Some of the group known as "the forty" *("die Vierziger")*, because that was the number the experiment was originally to have included, retreated to the part of the Coreth land on Comal Creek thereafter sometimes known as *"die Vierziger-farm"* (possibly identical with *"die alte farm,"* = "the old farm"). Among these young men were several who later became outstanding citizens, such as Gustav Schleicher, later a United States congressman, and Ferdinand Herff, first of a family of San Antonio physicians. Both Schleicher and Herff remained lifelong friends of the Coreths. Also among their number was Hermann Spiess, one of the sponsors of the hapless experiment and Meusebach's successor as commissioner general for the Society. From Mrs. Spiess's memoirs, one learns that the Coreth home was "a commodious dwelling with long piazzas and shady grounds," probably an idealized picture of the site of Dr. Herff's wedding celebration. Mrs. Spiess, a Mexican, had as a young girl been given to Herff by her captor, an Indian chief on whom the doctor had performed successful cataract surgery.[34]

New Braunfels, with a population of 2,000 and permanent houses numbering 300 when the Coreths had first seen it, had in their absence become next in size among Texas towns to Galveston, San Antonio, and

Houston. Along with the town's growth came a singing society, a target shooting club, numerous new industries and shops, a resident priest, and a school, which, though conducted in the Protestant church, was non-denominational. Later a *"Turnverein"* (an athletic club of a typically German sort) and a Catholic church and school followed.[35] Rudolf seems to have been most active of the Coreths in local clubs, having participated both in a singing society and in athletics.

In November 1851 the Coreths' friend Meusebach left for Austin to serve as a state senator. Ernst Coreth, whom the minutes of the commissioners court persist in calling Count Coreth, also entered community affairs in a modest way, serving on a committee appointed to lay out a road giving better access to the Comal Creek lots, including his own. The road seems to have facilitated Meusebach's courtship of seventeen-year-old Agnes Coreth, whom he made his bride in September 1852.[36]

The preceding winter the bride's mother, two years younger than the bridegroom, had given birth to Anna (27 February 1852). She was to bear two more children, Joseph (5 December 1854) and Ottilie (16 April 1858). There thus occurred an instance of overlapping generations as the two Agneses had babies at the Coreth farm where the daughter returned for her confinements. Three Meusebach sons were followed by eight daughters (including two sets of twins), four of whom died as infants and were buried on the farm. To his own children and to the Meusebach boys Ernst Coreth became a teacher, using the books he had brought from Europe. His intention of going into the mercantile business, whether or not it had ever been serious, was not fulfilled.

In 1853 German settlers throughout the United States began to show a desire for a collective voice in the political life of their adopted country. To some degree this was prompted by the antagonism directed toward them by members of other ethnic groups with whom they competed for employment. Also, the Germans as a group had entirely different attitudes toward the issues of practicing temperance, keeping the Sabbath, and working alongside slaves. These differences did not endear them to the predominantly Calvinistic Anglo-Saxon populace, which ultimately found political leverage in the anti-Catholic, anti-foreign Know-Nothing movement, extreme adherents of which wished to require twenty-one years of residence before an alien might acquire citizenship.[37]

It did not take long for political groups to spring up in the Texas German communities: *"Der politische Verein"* ("The Political Society") at New Braunfels, which made a reading room almost constantly available to the public; a similar group at Neuwied nearby, which elected as its president Louis Cachand-Ervendberg, first Protestant minister in New Braunfels and founder of the orphanage there; two groups in Gillespie County (the Fredericksburg area); and, perhaps most important, *"Der freie Verein"* ("The Free Society") at Sisterdale, then in Comal but now in Kendall County. *"Der freie Verein"* is thought to have had ties with similar organizations elsewhere in the nation.

Elected as president of the Sisterdale circle was Dr. Ernst Kapp, who had brought his family from Westphalia late in 1849 after his dismissal from his position as geography teacher for having published a political pamphlet. On his farm Kapp later established a hydrotherapy sanatorium which, along with the presence of the "Latin farmers" there, made Sisterdale the scene of very stimulating interchanges between residents and eminent visitors. The Meusebachs, being Kapp neighbors for a time, were occasionally included, as perhaps were Ernst Coreth and his older sons.

In the *Neu-Braunfelser Zeitung* for 24 March 1854 the Sisterdale group summoned all Texas Germans to meet for political purposes at San Antonio in mid-May during the second statewide German song festival. In response, various communities chose delegates, not for the purpose of organizing a party, they said, but for bridging the linguistic gap that hindered enlightened participation in public affairs. A platform was drawn up favoring popular election of most officials, supporting the Monroe Doctrine, advocating graduated taxes on income and inheritance, and opposing the grand jury system. What attracted widespread attention, however, was the Sisterdale group's public declaration that the practice of slavery was incompatible with democratic principles. There were also vague suggestions about federal aid. Before *"Der freie Verein"* could make clear that it had meant federal compensation should be given to slaveholders in a state that might itself determine to abolish slavery, a year-long controversy in the state's press had caused many a rift between Germans in Texas and had widened the gulf between the "Germans" and the "Americans."[38]

It was not long afterward that there began a gap of thirteen years in entries for the Coreths at the parish where they worshipped. After the baptisms of the two older Meusebach boys and the Coreth children, Anna and Joseph, on the same January day in 1855, there is not a single entry for the family until Ottilie was baptized in 1868 at the age of ten.[39] Except possibly for Johann, for whom hardly any records of any kind exist, only Marie and her mother are known to have maintained ties with the Catholic religion all their lives. In the fall of 1856, having already loosened his connection with his ancestral religion, Ernst Coreth swore to renounce allegiance to all foreign lands and sovereigns, and in 1858 first Carl, then Rudolf, followed suit.[40] The women of the family and Johann were never formally naturalized.

Before the inflamed feelings created by the San Antonio meeting had fully subsided, Ferdinand Lindheimer (editor of the *Neu-Braunfelser Zeitung*) and Ferdinand Flake (editor of the erstwhile *Galveston Zeitung* renamed *Die Union*) engaged in a printed exchange concerning the 1857 gubernatorial election in which Sam Houston was defeated by Hardin R. Runnels, a planter who wished the slave trade reopened, as most Germans certainly did not. What antagonized Lindheimer and many another Texas German was Flake's support of Houston despite the latter's past association with the anti-foreign element. By then the Know-Nothing Party was a dead issue on the national level, but in this state election, the pro-union Germans actually formed a coalition with this party. Predominantly Democratic from the beginning, the Germans became a less predictable faction as time passed.

In its very first issue, the *Neu-Braunfelser Zeitung* had proclaimed itself the official organ of Germans in West Texas, with the aim of making its readers more politically conscious and active, while also publicizing matters of local interest. Lindheimer's editorial policy was essentially aligned with the Democrats, but on the political issues leading to secession New Braunfels was far more inclined to follow his lead than the Hill Country German communities were. When he came out for Breckinridge's candidacy in the presidential election of 1860, citizens of the New Braunfels area voted better than 9 to 1 for Breckinridge versus Bell, casting not a single vote for Lincoln or Douglas. In Fredericksburg, on the other hand, Bell won by nine votes. Neither man opposed slavery, and in many respects Bell was the more conservative, which probably helped him win the nomination of the Moderate Constitutional Union Party, for which he competed against Houston. The principal difference lay in Breckinridge's belief that it was the right of a state to determine its own status on the slavery issue. With the coming of the war, both Bell and Houston withdrew from public life, while Breckinridge became Secretary of War for the Confederacy.

In the February 1861 vote on secession, Texas Germans generally opposed the move, especially those living in Gillespie County where the ratio was 24 to 1. Comal County, however, voted almost 3 to 1 for secession. Most Texas Germans never owned or wished to own a slave and would have preferred remaining in the Union with honor. The biggest German slave-owner in Texas had been the Society itself with twenty-five slaves in 1848. By the spring of 1860 feelings among the Germans in Texas, whom the native majority had so recently viewed as an alien and homogeneous threat, ran so high that neighbor was clashing with neighbor where recently their voices had been raised in contests of song.[41] The freedom, prosperity, and harmony that they had pursued so earnestly in coming to Texas only a few years before were to elude them for years to come. Remembering the ancient *Landlibell* of their ancestral homeland, Tyrol, the Coreths were probably solidly on the side of states' rights and felt they could not be compelled to serve outside the borders of Texas, which had long since become their home.

The "Woolentier"

Legally, every able-bodied male aged eighteen to forty-five who was a citizen of the United States or intended to become one was subject to military service on the basis of an Act of Congress establishing a militia on 8 May 1792. In actual practice, militias became state organizations that held periodic musters. As the nineteenth century progressed, enforced attendance was increasingly relaxed, and the musters more and more frequently and generally became jolly celebrations accompanied by much drinking. Army service was, for all practical purposes, voluntary in the United States until the Civil War; and even after conscription laws were instituted (in the late spring of 1862 in the case of the Confederacy), there was a brief period during which Federal and Confederate authorities permitted an eligible man to pay for a substitute.

Texas seceded from the Union on 1 February 1861. Hostilities had begun on 11 and 12 April 1861 when the Union decided to contest the assault on Fort Sumter. Separated from his family at this time of mounting tensions, the oldest Coreth son, Carl, wrote to the second son, Rudolf, on the day before the latter's twenty-third birthday.

Sisterdale
Monday, 6 May 1861
Rudolf from Carl

The reason I am writing now is your birthday, because I want to send you my heartiest and sincerest good wishes for it, my dear Rudolf. I would be spared a lot of worry if I also knew how the finances are going, whether they are also satisfactory. Father writes you want to present yourself if the militia is called up. I will do it too if necessary. There are people here who say they would not leave, they had not started the thing, etc. I feel duty bound to do it though, and what pleases me greatly is that Hedwig [Kapp] agrees with me. Up to now everything is still quiet here. Alfred rode to Blanco City to the petty jury yesterday. Yesterday Hedwig, I, Frau [Julie Kapp] Wipprecht, Wolf [-gang Kapp], Herr Dammert, and Fräulein Klappenbach went for a ride in the afternoon. We rode from here to Dresels'[1] and from up there into the valley above Ulrich's farm onto a hill. Hedwig got a little headache and so she and I rode home alone. The others still want to ride up another hill. We rode so slowly though that we got home after the others. I don't know what is to become of the addition [to the building] for us.[2] . . . It seems to me that political affairs will in the end delay the project again. Who knows after all what may happen any day. I am working on a shaft for Alfred's rifle now.   Carl

During the summer of 1861 military engagements were relatively favorable to the South, but from 1 September through early October battles raged around Cape Hatteras. On 11 October Confederate prisoners were brought to New York City.[3] In September 1861, after the militia had begun drilling in various communities of Texas, Col. Joseph N. Bates began undertaking the defense of the stretch of Texas coast from Galveston to Velasco for the Confederacy. On 4 October, a New Braunfels company under Capt. Gustav Hoffmann (ultimately Co. B of the Seventh Regiment Texas Cavalry) left for the camp on the Salado River near San Antonio. This group of men later took part in the Sibley campaign in New Mexico, the Battle of Galveston, and battles in Louisiana.[4] For some days following, Galveston was in a state of truce and being evacuated. By mid-month groups of soldiers were passing through New Braunfels on their way to join the Sibley expedition or assist in the defense of the coast.

Rudolf Coreth in dress suit, taken in 1860's

On 27 October, Rudolf evidently left for the army, the same day that a Union ship captured a Confederate brig off Galveston. Though one company was soon organized for defending Sabine Pass and three companies were assembled to protect the area from Matagorda Bay to Corpus Christi, the guns were not in place for Matagorda until December, and there were no effective ones at Aransas Pass.[5]

Traveling with Rudolf was an older and more worldly companion, Adolph Münzenberger, a Comal County rancher who had emigrated from Lübeck near the Baltic Sea. Twice as a young child Rudolf had crossed and recrossed the Atlantic, but since then he had probably traveled very little. His understanding and use of English were imperfect, since what formal education he had came almost exclusively from his father in the home. His previous contacts as an adult with people other than Texas Germans and a few Mexican laborers were surely not numerous or intimate. Reluctant soldier he might be, but still he was not entirely able to hide his eagerness for new experiences or to restrain his delight in being able to report them to his family, particularly his father.

Alleyton ["Arlington"]
30 October 1861
Rudolf to family

We aren't actually in Galveston yet but, since we have to rest for twenty-four hours, I want to use the time to communicate with you all. . . . In Seguin we had to wait that day because the San Antonio stage does not come until Tuesday evening. We roomed at Schuhart's.[6] Tuesday evening the stage coach picked us up there. There were so many passengers from San Antonio in it that we could only find room on the outside, but that is not so bad at all; one can lie down and stretch oneself as one wishes, after all. Wednesday morning we were in Gonzales, at noon in Sweet Home. In Hallettsville the wagon and the driver were changed. We ate supper at a German's by the name of Neuhaus[7] and got here this morning at 3:30. But since the train does not leave until tomorrow morning, we will have to wait until then. The passengers who are with us are mostly U. S. officers who are going on business to Galveston; one of them, a doctor, wants to take us to a captain in Galveston who is recruiting light artillery and is said to be a very good man. We are planning to take a look at everything for a few days first and to listen before we make up our minds.

Galveston
3 November 1861
Rudolf to family

This will probably be the last time that I will write to you as an independent man, because tomorrow we are going to enlist in Capt. Adgar's Light Artillery Company.[8] For now this is the way father wishes it, and so I want to report everything to you in the proper order. As I wrote to you from Alleyton ["Arlington"], we got onto the stage with three officers also going to Galveston who wanted to take us to the company which we have now chosen. From Alleyton there also went with us to Galveston another German company from the Colorado River. They behaved quite crudely all along the way, in a word, like a real bunch of German yokels. Yesterday we went to Flake,[9] to whom I was to bring money from F. Moureau.[10] There we found Colonel Oswald.[11] These two gentlemen took great pains to get us into the Galveston Battalion or, at least, into a German company, for example the one with which we had come. They said we would surely have seen that these were all respectable people, in any case they were the most respectable on the island. When we told them that we were willing to go into the artillery, they told us that artillerymen are being signed up for five years, which is absolutely not true, because they, like all others, are being enlisted for the duration of the war. Then we went to the camp, which is three miles from town, in order to have a look at what life there is like. It is not exactly delightful, but the people look pretty decent even if a bit messy. We talked to a number of them. They are all quite satisfied. They have a big frame house, several tents, and a horse stall which doesn't have a roof yet though. When we had seen all that, we went to the lieutenant who was at the place and told him of our intention. He was quite mannerly and told us what everybody in the camp told us, namely that this is the best company on the island. We promised to come back again this morning in order to talk to the captain ourselves and left with the intention that, if the captain is the way he had been described to us, we will enlist. This morning we went out there again and did find the captain in. He said he was very glad to get respectable men into his company, that he was quite satisfied with his men, that most of them were civilians who had just taken on army duty for the time being, that they were quite decent people, and that only a few were of the old army (these latter being less decent). In particular he praised the Germans in his company. In so far as one can determine a day ahead of time, we now are willing to enter this company. The trip on the train was generally very dull. We rode from 8:30 in the morning until about 11 o'clock at night, at first through prairie in which a great deal of water was standing. Then for a couple of hours the Brazos bottom was beside the track until Richmond, where one comes to the river itself. Up to that point the track goes rather smoothly down to the Brazos, but at the top there is a grade of perhaps thirty degrees. How they get up there again I do not know, but one goes down as fast as the wind. Then we rode through a big sugar plantation. The owner is said to harvest 500 barrels. We stopped there a few minutes, and immediately our German company rushed out of the car and stormed the sugar cane wagon where it was standing next to the track. But when the Negro driving it saw that white men eat sugar cane too, he instantly started to bargain and sold it to those people who did not simply help themselves to it. So in a few minutes the whole wagon was full of it and everybody was chewing. We gave the Negro ten cents, and for that he threw to us through the window as much as he could comfortably carry. It does seem to have much more juice than the Chinese cane, but it isn't sweeter, in my opinion. At Hallettsville[12] one changes cars but it was getting dark too, and I fell asleep. Münzenberger told me when I woke up a few miles before Galveston that the conductor had just asked all the gentlemen to help push the train back so that they could hang on an additional car. The Americans laughed at him, but the Germans let themselves be exploited. The first night we stayed here in the Tremont House[13] and preferred to pay a bit rather than keep running around a long time. It costs $2.50 a day to stay there. Now we are at Beissner's [Washington Hotel] and are paying $1.50 a day. Yesterday afternoon we were at Rump's.[14] He was quite friendly and willing to store our things. He doesn't think that there will be an attack on Galveston; he says it isn't as easy as they think. The ships could only come within 4½ miles of the town at one point, and that point was being held by the coastal batteries. Yesterday we saw a parade of infantry. They seemed to be a rough bunch. Tomorrow there is to be a general parade. We still want to see that as outsiders before we throw ourselves into the fray too. P. S. I won't be needing Johann's rifle here, because weapons are provided. Kindly write me whether I should send the gun itself or the money when I shall have sold it. In addition please send the English engineering book of Münzenberger's by mail. I think it will cost only 5¢. Münzenberger sends his regards.

Galveston
Wednesday, 6 November 1861
Rudolf to family

Today I expect to get the first news from you. You probably think we are soldiers already, but Fate has decreed otherwise. I wrote that we were going to enlist in Capt. Adgeir's [sic] battery, and we went out to camp on Monday after the parade of the cannons. The captain allowed us to be in the barracks a couple of days before we were to enlist. At first we didn't mean to take advantage of that but rather to sign up right away, so the men already took us for comrades of theirs and told us quite frankly that the day before two men had strung up another by the hands and had let him just hang there that way for three hours, and another one was hitched in stocks, and lots more, from which we could see that the people were not treated like civilians but rather like old regular military. Indeed that seems to us to be the case with all the troops on the island. I told Münzenberger that I thought it best to withdraw now while there is still time, and he was of that opinion too. We told the lieutenant who was there and went back to town. We are of the opinion that this is not the place where we can find something to do, and we do not want to expose ourselves to such treatment for an indefinite period of time. Therefore we want to go back to the mainland and see whether there is a place for us in Victoria. If we don't find a better place there, I am giving up the intention of going to war as a volunteer ["Woolentier"]. Our purse has grown quite small, so I am forced to take the money from Kauffmann[15] . . . because there is no opportunity to earn anything here. . . . We want to find out the cheapest way to get to Victoria. I hope you will be satisfied with what I have done; anyway there was nothing else I could do. If it isn't too late already, don't send the book to Münzenberger.

Mouth of the [St.] Bernard [River]
10 November 1861
Rudolf to family

Now we have been away from you for two weeks, and I still don't have a letter from you. . . . We are on the way to Lavaca, but it is possible that we will enlist in a company here on the coast. We hear that the captains here give the people credit with which to buy themselves horses. In order to make sure of that we are going to a camp six miles from here this afternoon and talk to the captain himself. . . . The coast here between the Brazos and Lavaca Bay is guarded by cavalry. There is a station every five miles which patrols constantly. We came across three such stations on the way from the Brazos to here. The soldiers here, in contrast with the troops in Galveston, make a very pleasant impression on me. These seem to be farmers. They don't wear uniforms and they bear their own weapons, whereas those in Galveston are almost all dock workers (mostly Irishmen) and quite a dissolute gang[16] that can be kept in check only by means of great strictness. If we could get stationed here I think we would have found a pretty good situation. Now I want to tell you how we got here. At first I intended to draw the money at Kauffmann's and be as frugal with it as possible, in order to be able to send you back the remainder. Kauffmann had however not yet received the [money] order from up there [New Braunfels], so we tried to figure out how we could leave without the money, because it would have cost us too much to stay in Galveston any longer, and decided we would sell our sixshooters. Münzenberger sold his for twenty dollars. I still kept mine because we thought we would get quite far on the money. Then we bought passage on a schooner that was going to Quintana (that cost four dollars each) and expected to be there the next day (Thursday), but the wind was bad, so we did not get to the Brazos until Saturday, and to do even that we had to do like the Heidelberg apprentice, push the ship forward a long stretch by hand. Also on the ship was a Frenchman who is ferryman over the [St.] Bernard, which flows into the gulf ten miles from the Brazos, and at whose place we are living now. He had quite a lot of baggage and took ours along too on the wagon going here. We walked. If we don't stay here we shall have to walk on to the Caney; then we hope to be able to go on to Lavaca by ship. How we will get from there to Victoria I do not know yet. Here I am playing doctor for a change. The woman here in the house has a fever and can't get rid of it. I gave her two pills of Apis[17] last night; whether it will help her or not I do not know. We will have to decide in two or three hours. We have a very good opportunity to eat oysters here. Fifty paces from the house there is a big oyster bank. I can't seem to make them taste very good though. Rump send greetings to you, Father. He has always spoken of you with great warmth. Besides him we have found only one other person who has treated us with good will, and that was Wagner, the intended of Alice Nohl,[18] but then we did not pay much attention to people.

Monday, 11 November [continued]

We have now enlisted. We went into the camp yesterday afternoon and talked to the captain about whether it was possible to sign up with a company here. He promised to buy us horses and saddles on credit and swore us in right away. I think we have found quite a good situation. The behavior of the men is as good as civilians can expect; the company is made up of farmers who, like ourselves, only want to defend the coast of Texas. . . . I have to go to camp right away, which is five miles from here. . . . The letters you have sent us thus far Wagner will forward to us from Galveston.

Caney Rifles Camp
13 November 1861
Rudolf to family

We are treated as well here as we could possibly wish. The company consists almost entirely of Americans; we are the only Germans here. The other people, officers and enlisted men, are all acquainted with each other. They are almost all planters from Brazoria County, who, it seems to me, only went to war to lead quite a comfortable life. Now they are finding out though that it isn't as easy as they had thought after all, and rules are repugnant to them, of which they make no secret, even though they carry out the orders they are given. The captain, everybody is convinced, is a perfect gentleman. He is very nice and accommodating toward us. He has never been a soldier before and may perhaps require a bit more than is absolutely necessary; for example, somebody has to stand watch every night, and anyone who cannot give the password is forbidden to go into or out of camp. That is leading to all sorts of scenes, up to this point, since we are forbidden to take care of certain matters in the camp but nobody seems to perpetrate or to expect any further clashes beyond that. The supply house is open day and night, and it doesn't occur to anybody that it should be guarded. On the other hand, we aren't getting our full rations up to now. The first few days we lived really miserably. We got only beef, cornmeal, and [sweet] potatoes. In addition there is still a lack of cooking utensils, but there was no dissatisfaction anyway because it was evident the captain is doing what he can to procure everything and hasn't any more than all the rest. We do have to wear uniforms. We have dark gray jackets and pants of the same material and caps of light gray flannel with a black stripe. The officers wear exactly the same clothing and are distinguished only by stripes on their shoulders, the captain three, the first lieutenant two, and the second lieutenant one. We haven't drilled but once and then it was on foot. It went quite well, and with the friendly manner of the officers it just can't be unpleasant for anybody to spend a couple of hours of his time this way. We haven't drilled mounted yet, primarily because we haven't got any horses yet. . . . Letters for us must have arrived in Galveston addressed to Huck and Company in Lavaca.[19] Münzenberger wrote there yesterday and had them sent here.

[Caney Rifles Camp]
[23/24 November 1861]
Rudolf to family

We have found out that we have rather heavy duty. Sometimes we only get one night of rest and then we have to stand watch the next. By day we have to drill 4-5 hours and the rest of the time we sometimes have other work such as fetching wood, making horse troughs, cleaning camp. It does not matter to me, because I still think we have the best company that we could find, and we are always treated decently here, and we know that we are not being betrayed by the officers, and that is all I require.—The heavy duty comes from the fact that our company is only half full. There are 42 of us, of whom there are twelve on duty every day. Then there are several sick and some absent for other reasons. One of our lieutenants is out in the environs recruiting more men. If only he were to get some more, things would be a lot better for us. Last Friday our horses arrived, a light bay and a dappled gray. Münzenberger took the latter and I the bay. It is a rather big but also a very long horse. Münzenberger's horse is an ordinary Spanish pony. The Negroes who brought them said both of them like to throw off their riders. Friday night a dispatch arrived saying that Velasco at the mouth of the Brazos had been fired upon. While we were drilling on Saturday morning we were interrupted by a sail that came into view before the mouth of the Bernard River. It was thought that a landing was being attempted there. That caused great excitement. We were ordered to saddle up, and after we saw that the boat had actually begun to sail up the river, we rode there as fast as possible. But it was a completely harmless schooner flying our flag. Münzenberger was ordered to stay at home and look after the camp. I rode my horse for the first time and had a chance to see that it truly isn't altogether tame. Somebody had lost a powderhorn. I was far in the rear, dismounted, and picked it up. But when I wanted to hurry to catch up with the others, the beast put its head between its legs and tried to throw me off, but it did not succeed. Since then I have tried several times to get him to do that again, but he doesn't seem to feel like it any more. . . . We have got three more men in our mess, two Irishmen and one American. I think we will get along pretty well with them. In case you do not yet know about the incident in Velasco, I think it was last Friday that the schooner *Sam Houston* came there and shot at the battery five times.[20] The battery shot back six times. Neither hit the other. We know that for certain about Velasco, and the *Sam Houston* sailed back and forth in front of our noses all week long.

[same place]
Sunday, 1 December 1861 [error?; cf. following letter]
Rudolf to family

At last I have received news from you after all. The night of 28 November I got the letter from Father that . . . was underway five days. . . . I was interrupted just now by a big noise. The *Sam Houston* is in view and several times smoke was seen coming from its cannon. We thought she had been shooting at the battery on the Bernard. We were given orders to load the rifles and take the horses to the rear. I didn't think it would come to anything, but a lot of people did think so, so the excitement was quite great. Some were glad that there would finally be a fight, and some spoke quite openly of their intention to run like scared rabbits. After the orders had been carried out, those who could find room sat down on a framework around a cistern from where one could see the boat and a long stretch of the bank, from which one could see seven riders coming. When they came closer we recognized them as being the son of our captain and three other boys who are visiting here and had gone for a ride. They said that about two miles from here shots had been fired at them from the ship four times. The shells had struck in front of and behind them. Then two more people came, our sergeant and another man. They said the battery on the Bernard had shot at the boat and one shell might perhaps have struck its mark. They had only seen it strike the water just in front of the ship. I don't think so though, because the boat is still lying there perfectly motionless in front of us about 1½ miles away. We can see the people on board with the naked eye. The man who came with the sergeant said he shot at the sail of the boat in a big trajectory with his rifle, and that right after that a rifle ball had whizzed past his head. Whether all this is true I do not know. I only know that the ship fired; that I saw myself. Then I saw too that a little rowboat was set out, moved a little distance away from the *Sam Houston,* then went back and was taken in again. We thought she had dropped anchor. Just now though, somebody told me that she is leaving again. But I think that I have described the false alarm adequately. The company has grown a bit, I think by six, but now we can regularly get two successive nights of sleep. . . . We have lots of fleas here. They don't let us really get to sleep at night. . . . We have had northers a couple of times but no frost here yet. Behind our tent there are several tomato plants which are still quite green. Our fare has improved. Daily we get a pound of molasses and ½ pound of sugar for six men. One can eat the cornmeal pretty well that way. We do get a bit of very nice wheat flour too, actually, but not enough. . . . Münzenberger's horse was appraised at $50, mine at $90. That is very high, but we won't be charged that way though. I can get mine for $70, which is actually still expensive, but I mean to take it anyway. I thank Father kindly for the money order to Kauffmann; for the moment I don't need anything. We do mean to write to Galveston to see whether Münzenberger's sixshooter is still available.

Monday, 2 December 1861 [continued]

We are going to write to Wagner about the letters. . . . If he has [sent them to Lavaca], they must be at Huck's. We have written to the latter once already. . . . Yesterday evening the wagon with flour arrived here and now we'll get more of that too.

[same place]
Sunday, 7 December 1861
Rudolf to family

Last Wednesday a man from the company on the Bernard came here in the utmost haste and said a much bigger ship was coming, one that probably intended to avenge the *Sam Houston.* We could see it quite well from here by then. It was a frigate. It approached rather fast. We saw that it was going past the Bernard without shooting; then it passed by us at a distance of about two miles. One could see the people with the naked eye—but it did not do anything to us either. At about seven o'clock in the evening a man from the station on the Caney about seven miles from here came with the information that the ship had shot at the shore and then had set a boat in the water in order to land the crew. That called forth a great excitement in our camp which was significantly heightened by a storm with rain that set in at the same time and tore down several tents. . . . The rain came so fast that the dry tents didn't keep it off anyway. There was a lot of noise; some men were cursing that their things would get wet and others were expressing fear on the one hand and anger on the other. There was a call for volunteers to be the first to approach the enemy. Münzenberger was one of those that offered themselves; I could not, because . . . I was on guard duty. Our guard unit was doubled and urged to be particularly alert. Our volunteers rode to the mouth of the Caney, where the ship was lying. When they got there they saw a big fire on the shore. The lieutenant explained that they must have already landed and have taken as their prisoners two of our men who were scouting. Münzenberger laughed at that and said he thought the Yankees were too clever to make a big fire when they landed at night. When they approached the fire with great caution, they discovered to their great astonishment not enemies but the watch post, where two of our people were sitting and drying themselves. The next morning the boat went on without having tried to land anybody. We think it came landward just to measure the distance. Some of us believe that it was shooting at the beef cattle there. I do not know why they might have done that. The next morning our people came back. They were wet through and through, because they had to stand watch all night too. That the ship put out a boat is said not to be true. The messenger probably said it in order to give his message more importance. Our company has grown a bit again. We got these people in our mess. They are two Americans, very quiet people. We are now eight men in our tent, but we have plenty of room. Our captain is doing what he can to give our people as comfortable a life as possible. Now he has had boards sent here out of which we can make bedsteads. He would like to provide for the needs of his men in quite a paternal way, but he does not succeed in making everyone content. . . . We now get quite a lot of provisions. For us eight we get 4½ lbs. of flour and 1/2 lb. sugar, a bit more than a pound of molasses, as much beef as we want, and [sweet] potatoes, as many as we want, whenever there are any. Otherwise we get split peas. We do not get enough bacon, and what we do get of it is bad, but we will get good bacon soon. We don't get coffee, but on the other hand we get as much tea as we need. Quinine is a special ration, but there is a great deal. Huge quantities of it are consumed. We have three doctors here, who are very generous with the ordinary medicines: calomel ["*Calomehr*"], Blue Mass, oil of cinnamon, and Spanish flies.[21] Then too, the first lieutenant plays at curing. The main thing consumed though is quinine. Every few days one of the physicians, the lieutenant, or the orderly sergeant goes around in camp with a big bottle of it and calls into every tent, asking if anybody wants some. Anyone who gets a fever always gets red pepper with quinine, and in addition a great big dose of calomel in order to clean out the bowels. But then they give quinine incessantly until the man is rid of the fever. If then he has a very swollen liver, he gets a poultice on it. The general conviction is that these are the best physicians of the area. It is much quieter in camp here now than at the beginning. At first one kept hearing noise. Some sang, others crowed like cocks, which they really could imitate very well; in short each made noise as best he could. Now all that is left of that is card playing, and dance music that a Negro makes evenings. Almost every evening the music making goes on in the Negro house. There are seven or eight Negroes that belong partly to officers and partly to the owners of the house and cook salt here. When I hear that there is a lot of stomping, I go there too to watch. . . . The two oldest of the Negroes are the main dancers. The one looks by day as though he could scarcely walk any more, but once he starts to dance he can shake his feet so fast that one can hardly see them. Then sometimes two Americans who want to be admired too step up to perform but they cannot equal the Negroes in limberness. Some time ago we saw a remarkable sight. I believe it was something like a *Fata Morgana* [sic]. Behind our camp there is a lake and a few miles behind it one sees the bottom of the Caney. One morning it shone there as though the land beyond the lake had risen up, so that the bottom looked like a forest on a mountain range. On both sides of the camp one could not see where the water and the land come together. One saw there only a completely strange area with much water, and on the land between one saw lots of cattle. That lasted a couple of hours and then it gradually disappeared. Political news you surely get faster from the *Neu-Braunfelser Zeitung* than through me. Here some expect an attack on Galveston. Today Münzenberger received a letter from Wagner from Galveston that stated the sixshooter is no longer to be had, that the man who bought it has had it improved and that he wants us to make that up to him now. It is a completely unacceptable demand. We have quite a good reputation here, though we are the only Germans in the company. We don't pay much attention to the people, and they let us alone too. A couple of times we have done elementary acrobatic stunts and have caused them to believe we are the strongest people in the company. Then yesterday or the day before some emptied their rifles and shot very poorly. I had to empty the sixshooter too and three times shot the best shots. That put them in a state of great amazement. I believe that this can only be to our advantage, because they will always guard against starting any trouble with us. I thank Carl heartily for his letter. I hope and wish for him that he won't be interrupted now that he has gotten well underway [with building his house].

[same place]
Thursday, 11 December 1861
Rudolf to father

Unfortunately now when it is too late I realize that I forgot your birthday. I therefore have to ask your forgiveness and ask you to accept kindly my good wishes just the same. Monday or Tuesday a man came through here from Velasco. He was on his way to Indianola. He said that a steamer, of which he was a crew member, intended to run the *Sam Houston* aground. I think it was his mission to inform the battery not to shoot at the ship if it comes by. I am really sorry that I have to write for money now, but it is now the general view that we are going to be transferred, and that we might need money then; therefore we want to have $10 sent us from Galveston and then Münzenberger wishes to pay Wagner the dollar in order to have peace in that matter. . . . We won't need more, so you take the rest of the money back from Moureau.

Camp Winston [evidently the same place as before, now named]
18 December 1861
Rudolf to family

In the direction of Indianola some have heard cannon shots. . . . Somebody who came through here said a blockade ship had shot at the settlements on the Matagorda Peninsula and that the people were busy pulling out of there. This morning some say they heard shots in our camp. . . . Sometimes the surf makes a similar sound; it could have been that too. Last week our colonel was here. He said he would arrange for a parade in Velasco for Christmas and give his regiment a party on that occasion. If I can, I intend to stay away from that. . . . In a letter or package send me a bit of insect powder. We have noticed that some of our comrades have lice . . . and we would like to be prepared.

Camp Winston
21 December 1861
Rudolf to family

In Galveston, they say, an attack is expected. If that were to happen we would probably be pulled over there . . . otherwise we will probably stay here all year without smelling powder. Some people say almost every day that they hear cannon shots. . . . I think it is mostly thunder or the waves. The postal rider brought us an issue of the *Galveston Union* last week. I read in it that our [home] area is suffering from drought again. Here we haven't had any significant rain either. . . . I would have had an opportunity to come to you now, but unfortunately could not make use of it. The proposal was made to us, you see, that we go up to recruit people. It cost me a hard struggle until I could make up my mind to turn it down, but I am determined now not to accept it. Do please write me whether you agree with me on that. Many are going on leave now to have Christmas at home. I have promised the captain, who was here just now in order to talk the matter over with me, to write to you all to say that you might possibly send people here, and I can do that with a clear conscience. If you know of anyone who wants to go to war, be so good as to tell him the address. Tell him that we are satisfied, and that we are supposed to get between twenty and twenty-six dollars. In exchange we have to supply horse and weapons. The reason for all these efforts to get people is that the company is not full. If in two months it is not full, it will be divided and used to fill up other companies. That would be unpleasant for us all, because we could not get any better officers and furthermore most of the decent people are together here. Yesterday and today we had quite an unpleasant sight. An escaping Negro who had stabbed his overseer was brought in here. He belongs to a planter named Hardeman, who is in our company.[22] The report that that had happened had already reached here some days ago. Hardeman went home immediately to check into the matter. During the time another man from our company caught the Negro on the way between here and Hardeman's farm and brought him here yesterday. Then the Negro was bound and taken to a hearing. He said that the overseer had told him to do something, but that he had not done it. For that the man had wanted to strike him. He had gotten enraged about it and had stabbed him. He still had the knife with him. It turned out that it belonged to the man who had caught him. He stole it and gave it to him [?]. He went on to say that *that* Negro had taken other things from camp too and brought them along, things that have been missed here. Münzenberger had a pair of shoes stolen too. The Negro was tied up very tight and brought to his master this morning. He will be hanged. The overseer will evidently die too. He is said to have been badly wounded. Our captain could not cash the check to Klaener[23] in Velasco and therefore sent it to Galveston. . . . If in the course of the year you have a reliable opportunity to send my watch to me, it would be very pleasant to have it while standing guard. . . . Secondly, I would like you to send me something for lice. . . . One can get nothing of that sort here, and even if I did have a comb, I would not like to stand out in the yard and comb my hair with it.

Camp Winston
25 December 1861
Rudolf to family

Yesterday evening at 9 o'clock I got Father's letter of 6 December. The postmark was from 8 December, so it was underway sixteen days. . . . Münzenberger had the first and I the second watch. I knew that the postal rider had to come through and hoped again to get a letter at last. I think I was one of the most alert sentinels in the army. I let all of you pass by before me in review until 9 o'clock, when I accompanied you to bed, and then, sure enough, the postal rider came and brought me the letter. The corporal was nice enough to give me time to sit by the fire and read before my two hours were up. Even though I did not get entirely good news from you, it made me very happy anyway, because by and by I had worked myself up into a state of anxiety, and so definite news was very welcome. . . . I have got the money [from Galveston] now and I thank you very much for it (if only you won't be missing it too very much). Today there is a lot of noise here in camp. We went out and got whiskey for the party, you see. It came last night and the whole company with only a few exceptions was drunk even before breakfast and played Canaille. However, everything is going rather peacefully and then too, there isn't any more liquor. I couldn't get around drinking a bit too, and I think that is why my penmanship is even unsteadier than usual, but in a half hour the postal rider is coming through again and so I do want to take advantage of the opportunity. . . . Every moment or two somebody comes and throws himself on me and assures me of his friendship, putting the inkwell into great jeopardy. Belated best wishes to [brother] Josef on his seventh birthday. When I come up again I will bring along some red shells for him. Farewell now to you all. I wish you all really cheery holidays. Postscript to Father: Do be so kind and send me a list of the family birthdays between now and 10 November 1862. When I was at home, enough others always knew the dates and now I would like very much to know, because on those days I could have a clear conception of what you are doing.

Camp Windston [sic]
31 December 1861
Rudolf to family

The *Sam Houston* went by once but pretty far away from here. We had holidays last week, from Christmas Day until the day before yesterday. But everything went along rather quietly after the first day, and I have to admit to you that I have already said too much about that one. . . . I thought that practically everyone in the yard was drunk. . . . When we checked up later, we discovered quite a few others had stayed sober. Some people came from the camp next to ours to race their horses against ours. . . . They only won $10 though. They would have won $25 more if the man they had bet against had not been so clever as to bribe the judge. He told us that himself with a very sly expression. We seem in general to enjoy the confidence of these people anyway, because we don't take part in the business. So, for instance, another comrade sat down next to me and marked his cards with a knife. . . . He says those who play only for the fun of it can afford to do so, he supposes, but it isn't appropriate for a professional card player. But that seems to be the general view, because everybody plays with him anyway, and does whatever possible to cheat others. If one catches another doing it, he simply rakes in the winnings but they play on without any disturbance. Yesterday they discovered marks on a deck of cards, but that didn't shock them. They scratched out the marks and probably put their own in their place at the same time and went on playing. . . .

1 January 1862 [continued]

Happy New Year, all of you together, my dear ones. At this distance it is very easy for me to wish you a happy New Year before you can wish me one. I hope it will be harder to do the next time. Last night I got a letter from Father. It is from 13 December. . . . I can't, unfortunately, be really cheered by it, because I see that Father is still not well. . . . Here everything is quite still. Nobody seems to care about the festival day. All that happened was the captain was asked not to drill us, which he agreed to. I thank Father for the offer of having political news sent to me. I will be greatly pleased if I get news from up there [New Braunfels and the Hill Country] because those items are what I value most, and I would not get them otherwise. We get the *Galveston Union* from the postal rider, a German, but there isn't much news of our area. Father writes that one might expect important developments. I wish it would be so. . . . However, I have accepted my fate of staying here an entire year. . . . Our cuisine is quite simple. We get flour, cornmeal, peas, beef, molasses, and sugar. We ought to be getting tea and bacon in addition, but that is not available now and . . . without fat one cannot do much. We bake bread for ourselves, cook the peas with the meat after it has been drained, and that is all. When we have fat . . . we make pancakes, take the peas after they have been cooked, and bake them with fat like bread in a bread pan and fry the meat a second time after it has been cooked. Until lately we had [sweet] potatoes too, but they are all gone now. I hope we will get new ones. They are fried, boiled, or added to food in other ways. We usually get so many vegetables that one would not have to eat meat if one did not want to. That is what I usually do. My main nourishment is bread and molasses, and I think it is making me fatter. Up to now our laundry has been washed by an old Negro for 75¢ a dozen. But he has been taken away now. He handled the laundry very roughly. . . . Now a Negro boy has offered us his services. First we will see how well he does. We really don't have time enough to do our own washing. . . . In the last issue of the *Galveston Union* there is an article about Nicaragua that appealed very much to us and which I am enclosing here.[24] That might be the place meant for us in the South someday, when the war is over.

The war had scarcely begun, but Rudolf Coreth's longing for distant places rarely left him entirely during the remainder of his life. The wanderlust he felt did not, however, match very well the travels in his immediate—or even his distant—future.

Ebb and Flow

New Braunfels
2 January 1862
Rudolf from father
addressed to Mr. R. Coreth/Caney Rifles/E. S. Rugeley Capt.
P. O. Kenner, Matagorda County, Texas

Dear Rudolf,

. . .We are all well again now; the others were so without interruption.
I am completely straightened out, and Carl, who had a spot of erysipelas
. . . , is completely well now too. There is nothing new of significance in
civilian life, but there's all the more to make up for it in politics, which
you probably know already, namely the demand that England release
the captured emissaries or be ready for war.[1] Here nobody doubts that
the latter will be the case. The result will be a violation of the blockade,
and therewith the importing of weapons and munitions and then probably general peace. Lincoln's mission, which obviously advocates aboli-
tion, may help a lot in transforming the mood in the North to the
advantage of the South. Now back to the report from the home front.
When Carl was able to move about again, he set about the job of strength-
ening the plow with steel and repairing it. The thing worked very badly
though. The old soldered parts came apart and nothing was of any use
anymore. We started to buy a new plow and Carl chose a very nice and
evidently good one from among Runge's stock in New Braunfels at a
price of $16.[2] They are just now in the act of hitching it up and at the
end of this letter you shall hear how it turned out. Carl just brought
news from New Braunfels that Theodor Butz, the son of the New Braunfels watchmaker, who was in a company, deserted, was caught again, and
is to appear before the court martial.[3] Also the Elsner child is said to
have died. We spent New Year's Eve and Day very cozily in the family.
Only Johann and Franz had company from Galveston. Agnes expects
her confinement any day and told Meusebach he should not come down
until it is all over, so he didn't come down here. Meusebach is all enthusiastic again about distilling mescal and wants our apparatus. I told
him I did not want to stand in the way of his happiness and success, but
I did wish he would observe the Mexicans conducting an experiment
first. My view is that distilling fruit on a small scale as is done in Tyrol
might lead to one's making quite a nice little profit, but to start an
operation on a factorylike scale with strange people, with the water
shortage, and what water there is having to be hauled in equipment
belonging to a thousand and one people can only result in a loss. . . . I
agree that under the given circumstances you cannot come here (as much
as we would have been pleased to see you). You would not have found
any volunteers here. Whoever wanted to go has gone already and the

others expect to be drafted into the militia any day. Your watch I shall hardly be able to send you quickly. How would I be able to find a secure chance anyway? I am glad that you have the money. I think you can get more if you need it, in exchange for a check of yours, as I wrote you before. I cannot send you more louse powder at any one time, but I will put a little in every letter until you say you have plenty. If you should not receive it, then maybe you can get a few drops of anise oil in a drug store in Lavaca. Your mother and brothers and sisters send you heartfelt regards. The old dear cries for joy every time a letter from you arrives, and we were just as sorry that one was missing from our midst as we were happy not to have too many outsiders bothering us on New Year's Day. . . . For today farewell for eight days, if I have life and health. Your loyal friend and father E. Coreth.[4] P. S. The most cordial regards to Münzenberger. Do you know that I am writing with the pen Carl made out of paktong?[5] It writes very well and does not scratch like steel pens.

Rudolf from Carl [continued]

Dear Rudolf,

There is a little room left for me here to send friendly greetings to you and Münzenberger. Father just gave me the assignment that I should tell you how well satisfied we are with the new plow. It works very well, is 13" wide, fully polished, and very light for its size. If only it can take the stumps. The stones, I fear, will make it very dull before the piece of land in front of the house is ready. It is now being worked on. Then the plot of durra is to be plowed and then the wheatland.[6] Johann and Franz are quite industrious. They have plowed and harrowed the land between the house and the pond. But the wheat and the rye have not come up yet, since hardly any rain has fallen. The year appears to be developing into a rather dry one. That would be bad. There is, of course, still time enough and we can hope that the weather will make up for what it has failed to do so far. I am entirely well again. Things turned out pretty well. It could have, under some circumstances, ended badly. Tomorrow we (Johann, Franz, and I) want to ride into the hills in order to brand the calves that run free. Whether we will finish that I cannot say, naturally. If so, I am thinking of riding to my land on Saturday or Sunday and getting the house finished as well as possible, or at least continuing with the building. I have to nail on the rafters and then cover. I have used the rafters from the other house.[7] They are cut. I hope that the roof will be a good one. I think I have enough shingles. So farewell. Keep well. I hope the oysters with vinegar and pepper taste good. Keep writing regularly. Regards to Münzenberger. And cherish your loving brother Carl. All of the striking out of words came about because Father is reading aloud and I keep being interrupted.

Camp Winston
4 January 1862
Rudolf to family

We are well and we are contented, in so far as one can be under the circumstances. One could, of course, imagine a pleasanter existence. Our company is said to be the best one here on the coast; we are very well taken care of; we have good clothing, double tents, bedsteads, and always a clean yard; and I think that we have the last-mentioned item to thank for the fact that none of us is in the hospital, while seventy men from other companies are there. Cleaning the camp is sometimes a bother, to be sure. I see the need for it quite well though. Individuals don't take any pains to keep things clean. They throw meat and all sorts of things down wherever they happen to be, and after a while that would really begin to stink. . . . During the week we drill industriously (4-6 hours a day) for a big parade that is to take place soon and at which we are to show what we can do. They say we are the best-drilled company in the regiment already, but we are to learn even more. Actually, we need to do that, because mix-ups still occur often enough, and if we are the best, the others must be very poor. I thank Father very much for offering to let me draw more money from Galveston, but I really can get everything we need from the commissary on credit, and then we won't get anything but Confederate bills anyway, which are hard to change. Father wants to know how the temperance law is observed here. With the exception of the one Christmas holiday, it is kept to very strongly because there is no whiskey to be had here, and in Brazoria a gallon costs $3. Under those circumstances it probably has to be observed and that is just fine with me. Also you all want to have a picture of our captain. We both have tried hard to draw a good one, but we did not succeed. So I will do my best to describe him to you. He is about my size, has blond hair, a wavy beard, and blue eyes. He is, I think, about forty years old. If we manage to finish a picture before the postal rider comes through, I will enclose it. Just now Münzenberger arrived. He drew a picture of the camp. He gave it to me to send to you all. It is from the vantage point of the coast. If one stands behind the camp and looks toward the Gulf, our tent is the last one on the right. The guard tent is on the other side of the camp but that is not on the picture.

Sunday, the fifth [continued]

This morning we had a parade. But there is a bit of time left before the postal rider comes. Münzenberger is trying to sketch the captain. I have given up trying to capture a good image. . . . Postscript to Father: The business of the lice gave us such a bad scare that, for lack of another remedy, we used mercury salve. Now we are free of them. Do be so kind and write if that can be harmful and what to do about it instead, if it is. We smeared a bit about half the size of a pea on a comb and combed our hair with it. That way nothing could get to our skin.

Camp Windston [sic]
10 January 1862
Rudolf to family

The day before yesterday, 8 January, I got the letter from Father and Carl, dated 28 December 1861. Unfortunately it brought me news that is not entirely good again. . . . We don't have a single person sick at this time, whereas all other companies have lots. Of course some people are always dissatisfied anyway and take issue with everything they possibly can. They can probably never be satisfied anyway. Last week, and until yesterday, we lived a bit meagerly. There is no more tea to be had; the meat we salted down spoiled, so that it could not be eaten; there aren't any [sweet] potatoes either; and we got so little bacon that I think there will be about an ounce per man daily. So all we had was flour, beans, sugar, and molasses. Instead of tea we use sassafras wood that we find here by the sea. It isn't very good, of course, but it is possible to drink it and we drink it three times a day. At noon we had beans and mornings and evenings bread, molasses, and sassafras tea. Things might have been better. But otherwise we can be so satisfied with our situation that one puts up with that. Even though we may have been betrayed, we are absolutely certain that it isn't our officers who are cheating us. Yesterday afternoon we got fresh meat again; we rendered quite a lot of lard from it and so we have enough fat again for cooking for some weeks. The company is to be filled up now too. A man who recruited thirty men is being assigned to this company under the condition that our first lieutenant will resign to make room for him, and that is the way it's going to be too. We all like that very much because firstly, guard duty will get much easier for us and then, the lieutenant who is leaving is the very one who is least liked of our officers. The people are to arrive on 1 February. . . . The day before yesterday we were invited to a regimental ball in Velasco and almost everyone who could went there, but we did not, although we were much urged by several here. . . . The people who went to the party were given notice that absolutely no hard liquor ["Schnaps"] was to be drunk there, and the colonel had put up a notice in Velasco according to which nobody was allowed to sell spirits, but it happened anyway, only people were careful not to get too very drunk. Also the fun was too expensive, because a quart of liquor costs $1.50. Yesterday evening our people came back and some, who had lots of acquaintances, had a good time, but some did not especially, which probably would have been the case with us. . . . In the *Galveston Union* there is an article about Nicaragua again. I want to send it along to you again, because I think it will interest you. At least it will give us something to chat about. . . . Here everyone wishes very much for [support from] England. If that were to happen we would probably not have to stay here for our entire year, which would be very nice for me too, because here we surely aren't going to have anything to do anyway.

Camp Windston [sic]
10 January 1862
Rudolf to Carl

My dear brother Carl!

Your letter of 28 December did not make me very happy as letters from you do otherwise, because it brought me news of your illness. I hope by now all is well again. I can well see how unpleasant it was for you, aside from the pain, because I know how important it is to you to finish your farm. You must have been very busy while we have been away. I can't really imagine how it looks. When you write me again, do write whether the spring water has held up till now. If it does, you will really have a very nice estate, and if it doesn't surely it is not possible that you will be cut off from the water of the Blanco or the Cypress, which are not far away. But I think the spring will last. If the militia is called up now, as is being discussed everywhere, you would probably be able to stay up there on the Indian frontier, and so you wouldn't be so far from home that you could not get to your family often, and so you will find it bearable, after all. While I am quite contented here, it would be worth a great deal to me if, like the others here, I could get to my family sometimes. It is truly unpleasant that it takes twenty days just to get news from home. But now I have entirely forgotten that I wanted to send best wishes for your birthday. That, I think, should have been at the beginning of the letter. But I mean it just as sincerely here, and I wish for you what I think is worth most to you, namely that your farm may be completed quite soon. I think very happily back to the time that we lived together on the Blanco and I am reminded of it quite often, probably because we live a similar life here, but in the culinary arts we don't accomplish as much here as there.[8] Here there are six people with us in a mess unit, all of whom are a matter of total indifference to us, for whom, consequently, one doesn't care to go to any trouble. One uses the time as well as one can for oneself and takes care of the cooking in the simplest way possible. I have written all of you about our circumstances as clearly as possible, and there is nothing left for me to write. I would have answered your first letter already, but so little has happened here up to now, and I kept hoping for more important developments, but they kept me waiting in vain. Now, though, your birthday will be in six days, and I do want to send you my greetings for it. For now, farewell, my dear brother, and don't get sick again, at least not until we get together again, and write me soon again, if you have time. You know, after all, how much that means when one can have the pleasure so seldom. Rudolf. My friendly greetings to our acquaintances, especially the Kämmerlings.[9]

Camp Winston
Wednesday, 15 January 1862
Rudolf to family

. . . The news that the two Confederate emissaries were turned over to
England had a very depressing effect on us all here because here there
were high hopes that England would step in. Thus the matter, which
had begun to brighten up a bit, has become just as dark as before. The
general opinion is that we won't be kept here for the summer, but what
is to happen to us is a matter of opinion. Some think we will be sent to
the Rio Grande, others think we will be sent to the Indian frontier, and
still others think we will be dismissed for a few months not to be reas-
sembled again till the fall, but nobody knows anything for certain of
course. We are having very unpleasant weather now. . . . Our captain
gave those on guard duty a raincoat and the lieutenant gave us a pair
of fur gloves, so it was quite tolerable. . . . There hasn't been a freeze
yet, but it has snowed a bit sometimes. . . . Mother is probably baking
cake for Carl's birthday today and the others are probably sitting around
the stove discussing politics, maybe talking about Nicaragua too. I am
quite curious to hear what you think about it.

Camp Windston [sic]
19 January 1862
Rudolf to family

. . . Haven't you had any rain yet? Here it rained quite hard and the
numerous puddles around us gave promise of lots of mosquitoes, if we
were to stay here for the summer, but that is not likely. The company
will probably be broken up because it is not possible to fill it. A couple
of weeks ago they said that a man would bring thirty men . . . but now
still more troops are being recruited in the environs and so he will probably recruit a company of his own. There is a law which states that, if
a company is not full within three months, it is to be dissolved again. I
don't think anybody may be sworn in during that period. I think our
colonel made a mess of things. He swore the company in before it was
full and gave no accounting to headquarters after repeatedly having been
ordered to do so. Now, though, people are coming to him most urgently
and he wants to stick us into one company or several before he makes
his report. . . . We want to do whatever we can to prevent the company
from being divided. For that purpose we want to send a petition ["Pe-
dition"] to General Hébert.[10] What will come of it nobody knows though.
I really don't care much. Any change will be welcome. Yesterday Velasco
was bombarded. Two ships, I hear, shot thirty shells but caused no
damage. The battery answered the fire, I think without hitting them
though. There are only three or four steel pens in camp and we own one
of them. Everybody who wants to write borrows it, and all it takes to
spread it to pieces is that they write their names with it. We were having
some sent from Velasco, but could not get any. . . . We did not drill much

last week; partly the norther was to blame and then too, it seems to me, it is not being pursued with the same enthusiasm anymore. The last times we learned to load shells in unison. I don't know for what purpose, since neither our guns nor our shells are identical.

Camp Winston
25 January 1862
Rudolf to family

Today is Mother's birthday. I send my best wishes. I don't know myself what all I should wish, actually. I do wish this though: that you may have a very cheerful day. . . . Father writes that Mother wants to send me underwear. I thank you very much for your friendly concern, but I don't see how I can make use of it. There is only a poor connection from up there to here. It would have to go by way of Galveston, which would be expensive and unreliable, and then too, I can buy underwear and, in fact, all clothing here, even if at prices that are too high. . . . Father wants to know how the smoking and chewing are going. I have given up smoking since I ran out of tobacco. We bought $5 worth of leaf tobacco shortly after we arrived here at half a dollar a pound. We thought that would last us a long time, but with the help of a couple of communists,[11] we finished it up already a few days ago. The tobacco was not good, by the way, and I'm not sorry it is gone. I chew a little but not much. I haven't made up my mind if I ought to give that up too. Then, Father writes that he is not ready to agree to the Nicaragua idea yet. It isn't entirely clear to me either; it's just always been my favorite dream to get to the South, and that seems to me to be the most advantageous way.[12] And if the North should be victorious, which seems to be quite possible with the South making such a feeble effort, civilian conditions here won't be very good; and then, I think, one would find a pleasanter existence down there. What Father writes—namely that the article says June and July are winter there—either wasn't in the newspaper we had or we overlooked it; and that our fellow-countrymen are already in a fight wouldn't matter much to us if we had no more to do with them than we have now. But now there is still a war on, and when it is past we can talk it over. The lice powder arrived in good condition but too late, unfortunately. We had wanted it sent to us from Matagorda, but the postal rider . . . couldn't get any and brought us the gray salve instead. . . . In the watch tent one always sleeps with another person in the same bed, and we would have supplied the entire camp with the bugs that way. . . . We had a very strong north wind last week that tore down our tents and ripped almost all of them. And we had to repair them almost all day yesterday. Toward evening some people wanted to go get oysters. I have often eaten some before but never have helped fetch them and so I offered to go along, though I did not expect to get great pleasure from it. The water was quite cold and we had to wade around in the mud up to our stomachs to find any. We hired a Negro a couple of days ago who is to cook and wash for us. Münzenberger and I actually weren't for it, but all the others in our tent were, and so we did not want to be the exceptions and wanted to avoid their thinking that we are too stingy to pay our part of it. We pay $20 a month for him, that makes $2.25 each. I don't think we'll have him long though; he seems to be a pretty lazy fellow. I don't have anything to do with him; I pay my part and that's all. The time we have left over, I use to study Spanish. I know about three hundred nouns and can conjugate several verbs. We bought three books in Galveston, you see: an English dictionary, an artillery book, and a little German-Spanish textbook.[13] The captain has gotten news that the thirty men I wrote you about earlier are coming after all. We are all very glad of it, because then we will stay here until the whole regiment is taken away and our location, everyone thinks, had the advantage of being the most healthful on the coast. The political news which Father wrote me about is the latest I have had. . . . Congratulate Otto [Meusebach] for his birthday for me. . . . Friendly regards from Münzenberger.

Camp Winston
2 February 1862
Rudolf to family

Father writes that the war tax is being collected now.[14] I think it may be paid with paper money. I would be pleased, if you do not have any, if Father were either to postpone payment or would borrow as much in Confederate notes as are needed for that purpose, which would undoubtedly be easy to do. 10 February is our first pay day; I probably won't have any surplus left over yet. What there may be has to go for horse and saddle. But the second time, 10 May, we will in any case get the $50 bounty. If Father were to do so I would be pleased, because I could contribute a little anyway, since as Carl Münzenberger wrote his brother, you can get 30% discount on paper where you are or in San Antonio. [Adolph] Münzenberger was made a corporal yesterday. The money we sent for from Galveston we received in the form of a $10 Confederate note, with the assurance that it was as good as gold, but we could not get it changed till yesterday. Yesterday at last the person whom we had given it to take along for converting brought it back changed; he had had to take 50¢ less for it. You write that Carl is going to enter the militia. That is sure to be unpleasant for him, but I don't think that the affair will last long . . . then Carl can get back to building his house again. . . . The people seem to have gotten the laugh on us with that business of thirty men who were to come to fill up our company. Now they say that they aren't coming after all. I cannot grasp why we never get a definite statement about it. But by the tenth there will have to be a definite decision, because our three months are up. . . . Yesterday we got provisions to supply us for quite a while, which they surely would not have sent if they meant to remove us from here in a couple of days. . . . I almost forgot: Father asks whether the corporal here too reports to the watch, "Nothing new."[15] That is not the way it is done here. A report is made only if something has happened, which has never occurred as yet.

Camp Winston
9 [8?] February 1862
Rudolf to family

. . . Tuesday I got the letter from Father and Carl which brought me the news that I have become the uncle of one more niece. I send congratulations to Agnes; I think she probably hoped it would be another girl. . . . Father writes me sad reports about Indians.[16] I am very glad to know that Agnes and her family are down there with you. We got the news a day later in the *Galveston Union,* but there it is stated that several more are still missing. . . . Our camp looks quite ranger-like today. Otherwise, when there is good weather, the people are too busy. First we usually drill four hours now, and then there are always a few busy with hauling wood, cleaning the yard, unloading corn, and other such work. But today there is none of that. Of the officers none is to be seen and no work is being done either. There is a big fire in front of each tent. Ours is smoking up the tent a lot, but it isn't warming it much. I am sitting in bed with my legs wrapped up, so only my fingers are freezing, actually. Here and there somebody goes from tent to tent to watch the card players, and that is practically all the company. A few players always start and thereby enrich those who know best how to cheat. But it doesn't matter; they never get into serious fights. I don't know whether or not I wrote you that we have a new German recruit. I think he is a Silesian, a boor. We would have been just as happy to be the only Germans in the company. But the others know the man and seem to like him quite well, and then we don't pay him much attention so that we won't be held responsible for his actions, and so I don't think he will detract from our status here much. Last night . . . the scouts weren't sent out at all, and I was glad about that, since I was one of them and it would have been quite unpleasant to ride sixteen miles in the wind. We weren't called to roll call this morning and the parade we usually have every Sunday didn't take place either. We were quite comfortably warm last night. We closed the tent at the front with a blanket and brought an iron kettle with coals into it. It was as warm as a room that way. Now the men are making a wood fire in the kettle, which is less pleasant, because it smokes quite a bit. . . . Münzenberger sends friendly greetings.

Camp Winston
12 February 1862
Rudolf to family

Father writes that Ernst [Meusebach] has an attack of measles. These sickness reports are quite depressing to me, because I can do absolutely nothing but hope things get better. . . . In the camp there are a few who are sick again. . . . One, who had had the fever for quite a long time and could not get rid of it, we cured with Apis, and he hasn't had any fever for some days now. You must have plowed quite a bit already, and must have been quite busy all around since I left. It seems you are having to work on the fence this year as never before. I hope the last rain has filled

the creek. (Here it rained quite hard and we had a freeze at last.) . . .
Johann must be quite a good smith by now if he has to do all the work
alone on the farm now; even if Franz does help him, he isn't a master
at it yet. I didn't think the [sweet] potato crop would turn out as badly
as Father writes it did. . . . Another report that I dislike hearing is that
about the taxes, but actually only because I have no answer yet about
whether Father will use my pay for that purpose. If he does that, which
I hope he will, I won't miss it, because then my being here would not
have been completely without use to you. . . . At this point I still owe a
bit on my horse and saddle. We were promised we would be paid on 10
February, but the day passed without our hearing a thing about it. . . .
The colonel had no right to swear in the company before it was full. He
knew that too, and therefore never sent a report about the status of the
regiment. So no money was sent to us. Now he finally was pressured into
reporting that the company isn't full. On the basis of that Hébert ordered
him to Houston to defend himself in this matter. . . . I have for some
time given up chewing tobacco and for about a week smoking too. But
I took that [smoking] up again when I discovered I could easily get along
without it, because I do want to enjoy as much as possible whatever
doesn't hurt me. . . . It has been a very long time since we last saw a
ship, and nobody hears cannon shots either. . . . How tense everything
is you can conclude from the following: a few nights ago—I was on
watch—the whole camp suddenly got restless. The captain and the lieutenants dashed out into the yard and to our tent but then went quietly
home again right away. The cause: somebody had—to put it bluntly
["*auf gut Deutsch*"]—broken wind. That at first made the nearest ones
scream, then a couple of others outside the tent screamed just to be
companionable, and the officers heard that and thought heaven knows
what might be wrong. Just now people were saying there is a ship in
view. . . . The colonel was here in camp yesterday. . . . I don't care where
we go, if only we get away from here. I have nothing against this place,
actually; but we have been lying here long enough, and I would like to
see something else. The ship that came by here on the twelfth was, we
later heard, the *Niagara*.[17] It passed us at a distance of about 4-6 miles.
One couldn't see anything except that it must be a pretty big ship.
Yesterday news came that eighty men would be coming from Columbus
to fill up the companies down here . . . but the postal rider who came at
noon said the people had come all right but had filled up other companies
in Velasco and we wouldn't get any of them. . . . In five days our time
as slaveholders is up; our contract is up, and we have all agreed to let
the Negro go. He is a completely useless fellow. We are almost sure he
filches provisions on the side, and then he always knows how to arrange
very cleverly to get as much to eat as two or three of us. We often left
the table hungry. Then too, he was to wash for us, but all one usually
could see to indicate that the clothing had been washed was that it had
had holes beaten into it. It wasn't made much cleaner. But in five days
now we'll be rid of him, and I prefer doing my own things or paying
another Negro for doing it. Then they do it with pleasure and do it well.
I don't think it will cost more either.

Camp Winston
22 February 1862
Rudolf to family

. . . Tuesday night I got your letter. Unfortunately I had to learn from it that you are still not all over the measles. . . . I thought I had heard that one can get this illness only once. . . . I send Johann best wishes for his birthday, which is today. I must congratulate Anna ahead of time, because her birthday comes during the week and I have no opportunity to write then. . . . Today it is rainy here again and so I can imagine very well how everyone at home is sitting in the house and is happy about the rain. . . . Many are sick again; they all have colds, and so we are getting only one night of rest quite frequently again. . . . It did me no harm; my runny nose was gone just as soon as it usually is. I dressed warmly and took Aconitum[18] and Apis. . . . A couple of days ago they said on the Cedar Bayou, below Indianola, Northerners had landed. At first they said there were 1,200; then there were 12,000; and then they said there were only 12-14 men in two boats who had come to shore and taken beef, eggs, and butter from a farmer. They wanted to pay for them, and when the man declined to accept any money, they left the money behind and went away again. Then, they say, groups did land there after all and rangers were being assembled there. I believe that story about twelve men. They have done that a few times on Galveston Island already, before so many military were there. It seems that the company will stay here. Our captain went to Houston yesterday, where they will decide what to do with us. . . . We have tried often to draw a reasonably good picture of the captain . . . maybe there will be an opportunity sometime to have him photographed. I think that when we get paid, which is bound to happen sometime, enough daguerrotypists and people like that will turn up. . . . The last news we have is that the Yankees landed in North Carolina and took 3,000 prisoners after a tough fight, and that Mason and Slidell were not at all well received in England. All in all, it seems to me there hasn't been much good news in a long time, and the bad news, I think, is probably even worse than the version we hear. Then there was a report from Washington that the Congress had decided to get rid of slavery in any case; the good citizens should be allowed to keep their Negroes for five years more, but the rebels should have theirs taken from them right away. I don't believe the report; I think it was only made to arouse a little spirit in the soldiers again. It won't help for long though. There are, after all, very many who don't own any Negroes, and they are already asking now what they are fighting for anyway. And if the war lasts another year more, and more people say that, then I think it may be possible that we might lose after all. I cannot conjure up a pretty picture of our future in the Confederate States. I simply don't think we will get back to our former state of tranquility again; even if we win, it would surely be a very long time before we get back on the former track. I don't actually know where things are better, but to me, at least, it is a practical certainty that we will not stay in this country much longer.

Camp Winston
no date [probably 2 March 1862]
Rudolf to family

. . . Unfortunately I discover that the measles are not sparing even a
single one of you . . . I had a rather bad head cold the week before last.
I took Apis and Aconitum, and so it was gone except for a cough in a
couple of days. Then I thought of Hepa. as something that might perhaps
be the right remedy for it.[19] I don't know for sure whether it was, but
now the cough is almost gone too. You seem to have been concerned
about the landing of the Northerners, but surely have heard by now that
it was much ado about nothing. . . . It has not rained in several days now
and there was not much dew at night, so all the sand is dry and is blown
about in big clouds. Our bed is already completely covered with it and
it falls on the paper as thickly as if someone had strewn it on it. You
wish to hear a bit about my horse and are quite right in suspecting that
he has not won himself an especially big place in my heart, but since
you want me to, I will describe it for you. It is a bay about ten years old.
He has one good trait, which is that, up to now, he always allows himself
to be caught out in the open. I forgot to say that his form is not beautiful.
His hindquarters are not strong, and his back probably even longer than
that of Vaio [It. *vaio* means blackish, brownish, or spotted]. He doesn't
have any really bad traits. . . . His gait is not exactly unreliable, but to
be described as sure-footed he would have to quit bucking sometimes,
but he can't even do that well enough to distinguish himself. In short he
is too insignificant to be worthy of serving me as a battle steed. Without
wanting to detract from his value, I want to point out that his willingness
to be caught could be a result of his not eating properly, while the other
horses are almost all in good shape. When I get home, I want to hitch
him to the plow, his real calling, in which, according to his former owner's
Negro, he is a master. We still don't know definitely what is to become
of our company. Our captain is not back yet. He wanted to go recruiting
and come back in a month, but I heard tonight he is already on the way
back here from Galveston or Houston, and Gen. Hébert has sent somebody else to recruit. If that is true, we will probably stay here. . . . The
Galveston Union states that Sibley's Brigade in New Mexico has been
beaten, and an English newspaper said that they [Sibley's forces] beat
the United States troops.[20] . . . A couple of days ago a big steamship
went by here. The experts said it was a transport ship. It must have been
about three miles from land at this point. The same day some of our
men were in Velasco. People said it had passed so close by there that
one could have reached it with rifle fire. Why didn't they shoot at it, do
you suppose, since they have cannons after all? Probably because they
were afraid that a few of their pitiful wooden huts might be spoiled. Last
Tuesday Münzenberger and I were in Velasco and Quintana to buy a few
things. There are two stores, a sutler's and the commissary. But they
have hardly anything anymore. The smallest shoes that they had are
size 9. We bought a pair of boots for $10; a pair of shoes for $3.50; two

hickory shirts, rather poor quality, at $1.25 a piece; two pairs of cotton socks at 75¢ a pair; and two silk handkerchiefs at $1.00 a piece. Really poor quality cotton ones would have cost 75¢ a piece, and the silk ones seemed to be not exactly bad. . . . I think that today you all probably are sitting comfortably in the room and are celebrating Max's [the youngest Meusebach son's] birthday, for which I send him good wishes.

Camp Winston
5 March 1862
Rudolf to Carl

. . . I am really glad to see from your letter and from Father's that you are well again and now do at last have hope of finishing your house. How unpleasant it must be for you that you are making such slow progress with the building, for I know how much you wish it finished. But now, since you have money, I think the project will surely go much better, and so I think that now, when labor is surely not expensive, you can make fast headways, having money. I hope the militia law won't hold you back much; even though you have to go drill every fourteen days, I don't imagine you all will carry on so vigorously that it will take you all more than a half day. We are drilled energetically now and then, depending on whether the weather is good; that is to say, by the officers, especially one, the first lieutenant, brother of the captain[21] He is a terribly silly man. It is his business to drill us when the captain is not here. He does it as often as possible too, but since he knows absolutely nothing, he always lets us do certain drills which we knew how to do after we had been here a week, sometimes for four hours a day. You can imagine that that is not exactly entertaining. When the captain is here, or if he is prevented by something and one of the other lieutenants is in command, I rather like doing it; even if they don't teach us anything new very often, at least they do vary the drills, and then it is quite a good way to pass the time. I suddenly happened to remember, the lieutenant did happen to make an exception to the rule today. He let us practice attacking, which we have done only once since coming here. He did it in much the way Father said they had done it with their major. We were supposed to be guided by what the man on our left flank did. But his horse bolted and we did our best to stay at his side, so that didn't work out well, and we got completely mixed up as we reached the goal. That made him very unhappy. He ordered us to go back and do it again, but it didn't work out much better, so he gave the order to attack in only a medium gallop. Then it went to his satisfaction. Yesterday a special messenger came here from Aransas Pass with a dispatch for Galveston. One of our men took it to Velasco. The man who brought it did not know what was in it, but he said that a man and a woman had been put on land by one of the ships that keep crossing the gulf, and they said that the ship's officer had bade them tell the people that Galveston and Aransas Pass would be attacked simultaneously soon. Naturally people think the ship's captain was simply wanting a laugh at our expense. . . . Here people are already talking with great longing of peace, and almost everyone is happy that some newspaper states the war surely must be ended within two months, since neither party can endure it any longer. I don't know whether that is correct, but I think it is not impossible. But then I think it more probable that we will be conquered than the opposite, if foreign powers don't get involved. I still keep hoping for the latter, but if it doesn't happen, then I think we will see really quite bad times. I would be glad to contribute my share to making a peace soon that would be favorable to us, if only we were to have the chance. But here in Texas there doesn't seem to be any prospect of that. I must say, of course, that I cannot get enthusiastic about our cause, but I really do see our winning or not as a matter of life and death. If we had prospects of getting away, I wouldn't care so much, but since there seems to be no way of our selling our farm, I really wish that the South would pursue the matter a bit more energetically than it has so far. . . . No matter how the war may end, I will have gained from it the chance to take you all by the hand in reality again, but till then I must try to be content, even if I hear that you all are up to your ears in work and could surely use my help now. There is simply no way I can change that now. Now farewell, my dear Carl, and cherish your loyal friend and brother Rudolf.

Camp Winston
9 March 1862
Rudolf to family

. . . It is finally known for certain that the company will remain together. We will soon get recruits now. The militia law seems to drive people here to us. Last week three men enlisted here on their own and said that several more would be coming. Besides, a man who brought recruits to Velasco to fill up companies there a couple of weeks ago has been sent on his way again by Colonel [illegible name][22] for the purpose of getting some for us. . . . The political reports that we got last Friday are no better than those we always get now. The next-to-last newspaper stated that Nashville would be defended to the last man; but the last one stated that it had been surrendered without a shot being fired. However, it stated that it was surrendered in order to lure the Northerners into a trap. I really cannot quite believe that though. It seems to me that they saw that they could not hold it. It is my opinion and that of many Americans here that things are going down hill for us. The North has made very great progress during the last two months, after all, and it still has the chance to strengthen itself, whereas it is impossible for the South to make up for its losses. Everywhere we read of a powder shortage, and how can that be compensated for? Here it is forbidden to shoot a gun without the captain's permission. The rumor reached here that five or six ships landed troops in Aransas Pass; but there doesn't seem to be any truth to it, because nobody bothers about it. Yesterday a few of us, Münzenberger and I included, went to eat oysters. We got to quite a good place this time too. In half an hour we took out more than we could eat. Gradually I am learning to eat oysters too. I am already rather liking to eat them. The people here throw the oysters into a fire and leave them there until the water cooks out through the gap in the shell. Then they are very easy to open and taste quite good too. But I like eating them raw better anyway. One can eat more of them too than when they are cooked. Friendly greetings from Münzenberger.

Camp Winston
15 March 1862
Rudolf to family

You probably have already read about the progress of the Northerners too, and probably also what there was to the story about Aransas Pass. Yesterday and today a couple of cannons were transported by here to there from Velasco, twelve-pounders, I think. . . . The grass is beginning to grow and snakes are letting themselves be seen. Here it hasn't rained enough either; the planters are complaining that they cannot plant corn. That's all we need to help make times even worse—not being able to make a crop. . . . I am glad that you did not go along with my proposal to pay the taxes with my pay; that might have put you on the spot, because if the South loses, we surely have no prospect of getting anything at all. . . . I do want to write you another opinion of the Southerners though, that reached our ears here and that you may not have heard. They say about the German Northerners whom they beat in a battle, that they had stood quite still and exposed themselves to their fire and did nothing but keep loading and shooting because they were too stupid to run away. Then I heard something here too which might be useful to you. If rabbits damage a garden, the people lay down a hollow tree that is supplied with a flap like a mousetrap. It is the nature of the little rabbits, they say, to inspect every little hollow and shut themselves up in it in case of need. When they do that with the trap, the flap drops down and they are caught; and the Negroes catch quail here in a little log hut with a low doorway, the way one catches turkeys. A couple of days ago I weighed myself and discovered that serving the state must not have been much of a strain; I weighed 169 lbs. (That is quite a substantial weight, you must admit.)

[Camp Winston]
16 March 1862
Rudolf to family

. . . Father writes that the Tolles paid you a visit; I would like to know why they are acting nice all of a sudden just now again.[23] Do you suppose they have any intentions? I wish they were making overtures about negotiating for the farm. It would be a real relief to me if our entire means were not tied to the land. In the *Houston Telegraph* we read that in Paris Mason and Slidell said there were prospects the Confederate States might be made into a monarchy. If the government wants to do that, I think it has quite good prospects of putting it through. Soldiers haven't got the right to vote, and if the planters think they can keep their Negroes under a regent, surely they will be for it; and if they take the referendum about it before they dismiss the army, they just might get the majority. There are people here too who say: we would rather go over to the Emperor of France than back to being under the Yankee government. If that proves to be the case and we find it out for sure, then I would try to get out of the army, at any rate.

Camp Winston
20 March 1862
Rudolf to family

. . . From your letter I can tell you are concerned about me. We are well and contented and are still very quietly sitting here without prospects of being transferred farther than maybe to the [St.] Bernard [River] or to Velasco, if the companies that are stationed there leave the state voluntarily, because, like ourselves, they are with one exception sworn in for service in the State of Texas only. The call for the 18,000 men does not affect us directly at all. If anybody did actually want to, he probably could get himself transferred to one of those companies, I suppose. It may be that we will be asked whether we want to go, but we cannot be forced to do it; and for the moment, I won't be going voluntarily yet. At least I want to wait for a while to see what conditions our emissaries to Paris arrange. As I have written you already, the *Houston Telegraph* stated that they have spoken there of the founding of a monarchy. If that should prove to be the case, then I am quite glad that they have only such limited power over me, and I won't submit myself to them any further. That is also my reason for believing that we are not moving toward a very nice future. This project seems to be finding a good response among the slaveholders. Here a couple of people loudly declared themselves in favor of it, and the kind of shock that a report of that kind ought to call forth was not seen at all. It seems to me to be a bad sign when a proposal of that sort can come from the government. Five years ago hardly anyone even dared yet to talk about a separation of the old Union and now the entire South is fighting for it. . . . I hope we will be able to discuss this matter orally in a month and a half. Yesterday the captain gave us relatively certain prospects for a leave at that time. It is now definite that the company will be filled. The report has come that the recruiting officer has gotten thirty-two men together. On the strength of that the colonel gave the order that no more new recruits are to be sworn in here anymore, in order to leave room for those people. . . . This week we got ten days' supply of coffee, about two quarts. We decided among ourselves that we would rather have good coffee only a couple of times, and that until we get some new coffee again, we would return to our sassafras tea rather than to make bad coffee all the time, so we really enjoyed it. Do you still have coffee regularly, or are the times too bad? . . . I have given much thought to the subject of magnetism and I think I am on the way to a solution. However, it is not clear enough to me for me to be able to write it up.

afternoon [continued]

Just now our captain came from Velasco with the report that we have to decide whether we want to enlist for the duration of the war in order to march to Arkansas directly, or whether we want to be released and expose ourselves to being drafted from the militia. We—Münzenberger and I—decided for the above reasons to do the latter. Therefore we have prospects of being released in a few days. We will come up there then, and I will make further decisions up there after we have had time to consider the matter together. In any event, I have the happy prospect of being able to clasp you in my arms soon.

Camp Winston
25 March 1862
Rudolf to family

. . . We have been told that we are to be released on Thursday. . . . All troops that were recruited for a twelve-month period are being released now and the entire army is to be sworn in for the duration of the war. We can't understand what the reason for that is, but since we happen to be suspicious, we are trying to adjust our thinking accordingly, and so it seems to us that they want to extract the oath from us in order to be able to use us for whatever purposes and for however long they want. To make that even easier, they have restricted the freedom of the press.
. . . At the request of Major Colonel [sic] Brown we were asked by our captain how many of us, if any, want to sign up for the duration of the war in order to form a battalion under him. The captain did that twice in very energetic speeches. The first time perhaps twenty stepped up and the second time 24-25; it is a bit unpleasant for me to have to step back at just the right moment, but I can't do otherwise, after all. Since it is almost certain that we will break up in a short time, all discipline has stopped. It seems though to be going a bit too fast to suit the captain. This morning he had some of us drilling and put the rest, of whom I was one, to work mending tents and cleaning. I was given the hospital tent to mend. Tonight I am on watch. I think it will be the last time that I have to walk back and forth between two posts. . . . According to what Father wrote in my last letter, you think I am already on the way to Arkansas. I hope to be able to write you next from Gonzales.

Camp Winston
29 March 1862
Rudolf to family

. . . Time is certainly entering into our circumstances in a very sad way.
. . . We still have not received our release. . . . When we are released, we will immediately hit the road and can, if all goes well, be up there in 7-8 days, and then it would be possible that we might still arrive in time to be able to get into the same company with Carl and Johann. Our rations are growing scant. We are getting only cornmeal, sugar, molasses,

and a little bacon. The beef that was delivered to us the last time was not edible. This morning the suggestion was made that we go oystering, but each person had something that prevented him and so one of our mess members and I went alone.

Camp Winston
no date [probably 4 April 1862]
Rudolf to Carl

Dear brother!

Your decision to enter the army really surprised me, and I can grasp quite well how hard it must be for you, now that you are essentially through building your house, suddenly to have to leave everything for an indefinite period. The way I see the situation now, I would prefer it if you all would not do it, but after all, you have reasons for your opinion too, and so I cannot take it upon myself to interfere with you. We were told here at first that, if we did not take the oath for the duration of the war, we would be released in order to be drafted from the militia. So we made plans to travel up there and join a company with you all, just to be with you. But now the same people who at first told us that we would be disbanded have cast some doubt on it and say that no such order has arrived yet. It is possible that that is happening from private motives, because they discovered that many were glad to get away, and that they want to swear in as many as they can for the duration first and then let the remainder go. But because that may take some time yet, we prefer applying for a leave in order to see you all before you depart, if possible. We have positively made up our minds to sign up for the duration of the war only if we are allowed to go with you all. If they do not want to give us any opportunity to do that, they can defend their cause without us. The captain, whom we asked about the leave today, promised to support our request before the colonel. The latter is to come here tomorrow and so today we have high hopes again of being released, all the more so since forty-two men came to the company yesterday, and consequently the duties will be light even without us. The men are from Navarro County. They all seem to be farmers but not Negro-holders. It is a very fine troop, almost all of the tall sort of Americans and very well mounted.[24] I don't think though that many of them will enlist for the duration of the war. Several said, with rather sad expressions, that their fields were looking very good, but that nobody was left at home anymore who could harvest them. I hope we will manage to get up there soon enough to get together with you. Even if we couldn't go together, we would have so much to talk with each other about. Writing is, after all, only a very inadequate substitute. In that hope I remain, with the sincerest wishes for the well-being of you all, your loyal friend and brother Rudolf. My heartiest greetings to Johann.

Camp Winston
10 April 1862 [postmarked 9 April]
Rudolf to family
return address: Capt. Rugeley's Comp.
Baits [sic] Regiment
Texas Wollentiers [sic]

. . . I have a rather annoying rash. I don't know whether I came in contact with a poisonous creature or whether it is an illness. On the left side, at the tail bone ["*wo das Kreuz den ehrlichen Namen verliert*"] there is an area about as big as a silver dollar, which is red and completely covered with blisters. Besides, my whole left side hurts a bit. I took Hep. Mercurium from time to time.[25] I think it is probably of no importance and will be all right soon. When I wrote you that we would be coming up there, I thought that the officers were telling the truth, but I seem to have been mistaken about that. They seem to have told us that we would be released simply because they thought that was the best means of getting us to sign a new oath. But when they saw it had no effect they revoked it; at least they said that they had not received orders yet. . . . The day before yesterday the group that the recruiting officer recruited for this company (forty-two men) arrived. They don't seem to be fire-eaters either. One of them, the brother of the recruiting officer, is now our first lieutenant. He is just a simple man. He sleeps among his men in the tents, helps with the cooking and grooms his horse himself, whereas the other officers live in the house and even the sick have to be in a tent. That makes quite a pleasant impression. Our captain is leaving here and going along to Arkansas, and if the rest of the company stays here, then he probably has the best prospects of becoming the captain. If we get away and if we possibly can, we will bring along sabers, but there are two *if*'s in that, so you cannot rely on it. . . . Friendly greetings from Münzenberger.

Roll Call

Early in 1862 a New Braunfels merchant, the Prussian Robert Bechem, had been appointed Comal County provost marshal and brigadier general of the Thirty-first Brigade Texas State Troops, a position that put him in charge of certain affairs in a twenty-county area.[1] During 1861 numerous army companies had been organized, and even before eligible men were forced to enter active service, there was increasing pressure upon them to volunteer. Among such groups organized at New Braunfels was one under Theodor Podewils, a Prussian emigrant with European military experience. The original forty-two man nucleus, calling itself the Light Cavalry-Comal Horse Guard, along with the home-guard infantry and some Guadalupe County units, had encamped for four weeks during the late summer of 1861 for training on the George family's farm. Many of the original members had emigrated at about the same time as the Coreths and were well known to them. The company, commissioned on 20 September 1861, did not at first include any Coreths on its official rolls.[2] Carl was then living at some distance from New Braunfels in an area preparing to separate itself from Comal County and reorganize as Kendall County. Johann was not yet eighteen. Rudolf, of course, was already serving on the coast when conscription loomed.

On 29 March 1862, a farewell dance was held in honor of the Podewils company before it marched to the nearby camp on the Salado River. After arriving in Camp Salado, Podewils's men, mostly Comal County

Carl Coreth with army hat

residents and almost exclusively German, ceased to be known as Texas Mounted Riflemen. Two days later, Col. H. W. McCulloch called the troop into service as Co. F of Col. Peter C. Woods's volunteer regiment. Woods's regiment was officially the Thirty-second, but was known very generally as the Thirty-sixth Texas Cavalry Regiment—a misnomer not disputed by the real Thirty-sixth, which was itself quite frequently called the Fifteenth!

On 31 March 1862, Carl Coreth, twenty-five, and his brother Johann, eighteen, enlisted in the army as privates. At Sisterdale a week later (7 April 1862), Carl's marriage to Hedwig Kapp, for which the license had been issued the previous July, took place.[3] The next day, Carl and Johann's company was mustered into the Confederate army at Camp Salado, and two days thereafter all members were signed up in San Antonio for the customary three years or duration of the war.

For much of the month of April, Rudolf and Münzenberger were trying to arrange transfer in order to be with friends and relatives. On 27 April, as New Orleans was falling to Federal control, Rudolf enlisted in Co. F of Woods's Regiment, and on 3 May Münzenberger joined it also. Then Rudolf, and evidently Münzenberger, went in search of their old company, perhaps to gain official severance from a unit that, according to existing muster rolls, never considered them members in the first place.[4]

When Rudolf received the first of the following letters is uncertain.

New Braunfels
19 April 1862
Rudolf from father

Dear Rudolf,

I am writing this letter to you in the hope that you won't get it, which is to say that you will already be on your way to us when it gets to Camp Winston. . . . We got your letter of the tenth on the twelfth. The mail goes very quickly by way of Velasco. We had been craning our necks for eight days whenever anything moved toward our house from up at Scheel [e]'s in the hope that it might be you. . . . Franz will mail this letter and perhaps bring us the happy news that you are on the way, and if not— well then we shall have to reach for that familiar household remedy: all's for the best. All of us here are well again for a change. Mother caught a severe chill eight days ago and suffered quite a lot for a couple of days. Now, however, she is pretty well. Since then two heavy, that is to say hard rains [have fallen]; whether they amounted to anything is not entirely clear. They were very hard but short and with much hail. The creek began to flow, and, as the Pomeranians say, it washed away all the fun.[5] So far one does not see much of the results in the vegetation. Much of the corn is eaten up, and we shall have to plant almost everything anew. Wheat and rye are blown away. . . . Last Saturday Johann came home from camp for one night. Carl and [Alfred] Kapp were in Sisterdale on leave. Franz rode back home with him [Johann] and stayed for the night in camp. That was when the first terrible storm came and almost flooded the camping place. There are five American cavalry companies and one German one there, and they are said to get along well with one another. Toward morning they built a fire and dried themselves and everyone was in good spirits again, as Franz reported when he got home. Johann has a saber, all of them are getting pointed hats like the Tyroleans, trousers, packs, blankets, etc.[6] I have bought an old carbine for you, one that loads from the back, for which you will have to make yourself a new shaft though, if you want it. The way I hear it, Carl and Kapp are back, but I have had no news from Carl himself yet. There is mail in Austin in the camp.[7] The company was mustered in but is not complete yet. We have had no war news for two weeks. Indians were in Fredericksburg and killed three Germans and stole horses.[8] Otherwise I don't know anything of consequence to report. The cattle will probably stop dying now, but they have very little feed so far. Elsewhere, Blanco for example, there is said to be lots of feed. The four mares—Caty, Catrin, Trinette, and Morette—are near foaling time. We are using Zarwash[9] and the mule for the harvest. [Fritz or Wilhelm] Vo[i]gt's mare with the broken foot is still alive and looks quite well except for the foot. It was four weeks yesterday. I kept waiting for you to take off the bandage, but if you don't come, we shall have to have a go at it ourselves, I suppose. I hope your suffering from the tenderness [*"Liebwerthen"*] has let up by now. Apis would have been a good remedy in this instance too. So for today Adio; in the hope of being able to embrace you soon I am looking at the map. The road goes by way of Texana, Hempstead, and Gonzales. I ride along it daily with my eyes. Everybody sends you the tenderest greetings and wishes you good fortune for your birthday, should you not be with us for it. Your old friend, E. Coreth. Give the friendliest regards to Münzenberger.

Sandis Creek [elsewhere on maps called Sandy or Sandies Creek]
early on 6 May 1862 [the eve of his twenty-fourth birthday]
Rudolf to family

Last evening we met several people from our company here. They told us that the company is not down at the old camp anymore, but instead is stationed somewhere on the Bernard 80-83 miles from here. The way they tell it, the company has been completely re-organized. All but two took the oath for the duration of the war. Some got transfers and so we hope that we can do that also without difficulty. We have to hurry though to get to camp on time. . . . The man who is to take the letter to Hallettsville is waiting.

Velasco P. O.
Capt. L. T. Bennet's Co.[10]
at the mouth of the Bernard
11 May 1862
Rudolf to family

. . . On our arrival in Quintana we were disappointed to discover that
there is no legal way open to us anymore to get away from here, not even
in [Reuben R.] Brown's Battalion. General Hébert has issued the definite
order that no transfers are to be approved anymore. What right he has
to act so dictatorially I do not know, but because of our oath, we are
obliged to obey for one year, and so we have to adjust, unpleasant as it
is. . . . The first day we got not quite to Bellmont. We camped at a farm,
where we got corn for our horses. The pretzels that Mother sent with us
tasted very good. The next day we fed our horses at noon at Tunkan's
and in the evening we camped on the big prairie between Peach Creek
and Hallettsville.[11] We had almost emptied our bread bag by then, and
when we inspected the other provisions, we found to our really great
pleasure that we had meat too and were very thankful to Mother for
taking care of us. We cooked cocoa there for the first time, and thus had
an exceptional supper. At night it began to rain but it did not hurt us
much. We had hung up our things under a blanket, and nothing got wet
at all. The next night we camped on the Sandy seventeen miles this side
of Hallettsville. There we met some people from our company. They told
us that there was no problem getting transferred to another place anymore, and so I wrote you right away in my first delight. The next night
we slept on the Colorado just on the other side of Egypt. The next noon
we got to old Horton's plantation.[12] But it was raining so hard that we
accepted Horton's invitation and remained till the next noon, when the
rain let up a bit. He described the road to our camp in exact detail. It
was then twelve miles to Columbia, but the Bernard was so swollen by
rain that we could not cross it there. So we decided to stay the night on
a farm. The next morning we had to take a detour of several miles to get
to a bridge. After a very dirty road several miles in length, we met a
Negro from the camp who said that the Battalion was on the way to
Houston and just in the process of crossing the Brazos, where we could
probably still catch up with it. Then we met another man who said that
when one half had crossed the river, a counterorder had come and that
they would be going to Arizona now. We discovered that to be the case
too when we got to Columbia. We were very glad, because we thought
that we could surely go along there too at least, and that is where Carl
and Johann probably are going too. We talked to our captain. He said
he had not received Münzenberger's letter and had not done anything
about our request as he had promised to do. He gave us a note to Colonel
Bates ["Baits"], in which he requested our wishes be fulfilled if possible.[13]
We rode another two miles and then lay down. Yesterday afternoon we
got to Quintana via Brazoria and went to the colonel immediately to
present our request to him, but he said it was too late. He had received

orders not to comply with any further transfer requests. You can imagine how that made us feel. The regiment is completely disorganized. The officers are all gone and the rest of the companies are lying around without doing their duties and some people are trying to recruit companies from among them. If they have not organized them by the end of a certain period, as many as necessary will be thrown together into a company. But now each has free choice of going into the various companies. We rode here this morning because there are still six decent people from the old company. . . . We probably will have to stay here and wait patiently for our release. I cannot deny though, these matters have not particularly contributed to the heightening of my patriotism. When a government breaks [down], having paid so little attention to civil rights that it gives a general the power to decide what to do with volunteers, there is not much lost, and according to the most recent reports one would not be inclined to think that it [the government] can carry on much longer that way. I hope that Carl and Johann have not gone yet when you get these lines. If I should not find time to write them myself, please give them my best regards. I thank Hedwig most kindly for the trouble she went to with the valise. It has served me well. And I thank all of you again for all the trouble you went to in order to make my trip as easy as possible. The next time I write I hope I shall have adjusted to the circumstances. At least I am struggling to do that; and now again farewell, and cherish your son and brother Rudolf.

Velasco P. O.
Capt. L. T. Bennet's Co.
mouth of the Bernard
12 May 1862
Rudolf to family

I . . . was about to send you a letter when we discovered the new conscription law in a newspaper yesterday, and after carefully examining it, we agreed the colonel had no right whatever to hold us (Conscription Law, Section 13), and that we have the right until 15 May to go into any company we want. There is not enough time to go up there to sign up with Podewils's company, and there might be difficulties if we got there too late. Therefore we are going to join Brown's Battalion, which has orders to go to New Mexico, and that is probably where Carl and Johann are going too. Maybe then we can be transferred to the other company anyway.

Seguin
17 [19?] May 1862
Rudolf to family

In the last letter I wrote that we were going to join Brown's Battalion. On the way though, we considered that it would be better if we went to the Salado camp right away, since we have enlisted already, and now we are on the way there. Tomorrow at noon we will probably arrive. If I can, I will come to you and tell you how everything happened, or else I will

write you in detail as soon as I have time. We are acting according to
Section 13 of the Conscription Law. . . . An attorney and several officers
all said that the colonel has no right whatsoever to hold us. We rode out
of camp last Monday and have been on the way for six days now. The
road is very bad. Yesterday we had a heavy rain the other side of Bellmont. It wet us and our things through and through. So we just rode as
far as the town and at least got to sleep in a dry place. Now I have to
close, since we still want to get to Cibolo. Adio. Rudolf.

A few days earlier there had been naval engagements off Galveston.
It was becoming evident that the North, if not the South, considered
Texas to be an intergral part of the Confederacy. On 26 May the Trans-
Mississippi Department was created, and on 30 May martial law was
declared in Texas. For the moment at least, talk of civil rights and
freedom was pointless. Meanwhile Rudolf and Münzenberger arrived in
San Antonio to be united with friends and brothers.

Podewils's men had spent April and May at the Salado site, where by
11 May there were seven companies, A through G. During this period
the troops primarily underwent training, but in some cases also had
guard and patrol duties, since there was strong Union sentiment among
a significant number of San Antonio civilians, many of them Germans.
Not uncommonly the generous Woods allowed men to go to their nearby
homes for visits or to San Antonio to fetch ammunition. Despite some
losses through disease, accidents, and discharges, ten companies were
assembled by 1 June. About then the Coreths, and perhaps some of their
friends, were briefly detailed to the San Antonio Arsenal, which, though
begun in 1859, was not complete until 1866.[14]

San Antonio ["St. Antonio"]
4 June 1862
Rudolf to family

Saturday in camp I got your letter, which brings me the news that you
are well. We are getting along fine. I, at least, like it here quite well. Of
course we do not have much time during the day for ourselves, because
we work 9½ hours, but then we do not have anything else of importance
that we might miss doing on that account. From Father's letter as well
as Carl and Münzenberger's account I see that you still have a great deal
to do. Unfortunately I don't have much prospect for a longer leave now,
because in the arsenal there is a great deal of work waiting to be done
too, and so they probably won't let us go soon. Sunday our company was
given a flag by several ladies; ten or twelve of us accepted it at Münzenberger's. Münzenberger handed it over to our captain, who made a speech
that was so poor we were glad for his sake only close acquaintances were
listening. Working with us in the arsenal there is a very good violin
player, and he is very willing to play for us in the evening too. Unfortunately he is a drunkard though, and if he is exposed to drink, he drinks
so much that he cannot play anymore. But at least in this way we manage
to pass an evening very pleasantly. By day the time usually does not

seem very long to us. Usually we have to repair old guns, and we really like doing that. Last Saturday, before we rode into camp, we tried to get our pay, but did not get it, because Major Gray had already left earlier to campaign for his election.[15] He did not get a single vote in the camp though. Monday we got paid for the preceding week, $6.60 a man. That is the first money I have ever earned in my life. Münzenberger told me that Mother has offered to do our laundry. I thank her very much for the offer, but since we are now living in town, it is no trouble to have it washed, and then too, we won't be dependent upon C[arl]. Rückert [a Coreth neighbor]. Do be so kind and send my rifle to me up here via C. Rückert. I want to sell it to the government, because for the same money that I now can get for it, I can surely buy two after the war, and the money would be really nice for me to have now. I would like to write you longer, but nothing more at all comes to mind. . . . Therefore for today Adio, and cherish your son and brother Rudolf.

New Braunfels
no date [late May of 1862]
Rudolf from father

I am really happy to hear from Mr. Münzenberger and through your own letter that you are doing well, as are your brothers, to whom I shall ask you right away to give our regards, also to Mr. [Alfred?] Kapp. . . . The corn is standing quite tolerably and the cotton and melons are growing a bit too. Catrin has a foal, a little stallion. There is not much one can say about so young an animal, but, to be sure, at this particular time I would have preferred a calf. There is no news which you would not know earlier, when it comes to politics; and in the more intimate circle, Auguste Tolle's wedding is Saturday.[16] The high water broke Tolle's dam. It will probably take quite a while to restore it. Fortunately they have the necessary wherewithal. In our case such an occurrence would have had incomparably worse consequences because of the complete lack of anything to spare. In free moments I am reading about tanning leather in Krappf's *Chemische Technologie,* which gives me lots of entertainment. Farewell, dear Rudolf. I fear I will not get to see any of you for some time, but if the regiment were collected, leaves would be given more sparingly anyway. If you have a free moment, give me the pleasure of a few lines from all of you. Many would, of course, be even more welcome. Adio. Your old friend and father. EC.

On 13 June 1862 Carl and Johann signed an authorization for their brother Rudolf to receive the money due them for fourteen days' rations and went home to New Braunfels for a visit. Rudolf wrote that once they were all together again they were dismissed from the arsenal and were evidently made victims of the mounting tensions that arose as some Germans, especially those in the Hill Country, were becoming increasingly resistant or even openly antagonistic to the idea of serving a cause in which they felt they had no stake.

San Antonio
no date
Rudolf to family

We are still here in town today in order to collect our pay, which presents some problems, since they keep sending us from one office to another. Tomorrow we will probably go back to camp, where we hope we can get a leave, once the captain is back. We had quite a lot of excitement during the days when Carl and Johann were with you. Carl probably told you that we demanded a raise in our pay, and that our foreman advised us to get a leave and then get ourselves employed in the shop like the other workers, and that is what we did. Sunday we went to Colonel Woods ["Voots"] and told him our stand, whereupon he quite willingly signed our leaves. The next morning we went to Captain Samuel ["Samuels"] and showed him the leave permit and told him what we wanted.[17] He said not a word but instead left with the paper and came back after a while, called the foreman of the saddle shop and had him tell us that we should go right to work or he would see to it we got bullets and chains. We had not refused to work, but to be forced to do so in such a discourteous way did anger us very much. For the moment, however, we could do nothing but go so as not to give him the satisfaction of being able to carry out his threat. We remained quite calm, and that seemed to make him very angry. He asked where Carl and Johann were. We said that they had received leave and had gone home. So he wrote down their names, we think so that he could punish them for this. I told him to please give back the leave permit, that I had a right to it as our property, and that we needed it as proof of our rights, if he were to bring charges against us. But he did not give it back, and then I told him to please pay us our week's wages. He said he could not do that either. Then we left, and when we were dismissed at noon, we made a complaint at the lieutenant colonel's.[18] He seemed very upset about Samuel and promised us that he would straighten the matter out and told us quite definitely that Carl and Johann would not be punished. That was a great relief to us. In the afternoon he himself went to Capt. Samuel and seems to have spoken to him quite firmly, because when I went there in the evening to demand our money again, he said to me in a rage that he wanted to pay us and let us go, because for no amount of money in the world did he want the trouble we were causing him [Samuel]. But he only paid us the 40¢. We still do not have the 60¢ in wages, because he has refused to sign the authorization since, he says, it is not his place to do that. Today we went to the colonel and he said that he would straighten out the matter tomorrow. First of all we declared to him our intention of going back to camp if they did not pay us better, and we have carried that out now at any rate. I hope that soon we will come to you and then I can tell you everything in more detail too. Harry Tolle sold my rifle for me for $20. And now Adio until we see each other soon again. Rudolf Coreth.

When the regiment broke camp late in June to march northward in the direction of San Marcos, Carl remained at home under the orders of Dr. Theodor Koester so that he might recover from the erysipelas on his leg and an irritation in his eyes, perhaps an aftereffect of the measles that had swept through the family.[19] As the regiment marched through New Braunfels that extremely dry summer, the soldiers could hardly see the houses because of the dust and the screen of children who crowded the sidewalks.[20] Johann, too, stayed behind on the doctor's recommendation, and, as Alfred Kapp and Adolph Münzenberger had also managed to get sick leaves, Rudolf must have felt quite abandoned. On 29 June, Woods's regiment got to Camp Clark, located in Guadalupe County on the San Marcos River, close to Martindale near the Hays County line. The pleasant elm-shaded site was less than twenty miles from New Braunfels, to which mail service was probably available almost from the start,[21] but the Coreths' letters to and from camp at this period were generally delivered by members of the company and are frequently undated, making the chronology somewhat puzzling at times.

While still at home under the doctor's orders, Carl made a saddle that he sent to the saddlemaker Jacob Rose for covering. Rudolf inherited the old one, for like brothers everywhere, the Coreths practiced the time-honored custom of bestowing hand-me-downs. Since the family included a very wide range of body types, just as their hair varied from ash blond to almost brunette, from curly to straight, the saddle, if it had suited the very large Carl, may not have fitted Rudolf well at all.

Of Rudolf and of Carl, pictures and detailed memories have been passed down through the generations. Of Johann there are little more than the adjectives "raw-boned" and "reckless." Though none of the three Coreths was a truly enthusiastic soldier, the trappings of a cavalryman mattered to the younger two at least, probably because they had heard from their father about life in an Austrian corps. With half of what he had received for his rifle, Rudolf had asked Münzenberger to purchase sabers.

Meanwhile, Ernst Coreth's aging arms, more accustomed to wielding a saber by far, were learning to stir a caldron of soap. On 5 July, Ernst wrote of his success: "if we have an excess, which I don't know for sure yet, one could make a business of it, i. e. a moderately good one by our standards." He was feeling encouraged at this point for other reasons as well. "There is talk of a big battle in Virginia that we are said to have won, also of the recognition [of the CSA] by France, but all this has not been confirmed as yet. God grant that it will soon be over and we may be together again as we were."

Both the political reports and the estimate of the soap were to be disappointments. As Ernst stated in a letter to Carl, ". . . in these times ten pounds of tallow are a real item, and I have paid more dearly for the increase in my knowledge than I should have liked to do." Reflecting upon rumors that were circulating, he continues, "My reason tells me that we are spectators, an audience looking at the drama as supernumeraries. Our roles are unimportant, and yet the play could not be put on if we did not take part. Man can do what he will, but he wants to do what he must want according to his nature" (Ernst to Carl, 22 August 1862).

At the same time, life in camp was settling into a tolerable routine.

Camp Clark
no date
Rudolf to family

. . . I had a big laundry this morning. I washed five pieces clean to my satisfaction. . . . The high officers are proceeding quite slowly to imprison us in firmer rules. But just about daily we get orders that have that purpose. Then too our rations are being cut. Yesterday evening we were read an order from Richmond, according to which from now on we only have 1 lb. of beef or ½ lb. of bacon coming to us, while a ration used to be 1½ lbs. meat or 1 lb. bacon. In return we are to get a bit more flour than we used to, but up to now we have noticed only that they are taking away from and not that they are adding to our allotment. For the horses too we are getting only insufficient amounts of corn. We are supposed to manage with the last corn we got until Monday, but today at noon we fed them the last of it. Whether we get new corn before Monday remains to be seen. Our life is quite organized. Mornings at 5:30 there is roll call, then breakfast. From 7 to 9 drill; after the drill we ride to pasture, if one does not happen to be the cook, and come back at 12, when we eat our meal and then feed the horses. At 3:30 a bugle summons us to drill again, but in the afternoon the entire regiment drills together mounted until 5:30. Then we ride home, feed the horses, go to dress parade, eat supper, and ride back into the pasture, but in the morning we have to come back for roll call again. I am going to try to get a leave for 4 August and have good prospects for one too. Half the company is on leave now, and by then many will have come back.

At home, too, the worries centered around the corn crop. The family was having to cut out the non-bearing stalks—most of the crop according to Ernst—because of the dryness of the year. He lamented that there would be a bit of fodder, but not even two bushels of corn per acre, and that the cattle, unable to find enough in the pasture to eat, kept breaking through the fields and trampling what they did not eat, adding further to the problems. Before his return to camp, Johann, who cannot have been very ill, had rounded up the family ox from the farm of a neighbor where it had wandered and on that occasion shot three jackrabbits. Formerly something of a problem child, Johann was commended by the family for his eagerness to help and his efficiency while at home on leave. And Rudolf told of Johann's skill in cooking, a job that Carl especially disliked, and sent home the following report of his young brother's bravery and modesty while in camp.

Camp Clark
no date
Rudolf to family

. . . Here everything is as ever; yesterday the captain's wife and the two Misses Henne came here with their brother and they will leave again today or tomorrow, so I don't want to miss the opportunity [to send news], though there is not much to write. The important thing is that this morning somebody almost drowned and that Johann was the first to pull him out. We, Johann and I, were both close to the water, when I saw that a man was running along the opposite bank and was throwing a rope to a man who was struggling in the water. As fast as possible I pulled off my shoes with spurs, my leggings, and watch, and then ran into the water. Meanwhile Johann had already stripped off almost all his clothes and was in the middle of the river and reached the man just as he had stopped struggling and was going under. But he had grabbed him right away by the head and raised him up. Meanwhile several other people and I helped pull him to land. Johann got praise, which he received largely with indifference.

New Braunfels
no date
Rudolf from father

Münzenberger is riding into camp today and the thought that this paper on which I am writing here can and will be in your hands tomorrow morning has so much charm for me that I cannot deny myself the pleasure of sending it to you, although it contains little or nothing that is new. We are in good health and hope the same of you. We are having very warm weather and suspect you are not very cold either. The following has happened: The black cow is dead, and the skin is at Brown's [Braun's?]. Wolfgang Kapp came yesterday to fetch Hedwig, who has left quite a pleasant impression with us all. It still has not rained. Meusebach drove away from here yesterday. When he returns he means to take his family back with him for some weeks. The political news is that the Conscription Law contained very many leniencies, of which I am very glad. The reports from the *New York Herald* are that an intervention of European powers is viewed as imminent, which I like very much hearing, because if something of that sort does not put an end to the affair, it seems it will stretch out endlessly like noodle dough. For now, my wish for an armistice and indefinite leave with half pay until the definite conclusion is reached. Your mother, sisters, and brothers embrace you tenderly and are looking forward to the time of a reunion. In Mexico the French are said to have been victorious again. If anybody rides to New Braunfels from camp, do send a couple of lines along in the mail. Till then, Adio. Kreuz and Kessler are running for sheriff.[22] Carl does not know yet when he is coming to camp. His eyes are still not well, especially mornings. Your old friend and father. E. Coreth*

Between excursions to "San Marcostown" and Springtown and to [Allison?] Williams's farm on York's Creek to buy goatskins from which they planned to make riding pants and perhaps jackets, the men had assignments in camp. Rudolf wrote on more than one occasion of his work as a farrier. "I have quite a pleasant job now; I am employed as a blacksmith. I like the work on its own account and on this occasion am also learning to really acquire the craft. The Schulzes are very skillful workers and so one keeps learning methods one only stumbles on very slowly when one is on his own."[23] On 30 July he added: "I am pretty useful to the company. Old Schulze and I shoe the company horses from morning till night, and everyone considers that hard work, which it is too. . . . I am very pleased that I had the opportunity to practice this trade, and I have made good use of it too. I usually now shoe twelve horses a day, when Schulze makes the shoes and the nails for me. . . . Three companies have marched away, I don't know to where."

It was also on 30 July that Rudolf wrote to the family of money, a very serious matter. "The big news is that we were paid this morning. It was not possible for me to draw Carl's pay. They would not let me sign for him. Johann got $78, and I got $46. What we actually get per month I do not know though. If Carl can possibly come soon, I think it would be a good idea. Otherwise the money might run out in the end." And talk of money led to talk of trading, as the father wrote of having given the family mule to Meusebach to sell for him. Of the $125 that the mule brought, Ernst Coreth received $30 in newly printed money. The remainder his agent used to buy a bay horse. Apparently Johann, dealing directly with his brother-in-law, acquired the bay as his mount, where-upon Rudolf recognized the creature as a familiar one, perhaps the same bay that Rudolf had disparaged in an early letter as unworthy to serve him as a battle steed! Just when and how Rudolf may have disposed of the horse is unknown. The fillip to the amusing, though incomplete, tale is that, after trying out the bay for a while, Johann managed to pawn it off briefly on Rudolf again.

There is also one report by Rudolf of cavalry drill: "The day before yesterday, according to Sherwood's wishes, two companies, ours and Co. A, were to present a mock battle, but the officers let the men get into hand to hand struggle, and they struck at each other very energetically, though in a spirit of friendship, with flat sabers and guns.[24] I could take no part in it. I was riding Schramm's horse to York's Creek before noon, and Johann was riding my horse for drill.[25] Yesterday the same business was conducted with Millett's company.[26] I took part that time. I rode the bay; Johann says he prefers the gait of my horse and was riding mine. I don't actually know who would have been the victor, because the men are so brave that if they were to fight in earnest, there would surely be no survivors on either side. I don't think though that that kind of exercise will be conducted anymore" (no date).

In late July and in August the morale of many a Texas German began to sag, as friends or relatives who had participated in the unsuccessful

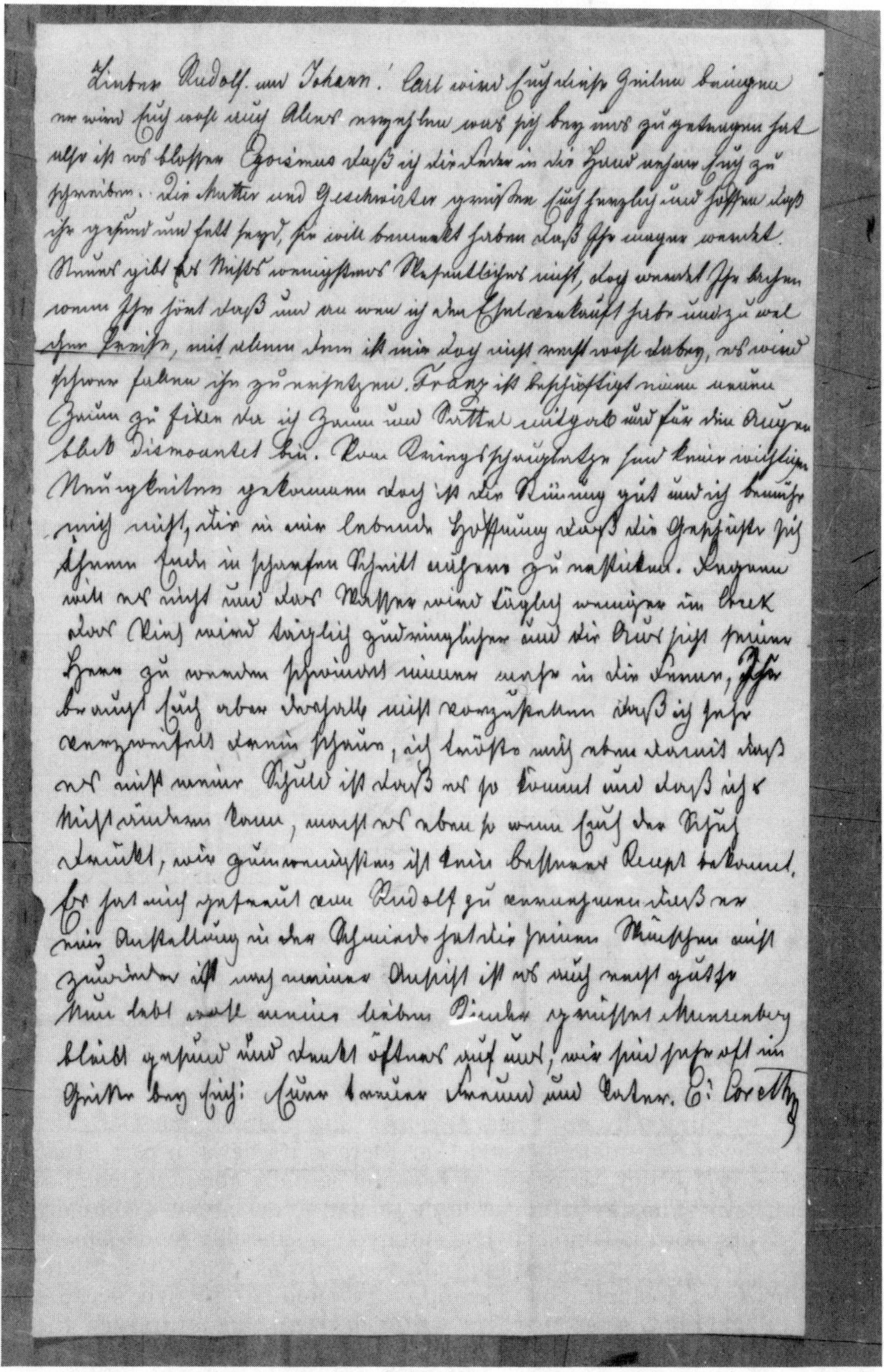

Letter from Ernst Coreth to Rudolf and Johann

Sibley campaign in New Mexico began to straggle homeward, some introducing smallpox into San Antonio, where Alfred Kapp, a patient of Dr. Herff's, was recovering from an unidentified illness and wrote to invite Rudolf for a visit during the latter's approaching leave (from San Antonio, 21 July 1862).[27] From a preserved permit, one learns that Rudolf's leave, granted him for the period of 2-9 August, was extended to 12 August by Colonel Woods himself. A baffling note from Hermann Kämmerling from the same month (partly indecipherable, but evidently 10 August 1862) conveys the depressed, restive mood of himself and several named comrades remaining in camp and strongly suggests that the circle of friends, including the Coreths, was toying with the idea of escaping further service, perhaps by going to Mexico. At almost exactly the same time, such an act cost the lives of a large number of Hill Country Germans in the most dramatic incident of its kind.

In the summer of 1862, Eduard Degener of Sisterdale, who had been an outspoken liberal in the 1854 political meetings, gathered around him a group of men, including two of his sons aged twenty and twenty-one, and made arrangements for them to travel to Mexico. The majority were German, but the group also included several Anglo-Americans and a Mexican. Some seem to have intended joining the Union forces after crossing Mexico; others merely wished to escape Confederate service. Approximately sixty, none over thirty-five years of age, set out for the border under the leadership of Major Fritz Tegener, traveling at an unhurried pace but by the most direct route possible. Of these, some twenty-eight, who decided along the way to return to Fredericksburg, were exposed to the epidemic of shootings and hangings that later gripped the Hill Country, as feelings there reached an even more irrational level than before. On 10 August a Confederate force attacked the remaining members of the escaping group at their encampment on the Nueces River, killing some outright and murdering the survivors, except for a few who escaped.[28] Reports of these horrors slowly filtered eastward to more densely populated areas, where fragments of information reached the ears of soldiers.

Camp Clark
26 August 1862
Rudolf to family

... You will probably have heard from Münzenberger that Carl and Alfred rode to Sisterdale; beyond that there is no news in camp that might concern us; but there are reports almost daily about the conflict at Fort Clark.[29] The day before yesterday a man from Carolan's company came, saying that the Unionists had suffered considerably more damage than our people, because their guns did not reach as far as the soldiers' sharpshooters.[30] I cannot give that report any credence though, because the man said that, after the fight was over, the soldiers dragged the wounded away from the camping ground and had them shot dead one by one, and that seems very improbable to me, really. Maybe it is put out by the Unionists in San Antonio. Yesterday a man came and wanted to talk to Alfred or Carl, to whom he brought a letter. He lives near Camp Verde,[31] and Saturday on his way here he got to Kapps. He told me that the two Degeners, Albert Bruns, and several others that I do not know, thirty men in all, had been killed, and we had only three dead and sixteen wounded, Beyond that he heard at Kapps' that old man Degener had been arrested and brought to San Antonio. He is said to have written a letter to somebody by the Rio Grande, hoping for a chance to take the Unionists to Mexico, and the letter is said to have been opened. If that is true, he may have lots of trouble ahead. I am curious to hear the official report.

Though the martial law that had been in effect in Texas since May was lifted in early September, the Hill Country felt little relaxation of tensions. Some of Woods's Regiment, but conspicuously not Co. F with its heavily German membership, was sent to patrol the area late in the summer, and it was in a camp on the Pedernales River some fifteen miles from Fredericksburg that a member of Co. G recorded having come across hanged human bodies cut down and left to rot as they floated on the water, an experience which was not unique.[32] These atrocities, it must be emphasized, were not the acts of Indians but of Caucasians against one another.

Probably for a combination of reasons—the slowness of Capt. Podewils to get back from San Antonio with clothing for the men (Hermann Kämmerling to Rudolf, Camp Clark, August 1862), the lack of urgent need for their services at this juncture, or the wisdom of dispersing the discontented men until the current tensions had diminished somewhat— the Coreths and their closest army friends were detailed to Sisterdale at the end of the summer to work at something they were all sure to have preferred. The timing could not have been better. Not only was Alfred Kapp in need of more time to recuperate fully, but also Hedwig Coreth had announced to the family that she was pregnant (Carl to parents, from Camp Clark, 10 August 1862; Carl from father, from New Braunfels, 22 August, with enclosed note for Rudolf).

Assembled to produce sixshooters for the army on or near the Ernst Kapp farm, not only the Coreth brothers, but at times also Adolph Münzenberger, August Schimmelpfennig, Hermann Kämmerling, and a somewhat nebulous character variously called "Wilhelm der Schmidt" or "Schmidt Willem" were involved in the project. All were under the direction of Alfred Kapp, who had special qualifications resulting from a tour of the eastern United States in 1856-57, during the course of which he had worked at the Colt factory in Hartford. Together these men produced a number of pistols (six, it is thought) which experts describe as combining certain features of the Colt, the Remington, the Smith and Wesson, and the Rogers and Spencer. Only one is known to exist today.[33]

Sisterdale
no date
Rudolf to family

You must excuse me for not having written you sooner. . . . I did not
know that mail goes through here only once a week, and then I was very
busy from the first moment here, and we have had light for only the last
couple of nights. Today is Monday. Wednesday the postman comes
through here. . . . We are getting along quite well. We are all in good
health, except for Carl, who has a boil on his hand. It isn't so bad though
that it keeps him from working. We are managing our own household.
Münzenberger cooks and Johann looks after the horses. We still cannot
all work at one time, because we don't have the necessary tools, but we
don't want to get too settled anyway until we know whether our work
is found to be satisfactory. The first sixshooter probably will be ready
this week; then Alfred will take it to San Antonio, and if the people there
are satisfied with it, we will make arrangements to do the work considerably faster than it went with this first. . . . We expected to cast a part
of the pistol of brass, but it did not work because we wanted to hurry
too much and had not let the forms dry sufficiently. After we had tried
that for several days in a row, Wilhelm the smith suggested to us that
it be made of iron; and when we saw that in the moist weather we had
last week it would always take a few days for the forms to become dry
enough, we did that, and have been working with the iron some days
now. We are progressing well and I think the pistol will turn out quite
well too. Here the report of a very big victory on the old battle ground
of Manassas [final days of August 1862] reached us. If that is true, then
one does probably have good reason to believe that the war might soon
end. Actually, though I can't find cause to want to change my days, I
wish it with all my heart. I cannot write you much about our surroundings. I very seldom get in contact with people other than my comrades.
I can say only that the people are quite polite.[34] The horses seem to be
doing quite well here. We bought them bran and feed them regularly
once a day. If I knew that it would be pleasant for Father to have Vaio
down there, I would send him at the first opportunity. Vaio stays in
place quite well here and can be left free all the time. The pack saddle
rubbed my horse a bit, but it did not get infected and has already healed.
The old bruise on the back of Johann's bay broke open and is infected
again. Johann washed it and gave him Hep. Salfuris but it looks quite
bad.[35] I almost forgot to say that we bought twenty-eight goats for slaughtering at $1.50 each. Three of them were lost as we were driving them
home. Münzenberger had to shoot one and two ran away. Now we still
have twenty-five. For today Adio.

New Braunfels
no date
Rudolf from father

. . . You made a good buy with the goats. Braun wants to give you a
dollar a hide. However, perhaps you will tan them yourselves, which
would be the most advantageous. They make very good shoes, the cor-
doban ones I have been dreaming of for so long. Your skins at Braun's
are ready and turned out beautifully. I hope to have news of the sixshooters soon. I am getting a bit worried, since after three weeks I have
not yet heard anything, and I learned from Agnes, who returned again
with Meusebach in good health and spirits, that Dr. Kapp and [Chris-
toph] R[h]odius went through Leon Spring on Friday but not Alfred.
About the horses: I would prefer to use your plug Vaio, if he can pull.
You might try that, but only if he can already do it, not if he can be
taught to do it; I am not up to that anymore. In political matters, you
probably know that Washington was taken by Lee [false]. I think we are
now at the critical point. Either the North will become enraged, then
the war will last a lot longer; or it is fed up, and then there would
probably be an end to it soon. Vedremo [It. = "We shall see"]. We are
well. There is no news. Our jobs progress at half a snail's pace. But I
don't know how to do the work any better. . . . For today Adio. Right;
you could try sprinkling dogbane powder on the bay's wound.[36] I think
it will do him good, and it wouldn't hurt to put a bit on Carl's hand
either.

This letter contains a postscript, one of the few instances of a preserved message from Agnes Coreth to her sons. From the penmanship
it is obvious that she seldom wrote, though the text is quite legible, and
the language is significantly more regional in coloration than her husband's. She obviously had a strongly Austro-Bavarian accent that is
reflected in her spelling, as is often true of Rudolf also, but not, oddly,
of the other members of the family. The older children perhaps had
some schooling in Austria, and the younger ones had more opportunities
in Texas than Rudolf had in either of these places. Agnes Coreth writes:
"Since your father left a blank space, I want to send you my heartiest
greetings, all of you: Karl [sic], Rudolf, and Johann especially. I am well.
At Agnes's all the children and Lisbeth [Schmuck] were asleep and this
morning a rattlesnake with six rattles lay by Lisbeth's feet. Meusebach
killed it. Farewell, all my dears, among whom I count Hedwig too. Your
ever-loving mother. We send greetings most sincerely to you all and send
regards to the Kapp and Wipprecht family. Kind regards to Hedwig."

Sisterdale
the sixth [no month or year]
Rudolf to family

. . . I got here yesterday at 7 am. The first day I got to this side of York's
Creek. . . . Johann and I have been working yesterday and today on a

new cylinder. I think it will be ready tomorrow. The day before yesterday
. . . Carl, Alfred, and Johann had poured the forms. The castings are
considerably better than the earlier ones, but they are still not quite
good. We will be able to use the one, but I think that it will be better
to make the parts out of iron anyway, because they can be thinner. If we
can, we want to make three more pistols, two big ones and a navy six. . . .
Up to now we have been eating at Kapps'. Tomorrow we are beginning
our own household though. Mr. Kapp sends the request that Father
order him the tri-weekly *Houston Telegraph* for a half year, and Johann
asks me to send his greetings. . . . For now good night. My light is going
out too. Degener's verdict is said to be in but not published yet. People
say things look bad for him.[37] . . .

New Braunfels
10 October 1862
Rudolf from Adoph Münzenberger

I was in camp on Sunday and did good business in so far as possible. I
drew our corn rations for two months in the amount of $122.50. And in
the absence of all colonels I dealt with Sherwood and received from him
a letter from him to Lt. Col. Benton in San Antonio, which recommends
to him to take up the matter for us with General [Hamilton Prioleau]
Bee, since Sherwood himself has money in hand for buying weapons and
to arrange for us a leave of indefinite duration, which Bee must sign.
Today, Monday, I am going to San Antonio and hope to return with the
leave permit. Please enter your figures, so that we can compare yours
and mine up there [in Sisterdale]. I am missing $5.00 that I cannot
account for. Yours. Ad. Münzenberger. P. S. I am bringing along the rifle
barrel.

Sisterdale
14 October 1862
Rudolf to family

. . .Our work progresses but still slowly. I think this one [sixshooter] will
be better than the first, which we delivered. . . . A few days ago we had
a hard rain here, almost two inches, and the night of Saturday to Sunday
and from Sunday to Monday we had two degrees of cold [?], so that
everything was pretty much frozen. Kapp already had a nice tobacco
crop, and it froze too. As we heard, it rained very hard in New Braunfels
too. I am curious whether the creek tore away the fence. The frost will,
I hope, not have reached down to your place. . . . Our household is not
really in order yet as it was in times past. First of all, we are lacking a
cook. One of us has to leave work and prepare something as fast as
possible, and then we are practically out of groceries. . . . The horses are
in quite good condition. . . . I discovered that he [Rudolf's] justifiably
carries the name Fat Black. The strawberry roan [Carl's] is in quite good
shape, and the bay [Johann's] is also fat and his bruise sufficiently healed
so he can be ridden again. Johann wants to ride to Comfort tomorrow

and buy himself a hat. [Christoph] Flach [a Kapp son-in-law], who was here the other day, told him that he still has a soldier's hat that is too small for him and Johann wants to buy it if it fits him. If Münzenberger should perhaps have gotten our winter clothes, I would like to request that you use the parts that do not belong to the uniform, and my two coats that are at your place, if you can use them, for I shall probably have enough with my leather clothes. . . .

With the winter approaching, the family was beginning to suffer shortages, and not just in relation to their wardrobes. Ernst Coreth, still struggling to make good soap, wrote that the last had been so inferior it had almost caused his wife to spoil the laundry and would probably have to be used as scouring soap because there was no salt to be had anymore. "Mother was in town and bought a few bits of cloth for $56 at Runge's, which should cover our nakedness for a while," Ernst wrote. He continued in a more optimistic tone: "He was selling out his piece goods . . . a good sign. People in trade have a nose for such things; maybe he figures that the prices have reached their highest point" (no date). They had discovered "the best coffee surrogate yet," a brew of mesquite beans, but a number of the family, especially Ottilie and her mother, had become quite ill from eating a compote of stewed cactus fruit (no date).

At Sisterdale, too, successes were mingled with failures.

Sisterdale
11 November 1862
Rudolf to family

. . . It is really very important that we make more progress than we have so far, because otherwise there is danger that we may have to return to the regiment again. . . . Alfred has gone to San Antonio, Kämmerling has a very bad finger [and] cannot do anything today. So there are only Carl, Münzenberger, A. Schimmelpfennig, and I, and of these August has to stay home as cook. But in his place, Wilhelm is working for us. We are now taking on two or three sixshooters at once. . . . Carl set up our lathe and altered quite a bit on the frame that improves it. The new drill and bit are also quite good. We bored the parts for one sixshooter and found that to be a big saving in time and strength. . . . Yesterday was a rather important day in my life. A year ago I became a soldier; that gave my life quite a different direction, after all, though I did not think at the time that it would last this long. And a year ago tonight I stood my first watch. Since then my circumstances have actually improved somewhat. I am leading an incomparably more independent existence than I did the first half-year of my service. It seems to me quite uncertain though how long that may continue. Here at least there is constantly talk about Texas being attacked from all sides, and if that should be the case, then none of us wishes to stay here any longer. That our regiment is going to Lavaca does not matter to us yet. They may be doing there what we did all last winter, which I do not wish for them though. That would be even harder for them with their equipment than it was for us. We at least had rather good tents, but the tents we have here are too small, first of all, and of such poor material that I am certain the first healthy wind would tear them to pieces. But if it must come to pass, I am ready at any moment to go along. It would be unpleasant for me, to be sure, if our company got something to do and we should not be there too. My life here is pleasant only so long as it is a way to avoid lying around in camp. What Father writes about the high price of corn is quite unpleasant. Münzenberger bought ten bushels of corn from [Dominicus] Werner [a Coreth neighbor]. . . . It is at your disposal. We won't be making use of it after all. . . . Johann sends greetings.

[Sisterdale?]
[early January 1863?]
Rudolf to family

. . . There is now a hammering and filing all day long that is a joy to hear, and also there is correspondingly more progress. Kämmerling can work again now, and Johann and A. Schimmelpfennig are working too with lots of energy. For Johann we have found a job that seems to suit him completely. He makes knives out of our worn-out files. In this way we can put our files to use again without harm and Johann has his amusement too. We arrived here on New Year's Eve. The first night we were in Comanche Spring, where Meusebach acted as our genial host. We left there at half past twelve and arrived here about nine o'clock in the evening. Alfred had already arrived on Sunday. . . . It seems to me . . . you all were in better spirits when we were down there now than you were back when I came down to see you for Father's brithday. I am ascribing that to the circumstance that you aren't quite as swamped with work as you were. . . . If only Münzenberger were right in thinking that by 15 January of 1863 there would be peace, then the year would surely not go by without event, but up to now there seems to be no prospect that this prophecy may be fulfilled. I only console myself with the thought that I can't do anything about it anyway, and that it is as it is. . . .

[Sisterdale ?]
[mid- to late January 1862]
Rudolf to family

Tomorrow Johann is riding to your place. He has to leave earlier than we because he still wants to have a pair of shoes made for himself. I think we will leave during the early days of next week, maybe on Monday. To leave earlier is hardly possible because we still have too much invested in our supplies and nothing has happened down there which would require our presence at the moment. I traded my horse for [Dr. Rudolph] Wipprecht's [a Kapp son-in-law]. I had to add $75. It had really become necessary for me now to have another horse to replace the black, which is very thin. I have to ask Father to give me the money, because our work did not profit us so much that we can cover more than the cost of our trip. . . . It is the only horse that I could get. . . . *Friday:* Johann's departure was delayed a bit. There was still some work to do that he had to help us with. We won't be leaving as early either as I had thought. The departure is set for next Thursday. For the moment, I asked that Father not draw the money at [Jacob] Schmitz's . . . I think I have about as much as the amount of the debt. . . . Adio until we meet again.

Münzenberger's happy speculations were, needless to say, somewhat premature. Actually there had been one good development for Texas, namely the wresting of Galveston from Union control on New Year's Day, but he cannot have known about that at the time. All along the coast, the Galveston-Velasco portion of which had been under the command of Col. Joseph Bates for some months, naval engagements were causing concern as Mexico became an increasingly important escape hatch and source of trade, the gulf ports being effectively blockaded. Early in October, General John B. Magruder had taken over command of Confederate forces in Texas, and late in November he had succeeded General Hébert as head of the area embracing Texas, New Mexico, and Arizona. Soon the Coreth brothers would be in a position to give their personal evaluations of "Gentleman John" based on observations at close range, for they were being sent to South Texas, back to their unit and a bit nearer the action.

Grains of Sand

Port Lavaca
10 February 1863
Rudolf to family

We got here the day before yesterday. . . . The first night we were at Schuhard's in Seguin, because it rained hard and we couldn't get any fodder for the horses otherwise. The second night we slept at Kent's ["Kind's"].[1] The third and fourth nights we slept in the open. The fifth night we were in Victoria in the hotel,[2] the sixth along the railroad [track] on the prairie,[3] and the seventh here in the barracks. We had already heard underway various rumors that our regiment was to be dismounted, and we considered that to be entirely likely too because of the great shortage of corn. Upon our arrival our suspicions were confirmed too, because the colonel told us with regret that we would already have to take our horses home tomorrow. He told us he thought that if the harvest were good this year we would get our horses back. I don't believe that though; I think instead that the people just say that to make the whole thing easier for themselves or us. Be that as it may, it is simply necessary and so we have to be content. The colonel and the lieutenant colonel did all they could to postpone this change at least, but without success. The colonel seemed to be very pleased with the pistol.[4] Alfred and I handed it over to him and we believe that he will help us in future undertakings. Carl and August [Schimmelpfenning] rode away with our horses yesterday. We did not care to live in the general barracks because we would have had only very limited space there and so we looked for quarters for ourselves and did find a rather good room where we aren't together with the entire company at least, which does, after all, have some very unpleasant sides. It is really disgraceful how the soldiers waste the property of the citizens here. The government supplies too little firewood, so that one must hunt for other wood for oneself, and one only finds that in buildings, but instead of taking only what they need, they take pleasure in destroying whatever they can. Oysters are quite cheap there, 100 for $1.50. Coffee costs $2.00. Tobacco is $1.50 a plug [*"Blok"*]. The area here is better too than where we were last winter. Here there is no sand and the town is situated much higher above the sea than our camp lay. If we stay here longer, I hope we will find additional good features to the place. Today the train leaves for Victoria and I hope that you will get these lines soon. Adio. Friendly greetings to you from Johann, Münzenberger, Kämmerling, and your loyal son and brother Rudolf.

Port Lavaca
16 February 1863
Rudolf to family

Till now the postman has not brought me a letter from you. . . . We got the *Neu-Braunfelser Zeitung* yesterday; there is nothing much new in it though. . . . We lead as pleasant a life here as soldiers can expect. Our rations are quite good and we can make good use of the few dollars we saved from our traveling funds. The duties are not heavy, though a third of the regiment is away. One gets watch duty and trench work about every fortnight. Johann and I were assigned to each one time together. . . . There doesn't seem to be any drilling done. . . . Our duties consist only of going to roll call in the mornings and cooking our food, which we do by turns. . . . Johann sometimes goes hunting; the day before yesterday he shot two jack rabbits, which Kämmerling roasted nicely yesterday. Yesterday Johann went again but did not find anything to shoot. We were lucky in our choice of a residence too. The house belongs to an Italian who at first seemed very distrustful and to whom it almost seemed unpleasant that we wanted to be here, even though it would be a protection for him if soldiers were to live in it, because then it won't be carried off as firewood, after all, which would be attempted at least, if it were to be standing empty. He said to us at first that we could use the room but should not go into the yard, because he wanted to keep it for himself, so we had to cook on the road. We were satisfied with all that and wanted to let the man develop confidence in us first, and we seem to have succeeded in doing that now too. He seems to realize now that we are decent people who don't intend to take any of his belongings from him. Yesterday when it was raining he told us we should just go into his yard and cook there under the roof. He said too that we could fetch water from his cistern. When we meet we now talk very cordially together and he visits us a couple of times every day. In short, the relationship is still in the process of improving. Up to now we have always had lots of spare time. From time to time we still have to work on the household furnishings, but that will stop before long and then we want to start studying Spanish again.[5] For this purpose our landlord wants to supply us with Spanish books. We spent some of our money on oysters. I always think of Father when we do that, but unfortunately that doesn't help him any, and I still have to eat them myself. Yesterday we ate three hundred. Alfred and I bought one hundred for lunch, and those Alfred, Kämmerling, and I ate right away. During the afternoon we helped our landlord's companion ["Companyon"] shell corn, and when that was over the landlord, who is named Fritze, bet Alfred two hundred oysters it would be twenty bushels.[6] Alfred lost the wager, so we fetched the oysters and opened them. Fritze brewed some very good coffee and so we had a very good supper. A soldier can't expect absolute freedom, and the only thing still lacking for me is news that you are getting along well, and I hope to get that soon. Johann says to ask you to send the knife down by way of Carl if possible and sends greetings. Also Münzenberger [sends the same].

Sisterdale
18 February 1863
Rudolf from Carl

I got here yesterday. In New Braunfels everyone is getting along well. It rained hard and the grass and grain are doing quite well. . . . The cattle look pretty good . . . only Charlie [an ox] is dead, and that is because he either overate or for some other reason, not because of skinniness. . . . I stayed in New Braunfels one day to let the horses rest. . . . We got there on Saturday evening. On Monday I rode away from the house at six o'clock and intended to ride up to here but couldn't manage it in one day, so I got here yesterday at ten o'clock soaked through. I really wasn't at ease about it either, because the norther had made me quite cold too, but I hope that that will let up again soon. But what really is uppermost in my mind is Hedwig, who, as I have also written to the commander of the camp, is sick and expecting her confinement soon. I can't leave her this way in any case. I have therefore written for an extension; do talk to our friends and you all see to it that this is accomplished. At the same time as this letter, either Schulze or the captain [Podewils], whichever is in command, will get a letter from me requesting an extension of my leave. I did not want to attach a medical certificate, because if it is from Dr. Kapp it might look one-sided or prejudiced. See what you can do about the situation. I don't think the colonel will make an issue of it.[7] I want to stay here until I get an answer. If I should not get an extension they can just cut off my head, for all I care; I won't go. As always, hoping for the best, I remain your loyal brother, Carl H. Coreth.

Port Lavaca
24 February 1863
Rudolf to family

There is still no letter from you. . . . We spend one day after another on the edge of boredom, because we haven't found a steady job yet. Alfred and I were at a steam mill that is here, which is by a cast iron foundry and a little workshop, and offered our spare time to the owner, but he said he had nothing to do now. There are hardly any books here, and whoever has any does not like to lend them. We kept looking for Spanish books. . . . Yesterday in the artillery mess, where Froboese is, we found a grammar, which they lent us.[8] So now we have a cure for our boredom for some time to come. We wouldn't be bored at all, if we could be alone; but we are hardly free for an hour daily from visitors who want to delight us with their own boredom. Just now we have five of them in the room. We haven't received any money yet. Captain [Wm. O.] Martin [Co. D], who has gone to San Antonio to get funds, is expected daily. The two companies of artillery from Shea's battalion that are lying here were paid out last week.[9] One of the companies consists almost entirely of Irishmen, and they are doing their best to invest their money in whiskey, and [Lt. Col. Nat] Benton is doing everything in his power to hinder the sale of whiskey. Almost daily he holds an inspection of the house, and if he finds whiskey it is confiscated. That is good though, because when the Irishmen get drunk they are just like animals. Yesterday Ireland's company from Corpus Christi arrived here. The only person I know in it is Ferdinand Dietz.[10] He looks quite well but has lost his belly. They are quite well satisfied with the situation here; they would rather have stayed in Corpus Christi though, where they say it is quite beautiful. . . . No political news seems to get here. There is talk again of an armistice by 1 May, but I think that report originated here. . . . Then too it is said that Russia is invading Turkey and that as a consequence France is ordering its troops withdrawn from Mexico.[11] I, for my part, have accustomed myself to the idea that the war might last another couple of years, because it seems to me the end is as little in sight as it was last year at this time. Now farewell, and write me soon about how you are. Rudolf. P. S. Johann and the others send cordial greetings.

New Braunfels
24 February [postmark]
Rudolf from father

Yesterday evening we got your dear lines, which made us very happy, especially me. In it [the letter] there is expressed a spirit of peace and an attitude of sensible content with what life brings that I so very much wish for you and for all my dear children. . . . We have planted some corn, peas, and durra and now intend to continue with the planting. The draft ox Charlie died. He got bloated, which we failed to notice at first, and then nothing did good anymore. Now we have hitched Brandy to Ben [oxen?]. I drove them yesterday. Joseph prodded them, so we can manage. Of political news, thanks to your efforts to order the *Almanac Express [Alamo Express?]* for me, I am as well informed as one can be in Texas. As well as I am able to understand, we seem to be in good shape and the hope for peace is not too daring. Two things struck my attention: one, the boring legislature, which has determined that Texas will take over its part of the Confederate debt, even if it should separate from the Confederacy; and the other, from the *New York Herald,* which states that [Louis] Napoleon wants to divide Mexico between himself and President Davis. I cannot make good sense of this, *yet* these are statements that really attract one's attention. The parity for the rate of exchange of Confederate money was not accepted, because it is against the constitution. So farewell now my dear Rudolf. Mother, your sisters and brothers embrace you and Johann in spirit. We send cordial regards to the rest of our friends. Franz saw some of your men who are up here. They said they would not be leaving here until the first of March. Don't let time lie heavy on your hands; and eat lots of oysters and think of me with every other dozen. Maybe then I will sense it magnetically and have a bit of a change from burnt flour soup and mash and mash and burnt flour soup.[12] Adio, my old fellow. Your friend and father E. Coreth*

Port Lavaca
4 March
Rudolf to family

Today I got the first letter from you all and one from Carl. . . . There
are no news reports, actually, except that there are some prospects of
our getting our horses back if the grass is good enough so that they can
get along without corn. . . . The death of Charlie probably does not matter too much now, since most of the work has been done. Our captain
returned today and was very glad that he was not punished. That also
made him sympathetic towards Carl, who can stay as long as necessary
up there now. Adio for today. I will write more again next time. Rudolf.

Port Lavaca
11 March 1863
Rudolf to family

. . . August Schimmelpfennig came back the day before yesterday. He
said that the high water tore away the creek fence [at the Coreth farm]
again. . . . Unfortunately I have no prospects of helping you improve it
this time. We are well, and the marching orders to Brownsville that were
read to us a couple of days ago give us material for suspicions and
speculations, if we have nothing else to do. We have prospects of getting
our horses again, and if that is the case we will be glad to go anywhere.
Lt. Col. Benton traveled to Houston yesterday to ask whether we are to
get our horses again now. He may get back by Sunday, and then I will
write you immediately what he has found out, so that Carl can act
accordingly when he comes down. We will probably be transferred to
Victoria soon, the captain says as soon as next Monday; and from there
we will either go by foot directly to Brownsville or first go for the horses.
If that were to be the case I might get up there to see you again. We are
always glad of orders, because even if we were to have to go on foot, we
always like seeing something new. There is lots of talk of peace here, but
whether with reason or not I do not know, because we only get the *Neu-
Braunfelser Zeitung,* and there is nothing about that in it. It is said that
the generals in Tennessee have orders not to attack anymore, because
negotiations are underway. I, for my part, do not believe it for the moment yet. I am preparing myself to be a soldier for at least another year,
because it seems to me that the North is not as bad off yet as we were
a year ago at this time, and it seems to me that it, like the South, will
carry on as long as it can. Even if the new Congress is inclined to peace,
Lincoln is not required to convene it until next December, and so he has
the power to continue the war until then at least. . . . I am afraid there
may have been a freeze up at your place. . . . The corn is not so high yet,
I think, that it would have been greatly harmed by a frost. Woods gave
the command of this place to Major Shea, who seems to be going to the
trouble of making us feel his power as long as we are still here. Up to
now we have smoked or eaten or stood as we pleased at our posts. Just
now A[ugust]. Schulze, who is officer of the day, came with an order

from Shea in which he commands that no man may smoke, sit, or speak with anyone when at his post. He said that Schulze should bring anybody who does not follow the order to the guardhouse, or else he would punish him himself. I doubt that our men, officers or enlisted personnel, will pay any attention to that and instead they will do just as before. Today the train from Victoria is coming again. I think it will bring me a letter from you. Farewell to you all, and cherish your son and brother Rudolf.

vicinity of Brownsville
no date [April 1863][13]
Rudolf to family

We have finally arrived at the end of our trip in good health. We are lying in camp six or seven miles from Brownsville on the San Patricio Road and are waiting for Benton, who rode ahead in order to look for a permanent campground for us. Carl was in town yesterday to ask about letters and got one from his wife. He told me things are going badly, that she is sick. It seems to me that the active life is having a good effect on Carl; he is generally in a good humor. Actually he was so at all times on the trip until yesterday when he returned depressed. Now though, it has let up quite a bit again. . . . Our march was, for a military march, a rather hard one. We had to make long stretches per day in order to get to water, and that often turned out to be very salty, and the stupidity of our captain did not contribute to making the way much pleasanter. Now we are separated from our horses again. They are being herded by our men about thirty miles this side of San Patricio, because there is no more good grass or water nearer here. At the beginning I was not altogether content with this change; now though, I have come to see that it is best, because here there is no grass at all that a horse could eat. Between here and King's Ranch, where our horses are, there is a stretch of maybe forty miles of very deep sand. The only water that one finds is in wells and that has a strong taste of salt. At the beginning of this desert [Maj. Gen. John Bankhead] Magruder and his staff caught up with us and moved into a camp not far from ours. The same evening Capt. [Wm. L.] Foster ["Forster"; of Co. D], who at the time was commandant of three companies including ours, gave the order that two men from each company should ride ahead under the command of a lieutenant from Millett's company and look for a suitable campground on the Arroyo Colorado. From our company H[ermann]. Conring and I were ordered to go along. We rode away that same evening before sundown and got out of the sand at noon on the second day. Magruder's advance group caught up with us a couple of times and told us that Magruder had dismounted the regiment and that our men would have to make their way through the sand on foot. We rode as far as the Colorado, where we were able to convince ourselves that there was no grass to be found in the area, because it is horribly dry so that nothing can grow but mesquite, cactus, and salt grass, which the horses don't eat. Our horses ate hardly anything for thirty-six hours, and we had to ride quite hard, after all. So I longed to dismount and felt pity for those people who, as I thought, were having to walk through the sand. On the way back we met Magruder. Our Lieutenant asked him what had become of our men and he confirmed everything that his men had already told us earlier. He has fifteen baggage wagons in his entourage, not counting the wagon in which his staff is following. When our lieutenant said that it surely was hard for the men to march through the sand, he said that was just a minor matter. He made a very bad impression on all the people I talked to. It sickens the men that a soldier should make such a fuss while we had to suffer such comparative want. In every wagon they have a big bottle of whiskey. He looks like a real drunken innkeeper or brewer, and his staff looks like an English riding party. I have never seen a company of such conceited and jaded faces together at one time. Riding with Magruder is a young woman, and while the lieutenant was talking with him, she was conversing in quite a common way with the teamster who drove the wagon behind theirs. Soon thereafter we met C[hristoph]. Pfeuffer, who brought us a letter from Col. Benton, in which he commanded us to ride back into camp before that day was over, since the horses were to be sent back the next day. He had taken the responsibility of not dismounting our men but rather letting them ride through the sand, and only then would he send back the horses. We had to ride over forty miles that day to get to the place he indicated. As if that were not enough, one of our horses gave out and we had to simply drag it for the last eight miles. Conring had the lariat on the saddle horn and another man and I pulled as hard as we could. We got to the designated place quite late at night. The companies didn't get there until the next day. We stayed there until the next day, then the horses were sent back and we went on toward Brownsville. Two companies left in the morning under the command of Col. Benton, and we stayed until evening in order to wait for wagons that were to take our things away. We made three more miles that day but didn't catch up with the others until we reached this camp. It is a stretch of about fifty miles, and we made that in three days. The walking wasn't hard for us. The road is good and firm, and whenever one of us got tired there was still room in the wagons so that he could ride for a stretch. Some rode all day long. The rations were good. We always had fresh meat, flour, sugar, bacon, and often had a chance to buy coffee for $2.00 or $2.50 a pound. The rations we get here seem to be very good. Today we drew bacon, rice, coffee, sugar, flour, and soap. I know only very little about the town so far. If I get there before the letter goes off I can write a little about it. For today Adio.

Camp on the Rio Grande
30 April 1863
Rudolf to family

The day before yesterday we got Father's letter of the thirteenth. We were happy to see from it that things are going well for you at home. Carl got less good reports from Sisterdale. He told me that Hedwig is badly sick, that she had a very badly infected breast and is in poor health in other ways too. I hope that he is imagining the circumstances to be worse than they actually are, which, it seems to me, is very much his inclination. Carl has been somewhat sick for a few days. This morning he broke out with a rash. He has a little fever with it, but not much. I think that everything will be all right when the rash goes away. We are attributing it to the diet, because since we have been here we have received no fresh meat anymore but only salted meat and salted bacon, because our commissary has not been set up yet. The rest of us are all well. Carl sent my last letter off before I wanted it sent; I meant to send it only after I had been in Brownsville. Carl sent it while I was in town. Alfred, Johann, and I had leave for two days and a night. The first day and night we stayed in Brownsville, and the next day we looked around Matamoros, which has earned itself the name "la heroica." Brownsville is not much bigger than New Braunfels, but it has bigger buildings. It has very lively traffic. One can get almost anything for silver; paper is worth from 12½-20¢ on the dollar, and even the specie exchange rates are higher than formerly. In Matamoros this is how things stand too, except that many won't accept paper there at all. Among the military men the army regulars prevail, and an ordinary soldier is just a very insignificant creature here, because the officers are very much convinced of their importance, and the merchants easily figure out for themselves that one cannot do anything grandiose on a monthly wage of five dollars at most, and they are just as pleased if you buy nothing at all as when you buy something for paper, because one bit [$.125] in silver is more to them than $1.00 in paper. We found a couple of acquaintances here in Kampmann's company: Franz Daniel Gepart and Th. Butz, who seemed glad to see us and took pains to help us pass the time pleasantly.[14] Then we saw August Heick ["Heik"].[15] Alfred found the merchant Jordan in Matamoros.[16] They did not seem to place much value on our company, and you all can well imagine that we did not run after them. In Matamoros there are quite a few beautiful date palms and royal palms. Of the latter there are quite a few right here at camp. At the market over there one can get some tropical fruits, but we didn't buy any. It rained quite hard during the last nights and it is still raining quite often now, but higher up it must have rained a lot harder, because the river has risen several feet. I hope it rained at your place too. Yesterday we had a big parade. General Magruder did not come himself but just sent two adjutants out here. I think they were satisfied with us. Today we are supposed to have muster in order to get our pay. Then we shall see whether many of our men desert. Up to now only three from Maverick's company have run out, but it is possible that the men are waiting for money in order to have a bit of travel funds. They say we are supposed to be getting paid a bit of silver too, but that is still very indefinite. Our camp is situated about two miles below Brownsville on the river in a bottom that has a type of Brazos cane instead of underbrush. I think it is one of the most healthful places in the area; at least the south-wind can blow into the camp quite well, because on the south side of the camp there is a big prairie. Our mess has two tents, and yesterday we made ourselves a roof of branches, a table, and benches, and so now we are as comfortable as we can be in camp. Carl, Johann, and the others send greetings.

Rudolf.

Rudolf to father [continued]

Our captain [Podewils] acted quite like an enemy to our whole mess on the march down here without our having given him any reason, just because he was so bored he did not know what else to do. We did not put up with that and had a couple of rather serious confrontations with him, as a consequence of which he avoids us a lot now. But we are going to collect facts with which we can protect ourselves later from being plagued, by our threatening him with publishing them. We have quite a bit collected already and we have now managed to provide ourselves with some rest that way. It occurred to me that you told me once of some dirty business he had pulled with the Protection Society. If you learned of this in a way that one can make use of, and you tell me about it in detail, I would be pleased. It would not occur to me to attack a man in this way if I could settle the score with him in any other way. But he expressed himself in a way that makes it impossible to think of a direct attack; one does not, after all, like to let oneself be deceived [*"sich schikanieren lassen"*] in this way by a man like him. In one camp Alfred's horse ran away. The company was supposed to march at sunrise, so I requested the captain directly to allow me to help Alfred search, and he denied me that, whereas the others who could not find their horses, among whom was A. Schulze, got people quite effortlessly to look for theirs. He only told us that if we did not find our horses before daybreak it would be our loss, and we would have to go along on foot. When I threatened him with complaining to Benton, he gave in to me completely. In this way he did something or other every day until we threatened him with taking stern measures against him by forcing him to courtmartial us, where we would then be able to bring out our accusations against him as a defense. He answered we should just go ahead and do that; they would not be able to do more than chase him away, and he would be quite content with that. Münzenberger had this conversation with him, and since then he has left us alone. But one never knows whether he won't start that again sometime, and we want to be prepared. So, if you know of some bad trick he pulled that you can tell me of and you wish to do so, I would be pleased. I do not want you to expose yourself to unpleasantness though, because somehow it will be possible to manage with such a wretched person in another way. Adio. You may be imagining that we are in a very unpleasant mood, but that is not at all the case. We are as cheerful as ever, and somebody would really have to make a big effort if he wanted to deprive us of our good humor.

Camp on the Rio Grande
10 May 1863
Rudolf to family

Last week Froboese [sic] came to our camp. He brought along a letter
from Father to us. . . . Carl has been well again for several days. I think
it was our diet that was responsible for his condition, since it consists
of only salted meat and flour. We do, of course, get rice, beans, and peas
too, but they last only a couple of days, and then we have only meat,
bread, and coffee. The rest of us are getting along quite well that way,
and Carl seems to have grown used to it now too. Also we have located
a place in town where one can get a rather large serving of apple juice
for 50¢ paper, and when we get to town we usually go there. I saw H.
[probably Henry; possibly Hermann] Runge in town once. He acted very
cool. I greeted him, and then he shook hands with me without saying a
word and then spoke to other people. I didn't pay any attention to him
after that either. There is not much news from here. The political reports
almost all come from New Orleans, but they contradict one another so
much that one can't make sense of them. First Sibley was supposed to
have won a big victory over the Federals; then again he was supposed
to have been terribly beaten and have lost five hundred men. And General [Sterling?] Price was supposed to be no more than forty miles from
the Texas border; then came a report that [Gen. Edmund] Kirby Smith
had attacked Price from the rear and had completely disrupted his army.
What is the truth in all this we naturally cannot know. Probably all the
reports are exaggerated. That is also how things are with what is to
become of us. One day we are told this and the next that, and always
the people claim to know it from reliable source. A very general view is
that we will be ordered to go to Louisiana. Magruder is supposed to have
said in a speech that recent events have made it necessary for him to
send two cavalry regiments to the border of Louisiana. In short, everybody thinks we are going to be sent to Louisiana; for what reasons the
infantry thinks that, I do not know, and most very much dislike going.
The infantry is deserting on a very great scale. Yesterday twenty men
are supposed to have left the fort [Fort Brown], and our officers are
resigning with all their might. Last week three resigned. Our officers,
with the exception of [originally Third Lieutenant Edgar] Schramm, are
also proceeding with the hope of getting out. I heard that they have
already applied for their discharge. But people are not talking about it
yet. Our Germans from up there are still holding up quite well. Of Bose's
company only three have deserted so far, and none of ours has left yet.[17]
I will be glad to go anywhere; that way one gets to see a bit more of the
world. We are getting our horses back now. The men who had horses
here in camp, of whom Alfred is one, have been sent away to drive our
horses toward us. When we are to march away we do not know yet; in
any case, we won't be staying down here for long anymore. At first it
was said we would still be paid out here before leaving; but nothing
seems to be coming of that. If we were to be stationed farther away from

the Mexican border again, it would probably be quite good for us if we were not to get the money until later, because here it is becoming worth less day by day. Now it is said that the merchants won't accept the dollar for $.125 anymore. The last nights here have been very cold. . . . I am waiting with great curiosity for your letters and hope to get good news. People who have come from up there say that grain prices are falling very rapidly. For today Adio. Rudolf.

New Braunfels
15 May 1863
Rudolf from father

We got your two letters of 1 May on 13 May. You can imagine what joy it was for us to get news of you all, news for which we had longed for quite some time. That is not meant to be a reproach. We were the first if not the only ones who had news of the march and of the arrival from Beeville, and from 21 April from Carl from Brownsville. I discovered accidentally some days ago that letters from Matamoros always arrive on Wednesdays and to Matamoros always leave here on Saturdays. Franz waited [at the post office] for the somewhat delayed arrival of mail and actually did bring us the longed-for news. The information that Carl has a rash made Mother worry a bit. . . . I did not know just how to write to Amalia and Hedwig . . . that Carl was not well, since Hedwig is still said to be very sad, though bodily in good health. So I wrote that you all had reached your destination in good health except for a slight rash which Carl had *too*. All the other news left a more or less good impression. It pleased us to hear that you have good provisions, a nice camp ground,

Ernst Coreth, taken in Texas

have poked your nose into the often-discussed Mexico, and, as you say, are in good spirits. On the other hand, shadows pass over the picture of your existence as you sketch it for us. The undemocratic manner of a soldier's life, the meanness. Dear Rudolf, life strips away one bit of faith in incarnate beauty after another. You are lucky if you manage to undergo this peeling process while young instead of having it happen to you in your old age, when it is too late for one to construct a philosophical system on the basis of these experiences that you have had. What you wish from me I cannot provide, since what I know and have said has nothing to do with the situation. Then too, I hope that you will not need to make use of such weapons. In the course of the next week we hope Froboese will return and tell us about you all, or that the mail will bring us new reports. A letter, it seems, takes twelve days to get here. We, dear Rudolf, are getting along pretty well up to now. We live a rather lonely and peaceful life together; we all work, Mother above all. She has a very beautiful garden. Our peas have been giving us good food for quite some time; greens are coming along; of tobacco she has about a hundred plants. We have planted only about one fourth of the field in [sweet] potatoes because of a shortage of plants. Cotton is coming up, plus quite a lot of melons. Rye and barley are normal; the corn is up nicely, where it is not missing, which fortunately it is not to a great extent. Next week we will presumably be mowing with Tolle's machine. We have five young calves fenced in, and we have all the milk, cheese, and eggs we need. Franz, in addition to his other work, is always busy making shoes. He has already made fifteen or sixteen pairs. The two girls [probably Marie and Anna] are quite industrious and get along pretty well, learning something every day. Joseph and I work in the field and Ottilie ["Ottle"; stress on first syllable] is healthy and eats and drinks quite nicely. The fodder is very good because of the favorable weather conditions, and other people's cattle have not been annoying lately. In politics things look a bit gloomy lately. The Northerners have taken Alexandria in Louisiana. One does not get any report from farther away, only rumors. You probably hear more but only from Northern papers, and those are one-sided views, to say the least, if not intentional lies. From Agnes we get news regularly. They are well, and with the very good weather and the renter, they hope to have a good crop. Amalia has gone to Sisterdale, but we expect her home again soon. According to her last letter she is often homesick. The prices of things are taking a really funny course here. Thus, some time back a pound of coffee cost $3.00 one day, and $5.00 a day later, and $7.00 some days later. A pair of shoes $10.00, tomorrow $15.00. Things almost seem to be going the way they did during the time of the French Revolution, when a pair of boots cost $6,000 in paper, as I recently read in an old book. I waited with the letter until Mother was ready to ride away to mail it. That collection [of mail] now occurs at half past one. Nothing more that is worth mentioning has happened, so farewell for today, my dear Carl, Rudolf, and Johann. Mother and your sisters and brothers and I embrace you. Heartiest greetings from us, your friends as always. Your old man E. Coreth*

— — —

San Fernando
June 3rd

John Coreth a private of Co. "F" 32nd Regt having applied to me for a certificate on which to ground an application for a furlough I certify that he had Dysentery which has so debilitated him that I deem a furlough of 25 days necessary to his complete recovery

Approved   W. D. Kelley
PC Woods   Surgeon to
Col 32 Rgt. Tex. Cavalry   32nd Regt
                                            Texas Cavalry

— — —

Regimental Head Quarters 32th T C
Camp on San Fernando June 4th 1863

Private Rudolf Coreth is hereby detailed from Company F of this Regiment to accompany and be an attendant on Private John Coreth on sick leave and of the same Company. Said R. Coreth will continue on this Service until the patient shall reach his home in Comal County Tex., after which he will rejoin his Company at or, whereever it then may be without delay.

F. Schulze II Lt *Co* F
Commandg Compy

The above Granted with the Condition that he join his Company in 20 days or sooner if practicable.

P. C. Woods
Col 32rg [illegible]

— — —

no place [New Braunfels]
no date [June 1863]
Rudolf to father

Dear Father,

In a few minutes I will be with you myself; unfortunately I am bringing along a very sad report; what it consists of you can already imagine when you hear that I am coming alone.

I am sending these lines ahead so that at least I won't frighten you by my arrival. Rudolf

⭐ Drops of Water

The news that Rudolf was bringing was sad indeed. On 7 June 1863, Johann Coreth, who had passed his eighteenth birthday just the preceding February, died on King's Ranch, where he is buried at an unknown gravesite. It was the second loss the family had sustained that spring, Carl and Hedwig's first child Ernst (named for both grandfathers) having died at Sisterdale on 21 March, nine days after his birth. Carl, who had returned to the army briefly between his wife's confinement and a second leave he had been granted in order to be with her when she became ill, had not been with Rudolf to help when Johann had sickened and died. After a very brief visit with the family at New Braunfels following delivery of the death message, Rudolf was on his way again, once more alone and in search of his army unit.

Camp on the Rocky
27 June 1863
Rudolf to family

I arrived here in camp on the evening of the 25th; everything is going well in our mess. It got hard for me to find the regiment, because everybody I met along the way told me something different about where it was supposed to be staying. Some said it was on King's Ranch, others said in Columbus, and the rest said it was at some place in between. It seemed most likely to me that it must be where it is, and therefore I changed my course above Rancho [?] and came here by way of Gonzales. It rained quite a lot all the way and made the road very dirty. I got quite wet several times. I was always in houses at night. The camp is in quite a good place. We have everything we need: wood, shade, good water, good grass for the horses, and quite good rations. It is perhaps eight miles from Peach Creek, and if we ride there we can also get enough green corn and melons. Yesterday we were paid out again, $61.00 a man. I drew Carl's and Johann's money and will send it home by the first safe opportunity. The people who owed Carl and Johann also paid me the money. I have to break off, because the mail is leaving right away . . . but there is actually not much more to say. . . . Rudolf. Greetings from the mess. Be so kind as to send the letters to me to Sweet Home, in Lavaca County I think.

Camp Rocky[1]
1 July 1863
Rudolf to family

. . . I fear that the creek washed away the fence again, because I heard the Comal has been very high. That makes me very unhappy, because

I see no way that you can manage to do the work, and I have no prospects of getting a leave now, because there are so many who want one. We are getting along quite well, better than ever since having entered the service as far as diet is concerned. Our rations are the same as always, but lately we have had enough butter, green corn, watermelons, tomatoes, and all possible sorts of vegetables (though, to be sure, we have to fetch these things from rather far away) and at very low prices, or even free of charge. The farmers have a great quantity of them. The day before yesterday Alfred and I were away all day in order to look for such things and did not get to a farm where there was enough of them till evening, because we had taken the wrong way. We loaded up our horses as much as we could. We had roasting ears, tomatoes, squash, okra, melons, and some butter. The man did not want to take anything for them, so we hit upon the idea of offering him what was left of our flour, and he accepted that with great pleasure, because flour is the rarest item among the farmers here. . . . Last week we were paid out, except for two months. Up to now, though, I have not been able to find a good opportunity to send Father the money. It is possible that [Franz] Moureau will pay out the money. Kämmerling wants to take the money from me in order to buy himself a horse and then have money deposited for Father at Moureau's. I don't know yet how much he will take though. Horses aren't as expensive here as up there [in New Braunfels] because paper is still worth more. Here they give you $1.00 in silver for $3.00-$3.50 in paper. Münzenberger wants to buy himself a different horse too because the saddle bruise on his isn't healing as fast as he expected. We had muster yesterday. A lot of ladies from the neighborhood had come to watch us. Afterward the soldiers were plied with food ["wurden abgefüttert"] but we did not go there. The people who were missing were reported absent without leave, and I believe things will go somewhat worse for them this time than before. They are supposed to be turned over to a general court martial. Lt. Schramm and H. Conring are being sent away to fetch them, but it seems possible to me that they themselves will stay away because the captain will certainly try to persuade them to do that, just as he did in my case and those of other people who went up there with him. What is to become of us . . . nobody knows. Most think that we will go back to Beeville. . . . Surely Carl is at your place. Alfred sends him best regards and wishes he would write him. . . . Two letters for Carl have arrived by way of Brownsville since I came here and one to me from Father with the enclosure from Franz to Johann. So now farewell to you all and don't work too hard. Rudolf Coreth. Regards from the mess.

New Braunfels
no date [early July 1863]
Rudolf from father

You can well imagine that the receipt of your letter from Sweet Home gave us all great pleasure. We had followed you step by step in our thoughts and got wet in our thoughts with you. By now though you have been soaked through by rain again and dried again a long time, because the rain is very generous this year. You know the hackberry ["*Hegbeer*"] tree in the bottom that was marked. The water rose a good five feet above that mark. Fritz Vogt's and William Vogt's fences went to the devil; Tolle's threshing machine floated in his bottom land; two full wagonloads of rye washed away from the Merz place.[2] Fortunately they were chained to trees, or else the wagons would have gone along, but this way they were simply turned over. At Neumann's the alley was so full of water that the stone fence lacked only the length of a hand of being covered by water. . . . So we had our hands quite full and the fence is still broken, but so far no cattle are coming in, since on the hill there is enough feed and water, and in the valley there are droves of unbearable flies. We keep moving the rye; Carl helped us make a shed[3] which soaked through again the same night. . . . So only damage teaches us wisdom. During the rain Kämmerling's brother [Otto] spent the night with us. . . . The thirtieth Carl came with Hedwig, which pleased us very much. Carl has already recovered to some extent and is making visible progress. Hedwig looks rather well too, and, given peace of mind, will recover completely soon. . . . Your mother is generally well, only in the last days of working on the rye she strained herself very much . . . but I hope she will rest soon. Your brothers and sisters and I are well. We know nothing of Agnes. The roads down to here are probably too bad to be traveled. I don't suspect anything is wrong. . . . In politics we are looking to Vicksburg, but an impenetrable fog separates us from there up to now. I hope for the best, and incidentally, also because then you could lie quietly in your camp during the hot time of year, which it seems you like doing quite well. The militia is supposed to be called up in the state [of Texas]. [Brig.] General [Robert] Bechem [commanding Thirty-first Brigade, TST] supposedly, as I hear, has decided on his own to let his men stay home for now to do their work. From our barnyard the news is that Franz brought the blind cow with a calf from Tausch's. We have now brought in nine of this year's calves; one is still out, and three or four are still expected. . . . Mother, your brothers and sisters, and I embrace you with the warmest wishes in our hearts for your welfare, and so for today Adio. Your old friend and father, E. Coreth*. Yesterday evening Wolfgang Kapp came to get the wagon that Carl came in. He is going to town now and is driving back home again this afternoon.

New Braunfels
3 July 1863
Rudolf from Carl

On 30 June Hedwig and I arrived here from Sisterdale in the buggy. We had meant to travel a few days earlier, but on the day (or during the night) before we meant to leave, a heavy rain came . . . so that we had to postpone the trip. . . . My health is improving significantly, but I still lack the strength to work. I am always out of breath right away and get into a feverish condition, sweat very hard, and feel very tired afterward, but the rest of the time I have only a slight remnant of my illness, such as a little fever or something. I have gained considerable weight already. . . . On the twentieth I have to go to San Antonio to report. . . . I can't send any news about politics. The most recent newspapers have no reports. But something decisive will have to happen at Vicksburg soon. As much as one can tell from our newspapers, this Southern situation looks quite good.[4] . . . Regards to our friends and cherish your always loyal friend and brother Carl.

Camp Rocky
6 July 1863
Rudolf to family

Still no letter from you has arrived. . . . I have not been able to find out anything about Carl either. . . . Just the hope that everything is going well makes for a very meagre diet. . . . Alfred, Kämmerling, and Münzenberger have not yet returned from horse trading. We expect them tonight. Sunday C[hristian]. Pantermühl and I were at the farmer's on the Peach Creek to fetch melons and tomatoes. While we were away, a man of our company died, H[enry]. Puls; I think he had the same sickness as Johann. He got sick on the San Fernando when we stayed behind. Yesterday morning I rode with another man back to the same farmer's to make the coffin. We didn't get back until afternoon, but this time we brought back a lot of melons because we had a wagon with us.[5] We can't complain about our lives now at all; eating vegetables seems to have had a very good effect on all the regiment. There seems to be much more vitality among the men again now. I have not had a single newspaper in hand since coming here; and since we seldom have contact with civilians, we seldom hear political reports either. It seems to me that nothing important has happened either though; otherwise surely it would have seeped through to us anyway. It seems that the people who have overstayed their leaves are to be handled more strictly now than heretofore. They are all to be summoned by the court martial. The colonel offered to leave off the court martial if they would accept extra duty ["wenn sie freiwillig 6 duble Routs annehmen würden"]. They accepted the bargain, which I consider very stupid of them because the captain [Podewils] told them that they should stay up there [in New Braunfels] until he would send them away. To be sure, he did not have the right to give them the order, but I think he and not the men would have had to answer for that. . . .

7 July [continued]

. . . Kämmerling, Münzenberger, and Alfred came back last night. Kämmerling and Münzenberger got horses; they are right beautiful animals. They were ridden yesterday for the first time. Today I found a good opportunity to send the money of yours that I have in hand. A man named [Ernst] Klöpper will take it along and deposit it with [Ernst] Scherff. Kämmerling used up $50; he will deposit them to Father's account at Moureau's. I hope everything will get straightened out. Yesterday a letter from you finally arrived. . . . I thank Carl for his friendly letter. . . . I cannot fulfill his wish to know where the regiment is going. Every day they say something different. Yesterday I heard we would be sent to Galveston. . . .

8 July [continued]

Klöpper did not start out yesterday after all; therefore [Christoph] Pfeuffer will take the letter and the money along today. Pfeuffer is bringing $24. These $24 and the $50 which Father will receive at Moureau's amount to Johann's money. Alfred asked to borrow Carl's money in order to buy himself a horse with it. His father will pay it back to Carl. . . . the new horses are serving well. They already allow us to ride them well. Yesterday Kämmerling's broke the rope and ran off. I found it among other horses. It did not make a move to run off when I went up to it, which is quite a lot for a horse that has been ridden only four days in its life. . . . If you get the chance sometime, be so kind and send me my ink bottle, which I forgot up there. I have to borrow ink now all the time, and there is hardly any more in camp.

New Braunfels
10 July 1863
Rudolf from family

Dear Rudolf. The name-day of Amalia. Monday the said Amalia was in town and brought us your last letter with the news that you all are getting along well, that the body is made happy by nourishment and the spirit is not disturbed by any worries. We are getting along well too. Carl and Hedwig give us quite a dear picture of inward and outward contentment in consequence of the fulfilled wish for love. Carl's health is visibly improved. I wish this were less the case, because under these circumstances he has little hope for an extension of his leave. Carl helps us very energetically in restoring our destroyed fence, and we have the hope of putting it in order before the end of his leave. . . . Mother, your brothers and sisters, and I are well; all have enough work to do so that we never get bored, and still not more than we can endure. To be sure, much remains undone, but the world does not collapse, just the same. We heard that the little stallion was annoying people. Carl and Franz rounded him up and took him on a rope. He lets one approach him very well and is tame. The first night he got his foot caught in the rope and wounded his fetlock and got worms on it. . . . Next Tuesday is the auctioning of the stray mare. The rye is in; the threshing machine is to come in a week. The militia had to draw lots but is being allowed to stay here for now. As long as that is the case, everything will go quietly along. Dr. Koester is said to have bought a Negro family: a man, woman and child. Otherwise nothing new comes to mind. Farewell, dear Rudolf. . . . You know what a festival it is for everyone when a letter from you arrives. The regards of the mess are cordially reciprocated. Adio. Your old friend and father.

New Braunfels
10 July 1863
Rudolf from Carl

Father gave me his letter to read in order to prevent your being written things in duplicate, and so I saw that he has written practically everything worth mentioning. The fence on the creek is pretty heavily damaged. . . . We have made nails of fresh cedar wood, up to now about one hundred of them, but we probably have to make twice that many in all. . . . I am still lacking very much strength. Of course, I look stout, but it seems to me that it is more flabby than firm flesh. . . . My eyes are often quite red but do not hurt me, at least not much. Franz is going to ride to town today to get flour and also my things, which are at Scherff's. Do explain the business with the coffee to me; I hear that there is quite a packet of it among the things. . . . You probably all know that Otto Kämmerling has left [presumably for Germany]. I think he did write to his brother, didn't he? I did not see him. So farewell then. Give my regards to our friends. And cherish your loyal brother Carl H. Coreth.

Camp Rocky
13 July 1863
Rudolf to family

. . . I was away from camp for four days and got back last night. Alfred and another man (Emanuel Trefflich) and I were at the place of the man from whom Münzenberger and Kämmerling bought their horses. Alfred and Trefflich wanted to buy horses, and I rode along to help them bring them here. . . . I also traded my horse for one four years old, which had not yet been broken. I had to ride it all the way here—thirty miles— right away. It went pretty well. The first day we had our hands full getting the horses tame enough to be able to lead them, and I had to ride mine right away, because I didn't have another horse with me. The next day we headed home for camp. That day we only progressed eight miles. About three miles before we got to the pen where the horses were for the night, my horse did not want to go on. It began to buck a bit, and when he saw that that did not help him any, he threw himself over and got loose. I couldn't hold him by the reins, and I had carelessly tied the rope to the saddle. Alfred gave me his bay for trailing him, and Trefflich rode after him too on a little mule but couldn't keep up. I managed to get the horse into a pen after quite a lot of effort and caught it again. I mounted it again and tried everything I could to get it to buck again, but it wouldn't do it anymore. When I got back to Alfred, Trefflich had not returned yet and didn't come back either for another four or five hours; he had ridden back to the pen where we had been for the night and had waited there for me. When we were back together we meant to ride on, but then Trefflich's horse got shy and ran back as hard as it could. It took us maybe an hour to get back together and then we finally could go on. We put the horses in a pen for the night, and yesterday we got here without having had any delay. Today I rode my horse again; I think it will develop a good gait. It is a black [*"Sommerrappe"*], a little bigger than my old one was and it is now already quite tame. I gave an additional $25.00 for it, and everybody says I have made a very good trade. While we were away the marching order came. We are to march off for Beeville tomorrow morning. They say a drill camp is to be set up there. Beyond that, they say that P. C. Woods has been made a brigadier general. It hasn't been published yet, though. . . . Adio. Rudolf Coreth

New Braunfels
17 July 1863
Rudolf from Carl
addressed to Sweet Home[6]

. . . The bored fence is finished and has been made quite well. All the rails were newly bored, then the uprights were pulled tightly together with a chain and the nails welded. We are at present at work repairing the part up to Fritz Vogt's. The other parts of the fence are to be improved with brushwood. I hear that the Medical Board in San Antonio has been disbanded and will not issue any more sick leaves, so if that is true I would be spared the ride to San Antonio. I think I will stay here as long as possible, and that is till the forty days run out, to 30 July. . . . I was glad you bought a horse. . . . I wish I could trade my strawberry roan [*"Rothschimmel"*] too, because its back is still too tender for hard rides. . . . Last Tuesday Father and Franz were in town with the stray bunch [of horses] for the purpose of selling them, with the intention of purchasing them themselves, even if they were bid up high, because Father would, after all, have to pay only one-half for it, but that was not necessary, as it turned out. They bought all three horses for $80. Father only had to pay $38, because he was repaid $2.00 more for expenses. Stray-Schneider isn't much use, of course, but it is a horse, after all, and I would have liked to have it, actually, because nobody here places any value on him and I think that there is nothing to be lost on it anyway. Father contends he is too poor a horse for him to wish to give him to me. Maybe we will go fetch Schneider sometime and will see whether he lets us ride him. The little stallion's fetlock that he rubbed raw with the rope is still not healed, mainly because he often rubs the rope against it. Again adieu, dear Rudolf. Always your Carl H. Coreth

Rudolf from father [continued]

. . . We are well. Carl has recovered quite well. . . . Camp life has not left any marks on him. If he keeps on that way for the rest of his life, he will thrive; besides he is in a good mood and much milder. Marriage has had a very good effect upon him. Also Hedwig's health seems to be straightened out. . . . When you too will have gotten to the point that you can endure the quiet of domestic life again and take up your abode among us, then I will be glad to live to my hundredth year. From outside the reports are less favorable. That Vicksburg fell had a bad emotional impact on me. Actually, one ought to break the habit of being moved. There is nothing that is either good or bad (as such). All one can say is that it simply is. The threshing machine has not yet been here, but . . . we expect Hoffmann the first days of this coming week. . . . There is to be a new frame made for the sugar barley [*"Zuckergerste"*]; Franz has already made new combs in the cylinder and did it very well. Beyond that, Carl pulled the front gallery against the house and nailed it fast. It was on the point of running to the road that leads to the gate and was, if not halfway there, already pretty far from the house. . . . The Canadian named Roberling is now attached to a rope.[7] I like the animal quite a lot. I think it will turn into an animal that I myself can and will ride. God knows whether and *where* you will receive this letter. I am giving it to Carl, who will take it to the Post Office and inquire there about how to address mail to you all. Carl will bring your ink well to you, but I wrote up all the ink. That won't matter to you, probably. You can get ink anywhere, after all, if only you have the well. . . . Our compliments to the mess. Your old friend and father

Goliad
19 July 1863
Rudolf to family

The evening before we marched away from Camp Rocky, the letter from Carl to Alfred arrived with an enclosure for me from Father and Carl, which gave me much pleasure. . . . All the spare time we used to have we now use to break our new horses. . . . We may be staying here a bit longer. We never find out definitely in advance because it probably would not be military to acquaint us with plans. As much as we know, we are supposed to go to Beeville. It is generally believed, though, that if the report that Vicksburg has fallen is confirmed, we will soon get other orders. This report is disputed by many, to be sure, but I fear that it is true, because the *Houston Telegraph* surely did not enjoy publishing it. I think that if the Federals attack Texas, then they will not be strong enough to hold us, and we will get everywhere too late again, because it will take us at least a month to be able to get to any border. Colonel Woods did not become a real general but rather is just functioning as one, but is to keep colonel's rank. . . . Rudolf

[vicinity of Goliad]
27 July 1863
Rudolf to family

. . . We are located ten miles below Goliad on the San Antonio River. It is a rather good camp. We have enough corn and good grass. . . . There are no farms in the vicinity, and in this region there are no melons or other vegetables grown at all, which we could get plenty of on the Rocky. . . . It was uneventful on the way here. It is a rather boring road, always pasture and prairie alternating, and in spots there is very much sand. The corn that we saw in the fields on the way has stayed very small. The people won't make anything much anymore besides corn for bread. Here along the river it seems to be better. Goliad is quite a pretty place. There are many rather large stone houses here, which look quite decent because they aren't coming apart the way they are in most American towns. The foundation seems to be very solid. I inquired about our [acquaintances, the] Swiss family. They still live here, but the boys aren't at home anymore. Isaac and Jacob are teamsters. Isaac has driven to Brownsville and will be married when he comes back. The old town lies on the other side of the river about two miles from the new one. We were there and looked at the ruins. The church is still quite well preserved; divine services are still held in it. It stands on a side of the courtyard, which is a square with sides about 120 paces in length and which is enclosed by a wall ten feet high and two feet thick. On the other side of the courtyard there used to be rooms, but now the walls have been broken down in many spots. An old Mexican told us that Colonel Fannin's men had done that. The building must be very old, because the mortar is as hard as the stone. Around the ruin there live 20-25 Mexican families, who belong to a much more beautiful caste than those on the Rio Grande. We saw a couple of very beautiful women there. Today I was given the chance to go to Victoria and help shoe the horses of the brigade. Alfred and I decided to take them up on it, because it is a change, after all, in which one can earn a little too. We are to get $5.00 a day plus room and board. We are going there tomorrow or the day after. If we don't like it, we can always give it up too. The last few days very good political reports are arriving again. They say General Lee has taken Washington, but that does seem exaggerated to me.[8] I cannot imagine that the place is so little defended that it fell the first time it was stormed. Beyond that they say that Vicksburg was given up on purpose in accordance with completely new plans and that it would have been easy to hold it if they had wanted to. When you write me, do write me how things are with the horses. . . . Here the horses had the same condition as the bay, but they are all better now. An American veterinarian lanced them a bit around the eyes, but the horses that were not operated on got well too. I should like to advise Carl to try everything he can to have his leave extended, or else to get employed in a shop in San Antonio, because life in the company is sure not to please him. To be sure, the captain is away, but on the other hand Schulze and Schramm act stupider every day, and more conceited, which is sometimes quite a touchy business in men who used to be glad if one had anything to do with them at all. Now farewell to you all and write me soon to Victoria, and cherish your son and brother, Rudolf.

Victoria
5 August 1863
Rudolf to family

. . . All I have heard about you was told by W[illiam]. Scherff, who arrived in camp a couple of days ago, and he only knew that Carl would come to camp this week. . . . A few days before we (Alfred and I) came here from camp, all our mess's horses ran away with the exception of [August] Schimmel [pfennig]'s. We found Alfred's the next day, and Alfred and I rode continuously one day from morning till evening all through the area but found nothing, which led us to think that they had run home. The next day Münzenberger and H. Conring rode after them . . . I think that was on Saturday; on Sunday Alfred and I came here by wagon because we were to start the shoeing. An American has the contract; he seemed to be very glad that he got us. He is quite a decent man and seems to be respected too, because he is sheriff of Victoria County. One finds the work is rather hard again on the first days, but I think that it is quite good for us to get out of the lazy camp life again for a change. . . . I got quite a bad attack of colic during the night, which was gone though by this morning, but which has so weakened me that I preferred not to work today. . . . I really don't know from what I got it yet. . . . It is raining on my paper, and then too I have copying ink which keeps dissolving, leaving everything full of blots. I hope very much for news from you all soon. Rudolf.

Camp near Victoria
August 1863 [day unclear]
Rudolf to family

. . . It is said that we are soon to go to another camp. . . . We are simply to go somewhere the tax corn has not yet been collected. The story about Tolle really gave me pleasure. . . . I don't think, if he were to decide to buy the farm from us, that he will do it very soon. . . . I also don't believe that it would be a good idea to sell the farm now during the war, unless one were to get a very good price for it, because, first of all, it would be hard for you all to have to look for a new place to live now, and to move. Then too, the place would make much better sense once this question is settled, because the doubt about it keeps many people from paying such a sum; and then it seems to me too that after the conclusion of the war, many people will change their place of residence, and then the place would be big enough even for a little plantation [?; "Negerfarm"]. I would be of the opinion that one should be compensated completely for the buildings and fences and all the work that has been done. . . . Old [Otto von] Roeder lives a few miles from here. He was here in camp a few days ago and looked us up. He asked us to send you the regards of him and his family and invited us to visit him. Yesterday Carl, Alfred, and I rode there and stayed almost the whole day. The people were very friendly and made the time pass most pleasantly for us. The oldest son is in Sibley's Brigade. The daughters are at home. One of them is married.[9] They have all gotten to be quite big women. Today the old man came to camp on business again and ate the noon meal with us. He said we should bring our laundry to his place for washing, which we won't do though, and offered to take care of everything for us that we need. So farewell for now. I am cook and must prepare the meal. Rudolf.

Victoria
9 August 1863
Rudolf to family

. . . I am completely well again. The day before yesterday Carl got here.
. . . He looks quite well, only his eyes seem to me to be somewhat inflamed even now. That could come from the dust though too. It seems
to please him very much that his wife is with you. . . . The same day
Mrs. Runge arrived, as did the two Froboeses and Reifert.[10] I have not
seen Mrs. Runge yet. Carl, Froboese and Reifert came to us where we
were working. It just so happened that we had finished with the horses
of one company, and so we quit working for the evening and went to a
wine-house Froboese knew, where one can get quite good wine for $3.00
a bottle. In the evening Kämmerling came into town, and so we spent
quite a pleasant night. We were a bit worried about the next day's work,
but it went quite well. We didn't even have a headache. Yesterday the
entire company came into town to accompany a German lieutenant who
had died here to his grave. Carl stayed in town all night, and when we
have finished writing, we will go out to camp together, where I want to
get part of the cheese and the peaches Carl brought along from your
place. Our horses still haven't come back. We heard from somebody who
saw Münzenberger and Conring though, that they had found the trail.
. . . We have shod the horses for three companies. I want to leave the
rest of this space for Carl. . . . Rudolf

Carl to family [continued]

. . . In a few days the horses will probably all be shod and Rudolf and
Alfred will return to camp, if they are not still to shoe for other regiments.
. . . The attack upon Charleston is said to have been repulsed, as I heard
today. That is good. There doesn't seem to be much to the story about
the Yankee ships. At least I have heard nothing more about it. Be so
kind as to air out Münzenberger's clothes from time to time. . . . With
many regards Your Carl.

New Braunfels
no date [August 1863]
Carl and Rudolf from father
addressed to Victoria

My dear sons Carl and Rudolf! The mail has been so scarce that it has
almost caused us to worry . . . Then on Saturday (the fifteenth) in the
morning Mr. Triesch [Peter, a neighbor; or his son Adolph of Co. F]
came and brought us Carl's letters, which, presumably as a result of the
good stuff at $3.00 a bottle, were dated at Camp Goliad instead of Vic-
toria, which totally confused us, since we had not yet received the earlier
letters. Finally at noon Sunday we got all your letters that contained the
key to the puzzle. Well, for $3.00 (paper, I hope) there grows a good
wine! 'Tis pity I've become so old already, otherwise it would be a daring
deed worthy of these excitable times, if I were to ride to Victoria and

break the necks of a couple of those bottles at $3.00 in camp in your company. Of political matters, nothing new. The [*Neu-Braunfelser*] *Zeitung* knows nothing, like ourselves. We have a cap of fog down over our ears, and when it is removed there may be a ghastly storm to be seen, or maybe sunshine too—both are part of the world plan—inevitable: *dunque lassiamo andar* [It. = "let it go then"]. In the household, nothing new either. We are all well and are working our boots down to the old last. Just now we are cutting off the cornstalks for fodder so that it can sprout anew, if it should rain. Rudolf writes that it is raining as he writes. Here we have had not a drop of rain since the big rainy spell. The dust is lying at least a foot deep on every road and path. Yesterday afternoon Mr. and Mrs. Iken were here for a visit.[11] We carried on an idle conversation. From Agnes we had no news again this past week. It turned out Tony and Max were sick; she had a little maid servant in place of Lisbeth, whom old Mr. [Otto] Schmuck [Lisbeth's father] had fetched home. Nothing else at all comes to mind except to say a hearty farewell to you from Mother, your brothers and sisters, and me. (Hedwig is going to write herself.) This business of writing is simply no good. If we were sitting face to face, the thoughts would not be so sparse in coming to me, even if it were over the wine at $3.00 that does not give you a hangover. Hangover is a rough time, as after too much beer, especially if it is too new, when it is cold piss. So Adio, your old friend and father, E. Coreth*. *Mes compliments à la Messe* [Fr. = "My compliments to the mess"].

New Braunfels
21 August 1863 (Friday)
Carl and Rudolf from father

Dear Carl and Rudolf, I am making use of the opportunity that Hedwig is writing to you to enclose hearty greetings from your mother, sisters and brothers, and me. We are well and hope the same of you; a short time ago the rumor that the Yankees had landed and that now absolutely everybody, the halt and the blind, would have to go was being spread here. But then none of these things happened. Then it was said that Luckett's regiment had been disbanded and that they had laid down their arms.[12] But on closer inquiry it proved to be as in the case of bats, which everybody fears getting caught in his hair but nobody has yet experienced personally. Hedwig, to our joy, has not been fetched from here yet; we grow fonder of her every day; she too seems to like being here and also she is putting on some weight. She looks quite well. Where in the world may you be marching around!? I hope though that Münzenberger and [Adolph] Triesch have caught up with you and that you will now be in possession of your letter. In the *Brownsville Flag*[13] there is now the official statement that the Mexican government has accepted the monarchy, that eleven persons are traveling to Vienna to invite the Archduke Maximilian to take the throne of Mexico, and, in case he refuses, to leave it to the Emperor [Louis] Napoleon to select a regent.

I would not like to accept the post, if they were to come to me. Adio for today. Yesterday evening there was thunder with a few drops of rain; today the Texas skies are blue again. Maybe the mail delivery will bring us news from you. Your friend and father, E. Coreth*

Victoria
no date [August 1863]
Rudolf to family

The day before yesterday Münzenberger and Conring arrived. Münzenberger brought us the report that you all are well. . . . They brought two horses, Kämmerling's and one of Münzenberger's; they did not find mine. These two had come home while they were up there. . . . A[ugust]. Schimmelpfennig and I had ridden to a place where they had been seen twelve days ago. At that time they were all three still together and it seemed they were on the way home. . . . A lieutenant who is familiar with the neighborhood means to ride along and help me search. . . . The horseshoeing has stopped for now, because there are no more horseshoes left. Some will be fetched from Seguin first, and till then we will stay in camp again. The work did me quite a lot of good. I feel much better now than before. The camp life makes one so limp that one can endure hardly anything. The work hurt us a lot the first few days, but when that was behind us we felt very well and we shoed up to eighteen horses a day without straining ourselves much. We haven't received any definite political reports in quite some time now. Now it is said that Lincoln has proposed an armistice of ninety days to his cabinet. Here in the vicinity there is a very bad mood prevalent. The men acknowledge quite openly that they are Unionists, Germans as well as Americans, and all Unionists as well as Secessionists wish very much that the war might soon come to an end, and I hope that most emphatically too. . . . I hope the business is over with soon, so that we can get together again. Rudolf.

Victoria
no date [August 1863]
Rudolf to family

Yesterday I returned to the regiment. I have not found my horse. I tracked it to the place where it grew up, and there it probably was caught and taken along by some Negroes who were on a big cattle hunt. . . . I have little hope of finding them. . . . The region in which they are said to be is simply too extensive. . . . Now I am riding Kämmerling's horse. . . . I saw quite a bit on my trip, about which I will write you in detail next time. Mainly I was interested in how indigo is rendered. I consider it possible that we could make use of indigo too. Adio Rudolf.

Kemper's Bluff ["Camper's Bluff"]14
28 August 1863
Rudolf to family

Father's letter of the twenty-first came yesterday. . . . Now the postal connections seem to be straightened out. . . . We are well; we have quite a pretty campground and are not much bothered by duties either. We are near the Guadalupe. I think that if we were to stay here long, sicknesses might begin, but up to now everyone is still in good shape. The men catch lots of big fish and one can also get enough jackrabbits, if one makes the effort of going a half mile from camp. We get quite good rations now and so there is really nothing lacking now. This morning three companies marched away from here again back to the old camp above Victoria, and we are going to follow as soon as all our wagons are together again, which will probably be the case again in a couple of days. Planting indigo keeps going around in my head all the time now. Unfortunately there are no books at all to be had here in which one could read up on the subject a bit. I remember having read, however, that indigo plays a very big role in commerce. The plant from which one derives the dye grows here in low-lying, sandy places and grows up to the height of a man. A man told me that he had found it in bottoms too, and that there it grew even more vigorously. The rendering of the dye from the foliage is rather simple. The plants are cut off and put in containers with water poured over the foliage and let stand until the fermentation is over. Then the greens are carefully taken out and the water stirred vigorously. First a green foam forms, which gradually turns blue. The stirring is continued until all foam has disappeared. Then a bit of lye is poured into the brew and it is left to stand until the indigo has settled out. Then the upper liquid is poured off and the sediment is hung up for dripping and drying (in a sack). The people told me one worker could make up to 5 lbs. of indigo a day, and that before the war a pound was worth $4.00. If just some of that is true, one would surely be able to make a lot from it, if one could get some big containers. Furthermore, in Clinton I saw a fence of huisache [such as] I think I told you about. It grows wild on the Nueces. The fence stood on a very dry place but seemed to grow very well. I consider it to be a better hedge plant than bois d'arc.[15] I haven't heard anything about my horse yet. I have now done everything I could to get it back. . . . I think I could sell it for $80-$90 in silver. Farewell to you all and cherish your son and brother Rudolf Coreth.

The letters of this period give certain tell-tale signs in the penmanship and the compositional logic that Rudolf is not as well as he believes himself to be. It is almost as though he were attempting to write quite methodically about practical matters to test his powers of concentration and, at the same time, to delight his father, who always took great pleasure in reading about chemical experiments and sometimes even conducted some himself, not always with success, as in the case of the ruined soap. His father, delighted by the informative letters from his son, who was always anxious to please him, wrote a reply that indicates he sensed nothing of the young man's illness.

New Braunfels
no date [3 September 1863]
Rudolf from father

Dear Rudolf! Yesterday, 2 September, we got your letters, I yours and Hedwig Carl's. From them we know that you all are well up to 30 August and in camp above Victoria. We are greatly relieved and happy to know how you are, and to know you are in relatively close proximity. We are all well too and are making slight progress in our work, but only moderately because it is still too early to harvest corn and too dry to plow. In your letter you complain of having no books that give you information about indigo.[16] . . . We have a nice supply of fodder for the winter. The horse stall and the vinegar storeroom are full, and we have a stack of corn stalks that average ten feet in length besides, that we have set up like a shock ["*Triste*"] covered with straw and hay. The stack is in a circle with a diameter of eighteen feet. I think this straw is a very good material for roofing. I don't think that reeds make better roofs, and after all, thatched roofs of reeds are quite usual in many places. In the more intimate circle of acquaintances nothing worth mentioning has happened, to my knowledge. Amalia was in town yesterday and at a central point for news, but without any significant yield. [Wilhelm?] Tonne is to return without emigrating to Mexico. The [*Neu-Braunfelser*] *Zeitung* has told you that Colonel Schmitz has rented his hotel to an American named Smith.[17] Adio for today. Mother, your sisters and brothers, and I greet you and Carl most heartily. As ever, your old friend and father E. Coreth*.

Victoria
18 September 1863
Rudolf to family

I hope you are well. According to Father's last letters everything did seem to be going well. I will be able to reassure myself of it soon, by the way; if nothing unexpected happens to me in between, I will be with you in a week. Carl wrote you that I had to stay behind here. I was quite badly sick, but everything is all right now again, except for a very great weakness. Tomorrow we—Alfred, Carl, and I—are going away from here to Mr. Roeder's; he invited us most cordially to stay at his place for a while. I mean to stay there only as long as absolutely necessary though and then come to you right away. On the way home I want to look once more to see whether I can get my horse back. The day before the regiment left, a man came back who had been looking for horses for quite a long time, and he told me that he had seen the horse, and that was at a place where I had expected to find it, and it isn't out of my way at all either. Carl, I think, will go with me. My illness became evident first as though it were malaria, but after a few days changed to a condition that the doctor whom we called afterward called cholera. When I came here my pulse was so fast that one could hardly count it and my hands were completely cold to the elbows and my feet to the knees.[18] The doctor had me rubbed down all over with whiskey and had poultices of cornmeal laid on my abdomen. That did quite a bit of good. The pulse soon became slower and the warmth returned to my extremities too. From then on my recovery went forward very fast, much faster than I had expected under the best possible circumstances, and now I am far enough along to be able to walk around quite well and in a couple of days I think I will be far enough along to be able to ride. Now I have written you enough about me though. That seems to be characteristic of most sick people though; they talk about themselves with the greatest of ease. We have found quite good people here again. The man at whose place we are living does everything he can think of that could be pleasant for us, and that surely not from selfish motives. The doctor was quite decent too. He charged $13 in specie for nine visits and some medication; that would not be much, except that because of the paper money exchange rate, it will come to quite a lot, namely $130. Nothing else that I could write comes to mind now, actually; so I will take my leave of you for today in the hope of seeing you soon, and then we can tell each other everything once again. Rudolf.

New Braunfels
no date [20 September 1863?]
Rudolf from father

. . . Seekatz, Conrads, Bruno Klappenbach, and Ernst Conring are salt-peter makers.[19] But since the kettles which were bought somewhere in the country are traveling around nobody-knows-where, the four gentle-men are on indefinite leave. I was in town three times, since Mr. Tolle summoned me (through Koester), though he did not really charge me. I went very willingly, because I knew that, if the matter were to reach the point of discussion, I would be recognized by everybody as being in the right, and that was how it turned out too.—Tolle had said that I had diverted the water, because it no longer was coming back into the river bed, and so he could not grind at his mill. When asked where I had diverted it to, he admitted that I had only directed it into my field and that *it* had swallowed the water up, and that was how I had diverted it. So now the matter is to be brought up before a judge, and I am really curious to know whether there exists a dumb ox who would decide that the irrigated land has to give back all the water again. I had to pay $5.00 in paper to have the case drawn up, which suits me very well, since just a ride to San Antonio to engage an attorney would have cost me five times that much and I suffer more from a shortage than from an excess of means and have enough now to cover the needs of the moment. So tomorrow, among other things, I will be buying wheat for the winter, six bushels, I think; they will cost me $12 in silver, and 200 lbs. of salt will cost $10 in silver; besides soap, which can be had only for silver. But the lordly Colonel Schmitz promised to give me back interest in the amount of $22 in silver in a few days.[20] Hurrah for the colonel!!! Now I am coming to the outermost circle of politics. In San Antonio a War Meeting Bar-becue in the grandest style has been announced for this coming Saturday.

So naturally there is also a War Meeting in Podunk [*"Krehwinkel,"* meaning New Braunfels]. It is enough to make one explode when one has heard each and every one of the shop-keepers individually and sees their shameful souls lie fully exposed before one, and hears them sing "War, Brother, War" [*"Krieg, Bruder, Krieg"*] in chorus.[21] It is less remarkable that several bags of wind cast a shadow than that so many zeros add up to something, namely a war meeting. Our affairs, under these and many other circumstances, are not at their best, but the peasant says, if the weather does not suit you, improve it.—I must also tell you that we have a very well-filled mesquite fence from Tolle's corner to the watering place, and in it a gate. The problem of the cattle simply got to be too great. When we stood guard morning and evening for three hours, twenty to thirty would come during the night, so that we slept by the creek several nights. Franz and I have now been leading the horses twice daily to the water, and that is the end of it. When there is more water again maybe we can leave the gate open again. Adieux, dear Rudolf. Mother and your brothers and sisters embrace you heartily, as always does your etc. E. Coreth*

Regimental Headquarters, Liberty
28 September 1863
Rudolf from Münzenberger

Dear Rudolf! We received the news that you are out of the woods. I have to tell you sincerely that I very much feared that you would bite the dust. So it pleased me all the more, especially because of your relatives, for whom it would truly have been too hard a blow, and for whose sake you too were more worried than about yourself! God be praised that the scare is over! As I hear, you—or you all—went home. I hope you left orders with somebody in Victoria to forward the letters that arrive there for you. I wrote two letters to there with the charge for Carl and Alfred from Hutchison that they stay with you, besides mailing a letter at Hallettsville to Carl from home;[22] and I mailed one from Houston with a copy of the order, for safety's sake. Meanwhile we have made some side trips. On the way quite bad weather, so that we often had to bed down in wet blankets and many got the fever. Schwantes caught up with us at Prairie Point and brought us the first news of you.[23] We left old Schulze [Friedrich, Sr.] behind in Hallettsville with cholera, but also recovering. At Columbus I got the fever too, quite badly. Had it three times, once terribly, so that I completely lost my senses in Houston. That probably was because I took my remedy—pill bugs—at the very height of the fever.[24] They defended themselves though, because I am as well now as a fish in water. I really need to be, though, because I am still alone in the office. On the days that I was sick Schwantes worked, got sick again though, and has given it up altogether now. And I am not merely captain, major, and regimental clerk now but also postal clerk. Since just recently the major [Hutchison] has taken command of the troops here, which consist of our regiment and six companies of militia cavalry, one company infantry, one light battery. Shortly the other companies will come too. You are bound to know that we are dismounted again. Our horse is at Alleyton. We had to turn in our few tents and are now lying about here in the rain having fun. Don't you dare come till you are entirely recovered. I am enclosing a copy of an order which might interest Carl and Alfred, so they can be under a roof for the winter. Let us hear from you soon, and give my most cordial regards to the folks at home from your A. Münzenberg.[25]

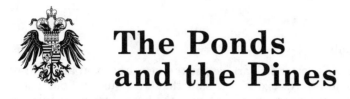

The Ponds
and the Pines

The crops were in and Rudolf's health was restored when he and Carl headed back to camp, now at a site in eastern Texas near the coast.

Beaumont
25 October 1863
Rudolf to family

... Yesterday two letters came, one to Alfred and one to Schimmelpfennig, and when they opened them they found that they were their own letters that they had sent off a couple of days ago and that had meanwhile gone to Sabine Pass and had been sent back from there.[1] ... We have quite a good life here, at least as good as one can expect under the circumstances. The morning after we got here it started to rain, and because we have no tents, we got the order that we should look around for empty houses. Our officers found a big steam mill which is not in operation now, into which we got just in the nick of time before the rain really broke loose. Almost all our things stayed dry. Since then we have been here awaiting marching orders. There seems to be a good chance that we will be sent back to Houston again. If I had something to say about it, I would vote to stay here because one moves much more freely than there. The regiment is lying spread out over the space of about a mile and it is still so muddy in town that nobody goes out who does not have urgent business. They cannot make us drill. And then too, I prefer the mill as a residence to the huts in Houston, because it is bigger and has only a good roof but no walls, which makes the accumulation of barracks vapors impossible. Both the last nights we have had a freeze, and it is cold by day too. . . . There is so much stagnant water everywhere that it must also cool the air off a lot. In the summer this area must be very unwholesome. There are lots of militiamen encamped here in addition to our regiment. They got enough good tents and are cavalry. There does seem to me to be very bad morale prevalent among them. They, as I hear it, do not want to leave the state and are supposed to march to Louisiana, and so quite a few of them are deserting. Yesterday the report came that twenty-one had left and are expected to be coming through here. We had to occupy the river crossings for a couple of miles around, but nobody has been caught yet. Of our regiment four also left last week; three of them were caught and taken to Houston. We are curious to know what is to happen to them. In Houston we did not have any time left anymore to visit H. F. Fisher,[2] but we will do it if we should get back there. I am entirely well again and strong, as in the past. . . .
Rudolf

Beaumont
2 November 1863
Rudolf to family

Through Hedwig's letter to Carl we got the news that you are well; we are too. . . . A few days ago it was said that we would get our horses back, but the order was revoked and now the horses are to be taken to the source of the San Jacinto and be herded there until there are other orders. We are perfectly content with that, because here the horses would be more trouble than use to us. . . . It is the laundry that one postpones as long as possible; that is what lies ahead of me too. Once I get started I am through in an hour at most, but the starting! . . . Rudolf Coreth

Beaumont
9 November 1863
Rudolf to family

. . . We are still at our mill. How much longer we will be staying here, nobody knows. But I think that our stay is more than half over. The local citizens say that in two or three weeks the entire area here will be under water, and so I believe we will be sent away before then. The day before yesterday Major Kampmann came through here on a trip from Houston to Sabine Pass. He told Münzenberger that he had read a letter in Houston from Kirby Smith to Magruder in which Magruder is ordered to keep 10,000 men ready to march in order to back him [Smith] up. If that is true, we will probably go to Shreveport too, because I think that except for the artillery there are scarcely 10,000 line troops here, and the militia has refused to go over the border. Last week we had quite a hard rain again that made the roads impassable for a couple of days. Now it has dried out a bit so that at least it is possible to walk between the puddles without having the water leak into one's shoes. For us that really is no disadvantage; what we must do, except for standing watch, we can do on water too, and we have quite a good boat for that. Yesterday there was quite a lot of excitement among some of the American companies. A young lady who was on a journey to Sumter ["Sumpter"] had to stay over in Liberty. There she made the acquaintance of an old woman who lives here and who persuaded her to move in with her here and stay until a good opportunity to travel on might present itself. Here she was constantly pursued and annoyed in the house of her protectress by a lieutenant of Elmore's regiment,[3] and she had no means of getting away. So then she found acquaintances in our regiment and complained to them of her poverty. They gathered together some money and took her away from the old woman and took her to a different residence. Then they caught the lieutenant and wanted to throw him into the water, but when he assured them of his pure intentions, they let him go again. The old woman was very much agitated and complained to the post commander, and yesterday evening he had an artilleryman arrested who also belonged to the group supporting the young woman. Everybody is very anxious to know how the business will continue. In any case, it has to come to trial. Gustav Artzt was commandeered last week to escort prisoners to Houston and returned again the night before last. On the same train on which he rode to Liberty, our saddles were being transported too. The horses, he said, were therefore expected in Houston yesterday. They are to be taken to Montgomery [Texas]; they are said to be in very fine condition. Recently I have heard the same identical story told several times by different people, namely, that Luckett's Regiment had their weapons taken away from them. There was a complete revolution. Luckett's men simply wanted better rations, because on this diet they could not do their duties. But Cook's Artillery, which is holding the fort, turned the cannons around with the mouths toward the town, drove out the officers who would not take their side, and threatened to blow up the town if their wishes were not satisfied. Colonel Debray, who wanted to go into the fortifications at night, had to surrender his saber to the sentinels. And they kept this stand until they got satisfaction. The newspapers were probably forbidden to discuss this matter.[4] . . . Rudolf

Beaumont
9 November 1863
Carl to family

. . . We are still here in the mill. . . . At your place you are now fewer by one, since Hedwig has gone back up to Sisterdale. . . . I was always relaxed about her welfare during the time she was with you, and each of her letters and my stay at home just added to my contentment. Then too, she was nearer me by fifty miles, and even if that . . . makes no real difference . . . it is pleasanter just the same. . . . Also Hedwig so enjoyed being with you and is very grateful for the warm treatment she received there. Sometimes she seems to me to have had a kind of homesickness for up there [Sisterdale], mainly for the grave of our dear child. . . . Of politics I can report nothing of consequence, and what I would write from here you would hear sooner from the [*Texas*] *State Gazette* [of Austin]. General Magruder has issued an order according to which all commanders of posts, especially from Niblett's Bluff, Sabine Pass, Beaumont, Houston, [and] Galveston, are told to confiscate all spirituous drinks, and to send them to Houston to Major Hyllestet.[5] This order has as its purpose, first to keep the soldiers from getting soused, and second to provide the hospitals plentifully with the stuff that is so useful and necessary to the sick. Last night a lot of wine boxes came up from Sabine already. In the night the sick probably fetched our boxes, though by then there was a guard. It naturally sees nothing it does not wish to see. Magruder probably also is suffering from an illness that he means to heal in this manner. There are supposed to be no Yankees far and wide with the exception of the blockade ships on the bay. Our horses came through Houston a couple of days ago on their way to Montgomery County. Our saddles are in Liberty. The horses are said to look good. My pipe was stolen yesterday while I was in the shop working on my sixshooter. I am at work on a new pipe, but the wood is too small for a bridge [between stem and bowl]. Now I have to go eat, because otherwise

I won't get anything anymore. Adieu. Just now I got back from the meal. It consisted of meat, coffee that we bought ourselves some time ago, and bread. It tasted quite good to me, except that there could have been more of it. This afternoon we may perhaps go by boat for [sweet] potatoes. Now farewell, all of you. With many and warm regards to Mother, Father, ecte. [sic], always your Carl H. Coreth

Houston
16 November 1863
Rudolf to family

. . . Last Friday we were supposed to march from Beaumont. We had already been taken to the train station before sunrise, but the train that was supposed to pick us up did not come until 9 o'clock in the evening, because it had run off the tracks on the way, which recently has been happening once or twice every time, and so we did not get away from there until morning of the day before yesterday.[6] We had ten cars such as are used in Germany for transporting wood, without a roof or side walls, and five enclosed ones. The flat cars were loaded with us and our things, which completely covered them. On the first car behind the locomotive there were our [music] band,[7] plus eight criminals from Louisiana with a guard that was to escort them to Houston, and a few additional people. Then there came our hospital ambulances, then the commissary, and then all of us. When we had ridden about twelve miles there was suddenly a big jerk and the train stopped. In a moment everybody was down from the cars and running to the front to get the dead and wounded they expected to find there out of the way, because the two first cars were lying in the ditch next to the track, and the people were lying there in a big heap with their crates. But it did not take long before the people had all crawled out from among their things, because they were afraid that the cars might turn over again, and they found to their great surprise that nobody had been hurt. The train was a real picture of destruction. The locomotive lay with its rear end in the ditch and was dented by the latter cars; then for a stretch the whole track was shattered and next to it lay the cars; and then there were a lot of cars that had jumped the track but were still standing. We had to stay there until yesterday morning, when another train came from Houston and picked us up. Then we rode to Liberty, where we arrived at noon. There was something wrong with the pump though, and the locomotive had to leave us sitting there and go on to the next station for water. It did not come back until sundown, and at last we got here at 10 o'clock at night without having had further delay. We think that our march is connected with the Yankee attack at Brownsville.[8] Our horses are at Camp Lubbock; we got the saddles back this morning, and just now Kämmerling told me that the wagons are supposed to be coming. So I have to go there and help load, so I have to say Adio for today. . . . Rudolf

Camp at Houston
22 November 1863
Rudolf to family

... We are supposed to march away from here tomorrow again. They say we are supposed to go to Matagorda. Yesterday the news came that Corpus Christi is supposed to have been taken by the Yankees, but it has not been confirmed yet as far as I know.[9] In the company there has been some change since I wrote you. Capt. Podewils's resignation has been accepted, whereby August Schulze became captain. The two other officers rose in rank, and we had to elect a new lieutenant. Candidates were Münzenberger and Philipp Bitter; Münzenberger was beaten by seventeen votes. If everybody had voted for him that promised to do so, he would have had a considerable majority, but a lot must have lied to him. Bitter is an arch-boor, and to that degree he fits very well into our officer class.[10] Last week we received our winter clothes: pants, jackets, hats, and blankets. The trousers and jackets are of gray woolen cloth ["Tuch"]; everything is pretty good. The order came that each man is to get two complete suits and, in order to complete these, another requisition for clothes was made, but they haven't arrived yet. I don't think we will have time anymore to visit [H. F.] Fisher. We have a lot to do in order to be travel-ready, and up to now Carl and I have never been able to get off at the same time. Since we got here we have both been on guard duty, had to herd the horses, and had our day of cooking duty. We might perhaps get to it this afternoon though. In Houston there is said to be smallpox, so it is strictly forbidden to be in town at night. It won't be possible for us to come to you for Father's birthday [2 Dec.], because now there are positively only sick leaves given, and we have no prospects for that, since we are enjoying very good health. There is no hope now of our coming together, unless the war were to come to a quick end. Our horses are not in good condition, and besides mine got kicked by another one the night before last and is of no account now. I hope though that it will be all right again soon. We usually get twenty ears of corn a day. By day the horses are herded; at night we have to keep them tied though, and that doesn't make them better either. Nothing else that might interest you comes to mind just now. . . . Carl may still write you too. . . . Münzenberger, Kämmerling, and Alfred send best regards, and above all your Rudolf sends greetings.

Camp on the Navidad
2 December 1863
Rudolf to father

Before it gets dark I want . . . to send my best wishes for your happiness on your birthday. I can only write you in pencil because we are on a forced march and the wagons have not caught up yet. Three days ago we got your letter of the fifteenth, the first since we left Beaumont, and you can imagine how glad we were to get good news from you. We are well. I wrote you all that we would be going away from Houston. From there we went to Columbia, and there we lay until Friday, when we got the order to go to Matagorda in a forced march in order to be transported from there by water to Saluria. We came by Alex Rugeley's on the Caney. I visited him; it seems he was pleased to see me.[11] Münzenberger was not with us. Artzt got lost while hunting near Columbia when we got marching orders, and so Münzenberger stayed behind with his horse until he returned. They caught up with us again the day before yesterday. From Rugeley's we marched away at 1 o'clock in the morning for Matagorda; that was the night from Sunday to Monday; it was quite cold. At about 9 o'clock in the morning we got to Matagorda. The steamships that were to take us to Saluria were waiting for us, but then the news came that our troops had left Saluria the night before, and that thus the entire bay has come into the possession of the Yankees, and we could not risk going over anymore. Now we are on the way to Port Lavaca or Victoria by land. From each company two men were left behind in Matagorda in order to set fire to the cotton that lay there, if necessary. Alfred is one of those. The same day we went another 5-6 miles up the Colorado because the first ferry is twenty miles upstream. The next morning we heard cannons shooting in the bay, but don't know whose and why they were shot off. We are now still thirty-some-odd miles from Victoria. We will probably get there the day after tomorrow. There are some very conflicting rumors going about concerning the advances of the Yankees; I don't think they are farther along than Saluria though. Of our horses many are already very tired, Carl's and mine included. They get corn all right, but they don't have time to eat grass. I think though that they will hold out to Victoria, and there they will get a few days of rest again, probably. Marching together with us is Pyron's Regiment, and the way I heard it, there are nine additional regiments supposed to come down afterward.[12] We now have all sorts of good guns. The no-good ones were surrendered, and we got Enfield rifles for them.[13] I have one of them too. Münzenberger drew one and gave it to me for mine. The rations on the march were quite slim sometimes. Probably you will get to hear lots of complaints about that again. I would be quite content though, if I knew for sure that we did not have harder times ahead of us. We rode thirty-five miles today; tomorrow we are to walk ten miles, and the next day the rest of the way. I am very glad that we are back in the west, because that is the place where we belong, after all.[14] I hope we stay here. We hope we can be together for your next birthday. One would think that the war would be over by then. Now Adio to you all, my dear ones. I hope we get news of you again soon. Rudolf

Camp on the Caney
9 December 1863
Rudolf to family

We are still without news from you. . . . Carl had liver pains and I had a little attack of vertigo ["*Sturranfall*"].[15] I last wrote you from Navidad, when we were on the way to Victoria. We thought at that time that we would be staying in the west, but we were very much mistaken about that, because we were still twenty-five miles from Victoria when we got orders to go back to the Bernard in a forced march. We had to leave the wagons behind and one day we had to ride forty-five miles. We stayed on the upper Caney one day. The next day, the day before yesterday, we went twenty miles farther down it and camped for the night at a plantation that is twelve miles from Camp Winston; our [Münzenberger and Rudolf's] old company was there too. Münzenberger and I went to their camp in the evening and had quite a good time. We had a lot to tell each other. The men seemed to be quite glad to see us again.[16] Yesterday we went an additional four miles farther down to a place where fodder and corn enough are available for us to hold out for several days. Where we will go when that has been used up, we do not know. An attack on Velasco is expected, and it is thought that we will stay in the area in order to be able to go there in case of need. We get quite good rations: sugar, molasses, [sweet] potatoes, beef, and the last few days we have gotten pork a couple of times too. The only thing we really miss is soap. We haven't gotten any since we left Houston, and nobody has clean clothes anymore. However, I would rather be without soap than provisions. The various reports of what was the cause of our crazy marching around all proved to be untrue. The only true part is that Saluria has been taken without our having been able to fire a shot, because the fort was not protected at all on the landward side and the batteries all were directed toward the water. At least that is what is assumed here to be true. The day before yesterday Alfred came back from Matagorda. He says they had right good times there. They stayed there until the government's cotton had been shipped off, and during that time they had nothing to do but cook and eat. The crops down here have turned out excellently. It is completely unclear to me though how we will sustain ourselves for the next year. The planters from the area here are leaving their places along with the Negroes that the conscription has left to them and are going farther inland. Thus the fields here are remaining uncultivated, and, furthermore, the Negroes alone won't accomplish anything but rather eat up a lot of provisions too which until now have been for the army's benefit, and that is all because of a great vagrancy, because Magruder has issued an order according to which all slaveholders with their Negroes are to pull back from the coast for seventy-five miles. And in the part of Texas that is cultivated by whites, the outlook for crops will be bad too, now that the militia has gone away. I keep hoping that the war will end before next winter. When we went to Victoria the other day and thought that the Yankees were on the way inland, because we had heard that they had already had a confrontation with the militia on the Chocolate Bayou, I gave thought to what we could do if it were to come to pass that our place [the Coreth place] might be in danger, and I thought that it would probably be a good idea to deposit a supply of flour in safe places, for example in the cave above Merz's stone creek.[17] One could keep a couple of barrels quite dry and safe and fetch them away quite unnoticed when one needed them. I am always afraid that it might occur to the Yankees someday to go from Brownsville to San Antonio and the upper [Hill Country] counties, where they will find like-minded people, and then [New] Braunfels wouldn't be safe anymore either. I don't think though that our regiment would stay here anymore then; I think the men would leave even if they didn't get orders. At least I would do that, but under favorable conditions it takes 5-6 days to get up there, and so in the end one could arrive too late anyway. I shall hope that those are unnecessary fears, but I cannot deny anyway that I would much rather be in the west [ern part of Texas] now. What I may perhaps have forgotten to write, Carl will probably write to you. Farewell to you all and cherish your son and brother Rudolf. Cordial regards from the mess.

Camp Wharton
24 December 1863
Rudolf to family

. . . Except for the wish that you may spend the holidays in good cheer, I know nothing to write except the trip to [place name omitted; the following unclear, almost illegible]. To recount in the order of their happening the events that we have experienced since I wrote you: the night before the day on which we left the last camp we were told to keep ready, since we might be needed. That gave us cause for all sorts of conjectures, but finally most people concluded that it was just a drill, and that is what it was too. It went quite fast, and I think General Bee was quite pleased with us, because nothing more has been heard. Then the camp was moved three miles farther down the [Caney] creek. There the entire division is camped together now and is supposed to drill every day. Up to now though something has interfered most of the time. Furthermore the order came that weapons were to be divided differently. The guns with the longest range were given to the wing companies, and the next-farthest-shooting ones to the second companies, and so forth, until the center gets the poorest guns. Our staff officers did not want to carry out the order at first. But they could not hold to that intention. So we lost our Enfield rifles and got Sangers in their place. Our duties are quite heavy now. There is hardly time to do anything for oneself. . . . One day guard duty, then we had our day to cook. The next herding horses, then yesterday fetch corn and rations for the company, and today we have a big inspection again. The day before yesterday we were paid out $48 a man. After subtracting my sutler bill and contributing to the mess treasury, I have $8 left. That isn't much really, but we haven't even got a chance to spend that, unless one wishes to gamble it away. The camp is very closely guarded in order to keep the men together. Besides the camp guard there is a provost guard that rides around the camp and arrests everyone who is found without a pass more than a mile from camp, and all roads and bridges are occupied by small groups. There does not seem to be much confidence in the western troops here. General Bee gave an oration to our regiment a couple of days ago, the purpose of which seemed to me to be to put us at ease about conditions in western

Texas. It didn't make a deep impression though. From Münzenberger we learned that Magruder told Colonel Benton that the Yankees have 25,000 men waiting on the borders of Texas. Of these 5,000 are on the Rio Grande; 10,000 are on the coast here; and 10,000 are off Galveston. For the 5,000, he said, there is still enough army in the west to hold them back, and here and at Galveston, he says, the ratio is like seven to ten, of which we have the seven. The plantations are in part already deserted, and the remainder are being abandoned now. Confidence in this war has now sunken very much, even among the Americans. I talked yesterday with several and they were all in accord with one another that they would rather have mules than Negroes and Confederate money. The health conditions here are quite good. I was in the hospital today to get medicine for Fritz Pantermühl, who got sick yesterday, and there were only a couple of people there besides me. Pantermühl has bad headaches. Yesterday we heard from a nephew of old man Roeder that the latter was taken captive on Mustang Island and has probably been transported to New Orleans. That must be quite hard on the old man.[18] Now I have probably written you everything I knew. I hope we will soon get a letter from you bringing us the assurance that everything is in order at home. With many greetings I remain your Rudolf.

26 December [continued]
Carl to family

How we spent Christmas Rudolf has already written you anyway. I cannot deny that I found myself in rather a depressed mood at times and had to struggle not to let it get the upper hand. I succeeded too and am rather content again. I hope we will be together the next time. . . . The reports from Hedwig are rather good . . . at least as far as Indians are concerned. That Meusebach's business [the store in Fredericksburg] is going well really pleased me. I send best regards to Agnes. I will write her sometime when I find the time. But one has a hard time finding any because of all the duties. Farewell. With warmest regards, I remain as ever your old Carl.

Camp Wharton
1 January 1864
Rudolf to family

First of all, my heartiest good wishes for the New Year. This is already the third New Year's that I have not been with you. We thought a lot about you yesterday and today. On such a day one can best imagine what the people at home are doing. You all are probably sitting in the [living] room and our thoughts may perhaps collide, because I think that you are probably pitying us very much today. We have had bad weather the last few days. It began with a heavy rain and to this there was added a strong norther with ice. Now the rain and wind have stopped, but everything is still frozen. Actually only the night before last was unpleasant. It was really cold then already, and the blankets were wet. By last night we were able to dry them, and then the cold did not matter to us anymore. Such a spell of weather is not exactly pleasant; but one imagines it to be much worse than it actually is if one is in the house. We received Father's letter of 10 December and were pleased that you are getting along well. In general we are too, except for Carl, who sometimes has toothache; I think that will stop when it gets warm again. There is now great likelihood that the immediate future will be an eventful time. The *Houston Telegraph* of the twenty-seventh brings the report that Texas is to be attacked on 1 January by about 60,000 men, and a Yankee who was taken captive at Matagorda and is now in our camp is supposed to have said the same. The day before yestereday we heard lots of cannon shots on the coast; as we later heard it, a ship came up to the mouth of the Brazos and shot some balls at the fort, of which two hit their mark but did not hurt anyone. At the same time a militia company that was lying at the mouth of the Bernard was shelled. They are supposed to have retreated in full flight. Of the remaining shots it is suspected that they were shot at Galveston. Yesterday during the violent storm one could hear a dull humming that some held to be shooting, and today a shot is heard once in a while again. It is strange the way that nobody pays it any attention here. Everything goes along in the usual way, as though we were lying here in the profoundest peace. Kämmerling and Schimmelpfennig went as guards with a wagon to Texana the day before yesterday. They aren't likely to be able to return before ten days are up. Carl and I had rather a good stroke of luck with our guard duty. We stood watch at just the beginning of the bad weather. I would like writing longer to you, but my fingers are freezing so that I have to give up. Farewell to you all. Rudolf. I think it would be good if you were to write "Bee's Division" on the letters in addition to the regiment, because the letters are now sent and received by way of the headquarters.

Camp Hardeman
21 January 1864
Rudolf to mother

Your friendly letter gave us great pleasure, especially though the report that you are in better health than usual, despite the many chores that fall to your lot. I hope by now you all will have received the letters too that will take away your worry about us. We withstood the bad weather quite well; in our house that Carl, Alfred, and I built ourselves, neither rain nor norther could do much to us. We three together have eleven blankets. Two of them form the roof; and of the remaining nine, three are laid on a thick layer of moss or grass under us, and with six we cover ourselves. Since we arranged it in that way we have not been cold a single night. When we got here we built ourselves such a hut right away again, which is indisputably the nicest in the regiment. On three sides we have braided walls out of twisted moss, and the fourth side, which faces south, is open. The walls hold off the wind perfectly, the roof is completely waterproof, and there is more room in it than in the little house [Carl's and Rudolf's pre-war] on the Blanco. In general we are getting along as well as we can expect in a time such as this, but I think that a great many letters of complaint are being written home anyway. The very people that in the past very often had to suffer want are now the first to complain and find fault if they do not get everything that they imagine they should be getting. The best measuring gauge is the hospital, and that is not visited more now than usual. A couple of men have measles; otherwise though there are no bad diseases going around. I do not want to beg that you write us again, because I know that you have quite enough to do as it is. But if you were to do it just the same, I would be very pleased. With many regards, I remain your son Rudolf

Rudolf to family [continued]

. . . We all hope to be sent west again, for which there seems to be some prospect too. They say that Magruder is waiting until the Yankees penetrate inland from Indianola, in order to get us there in forced marches before they expect it. Meat for three days is being dried, and rumor has it that it is to be stored for that march. Down here on the coast there does not seem to be any intention of an earnest attack, although a ship keeps our batteries constantly active. Our men are raising breastworks on the peninsula. What they are good for, I actually don't know, since they don't have any cannons that they can set up behind them. A few days ago the Yankee ship anchored off there and bombarded the workers all day long. It shot eighteen 150-lb. bombs at the land, of which three didn't explode. The remaining shots were fired from smaller cannons.

27 January [continued]

Up to now I haven't found time to continue this letter again. . . . We had to go in forced march to the mouth of the Caney and back. The night of the twenty-first to the twenty-second a bugler sounded an alarm at 2 o'clock. We got the order to cook provisions for three days to be in readiness, since our wagons would be left behind. They said the Yankees had landed on the peninsula in considerable strength. It wasn't possible for us to bake much bread in preparation, because we have too few bread pans, and we were to leave long before daybreak. The meat that had been dried was divided to be sure, but it was only enough so that each could have two portions. At noon we were still fifteen miles from the place where the Yankees were supposed to be. There we halted and waited for further orders from General Bee. At eight in the evening the order came that we were to go on. It was 12 o'clock when we arrived at our destination. We were very sleepy but were only permitted to lie down next to our horses but not take off their saddles. We were between the Caney bottom and Cedar Lake. It made a remarkable impression to see cavalry converging together from all directions. The moon was shining so full that one could see everything well at a couple of hundred paces distance. We stayed lying there the nineteenth [Rudolf's error]. Arms were issued, the weapons were inspected, and the remaining time each person looked for fodder wherever he could. A lieutenant from Van der Stucken's company told us that nothing was the matter, that the rumor had simply been flying about that five Yankees had been seen on the peninsula.[19] The twentieth we marched back toward Camp Hardeman again. About noon we met our wagons, which had come after us with corn and provisions. After we had eaten heartily, I was sent back to General Bee with a dispatch. I did not arrive at Bee's until midnight, and the next day I caught up with the regiment again in the evening at Camp Hardeman. Since then we have been lying here very still again, waiting for further orders and passing the time drilling. We were underway on Mother's birthday, and it was impossible for me to write. Therefore I must beg her to accept my best wishes kindly anyway, even though they are coming too late.

28 January 1864 [continued]

. . . all that remains is for me to answer the questions that Father put to me about rations and our horses. The rations, to tell the truth, have become scanter than ever, but nobody is made to suffer starvation anyway. They consist of cornmeal, beef, and salt; and then sometimes, if they happen to be available, we get [wheat] flour ["Flour"], sugar, molasses, [sweet] potatoes, and bacon or pork. We get enough cornmeal, in terms of weight. It is usually so coarse though that one must sift out a greal deal. The meat here is good, and also enough is delivered. Salt is scarce. Even the farmers are suffering from a shortage of it. We have run out of it a couple of times before the day a barrel is delivered. We have still always been able though to get some up to now from people who had more than they needed. Now we have enough of everything. We have a mess treasury, and expenditures from it are always disputed when we have a chance to buy anything. We always have enough to eat, and so do the majority of the company. But we all find fault, of course. . . . The horses get more corn than they can eat; nevertheless Carl's and mine are skinny . . . everything they have on their bodies is corn-flesh, and they have quite a lot of endurance. . . . I think when the green grass comes out they will gain weight rapidly. Carl is cook today and cannot write. He sends best regards. Farewell. Rudolf.

Camp Hardeman
4 February 1864
Rudolf to family

A half hour ago we got back from pursuing the deserters without having caught up with them. . . . When it became generally known that so many men had fled, Captain Schulze volunteered to pursue the men and do his best to bring them back. He took me along as scout. A captain from Pyron's regiment . . . attached himself to us. We rode almost all night. Toward morning we met four of the deserters, who had turned around. They said that we were about five hours behind them [the others]. . . . We were forty miles from camp and had no prospects of catching up with them for another twenty miles. The captains had orders to return within three days. That was too short a term for continuing our pursuit with hope of success, and so it was decided that we should turn around. The men were riding in perfect formation, as we heard from the people who had seen them. They seemed to be very much in a hurry. . . . When we got here to camp we found it abandoned; only one man of each company had stayed behind to watch the possessions of the men involved in pursuing the deserters. Of our company Carl is here. He told us that our regiment marched away this morning. He said it looked the way it usually does when just two companies march away. Pyron's men seem to have refused to leave. He says the bugler blew boots and saddles several times, but nobody paid any attention. At last the officers rode away; then one by one the men followed after, except for twenty men who rode out of camp in the opposite direction. What is to become of all this is completely unclear to me. There is absolute demoralization. I have to close, because we mean to ride on. Adio, all my dear ones. Rudolf. Colonel Benton gave the officers hope of going to the west soon.

Camp at Hawkins Plantation[20]
Sunday, 6 February 1864
Rudolf to family

. . . Capt. Schulze and I rode away from Camp Hardeman the day before yesterday and got here yesterday at noon. A couple of miles from here we met the horses of our regiment, which were being driven back. I was somewhat surprised, because I thought that the men would not surrender their horses without offering resistance. They had not resisted at all though. We now are camping seven miles from the coast, near Cedar Lake. . . . There is shade and enough good water here, and that is all we need as infantry, except for rations. How they are, I don't know yet. . . . General Bee has transferred his camp here too. Alfred . . . seems to think his [own] horse was stolen from him a few days ago; at least his searching was fruitless. He says that last night two fine horses of Bee's staff members were stolen too. . . . They say that a fight between a militia regiment that was on the way home and two companies of Debray's regiment[21] took place and eight or ten men were killed without the militia's having been forced to come back. Yesterday the Yankees shelled the fort at the mouth of the Caney and wounded some of our men slightly. For today Adio. Rudolf.

Camp on Cedar Lake
11 February 1864
Rudolf to family

. . . Carl came back today. He is in quite good spirits; he says that he had quite good times after the regiment left, because the few who stayed behind were able to get enough good provisions at the farms cheaply. When he got here he was given the opportunity to work as a carpenter in the fortifications. . . . But I don't think that he is going to accept the offer, because in the end it would be difficult to get away when one has had enough of it. . . . A great dissatisfaction with practically all high officers prevails, but nobody speaks out openly. . . . In Pyron's regiment there will probably be a rebellion by 20 March, because their time is up then and they want to re-organize, which they probably won't be allowed to do. The day before yesterday we had a big review in the presence of Kirby Smith. Our regiment was represented there by about 120 men. Gen. Kirby Smith makes a good impression upon the men. He did not look so very much like an actor, as other generals do.[22] He has issued an order since coming here that reduces Magruder's staff of fifty-odd men to twenty-five. On the coast everything has been quiet for several days. . . . With many greetings from Carl and me, I remain your Rudolf.

Camp Sidney Johnson
14 February 1864
Rudolf to family

Tomorrow we will have a good opportunity to send a letter to you quickly. Capt. Schulze is going up there; he got a leave because his wife died.[23] We have had no news from you in a long time. . . . Carl worried me the last few days; he had an attack of liver pains that was worse than he has ever had before. . . . We made him a wet compress around his stomach and covered him up warmly. . . . Today he ate some meat broth and some of the stewed plums that Mother sent along. Tomorrow he thinks he can get up. . . . Carl has the intention of wearing a binder around his stomach all the time from now one. I am very glad that he managed to get here before he got the attack, because he would have been quite abandoned in Camp Hardeman, and we probably wouldn't have heard anything about it. I am quite well now. . . . I was running round with bad headaches that dissolved in a head cold. . . . There are surely a lot of sick men here. Most have skin diseases: measles, itch ["eetsch"], various other sorts of rash, and many have infected vaccination pustules. It has been strictly forbidden to continue the vaccinating, because, they say, the stuff that they vaccinated with here was taken from very virulent pustules. The men have very thickly swollen arms, and the pustules are cauterized daily with silver nitrate. I am glad I did not have myself re-vaccinated, which actually was the order. In our company a couple of people have had the measles, but we have been spared the other stuff so far. . . . They say we are to leave here soon, as soon as the generals feel sure that no attack is intended here, of which they are said to be almost certain already. We think that we will be going to the area of Wharton and Egypt then, where our horses are, and where there is still plenty of surplus corn to be had because no military have been stationed there yet. Our meat ration has been raised from 1½ lbs. to 2 lbs., which will do us lots of good, because meat is now the best part of our ration. If one has lots of meat, then one can eat lots of bread with it too, and everything revolves around the food, because that is always our main entertainment. A couple of days ago Alfred had an opportunity to buy a side of bacon. We really needed that, because we had no fat. . . . Alfred is still on guard duty at General Bee's. He has heard no more about his horse. . . . We have almost nothing to do now . . . we don't have enough men to drill. . . . Farewell to you all and cherish your Rudolf. I forgot to write that since Carl is sick we are living in the company tent.

Camp Sidney Johnson
19 February 1864
Rudolf to family

When you get this letter Carl and Alfred will probably be with you already. . . . The last letters that we got, from Father and Amalia, gave me great joy. It seemed to me, judging from that, that you have lots of work, to be sure, but that the remaining conditions are rather good. I am very happy that Carl got such a long leave. First, he himself is very happy about it, and then, I think he will be able to help you quite a bit too. I congratulate Agnes on her twin daughters, and I thank Amalia for her friendly letter. . . . Yesterday some cannon shots were fired along the coast. We don't know definitely by whom, but [Vander] Stucken's men say that it was the Big Yankee *Columbiade* [sic], by which the fort has been shelled often in the past. They claim to have recognized the cannon by the sound. It would surely be remarkable, wouldn't it, if the Yankees had simply waited until our regiment had left and then had begun shelling the forts again, as they did almost daily before. . . . There are so few men here that if they really did want to make noise, one could not hear them very far off. Fritz Pantermühl and I represent our once so numerous mess now. We live simply but in general rather well. Our main nourishment is cornmeal and beef. I drink water with it, but Fritz usually gets himself a cup of corn coffee from one of the other messes. We are actually supposed to get molasses too, but just now there is none here. . . . Farewell for today, all of you dear ones, and write me soon. . . . Rudolf.

Camp on the Colorado
Saturday, 5 March 1864
Rudolf to family

. . . Thursday we left Camp Sidney Johnson. The trip was divided into two day-long parts, each of about fifteen miles. . . . I found the walking rather difficult. My feet are completely soft from lying around so much, and then I drew new shoes that I had to put on right away, because my old ones were so torn up I couldn't wear them anymore. My feet got swollen and got lots of blisters. They are better again today, only I am still somewhat stiff. The shoes we drew are quite good. . . . They are English ones again, but a different kind than the last ones. . . . The purpose of our march is not known to us. It seems to me as though we are going to go even farther. . . . Our horses are twenty-five miles from here; maybe we will get them back. Last week a man named Hove [?], who was an orderly in the Brigadier Office, was brought before a court martial because he was said to have read letters and torn them up. He was guilty, but in consideration of his youth he was merely dismissed from the office and the charge was proclaimed in his presence at dress parade. Our guardhouse is full of deserters who returned voluntarily. . . . Several of them are suffering the consequences of vaccination and they are strictly watched even in the hospital. . . . The disease is still spreading about and the doctors have no means of controlling it. . . . The beef is better here than on the coast, the water is good, and then here in the bottom we find a lot of onions that are just as good as the cultivated ones. Nothing more comes to mind that I might write now. So farewell to you all for today. Regards from the bottom of my heart from your Rudolf Coreth.

Camp Colorado
9 March 1864
Rudolf to family [letter badly blotted]

. . . Up to now we have had absolutely nothing to do besides stand watch every six or eight days and cook. . . . Our men are catching lots of quite nice fish here in the river. C[harles]. Mergele caught two, one of 48 lbs. and another of 40 lbs.[24] They would catch even more, if one could get poles and strings, but it is very hard to get them. . . . It is said that in the next few days we will be paid for six months, which would amount to about $200. Two months' pay, $48.80, hardly helps at all now. The least little thing costs $5.00, and so that is gone before one turns around. . . . The night before last a man escaped from the guardhouse. They say that he had been condemned to death. He had been court-martialed for insubordination and agitating. . . . Right after sundown he crossed the river on a raft, and so he would be able to get as far as Navidad before the night was over. He could hide there. . . . If all those who had made agitating speeches were to be shot, then probably one-fourth of the regiment would have to be shot, and since that is the case, it seems unjust to me that they single out an individual and execute him. I know of nothing more to write to you. . . . Adio from your Rudolf Coreth. . . .

Spanish Camp
14 March 1864
Rudolf to family

Tomorrow H. Weil is going to New Braunfels.[25] That is another opportunity to let a few lines get to you which must not be allowed to pass unused. We left Camp Colorado on the twelfth and made a march of twenty miles. It was not very hard on anybody . . . we were told that the horses would be brought to the camp. . . . I got H[ermann]. Conring's horse. Today we continued mounted, which was quite a pleasant change for us, especially since quite a cold norther with rain was blowing. . . . He [Conring] is driving the hospital ambulance and is in La Grange and probably won't come back soon. Yesterday seven people that A. Schulze freed from the jail came back to the regiment too. They were placed under arrest right away; but probably not much will happen to them.

Benton is supposed to have said that he intends to let the men get by with no more than extra guard duty as punishment. Today each company moved into the horse-camp intended for it, and they are so far apart that it was difficult for the men to have a guarding place in common, and so each company was given its own prisoners, and ours are doing exactly as they please and don't have to perform duties at all. . . . Yesterday A[dolph]. Triesch told me too that there was a good rain at your place and that there are prospects for a good harvest. All in all, everything has gone as I would wish during the last few days. First I got your letters; then we went on the march, and it seems to me there is nothing to fear in the west; and then I heard from home directly too; and finally I heard from the people in the horse-camp that my horse has improved a great deal. Now farewell to you all. . . . Be so kind and send your letters "care of Captain C. C. Clute" in Houston.[26] Rudolf. . . .

Camp at Hempstead
20 March 1864
Rudolf to family

. . . I am getting along quite well. For the moment I am regimental butcher. I got the job, actually, without knowing about it. We were asked who in the company wanted to help with slaughtering for a couple of weeks. I volunteered, but then the quartermaster told me that I was to be chief butcher, and that I was to get five men as helpers every day. That was five days ago. Since then we have been slaughtering two or three head of cattle daily. I am planning to give up the post soon; the work is not completely to my taste. The night before last we stayed at San Felipe. The town has grown somewhat since we were there [in 1850?]. A lot of poor people are living there: Poles, Bohemians, Germans, free Negroes, and some Americans. The men are in the army, and the families are said to be suffering quite badly from poverty, I hear, because the planters who live in the vicinity support them only very scantily. Today Colonel Benton came back from Houston and brought the order from Magruder that one in fifteen men is to get a leave. That made for several very happy people; from our company two are going, [August] Oelkers and O[swald]. Jung. They will leave tomorrow and take this letter along. . . . Captain Stevens and his commando are not here with us yet; they are expected daily.[27] Now farewell to you all, my dear ones. . . . Where we are going we do not know definitely. The first order said to Polk County. Now they say we are going to Louisiana. I don't know yet though, if there is anything to it. Rudolf. . . .

Hempstead
24 March 1864
Rudolf to Carl

Since you and Alfred left I have not received any detailed report about you yet. . . . Yesterday I got a letter from Father in which he wrote that you had arrived in good shape and had ridden to Sisterdale. . . . I heard

with regret from Kämmerling the reasons for his staying behind
[?]. . . . The prisoners were surrendered to a general court-martial which
was supposed to be opened in Hempstead on the twentieth. They were
divided into six different classes according to the degree of their offense.
Then one was selected from each class to stand trial, and the remaining
five are to get the punishment meted out to him. The men who reported
to the regiment here voluntarily, which includes the men our captain
[Schulze] freed from the jail, were court-martialed in the regiment. They
are getting thirty days' fatigue duty ["fatigue duty"], and they are fined
a month's pay. I fear that the men who are to come before the general
court-martial won't get by that cheaply. Benton wants to fetch the cap-
tives from town and bring them into camp. . . . Today all men belonging
to the detachment were ordered to come to town. They say Captain
Stevens wants to undertake another expedition to search for the remaining deserters. It may be too, though, that they only have to bear
witness at the court transactions. The actual cause of my writing is as
follows: yesterday the officers put the question to the company whether
we wished the company to get out of the regiment and be transformed
into an artillery battery, since . . . Magruder is permitting the cavalry
to transfer to the artillery. Now there is a new battery being recruited
in Houston, and so the officers want to see to it that the company, just
as it is, is transformed into artillery. Naturally the officers want to retain
their ranks. The men were told that there were big advantages for the
artillery. First, they were to get thirty days' leave (?). Then, they said,
artillery always camps alone; and then too, it is true, they are always
better supplied with clothes and provisions. Practically all of the men
were willing to go along with the proposal. The only ones opposed were
I, Christian Pantermühl, and, I think, Lüders.[28] C. Pantermühl does want
to go along though, if the battery is to go west. Only I am strictly against
it, and for the following reasons, you see. I do not want our officers to
get command over a camp, because they don't have enough sense to do
something for the men and they will just practice deception [*"chicani-
eren"*] whenever they can, which is what they always did in the past
when they got a chance. Beyond that, in the artillery strict discipline is
much more necessary than it is with us, because every man is part of a
mechanism and because the officers have greater responsibility, since the
horses and weapons belong to the government, and our officers are not
the people to attain discipline in a sensible way by a long shot. And,
finally, I don't like having anything to do with heavy artillery itself,
because I think that a well-maintained rifle has just as much real worth
as a cannon, and I can move about much more freely with a rifle, if we
were to get into battle, whereas, as an artilleryman one must hold to the
group, because otherwise one is left standing there completely unarmed.
I explained . . . that I would take steps to make my position in this
regiment secure. Then they asked me not to do anything yet until they
know whether it could be done at all. . . . Schramm and F. Schulze drove
to Houston today to ask about it. If it is possible, they want to get away
as soon as possible. I said for you, Alfred, Münzenberger, and Kämmer-

ling that you did not want to go along *until you all had written me about it*. Be so good as to write me as soon as possible what you want to do. . . . If the company were to leave and we were to stay here, I would propose signing up with Captain Holmes's company.[29] Father wrote me in the letter I got yesterday that he had brought Trinette and her foal to our stallion. If it is not too late yet, do be so good as to take it to any other stallion instead, because even if it is just a Spanish one, I think nothing good can result from such a close blood relationship.[30] When you come down here bring me along some stationery. This I am using here is just too very poor. Now farewell. I must go and dry my things. It rained during the night and I have kept hardly a dry thread. Now the sun is shining again. Rudolf Coreth. . . .

Camp near Livingston
28 March 1864
Rudolf to family

. . . We are marching quite fast to our destination. Usually we make over fifteen miles a day. This side of Hempstead the region assumes a completely different character from that which we have been hiking through up to now. The land is hilly and it is almost completely covered with spruce trees, that are occasionally astonishingly tall. In the valleys there is dense bottom ["Botton"] in which the trees have grown much higher too than farther to the west. There the people have hewn out their fields. The area through which we came is rather densely populated. There are quite considerable fields, but they don't seem to me to yield an especially good profit. The corn that we draw usually has very small ears. It seems that the people have lots of fodder crops, because they have to feed their horses all year long. . . . One can sometimes ride all day without seeing a single head of beef. Mainly the people seem to raise pigs, for which the area must be especially suited. Our meat rations are now always only bacon, ½ lb. daily. Our horses feel the total lack of grass quite badly. We got fodder only twice, once two bundles for each horse, and today only one however. We get enough corn, but without grass it nourishes the horses only poorly. In Hempstead we visited Schimmelpfennig and Artzt in the guardhouse. The courtmartial was underway, but they had not yet been called. The court was through with the men who, it is thought, will get the severest punishment, Hübotter and Daum from Co. H.[31] They were taken to Houston; but nobody knows yet what the verdict was. I think Schimmelpfennig, Storck, and Artzt will be punished rather lightly, because they still surrendered. . . . They are guarded by our men; they let them go where they wish, and pro forma one always accompanies them. Today [Ernst] Schwantes arrived. He told me he had seen Mother and one of my sisters, but otherwise he did not know anything to tell me about you all. Tomorrow we will continue onward. I think we must surely get settled soon. . . . With many regards I remain as ever your Rudolf.

Moscow
2 April 1864
Rudolf to family

. . . The only news I know is that we are not, as the first order said, staying in Polk County but rather are moving forward to Louisiana. . . . Dr. Kelley said he had seen the order and all arrangements confirm it.[32] From Coldsprings [Polk County] on we are going a different route. Up to there we went eastward, and now we are going almost due northward. They say our destination is Many, which lies between Shreveport and Alexandria. Since I last wrote you we are still continuing to ride through forest. The only prairie we have encountered was maybe a hundred acres in size. We camped there yesterday. . . . My tools have now been completely abandoned. I have volunteered for duty with the company again so that at least I will have something to do, but there is hardly anything to be done. We haven't put a man on guard duty for two days now, and recently we put more than one on. The last few days we have almost always gotten fodder for the horses; if that is too little, we fetch some cane and give the horses leaves from it, which they like eating quite well. . . . . The nights here are very cold, and mornings one frequently finds frost on the ground. . . . I think the forest is the cause, because the ground is so covered with shade all day that it never warms up. I forgot to write you the last time that nothing came of the business about the artillery. The company can go, to be sure, but if the officers want to go along, they have to take an examination, which they aren't capable of doing, and the company does not want to go alone. I am rather sorry. I hoped to be free of the company in that way. For getting away from the company in some other way—for example by going to a workshop in Houston or San Antonio—this does not seem to be the time, but I would like very much to get away. They are just such awfully coarse trash really. I could tell you a lot of things, but no purpose is served that way. Fritz Pantermühl was made a corporal.[33] He asks me to ask Carl to bring him along his watch from Wunderlich's. . . . I hope Carl does not feel obliged to leave up there [home] before he has to, just because we marched away. . . . From New Braunfels things must surely look more dangerous again than they really are. Here it is as quiet as in the most profoundly peaceful times. Farewell. . . . Rudolf Coreth.

Mary Ann on the Angelina River
7 April 1864
Rudolf to family

. . . The last few days we have usually gone twelve miles. People acquainted with this area say that it is another three hundred miles to the prairie in the direction we are going now. The detachment that remained behind in Hempstead for the court-martial is behind us; it will catch up with us in a couple of days. . . . Schimmelpfennig, Storck, and Artzt are coming here with the detachment. They have been turned over to the regiment and will be sentenced here. They will probably be punished little or not at all. Yesterday we figured out the distance between us and New Braunfels as best we could; we added up 335 miles. That is, in any case, the greatest distance we have been away from home since entering the army. Carl and Alfred have a long road ahead of them. . . . If this letter arrives before they leave, do be so good as to send me a comb; I have lost mine and can't get one here. Now farewell. . . . F[ritz]. Pantermühl and I have built ourselves a tent in which we will lie quite dry. With many regards to you all, I remain as ever your son and brother Rudolf Coreth.

San Augustine
9 April 1864
Rudolf to father

My dear father!

Since it is probable that we will have an encounter with the Yankees soon, and one can never know just what might happen then, after all, I want to tell you in detail about my financial condition (which, to be sure, consists exclusively of debts) with the request that you straighten them out in case these lines reach you.

Debts of Rudolf Coreth

to Carl [Coreth]	$14.50
to [Mariam] Appmann	1.00
to W[illiam]. Triesch	1.00
to [Fritz Panter]Mühl	1.50
to Ch[ristian]. Pantermühl	2.50
to [Hermann] Kämmerling	40.00
to Capt. A[ugust]. Schulze	2.50
to Dr. Collier[34]	4.00
to A[nton]. Elsner	2.00
to [Christian] Busch & Mess	1.60

The bill with Carl might be a bit in error. I believe it is a bit more than I indicated. $53.50 I still owe him from the time when the money exchange rate stood at ten to one. Likewise the debt to Kämmerling, at twenty to one. The horse I am riding belongs to H[ermann]. Conring. Should it be lost, I must ask you to pay for that too. According to my calculations, it is worth $40-50 in silver. I hope my estate, namely my horses, will be sufficient to cover these debts. But should that not be the case, I ask you to help along a little. Now I face the future entirely at peace. I don't believe anything will happen to me, but I consider it to be good to be prepared, and therefore I am writing this.

After twenty-nine months of soldiering, Rudolf Coreth was at last to see action.

Battles and Bayous

A former United States congressman and governor of Massachusetts, Nathaniel Prentiss Banks became a major general of volunteers in the Union Army in May 1861. At the end of December 1862, he replaced the tyrannical General Benjamin F. Butler as commander of occupying forces at New Orleans, which had fallen to the Union on 25 April of that year. Largely responsible for the fall of Port Hudson, Louisiana, in July 1863 and the consequent opening up of the Mississippi, Gen. Banks fixed his attention in the spring of 1864 on moving up the Red River to General Kirby Smith's headquarters at Shreveport, where Banks planned to join with General Frederick Steele, who was encountering considerable opposition from General Sterling Price's Southern forces in his move southward through Arkansas. By adding this strategy to the continuing blockade of the gulf ports, Banks hoped to isolate Texas even more than before and bring Louisiana under full Federal control. At Pleasant Hill and Mansfield (the Battle of Sabine Crossroads), Bank's plan met with sufficient resistance in early April to frustrate his northward advance and thus prevent his invasion of Texas from the east.

The early April battles made clear to the Union commanders that, based upon their information, a retreat down-river was the best course of action to follow next. However, they were inhibited by a very marked drop in the level of the river at several points, so that the flotilla, hampered by heavy damage to rudders and wheels, soon found going with the current to be about as difficult as moving upstream had been. On 12 April, General Tom Green suddenly shifted several regiments of Confederate cavalry from Pleasant Hill to Blair's Landing, the port for that community, where Union forces on a number of ships and on the river's banks clashed with Confederate land forces. The ships, some of them too damaged to proceed, became central to the fighting. Guns from three of the disabled transports were collected and used to open fire on Green's men seeking shelter behind trees along the opposite bank.[1]

On the road between Pleasant Hill and Natchitoches
17 April 1864
Rudolf to family

On the eleventh I got two letters in Mansfield . . . I see with joy that at that time you were all still well. It is just a shame that the letters are so old. Of ourselves I have news to share with you this time. On 12 April ["März" = March] we had quite a hot battle. We lost thirty-four men, of whom eight are dead; the remaining twenty-six are more or less seriously wounded. Colonel Benton was shot through the arm. The [right] arm had to be amputated. Louie [Ludwig August] Roeder from Co. G was struck close to me by a piece of a bomb; he died instantly. General

Green had his head torn off by a cannon ball.[2] The remaining names are unknown to you. I have very inadequate facilities for writing here, but I do want to try to describe the story as closely as possible. Approximately 10 April we got the report that a battle was being fought at Mansfield [La.], so we began to proceed in forced march. So that the column would be lighter, we left everything that we did not need quite urgently behind in San Augustine [Tex.] and everyone took his baggage on his horse. The same evening we got orders to cook rations for three days and to advance without wagons at 12 o'clock at night. The clothes were loaded back on the wagons. On 11 April ["März"] at daybreak we went over the Sabine. We got to Mansfield a little after midday. There we met the troops that were coming back from the battle, where they had won a glorious victory. They looked askance at us because we had arrived too late, and we ourselves felt very depressed in their company, because it is not the first time that we have arrived too late. On the same day we went on, on the road towards Natchitoches, where the battle was fought. Our troops took 3,000 prisoners, conquered an enormous number of wagons with provisions, and hospital ambulances. I have to break off about that so that I will still have room and time left over for our battle. I just want to say this. It is known that the enemy had five times as many dead as we. The twelfth we caught up with Gould's regiment and a part of Parsons' brigade, which were commandeered by General Green.[3] We were four miles from a place on the Red River that is called Blair's Landing; there the Yankees had landed and were to be attacked that afternoon. The horses were left behind and we set out on foot. First we had to cross over a bayou and then we had to walk three miles through forest. Then we came to a very large field that stretched out toward the ships. Between us and the ships there was a roadway down by the river. We ran behind that for a stretch, then the command was given to jump over the fences and go for the ships, which were still about 500 paces away from us. That is when the first bomb came flying over our heads. It was received with a loud shout of jubilation, and the regiment ran forward as fast as it could up to a place where we were a bit covered. There we rested a couple of minutes. Meanwhile two cannons were set up which fired upon the ships but did not, I think, hit them. Then we went forward again, running along the bank up to directly in front of the ships, and there we let go our fire. It made a din as if one were surrounded by all the street urchins of Antwerp with their wooden rattles.[4] When they saw us coming the Yankees took their soldiers to the other side, where there was brush, and we were lying quite in the open and saw nothing but the ships from which there came a hail of shells of every type. We sustained the firing for two hours, and it is completely inconceivable to me that we did not lose more men. The regiment, in my view, held up extraordinarily. It would not have retreated either, if it had not been ordered to do so. Now we are resting on the road between Pleasant Hill and Natchitoches. An advance by the Yankees is expected. Maybe during the next few days we will have a battle again. It certainly won't be as bad as the one by the boats though. Farewell all for today.

I will write again soon. Rudolf. Address your letters in care of General H. P. Bee, Mansfield, Louisiana.

Contrary to Rudolf's observations, the losses of the Union commander were not large, and only five of the enemy ships failed to escape to safety. Somehow, during the midst of the battle, the gunboat *Neosho* had freed herself, and, as she drifted past the bend in the river, she fired at the Confederates on the bank. The *Lexington, Hindman,* and the *No. 13* also rained grape and canister shots upon the bank for a stretch of two miles, adding to the terrors of the day. Rudolf's description of Gen. Green's death is lacking in the grotesque details that at least one account includes. According to that version Green's horse became frightened when its rider was fatally struck and, in spinning around, caused the shattered brain to be flung out by centrifugal force. Other witnesses contend that Green was under the influence of Louisiana rum at the time, that he was "with a raw Texas regiment (Wood's) [sic] that had never been in a fight before," and that the Confederates picked up by the Union forces that day had whiskey in their canteens, without which fortification they would not have attacked.[5] It was not a glorious victory for either side, whatever the condition of the participants.

On 14 April, Confederate General Richard Taylor made several decisions that had a direct bearing on the course of events that followed. Taylor ordered a majority of his infantry (including a New Braunfels company commanded by Capt. Julius Bose) to Arkansas, where Gen. Kirby Smith had already gone to assist Gen. Sterling Price in stopping the advance of the Union commander Frederick Steele. To give Gen. Bee's cavalry more power to resist Banks, Taylor that day also dispatched toward Natchitoches the division led by General Camille Arnaud Jules Marie, Prince de Polignac.[6] Then, on 20 April, Gen. Taylor himself went to Natchitoches, where he took command of the troops.

Gen. Banks, not knowing of these changes, decided not to move overland toward Shreveport, but instead retreated, a choice which led to the failure of his Red River campaign. Confederate forces in the area, authorities now believe, were insufficient to have prevailed. Soon thereafter Gen. Banks was replaced by Gen. Edward S. Canby, who, as a colonel, had been largely responsible for thwarting Sibley's New Mexico ambitions earlier in the war. Many of the old Sibley brigade men were at this time in Louisiana at the core of the fighting.[7]

Of the other significant reshufflings in the command at about the time of Gen. Banks's failure, the one with an immediate relationship to the history of Woods's regiment has to do with the incident at Monett's Crossing on Old River. During the ten-day period between 12 April and 22 April, many of the men of Woods's regiment were involved in almost daily fights, while at the same time marching down the Red River at night. The period ended with an engagement of larger proportions at a point known as Monett's Crossing or Monett's Ferry. On the morning of 22 April, several units of Confederate soldiers, including Woods's men and many another Texas German from other regiments, were engaged in a battle with Union forces that very much outnumbered them. For whatever reason—some say because he received false information, while others say he simply did not wish to suffer losses such as he had sustained at Pleasant Hill—Gen. Bee ordered a retreat in mid-battle, and the Union men were thus able to ford the crossing where the water was very low at the time. Gen. Taylor, who faulted Bee with poor generalship in having allowed the enemy to get away, was badly discouraged and asked repeatedly to be relieved of command, a request to which Gen. Kirby Smith acceded on 10 June. Bee was removed from command and on 14 May wrote a report of the battle from his new station, Seguin, Texas.[8]

While for many days in late April and early May Taylor's Southern forces were involved in almost continuous fighting, some 3,000 Union troops were detailed to the Pineville-Alexandria area to construct a dam, the water level having sunk to a depth of four feet in some spots. On 13 May, after the fleet had already escaped in the deepened water, Union troops started leaving Alexandria. Despite General Banks's orders, the retreating troops set fire to the city of Alexandria, gutting it completely. Before long, the stretch from Grand Ecore to Cloutierville was ablaze and ravaged.[9] Rudolf Coreth's letter of that period was clearly written out of range of the worst destruction.

Marksville [somewhat blurred], Louisiana
15 May 1864
Rudolf to family

. . . I have been well all along. . . . If Carl, as Father wrote me, did leave on the twenty-fifth, then he might get here during the next few days. I shall be very happy to see him again. The captain and those on leave aren't here yet either. . . . Our position here is still much as it was. The enemy is in Alexandria, and our army is standing around it in a big circle without earnestly attacking them. Every day little battles take place in which, however, neither party usually suffers great losses. A part of the cavalry, to which we also belong, is lying here by the river in order to hinder the Yankees from going up to Alexandria, and up to now we have been successful. The river is not deep enough for big gunboats above our position, and our cannons, of which we have quite a few well-placed ones, shoot the little gunboats and transports, sink them, and burn them up. The week before last our men knocked off three transport ships and a cannon boat that way. Our brigade has been lying here at Marksville for a couple of days. We are protecting a battery of light artillery that must shell the ships that go by. We have less good prospects of success than the troops upstream that destroyed the boats. The boats that come up as far as where we are aren't endangered by our cannons, and there is not a spot where one could set up cannons or gun emplacements for protection, because the bank is so flat. Yesterday our battery shot at two gunboats, a very big one and a little one. The little one got several big holes shot in it; then we quickly retreated back into the forest though, because they began to bombard us. Nobody was injured. The transports

that were burned upstream had come down from Alexandria. A great
many letters from the army were found on them. When we came down,
the road was still heavily sown with them. From everything we hear we
conclude that the Yankees have had much bigger losses than we every
time that we have encountered them. The news that Münzenberger is
not coming surprised me. Farewell to you all now, and just get your
worries about me out of your heads. I will muddle through all right.
Rudolf. Regards to Münzenberger, Kämmerling, and Alfred from me
when you get a chance.

On the morning of 17 May, Debray's forces joined Gen. J. A. Wharton's, which had already been attacking Yankee troops at Moreauville.
The next day Col. W. O. Yager's regiment and the Second Louisiana
attacked a wagontrain of Yankees. On 19 May, Taylor's, Polignac's, and
Major's divisions gave the *coup de grâce* to the Yankee forces in the
same area. Many were dropping from thirst and heat exhaustion in the
steamy sub-tropical atmosphere after repeated clashes between the armies. In horrible conclusion, the thicket caught fire as the Yankees made
their last stand before crossing the Atchafalaya on their retreat eastward.[10]
After Banks's retreat, Col. Louis Bush of the Fourth Louisiana had
received orders from General Taylor to set about the job of clearing the
jayhawkers out of southern Louisiana. During the fall of 1864, a group
of such marauding guerillas led by a slave named Bernard staged raids
that kept the devastated region from enjoying whatever relief it might
have felt because of the Yankee abandonment of the Red River campaign.[11] For much of the remainder of their service in Louisiana, Carl
and Rudolf Coreth were engaged in trying to drive out such molesters.

Washington, Louisiana
29 May 1864
Rudolf to family

Today three men from our company are going on leave. One of them,
"Mr. [Wm.] Hoym," is going to be friendly enough to bring you these
lines himself. . . . We are still lying at Washington and are awaiting
orders, thus have time to rest up quite thoroughly again. The rations
consist of cornbread, bacon or beef, and molasses. Since the blackberries
are ripe, we cook some every day, which makes the bread quite edible.[12]
And the peace along with this makes our life quite pleasant. One could,
to be sure, wish for some other things, but our recent booty has been
plentiful, so one seldom hears complaints. I have been feeling pretty well
all along, but now I feel absolutely outstandingly well. None of our men
on leave has arrived yet. Many of them sent in testimony from their
doctors, which probably won't be recognized as valid though, because
men have arrived who saw the others on leave and in good health. What
is to become of us is not entirely definite. Sometimes they say we are to
go down the Mississippi and rob the area the Yankees are exploiting.

That is quite possible, because the high officers have a chance then to steal Negroes. But it seems just as likely to me that we will go back to Texas. Farewell to all. Rudolf.

New Braunfels
29 May 1864
Rudolf from father [addressed to Alexandria]

Dear Rudolf! Two days ago, to our infinite joy, we got a letter again—a sign of life—from you. It is dated 8 and 10 May. We can see from it not only that you are alive but also that you feel better than in the boring inactivity of the two preceding years, and we are satisfied along with you because *you* are satisfied with yourself, though we see you constantly in apparent danger, to which we others are no less exposed, except that in your case it is more evident. But . . . you want to hear about us and things here. . . . The harvest has begun. . . . This coming week it will begin in earnest. The ladies—Mother above all, it goes without saying— are busy binding. A week ago we had peas to be mowed, hauled, and threshed. They turned out very well; we have 8-9 bushels of nice, clean, and—as a sampling proved—good peas. Mother was foreman again. Franz cleaned them, and, by the way, made a pair of shoes for Josef. Ernst Meusebach is working at our place and is truly good, energetic, and willing. Incidentally, I plowed the pea patch and laid it fallow in order to plant a bit of tobacco and [sweet] potatoes if it should rain, which it has not for a long time, to the detriment of the grass, and which it was about to do just now when a rather strong norther came up and restored the eternally blue sky of Texas. The corn can wait another 8-10 days for rain. The head grains are not progressing properly in their growth at all, but there is no danger in their case. They can wait for the rain. We plan to sow Mexican [pinto] beans too, supplied to us by Mün- zenberger, who, in addition to his job, is carrying on a lively trade in San Antonio. In return for these we have to sell him the resulting crop minus the amount we used as seed and the amount we need for our own house- hold; he expects to pay us $6 per bushel. Also we are buying up corn for him and will deliver part of it to him in San Antonio in the form of meal. We will take along 10-15 bushels of our last year's crop too. Corn is going for $2.00. Peas are said to be $5.00 a bushel. Freight is 30¢ a bushel, so we can make quite a bit of cash profit there. Do you recognize your father in this ridiculous epistle? Yes, dear old fellow, needs must, when the devil drives [*"Noth bricht Eisen"*].[13] When may we be together again! There is just this much more to report of domestic affairs: Agnes and the children are well and with Meusebach in Fredericksburg at his store. Politically the news is good, but unfortunately no sign of peace yet. The elections in the North are still Unionist, and the war is not being ended on the field of battle. In Fredericksburg, it is said, ten men, the murderers of the poor Germans, have been arrested; but those are just rumors, and there is nothing in the newspapers about it yet.[14] As if that were not enough, the newspaper is not appearing at all because young [Eugen?]

Lindheimer [a son of the editor of the *Neu-Braunfelser Zeitung*] is sick. We have a complete cap of fog over our heads, and we will surely be greatly surprised when one day it is taken off and the world around us shall have changed completely. Alfred [Kapp] is content in San Antonio, I hear. Kämmerling is working in the tannery as a master tanner and has to wash old skins and is said not to be especially cheerful. Münzenberger is setting up a Mexican store besides his employment at [Gustav] Schleicher's. Young Appmann is going to be employed in Kampmann's hat factory at La Grange.[15] So you all are the last of the musketeers, because I am assuming that Carl has rejoined you by now. The Rhenhauses' murderers, Alsens and Holz, were arrested by the new sheriff, Wikrett. They were surrounded in the house by ten or twelve deputies who were on the job, and tried to flee in their nightshirts. Alsens surrendered when Bodemann held a pistol on him. Holz got a head start, but was laid out by a shotgun blast to the shoulder. . . . He is lying in the courthouse. Alsens is in the jail. The outlook is said to be gloomy for him. A bad end lies before the mayoral candidate of New Braunfels, who is said to have committed three murders already, and in the last one is said to have revealed to the world a mob-like bestiality.[16] Otherwise no news in town. And now, Adio, dear Rudolf. Though I look forward very much to writing you, in order to be in contact with you by means of the pen at least, I shall be ever so much more pleased when this means of communication between us has ended. All of us embrace you with me in spirit. As ever, your loyal friend and father E. Coreth*

Carl from father [continued]

Dear Carl! Mother, I, and all of us were very glad to have news from you now from Washington [Louisiana?, Texas?]. Hedwig is sweet and dear, still suffering, but better I think. The thing will take time—much time. Farewell and give us news. Your old friend and father E. C.

Camp near Opelousas
20 June 1864
Rudolf to family

. . . I wrote you on the fifteenth but could not send the letter because suddenly we got orders to get ready for a big jayhawkers hunt. We marched away on the sixteenth and only returned home again last evening. That was the second time that we went away for that purpose. The first time we caught thirteen men who, in order to escape conscription, had withdrawn into the forest. The last time we did not get anybody though. We did come upon three real robbers, but they rode horses that were so good we couldn't catch up with them on our skinny and brokendown animals. People of this sort make the roads unsafe. They have already murdered a lot of our men in cold blood. Sometimes they do play quite daring tricks too. Once, while the Yankees were retreating from Alexandria, we had to march ahead a long stretch in the night, in order to attack their column in the flank the next day. A mile in front of us there was another regiment of our brigade on the same road. They sent five men with the canteens from one company into a house that stood close by, in order to fill them with water. The jayhawkers must have noticed that, because they captured the five so fast that neither we nor the regiment they belonged to became aware of it. Later one of the men successfully got back to his regiment, and he told what had become of his comrades. The next day they came and got themselves General Debray's horse during the fighting, and he had to do his best to get away on foot so that they would not take him captive too. Most jayhawkers probably have left with the Yankees. But there are still enough of them here to cause a lot of destruction of private property. We will leave here during the next few days. It is said that we will go to the vicinity of Alexandria, where it is supposed to be easier to provide the fodder for the horses. I would be quite glad of it. First of all, I would get fun out of seeing once more the places where we fought, and then it is also very much to be desired that something be done for the horses, because they are very thin and weak. Pabieco had held up quite well.[17] He was thin and bruised when he arrived. We could not spare the horses when we were after the jayhawkers. We had to swim and chase alternately, and still it was almost always possible for me to be among the first people. . . . I think . . . I will be able to manage until I get back to you sometime, where I hope that Ben will have recovered. Now farewell for today, all. I am, as always, your loyal son and brother Rudolf Coreth.

Camp below Alexandria
27 June 1864
Rudolf to family

. . . The mails must be in terrible disorder, because I wrote you rather regularly every week while we were busy with the Yankees, and so a letter should have arrived. Now you are surely over your uncertainty, because our men on leave must have gotten home long ago. As far as the war is concerned, things seem to be completely quiet now. One hears only very excellent reports of victories, which are supposed to have been fought on 5 and 7 June in Richmond, where the enemy is said to have suffered quite terrible losses.[18] In consequence of these victories and the fall of the value of Northern money, the opinion generally prevailing here is that the war will now rapidly approach its end. We willingly go along with this hope, as you can imagine. But it seems to me too that there are better grounds now than before for this view, because it is surely not to be assumed that the Northern army would serve the way we are doing if once the pay they get should reach the point where it is worth nothing, all the more so if their troops have no fortunate successes. Furthermore, some time ago it was said, and the report seems to be confirmed, that New York, Pennsylvania, and another state (Ohio, I think) have declined to contribute any more men or money to the continuation of the war. This report, though, is too good for me to believe yet. We have been on the march for several days and arrived in a camp about seven miles below Alexandria on the Red River today, where we will remain a long time, according to appearances. Our horses very much need rest, particularly Carl's and mine. They are both nearly ready to give up. The strawberry roan got swollen glands that burst, on top of all that. He is practically well again now, but he is terribly thin. Carl rode H[[enry]]. Pantermühl's horse on the march; Pantermühl hasn't returned yet [from detached service to catch deserters]. . . . I keep thinking that . . . I might be with you by mid-October, maybe even a bit earlier. I very often think of that. . . . Farewell to you all, my dear ones, and just do not worry about us. Everything is not as bad as it looks when seen from a distance. Rudolf Coreth

Osburn's Mill[19]
7 July 1864
Rudolf to family

. . . Carl wrote to Hedwig and so you surely found out about what we are doing. We actually have considerable reason to be proud. We were asked whether we understood how to get a mill to working . . . since there is nobody here who understands a thing about it and the brigade has nothing to live off of if this does not get taken care of. We relied on our usual luck and had the joy of making the mill grind too. The men said that it had never ground as well as it does now. There are two gears. One pair of stones is like ours are; the others are French stones that haven't been sharpened for five years. In chiseling the stone Carl got so many slivers in his left hand that it swelled up quite thick; now it is almost entirely well again. We actually haven't anything more to do here, but we would rather stay a couple of days longer here because we can do what we want here and aren't plagued by camp rules. Our horses don't seem to want to recover properly. . . . You wish, according to what Father writes, to hear exactly of what our diet and clothing consist and how we spend our time. That is going to be a very short story. Our rations consist of 1½ lbs. of cornmeal, a like amount of beef, salt, and sometimes a bit of sugar. The meal is baked into bread by two men detailed to that task for ten days and then is divided amongst us. The meat is divided raw, and each one prepares it according to his taste and means. Most people, ourselves included, roast it on spits; some chop it fine with salt and eat it raw, and some fry it in a pan, if they have fat, which often is not the case though. If we are near a place where blackberries grow, great quantities of them are devoured, but where we are now we have none. When the little ears of corn have reached the right point, they too will probably be added to our menu. We aren't very well provided with clothing anymore either. Many have only the suit of clothes on their backs. I am still so fortunate as to possess two shirts, a pair of trousers, and a pair of underpants, so that I always still have something to put on while my clothes are being washed; so does Carl. We usually have our clothes washed on farms, because we do not draw any soap. We have to pay $1-2 for a piece. We have only very few duties, but there are almost daily inspections. It would look bad if the men were to allow themselves to get depressed; but all are in good spirits, and it seems that each is proud of enduring the times with good morale. Kämmerling and Münzenberger have been struck from the rolls, because their detail was not sent to the regiment. If you all can let them know that so they can plan accordingly, do so. We wanted to write to them but have no paper here. Adio. With many regards to you and Hedwig, I remain your Rudolf.

Camp Stevens
18 July 1864
Rudolf to family

. . . We have been dismissed from the mill again and have been with the company since the night before last. The horses have recovered somewhat in that time, and if they get a couple of weeks' more rest, they will be in good shape again. The troops in the environs have orders to keep ready to march. They say that there is to be a raiding expedition made on the Yankee plantations on the Mississippi. Polignac's infantry left to march down that way a couple of days ago. Today I heard that they came back again, so probably nothing will come of that undertaking. Debray's regiment has already practiced robbing and stealing ahead of time. During the night they came to the residence of the owner of the mill where we were, got him out of bed, and, threatening to shoot them, asked where he had hidden his rum. When he asserted that he had none, some of them forced him to go with them and unlock the sugar house, while the rest searched through the house and took along everything that they might use. They stole six hides of leather and all the clothing they could find. When they were through with the white people, they went to the Negro houses and perpetrated several acts of violence there. There were about fifty men; the regiment is made up of 350. One can imagine what the men would do if they were to get to enemy territory. Therefore I would prefer too if nothing were to come of the attack on the Yankee plantations, because I never like to see robberies, much less take part in them. Our rations are supposed to be supplemented by fresh corn ears today. There are supposed to be six bushels a day delivered per one hundred men. Since it is already a bit too late for roasting ears, I believe that the intention in doing this is to circumvent General Taylor's order that no corn is to be provided anymore for horses in Louisiana. There is still a lot of talk of peace. Some even are quite definite in their expectations that Jefferson Davis will be invited to come to Washington and take up office in the White House. Several of our men on leave came back and said that things are looking more beautiful in Texas than ever before. The men from our company haven't come yet but are expected any day. . . . The rest I hope to be able to tell you orally before too long, because as soon as possible I shall try to get a leave. Adio. Rudolf Coreth.

Osburn's Mill
28 July 1864
Rudolf to family

. . . We are getting along well. We have recently been with the company
or here at the mill alternately and would have stayed with the company
altogether if the mill could have functioned without us, but when we
were away for a couple of days, they kept sending for us all the time.
The few days we were in camp we spent rather pleasantly. Carl may
have found the time a bit less pleasant, because he was company cook
during the time, and cooking is unpleasant work for him. Fortunately it
did not take much of his time; he always was through with his work by
eight or half past eight and then had the rest of the day completely to
himself. In the vicinity of the camp there was a blacksmith's shop in
which Carl spent much of his time and made all sorts of little things,
like fish hooks and knives. I spent my time for the most part looking for
bee trees, of which there are a great many here, and was lucky enough
to find two too. One of them I helped chop. We got about two water
buckets full of pressed honey from it. I couldn't help with cutting the
second tree because we had to go back to the mill. It did not have quite
as much honey as the first, but was worth the effort anyway. In the
evenings Carl and I went strolling along the river and smoked the cigar
that Mother sent along with Carl and chatted about the past when there
was still peace and of the future, which we hope will soon bring peace.
Then, when we were last in camp, prisoners came back from New Orleans. Among them was [August] Maske from our company—we didn't
know what had become of him at all—and old Mr. Roeder, who was
taken prisoner eight months ago on Mustang Island. He came to our
camp to visit his relatives.[20] He talked lots about the time that he spent
in New Orleans, from which it is evident that our prisoners are treated
badly by the Yankees. On the other hand, the ladies are supposed to
have done all they could to make life as easy for them as possible. Mr.
Roeder says that he has no doubt at all that the war will be over next
May. He asked us to send his regards. He has become much thinner than
he was a year ago, but his spirits, if anything, seem to be more excitable
than they were then. He speaks of battle almost with longing. I think
though that once he has been home a couple of weeks, he will think it
over before he leaves again. There is lots of talk about going back to
Texas. Whether there are prospects of doing that, it is not possible to
say, because nobody actually knows just what we have been kept here
for up to now. Our brigade commissary said here at the mill that within
a week we would either be on the march to Texas or to the Mississippi.
The latter is not at all likely, because a third of our men are sick, and
the horses are in very bad shape. . . . I have given up the hope of going
on leave soon for now; at least I probably cannot get away as long as we
are here in Louisiana. So many men are getting sick that I consider it
better that Carl and I stay together. It is the usual malaria, to be sure,
that the men have, but it is better just the same if two are together so

that one can help the other. . . . I think Ben [one of family's horses] will turn up and be fat again by the time I get home; then I want to take him down here. The grey is too weak for me in any case, because with my pack I weigh over 200 pounds. Now farewell all. In hope of soon getting good news from you, I remain your Rudolf Coreth.

Camp Stevens
5 August 1864
Rudolf to family

. . . I got malaria several days ago. Carl and I are with the company again now. Milling has been given up, and they said that we would be leaving this area in a very short time. Till now we haven't got marching orders yet. But they are expected daily. Lt. [Edgar] Schramm was at Debray's headquarters a couple of days ago. There Sherwood told him that it is almost definite that we will be going back to Texas, and that in the course of a few weeks; however, there was also a possibility that we might have to go to the Black River, which would very much postpone our return to Texas. Let's hope that won't happen, because though Louisiana is not as terrible a state as people tried to make us believe before we had been here, Texas is more beautiful, after all. I thank Mother kindly for the friendly favor she offered by wanting to send us her mosquito bar. If only she does not need it herself. If you have mosquitoes yourselves, I hope that Carl's letter will arrive in time. When the regiment camps in a forest and has burned a fire for a couple of hours, the mosquitoes leave and one can sleep quite well. I thank Agnes for her paper. If we don't have bad luck with it, we'll have a supply for a long time.[21] My fever seems not to amount to much this time. . . . I have tried to get rid of it with cooking salt up to now, the way the *Houston Telegraph* indicated, but it was not a success. Since it is unpleasant for me to be out of commission, I have now made up my mind to take medicine. Our hospital pharmacy does not have quinine. The pharmacist told me they give iron sulphate and camphor now. . . . He said that doesn't have such a violent effect as quinine but cures the fever pretty well. . . . The prospect of going back to Texas pleases us very much; besides, we are in quite a good humor even without that. Most people seem to be convinced that it is better to adjust to the inevitable with good humor than to complain, and if sometimes a sick man does actually lose courage, we take pains, and usually with good results, to liven him up again. With many regards to you and Hedwig, I remain as ever your Rudolf.

Camp Stevens
11 August 1864
Rudolf to family

. . . The fever has left me again, at least it has stayed away for two fever days.[22] Before I went to the hospital Carl and I made yet another attempt at the water cure [Kapp's?, Kneipp's?]. Carl rubbed my back with water until it was quite chafed, but it did not help. The fever came back,

perhaps more than ever. In the hospital I got quinine. It took away the
fever the very first time. . . . We still haven't received marching orders.
The major [Hutchison] wanted to transfer the camp to the fir [pine]
forest, but nothing is to come of that. . . . In case my horse has turned
up again and there is a good chance to send it here, . . . do so. I think
that I will have enough means here to pay any expenses the man bringing
it might have from corn. . . . We get hardly any political reports. . . .
Here and there along the Mississippi little outpost skirmishes take place,
in which nothing is either won or lost though. We were somewhat disquieted some days ago by the rumor that Hardeman's brigade had been
beaten by the Yankees and had lost two hundred men.[23] It turned out
though that this report was completely fabricated. Farewell for today.
With the hope of getting good news from you soon, I remain your Rudolf
Coreth.

New Braunfels
29 August 1864 [?, second digit of day badly blotted]
Carl and Rudolf from father

My dear sons! A week ago we got four letters at once from you, two from
Carl and two from Rudolf. The last news included up to 1 August; up
to then, consequently, you were in good health and spirits. We hope that
the last twenty eight days may have found you so also. Today Mother
and the rest of us figure that young [Daniel] Wolfshol will arrive where
you are, and you are dressing up in new trousers and are luxuriating in
smoking ["*schmauchet*" in the original; even then archaic] a little pipe
of tobacco while fishing. Here we are doing all right, generally speaking,
though indeed Anna has the eye sickness, but not very badly. Yesterday
at noon the threshing machine came. We threshed twenty-four bushels
of rye by evening, which is about half the entire rye crop; Monday and
Tuesday we probably will be busy with the rest of the rye and with the
wheat. Franz loads up the threshing machine; Triesch and Krueger
[neighbors] are helping, since Franz helped them earlier. . . . As for news
in the county, there is little. Old Mrs. Schimmelpfennig died. I hear that
she said toward the end that she was not fearful of the black night. I
find these words much wiser than those of a certain Goethe: "*Noch Mehr
Licht!*" I think everyone can get all the light here that he needs, and
needs no more.[24] In San Antonio Captain Gordon shot to death a certain
Captain Steel.[25] In Fredericksburg an Old Bushwhacker was shot dead.
A truly slender yield of news for a week. Meusebach is here. He is doing
quite well. His business, according to a certain barometer [his own?],
seems to be thriving brilliantly. Among the prisoners taken by us on the
Rio Grande, all are renegades: Prose, Bringmann, a son of the Foerster
who used to live next to Schramm, Uker. They were taken to Houston.[26]
[Harry?] Tolle is still sitting in jail. His sentence is said to be fourteen
days of arrest and then returning to the company. The confirmation or
reprieve is expected from Houston; the latter is hoped for. About our ox
we know nothing yet. I can console myself about Ben, but I would like

to have Charley back. Adio for today. Your old friend and father. Mother, your brothers and sisters, and I embrace you most sincerely.

no place [plantation twelve miles from Alexandria]
1 September 1864
Rudolf to family

It has been a long time since I last wrote you. I did not like postponing it so long, but wasn't really well able to do anything else. First, about fifteen days ago we went on a jayhawker expedition that lasted ten days, during which we had no opportunity to send letters, and then during that time Carl got sick and so I didn't want to write again until I could simultaneously report of his improvement, which I can now do with certainty. Carl is almost well again now. . . . Only he still feels very listless, and his head is buzzing, which is the consequence of quinine.[27] First he got malaria, which developed into a high fever, because he could not pamper himself but rather had to stay in the sun just like the healthy men. There was no thought of staying behind, because the area in which we were is made so unsafe by jayhawkers that it would be insane to stay there alone for a couple of weeks, since we know of cases where people in the same position were murdered in cold blood. On the evening of the ninth day of our expedition we got to an abandoned plantation twelve miles from Alexandria where all the sick of the regiment stayed behind the next day, and where we still are now too. When we arrived, Carl (he had ridden on a transport wagon during the march) had a high fever which never entirely left him until the night before last. Actually he did not quiet down until yesterday. Until then he still broke out in a sweat every few moments, and he was still in such a stupor that I did not trust myself to write that he was actually recovering. There was no other remedy left for getting rid of the fever except quinine. We had to choose between feeding him quinine or seeing him die, because all the other remedies that we used during the first two days of our being here (during which there was no medicine here yet) had remained unsuccessful, and four men had died of the same condition. C[hristian]. Pantermühl, who is with another one of the sick men, rode to town and bought quinine, which we gave him with good results. To be sure, it did not completely get rid of the fever until several days had passed, but one could notice an improvement right away. By today he was already asking for something to eat a couple of times, and the cleansing of his tongue and the awakening of his memory of things that have tasted good to him give me the firm belief that his appetite will soon return completely. Up until now, whenever he wanted to eat something, I have given him thin, harmless things. I took little ears of corn, which had not yet grown completely hard, and cut the kernels in slices off the cobs and cooked them with water, which results in a gruel that is just as good as barley porridge. Then too we had a bit of white flour bread that C. Pantermühl brought from town too, which he sometimes ate softened with water as a soup; and sometimes I cook him tomatoes. Up to now he has not eaten any meat or drunk any milk; I expect to be able to provide those things here as soon as he gets a craving for them. A two-quart canteen of milk or a pound of butter we can get for 25¢ in silver. We still have a little bit of money, and when that has been spent we can borrow some, and we will soon have meat delivered to us, and if that should not be the case, then there are domesticated doves and young pigs enough here, which I would slaughter with a clear conscience under the circumstances. I mean to stay here until Carl feels strong again, which may be another week. Wednesday evening H[ermann]. Conring came and brought us the lovely things that you sent us by Wolfshol. Carl had gotten a bit of rest, which made it possible for him to be pleased about them too. The things have been as nicely selected as though you had known what we need. Our trousers had met their end on the expedition, so that we both had to go about in underpants. We had been out of tobacco for three or four days. We hadn't had any handkerchiefs in a long time, and no soap either. But you thought of absolutely everything that we needed. Now we can keep clean, dress decently, and smoke tobacco. What more can a man want, except to be at home, and one simply has to put that out of his mind now. I thank you all from the bottom of my heart for your thoughtfulness. You cannot know how much good it does a person to get such tangible proof once again that one has people in the world who are more concerned with his welfare than are those he is with all the time. Farewell for today. . . . With many regards and thanks to you all and Hedwig, I am as ever Rudolf. . . . The people who come from leave say that it is more beautiful in Texas now than it has been in years. . . .

McNutt's Hill ["Magnotts Hill"]
3 September 1864
Rudolf to family

. . . Carl is making quite good progress in his recovery. . . . In the hospital where he lay we could not stay as long as we had actually intended. We were given the order yesterday to go back to the regiment because the camp is at a more wholesome place than ours. Carl would have been able to go in a wagon if he had wanted to, but he felt so strong today that he preferred to ride on horseback. It is only three miles away and the ride helped him rather than hurt him. At least his appetite seems to have increased. When we got to camp the regiment was prepared to march away. It had gotten orders this morning to march to the Black River. What it is to do there we do not know. It doesn't seem to be anything important though, because it is to go to Alexandria in a two-day march, which is only fifteen miles from here. I stayed here too and will not leave until Carl can follow, if I am able to do that, which I firmly believe. We are going tomorrow to a convalescent hospital which is some miles from here and where the men are said to be quite well taken care of. Our physical condition in general is very bad now. We have a great many sick with fever, but only a few are dangerously sick, and they are only sick when they have neglected themselves and suffered a relapse. The fault lies with the great heat and humidity. . . . I heard from our officers, today that all men who are detailed in San Antonio are coming back to the regiment. If my horse has turned up again, I would be happy to get it again. . . . I simply cannot really get along with my grey. We are always at odds with each other, every time we have to do something together. Our horses are both thin but are well again now. According to what Father writes, you wish to have a detailed description of our life so that you can form a picture of it. Our clothes are very simple. We still have two shirts each, two pairs of underpants, and the trousers you sent; also rather tolerable shoes. Carl has made himself a straw hat, and I still have the felt hat I drew in Houston, which is still good too. Carl still has a good jacket; mine is a bit torn but it will still make it quite well till winter. Carl has an additional pair of torn trousers, which we want to patch so that we do not always have to wear the new ones right away. The rations now consist of cornmeal, beef, salt, and sometimes a bit of sugar and bacon. The meat is quite good. The steers come from Texas and are still quite fat when they arrive. Part of the time we spend cooking. We toast cornmeal and cook coffee from it. We roast the meat now in fat in the pan. Sometimes we cook ourselves a soup of it and cornmeal. The bread is still being baked for the company together. We spend our time mainly doing nothing; but rather often one does have to stand watch, every 6-7 days. One has hardly anything to do there, but is just supposed to stay in camp. We have almost nothing to do with the horses, because we don't get any corn for them. One just checks a couple of times a day to see whether they are still there. We usually wash our laundry a couple of times in cold water and then hand the things over at a farm to have them washed, because we aren't supplied with soap and seldom have a chance to buy any. Most of the day one lies quietly in the coolest place one can find and is surprised in the evening that another day has passed. When it gets cooler I will fish sometimes with the hooks you sent. Now it is still so hot that I do not think the fish are wholesome. Now farewell for today. I will write as often as I find a chance. Rudolf Coreth.

Carl to family [continued]

All my dear ones! Rudolf has written you . . . so all there is left for me to do is to thank you for the good and useful things that reached us through Wolfshol. It is superfluous to mention each and every thing. It all shows so much parental, brotherly and sisterly concern for your dear boys who are at war, that it did me good to the bottom of my heart. Let us hope that the time will come when we are all reunited and the pleasant feeling of closeness to one another will never again be driven out. Soon, I think, I will find time to write in detail. Till then, cherish your old Carl.

They were all to be together again sooner than they imagined. The next several letters that Ernst Coreth wrote his sons in Louisiana reached their destination, but the ones to whom they were addressed were apparently already on their way home for a reunion with their loved ones.

The Slough of Despond

New Braunfels
Sunday, 4 September 1864
Carl and Rudolf from father

Dear Carl and Rudolf! Last week we had news from you; the last date was 11 August. . . . Here we are pretty well, except that the eye sickness has descended again. . . . Hedwig is convalescing now and stays in a dark room; beyond that her health is tolerable. Last week, Monday and Tuesday, we threshed. The result was 64 [bushels] wheat, 44 rye, 3 barley. We are satisfied with the success; the work went well and smoothly too. Wednesday I went to town to assess the ad valorem war tax. Ours amounts to $500 in paper and $12.50 in silver. The paper amounts to $33 in silver, with the value presently at 15 to 1; the entire tax is thus $45 in silver. Now we still have to pay the income tax, the tithe, the state tax, county tax, corporations tax, and the school-house tax. Where we are going to get that the gods know, I suppose; for my part, I haven't the least idea. The rest of the news from the farm: Bella had a calf that died the third day though. That is the fourth calf she has had and that has gone the same way. She herself is as fat as a pig ready for slaughter. We are cutting cornstalks for fodder by the pecan trees. There is enormously much fodder. Mother and Franz built a shed [*"Triste"*] out of the straw in the barnyard that is as high as the old house. It is very nice, but the work was really very strenuous. Preston on Merriweather's farm died of a cerebral hemorrhage. Scherff bought Conrads's Store for $1,500. Simon Tischler bought the store where Wheeler [?] is. Spiess is also going to run a store. He is in Matamoros in order to buy wares.[1] Whether or not the Yankees have completely left the state nobody here is certain yet. It seems they have left Brownsville, but that they are still on the coast. Emil Dittmar and Gustav Müller, saddlers in San Antonio, deserted to Mexico; Müller is said to have been caught again and brought to San Antonio.[2] From the battle front we have no bad reports; everyone is placing his hopes in the convention, which is supposed to give birth to a peace candidate for president. Wolfgang Kapp has been released from all military service and has been made foreman of an iron works. Franz and Ernst [Meusebach] are breaking horses; they have already ridden Franz's 1½-year-old Seppel; then Mary, the foal of the sainted Stray; Coal, the daughter of Morette; and Katinka, the yellow daughter of Latty [Lottie?]. Up to now everything has gone quite smoothly and happily. I think the result will be a great relief. Meusebach left the day before yesterday, but he is coming back soon. He is doing well. Münzenberger is here on business in New Braunfels. He is waiting to hear from the

Medical Board what his assignment will be. So now you have a substantial serving of news again; I hope it will agree with you. It is not entirely lacking in spicy ingredients that can stimulate the nerves. Farewell, my dear children. Mother, your brothers and sisters, and I embrace you heartily. Your old friend and father E. Coreth*

New Braunfels
Sunday, 11 September 1864
Carl and Rudolf from father

My dear sons! Today is the feast of St. Mary on the calendar and the nameday of Marie [their sister]. We are well. . . . A part of your group was to have marched to Georgia, but the order was revoked, which made us very glad, because to know that you are even farther away would have been a hard blow for us. This week is short of events. Nothing to report occurs to me. We had a bit of rain, of which Mother made use by planting a bed of turnips, which give promise of being very good. We hauled in a wagonload of corn fodder that half filled the barn, and pressed the rest of the imphee, which in terms of quantity produced very little (2½ gallons) but has a very significant advantage over the other sorghum in terms of quality. Mother cooked soap. Also the boys plundered a hornet's nest and brought a drinking glass full of honey that tastes much better than bee's honey. That is just about all that comes to mind. Ben [the horse that had been missing] came to the fence one night like a ghost. Somebody must have hitched him up and beaten him half to death. His comrade Charley has not come back yet. Amalia, Franz, and Josef rode to Bear Creek today to fetch wild plums [*"Taubenkirschen"*]. Even if they don't find any, they will have had very beautiful weather for a joy ride anyway. We conscientiously keep counting the days from one Friday to the next in the hope of finding good war news in the paper. Up to now, though, we have not had luck finding anything more than reports of skirmishes [*"Scharmützeln"*]. But we like to think that there is hope that it cannot take forever before we can clasp you to our hearts again. Only it is not clear how we can do the least little thing in relation to a horse for Rudolf. . . . I wonder whether you receive our letters! I write regularly to the address that Carl gave us last. . . . Maybe we should put some other name instead of Captain Cloute.[3] For today farewell; that is my fervent wish and that of your mother and brothers and sisters. I remain as ever your loyal friend and father E. Coreth*

New Braunfels
17 September 1864
Carl and Rudolf from father

My dear lads, yesterday evening we had the very great joy of receiving your two letters of 1 and 3 September from the camp fifteen miles from Alexandria, where you had gone to the convalescent hospital. Fortunately the first of the letters to reach my hands was the one telling of Carl's recovery, so that we could read with calm the report of his illness;

every word gives us joy. The satisfaction with which you received our poor little gifts and the way you express your joy in them, your sensible way of enduring your difficulties and the sacrifices which Fate in its unfathomable but inevitable judgement causes you to have to bear; and only this hurts me: that we are so far from you that we cannot often do little things that would make it easier for you. We are well and embrace you both most fervently. Hedwig departed for Sisterdale the day before yesterday with Meusebach. She will give Carl news of herself as soon as possible. She has now recovered completely; she had overcome the eye sickness completely, and she looks better than ever before, according to all. Her mood too was good and at times quite cheerful. In four weeks she expects to come down to our place again, if there is an opportunity. . . . We have sold quite a bit of wood and delivered it. The carpenter [Wilhelm] Clemens chopped it; we loaded and hauled it. Our part will amount to $25. Those are, to be sure, only drops of water on a hot stone [a standard German expression], but nevertheless we will pay our taxes in this manner and be able to cover our nakedness, and the harvest has provided for our stomachs. Unfortunately I cannot give any favorable report to Rudolf about his horse. We don't know anything about it. Münzenberger probably did write to inquire but got no answer, and Franz is too essential for us to spare him for a ride into the unknown that would last at least a week [to the Gonzales area]. I hope, dear Rudolf, that you will not resent that and hold it against us. What you heard about the calling up of the details will, I think, not come to pass; not on their own account but rather on account of those who are earning from their manpower [employers exploiting soldiers working for them on detached service]. From town I hear that there will be an addition to Torrey's mill, on the side toward town, to house the machines that are on their way here from Europe. On 1 October Hermann Runge is leaving for Europe. Landa is in Matamoros and is said to intend buying such machines too, and Mather is going to Houston this week to get machines for the paper mill.[4] You see how things are progressing in New Braunfels. Old [George Friedrich] Tolle had his [mill]stone made much smaller and has put a belt on his works, which allows his wheel to revolve eight instead of two times. Harry [Tolle] is still in [military] prison. There is great hope that MacClellan will be elected, which would mean, to be sure, only an approach to peace and not peace itself. But "The first step is the hardest" is an old proverb; and I am full of hope.

(From the following letters it would appear that Carl must have been at home on leave for much of October and that Rudolf's month-long leave overlapped his.)

La Grange [Texas]
9 November 1864
Rudolf from Herman Kämmerling [addressed to New Braunfels]

Dear Rudolf! I just now got up, after having already had the fever for the second time while underway. Schramm can ride on now, in God's

name. I am staying here and will await you, if you mean to come this
way at all. If this should not be the case, then be so kind as to let me
know. Tell your Papa that I sweated just as marvelously this time as the
first. Since the post office is being locked up right away, I shall close with
the request that you commend me most heartily to your folks. To you
yourself, greetings from H. Kämmerling.

New Braunfels
13 November 1864
Carl from father
[addressed to Comp. F., 32nd Tex. Cavall., Dubray's
Brigade, Bagby's Division, Louisiana; Care of Capt.
Cloute; Houston, Texas]

Today for the first time since you parted from us, I am taking up my
pen in order to write to you even though I have thought of you innu-
merable times, but I have had so much to do in the meantime I hardly
found time to live; partly I knew Hedwig was writing to you. The last
news we have from you is from La Grange; I presume and hope the
reason we have not heard since then is that you went a way that does
not coincide with the postal route. I want briefly to share with you what
has happened in the interim, my dear son, since we were parted. First
the most important. Your Hedwig was overcome by *Herbstrulei*, presumably as a result of *Verkässlung*.[5] She is almost restored now; her
illness caused me a lot of worry, because the main remedy for it, considering her pregnant condition, could not be used. So that which could not
be achieved by the straight road had to be attained by the detours,
which, as the word makes clear, takes longer. Now the trouble is almost
gone, which also must be brought about only slowly in this illness, since
sudden cessation is also dangerous. At the same time Mary [Marie] also
had it. Hers lasted much longer, since the attack was not so severe, and
the mother-to-be got the principal care at first. Now she too is well again.
Agnes's little Johanne got *Früchen* from which she died after three days.
Rudolf, Franz, and I buried her by her [twin] sister. Dr. Koester was
called right away at the beginning of her illness. It lasted three days and
nights. Meusebach had already left and won't know about it until he
gets to Fredericksburg. Agnes, though depressed, controlled herself sen-
sibly. Rudolf, on returning from Sisterdale, got a rash; this too was taken
care of successfully. But he still has the itching on his body, especially
toward evening, as you had it. Now it seems to be subsiding. Praise God,
I am through with the invalid report. This period has taxed me very
much. I do not think other people realize that and think that one simply
gives medicine for an illness, as a cobbler puts a patch on a hole in a
shoe, but that is very largely not true at all, and the choice from among
many remedies, and the inadequacy of our domestic arrangements and
means, the inability of the patients to make sense of their condition,
augmented by pain and impatience make my office as house physician
truly no sinecure ["sine cure"]. Add to this the thousand little domestic

matters that keep in a constant state of unrest my old body and spirit that long for rest, and I am at this moment not in a rosy mood.—When will the day come at last that will take these burdens from my lame shoulders and bring back my good sons to be a support to me. They are as necessary to my burned-out heart for my existence as oil is to a lamp if it is to continue burning—Rudolf has acquired a very good horse. I hope he will get it to the regiment in as good condition as *it* may get *him* there. He behaved very lovingly and attentively toward Mother and me during the time he was here, worked as much as possible, among other things built a really beautiful oven that since yesterday is providing us with good bread. Tomorrow he will leave with the clothing detail. We worked quite a bit, e.g. plowed a couple of acres. We had begun before the rain. Then there came an interruption because of the wet weather, and now we have been continuing for a week. The coming week we want to sow on top of the weeds and plow under and then only at the end sow on the ground that is already plowed, so we will see which method is more advantageous. Little that is new has happened in the area. The mill farmer Haas was killed by a horse while hauling. The horse came home with the empty wagon; he was found dead. In Kendall County on the Webb's [?] Creek several Indians stole horses. Otherwise, as far as we know, nobody was hanged or shot to death. Last week the district court had its session. There were three divorces: [Hermann] Zum Berge and two that we are not acquainted with. On 8 November our fate was decided in the North. We saw in a Northern newspaper that the military will vote too without going home to do it. How things will go in that matter one can imagine beforehand, but what is to be, will be anyway, an immutable law in which we only know the original threads of the warp, the weaving of which takes from us the overview; but we know that nothing has been added and nothing taken away, so that no change in the law is possible. In the same newspaper we read that, according to the reckoning of a Philadelphia newspaper, up to 1,600,000 Negroes have been taken from the South. I think I have told you everything now that I know, or at least occurs to me. (Hermann Runge is in Matamoros.) Speculations into the future are not possible for me to make concerning the departure, but there is foundation upon which to build them.[6] I would give a lot to chat with you, if we could look one another in the eye while smoking a little pipe, but talking to one another on paper seems to me almost like—onanism. *15 November.* Today Rudolf leaves and I close my writing to you with the hope that he will soon come to you and find you well. He is leaving us in about the condition I described at the beginning of the letter. I would, to be sure, like to tell you lots more, not because there is so much but just to talk a long time to you and be united in thought, but my head is empty of thoughts, so I say to you farewell, my dear—Carl. Your old friend and father E. Coreth.

New Braunfels
20 November 1864
Carl from father

Dear Carl! Since I wrote you a week ago in a letter that Rudolf took along for you, nothing significant and new has happened actually, but, just the same, there is this and that which might interest you. First, Hedwig's condition has changed for the better, but then she is going to write you herself, after all. Rudolf left Tuesday, praise God, with a good horse and in other respects well equipped too. I fear he had a norther and rain on his way to La Grange; Kämmerling reported to him from there that he was sick with fever and would wait for him there. In La Grange Harry Tolle also is said to be sick. Furthermore, in the course of the week there arrived in the local area, in addition to your letter from San Augustine, another one from [Adolph?] Triesch and also from [Daniel] Wolfshol [both of Co. F]. The former reports that the company is sixty miles from Alexandria on the Mississippi and was driving oxen through there, in which endeavor the Yankees were bothering them [between Simmesport and Morganza]. We have determined that you cannot yet be with the party and are quite delighted about that; one does not have to have a portion of everything. I presume that Rudolf will go by way of Houston and so forth, if the same reports have reached La Grange, which would probably be better for his horse and which would bring you together sooner than would be the case if he were to take the same route that you took. You seem to be satisfied with your new horse, and we hope that you had good fortune when buying it. Here little has changed; we have taken wheat and rye to the mill; it was nicely milled, but when we weighed it, a fifth of the weight was missing. But praise God, the fort has provisions for a few months, since we slaughtered a castrated boar [?; "Hokdurlerich"] yesterday that we hefted and guess may have weighed 450 lbs. Franz did his job quite well under Mother's supervision. We have plowed, but quite a bit remains to be sowed. We are planning to do that this coming week. What some people have sowed for the winter is coming up already. In town the reserve has had to keep watch for some days again, in order to stop all people. I think they had little success. Camels, the offspring of the same ones that were brought to Texas, were in town to fetch corn. They were carrying packs for the first time, each with 200 lbs. They are dromedaries and still quite small.[7] For the saltpeter operation at Vile's [Weil's?, Wille's?] farm more than 100 Negroes came through town; they are, according to reports, a miserable lot. Thank God that is fifteen miles away from us. We know nothing new about the war. Mother is active as always and always well, like your brothers and sisters. I too am feeling better than I have in some time, but I always wear out very fast. We have lost three calves already from lesions of the screw worm [?, "Rückenblut"]. The wounds are very worrisome. We will probably lose a lot of cattle. Our cows look like skeletons; and since we have the oxen, the horses, and the calves in the inner fence, we have to keep watch over the fodder piles by day, and pen up the cattle by night, because it is extremely stormy. Now Adieux, dear Carl, for today. Maybe in a week we will know how the election turned out and will get an insight into our future Fate. Mother, brothers, sisters, and I embrace you in spirit. Your loyal friend and father, E. Coreth*

New Braunfels
27 November 1864
Carl and Rudolf from father

Dear Carl and Rudolf! Maybe you will already be together when you receive this letter (at least if we are not running round in the world completely without sense) and are well and possibly in good spirits. First of all, we are less of the latter; the reports that we have received recently are not very cheering, at least to judge from appearances. Lincoln is said to have been elected by a big majority; and even if, as is generally held to be the case, there were monstrous election frauds, this does show that it was possible to carry them out without the populace having defended itself against such, because they have been overcome by weakness. To be sure, some people here, who claim to have a knothole to look through even if there is none, say that this is the truth and the best we can hope for, but it is not all that clear and obvious. Here the recruiting is being conducted with renewed strength; whoever is not completely dead is sent to Houston, examined, and stuck into the drill camp three miles from there. In yesterday's *Zeitung* [*"Braunfelserin"*] there was a report from the *Galveston News,* according to which a strong fleet had been seen at Sabine Pass with transport ships. Just think how peculiar everyone is becoming: I was almost glad, because I thought it would bring you all closer to us. How poor one must be in terms of joy to have joys like that. Yesterday Franz was in town at the enrolling officer's to be weighed and measured [?; *"topographisch aufgenommen"*]. He was the only one of several boys who had grown a year older during the last year. All the rest remained seventeen years of age, but I was completely in accord with him. I hate falsehood, and I am glad that he too considers it unworthy of us. But what will be the result does not look very lovely as seen through the fog that envelops the future. We had a letter from Rudolf from La Grange this week and are glad that he could continue the trip with Kämmerling as had been their hope. We hear that the clothing commando is still here and will probably still be here for a while, until it is warm again. Nobody wants to give them wagons. We were busy all week plowing and sowing, but we have only taken care of two acres just the same. One must walk slowly in order to be able to hold out. The oxen are weak, since there is absolutely no fodder anymore except that which one gives them, and one must give that sparingly, because there is still a week of November ahead of us, and I too must save my strength. My feet don't seem to want to act right anymore. I should have taken pains to write you a more cheerful letter, but to do that is simply impossible without lying. Mother and your brothers and sisters are well. The old dear works from early until night with unshakable endurance. The new oven is behaving very well; and without the improvement that

Agnes Coreth, née Erier, taken in Texas

Rudolf's letter dated 9 Dec. 1864

Carl undertook with the plow, the planting for the coming year would probably have become an impossibility. Following several quite cold days with four degrees of cold (as I am told) [28 degrees Fahrenheit?] we are having very mild weather again, only today a bothersome south wind is blowing. Well, now it seems to me I have exhausted what happened during the past week, and we are approaching a new week in which we expect to hear news, since we have heard nothing new from the scene of battle for a long time. For the moment I shall hope I can write you in a better frame of mind. As ever your loyal friend and father. Mother and your sisters and brothers embrace you.

Evergreen [Louisiana]
3 December 1864
Rudolf to family

Last evening we rejoined the regiment here. Carl is well, and all the conditions are better than they were when we left. The health conditions, even if they cannot yet be termed good, are significantly better than earlier, anyway. The horses are in moderately good condition and get twenty ears of corn delivered to them daily. It is very muddy here, but we live in houses, and so that does not matter much to us. Carl, Kämmerling, [August] Schimmel[pfennig], and I have a room to ourselves that is sufficiently big for us and our things. Carl and I were awake a very long time last night and talked a lot about you. We thought that you too would be awake and would be passing the time with a hand of mockin [a card game], which seemed the most probable, if you are all well as we hope. I send Father best wishes for his birthday. I would have been very glad if I could have celebrated it with you, but that just could not be. If I had stayed at your place any longer I might have gotten into difficulties. I had already been reported absent without leave for four days. Had I stayed away just one day longer, at least according to the orders, I would have had to be sent to Division Headquarters to justify myself. But as it was, everything came out all right. The men were glad that we came. Our trip was quite a good one. In Texas we did not sleep outdoors a single night, partly because the weather did not please us for camping, and then we both got the rash quite severely after we left La Grange, and so we did not consider it advisable to expose ourselves to the weather. We always had enough fodder for the horses, and they behaved to our satisfaction too. The rash got better rather than worse after it had reached a certain point. Lots of people here in camp have it; they say it goes away all by itself after a while. It is not supposed to be genuine scabies [*"Krätze"*]; they call it camp itch ["camp eetsch"]. Here there is talk that this part of Louisiana up to Alexandria is to be given up because it has been eaten out, and neither people nor horses can sustain themselves here anymore. Tomorrow we will try to see what can be done about a leave for Carl.

4 December [continued]

Carl and Kämmerling have ridden to buy fodder for the horses. One gets a dozen bundles for $2.50 new issue. Schramm and I were at Major Hutchison's just now to see about leave. The major has no time today. He said I was to come tomorrow, and then he would see what is to be done. Carl wrote you what happened in my absence. When I unpacked my things here, I discovered I had brought along Franz's instead of my blue pair of pants. It already occurred to me earlier that I had forgotten those for Schimmel. Adio. In the hope that you are all well again, I remain your Rudolf. Kämmerling sends regards. The mess is doing quite well. Only H[enry]. Pantermühl and Schimmel still have malaria.

Camp at Evergreen
9 December 1864
Rudolf to family

Tomorrow C. Storck is going on leave, and so we do not want to let the opportunity to send you news of us go unutilized. Unfortunately we did not learn of it until late, so that we haven't much time left, because the regiment is going on the march tomorrow morning. We are getting along pretty well. The rash seems to be getting better, but slowly. The horses have done very well till now. We drew considerable corn and bought

fodder for $2.50 a dozen bundles. We are going toward Alexandria to-
morrow. How it will be there with respect to fodder for the horses I do
not know, but surely not better I think. The way they tell it, the part of
Louisiana in which we are now is to be abandoned up to Alexandria. All
people who have Negroes have either left the state already and are in
Texas or they are preparing in great haste for the departure. Yesterday
a report arrived that would be very nice, if only it were confirmed. Five
western states are said to have seceded from the Union. General Bagby
is said to have had shots of joy fired.[8] We are having very unfriendly
weather. It is cold and it rained hard last night. Tomorrow we will probably camp in an empty plantation again, because there are lots of them
now. Unfortunately one is not entirely safe from bed bugs, but it is better
than lying in the open anyway. It is getting so dark that I must break
off here. Farewell for today. Cordial regards from your Rudolf. Kämmerling sends greetings.

Carl to family [continued on the back]

Dear parents: Please send news as soon as possible. Happy holidays.
Your Carl.

San Augustine
23 December 1864
Rudolf to family

Since I left you we have had no news from you except a letter from
Hedwig to Carl on 18 November. . . . Carl is well and I am well except
that my skin does not want to heal yet. It is significantly better though;
I can sleep peacefully again. The main news that I have to share with
you today is that we had a lieutenant's election and that I failed. The
business came up quite surprisingly. We had to elect two officers in place
of the two Schulzes. [William] Hoym and I were urged by many to run,
and there was nobody who wanted to run against us. Then Lt. Bitter
and his clique put up an American who has been in our company several
weeks and made him my opponent. They kept after the men, and at the
casting of votes he beat me by one vote. Almost all those who had asked
me to run voted against me. Some had very definite reasons for doing
so. One claimed he didn't want to vote for me because I had volunteered
too often when there was something to be done in the company. Another
claims that he once heard me say something at Seele's [recreation hall]
about "common people" ["*Pöbel*"]. He must have made that up out of
whole cloth, because I never had an argument there and did not even
know the man before I came to the company. And a third thought it
would make the company look very fine if we elected an American. And
now we have a lieutenant who seems to be a perfectly good man, but of
whom it is still questionable whether he can write more than his name,
Henry Smith. He is a son of Bill Smith who lives at Calhoun's. Since he
has been with the regiment he has spent most of his time driving mules.[9]
I can console myself about it quite easily. The advantage of it is an

expansion of my knowledge of mankind. A big reason too may be that I did not go around and ask the people for their votes, which the others did. I only said to the company when they were together, that, in consequence of their urging, I would be a candidate, and that it would please me if they elected me, because I would view it as proof of their trust. And I did not speak to individual men about it at all. The Americans are greatly surprised about it and say that, if somebody wants to become an officer, all he has to do is go to Co. F. After this occurrence, though, I am going to try to get out of the company and maybe even out of the army. Carl and Kämmerling, who took a great part in the affair, want to do the same. First we want to see whether we can be employed in shops in San Antonio. For this purpose Carl and I want to write to Alfred and Meusebach, and get them to try to put all the irons in the fire to bring that about, and Kämmerling will write to a man in the tannery with whom he thinks he has influence. If that works out, it would be good; if not, we will probably find something else. . . . We have had quite a bad time behind us. There was constant bad weather; rain alternated with frost, but we had to march anyway and often got only very scant rations. Now we are pretty well off again. The rations are not adequate actually, but they are good. We draw cornmeal and fresh pork, sometimes beans too. We get twenty ears of corn for the horses and sometimes a bundle of fodder per day too. Just now it started to rain again. Carl and I have made ourselves a house of blankets, but the roof lets so much rain sprinkle in that I have to quit writing. Carl and Kämmerling send greetings and join me in wishing that you may spend the holidays in good spirits. Rudolf Coreth.

San Augustine
30 December 1864
Rudolf to family

We still have received no news from you. . . . We are staying at San Augustine and get rather enough corn for the horses. We do not get fodder delivered, but up to now we still are able to buy it in the neighborhood. We can't complain about the quality of our rations, but there is not always enough. We bought ourselves [sweet] potatoes several times. They are getting very scarce already in the area around where we are. It seems to me that we eat more now because we are not accustomed to such good food, and soon will be able to manage on it. In a short time we are going farther northward again to a county where they say there is still a lot of corn and fodder. We keep hoping to be given back to the District of Texas, because as long as we belong to Louisiana we are not allowed to go more than thirty miles from the Sabine, and we would like to get where there is some grass. When there doesn't just happen to be bad weather, we lead quite a pleasant life now. There is no drilling and there is not much watch duty required either. I am doing nothing at all, by the way, because I am always on sick report. A large part of our time is now taken up with washing our laundry. Bed bugs turned up in Louisiana and one fine day we had the unpleasant surprise that, though we had kept away from other people as much as possible, we got some just the same. We now wash our clothes as often as possible in order to get rid of them again. Boiling kills them, but we have no basins in which we could boil our blankets, and so we can only get rid of them by persistence, because quite a few probably stay in the bed, and even if one is dressed in completely fresh clothes, one gets some again anyway. Yesterday I found that washing is made much easier if one mixes sal soda in the water in which the laundry is boiled. What the chemical composition of it is I do not know. But it washes very well and must be cheap, because for $1 in paper I got a whole tincupful ["Tin-cupfoll"]. It is the stuff that barbers use for shampooing and that is where I bought it too. One makes a saturated solution of it and, after one has dampened one's hair with clean water a bit, one thoroughly wets the head and rubs in [the solution] really well. It foams like soap, and after one has washed it out, the hair is as clean as it can be. Of politics we hear nothing now; only now and again a report that one can tell was made up in camp is circulated. So for example we heard yesterday that Lincoln had recognized twelve states.[10] What we will celebrate this New Year's with, we do not know yet; probably it will pass quite dry. It would really please me if I could believe that you will have a cheerful time. If wishes could help at all, you would surely not lack anything, but unfortunately I have little faith in that. Adio for today; with the hope that we may be together longer in the year 1865 than in this one, I remain as always your Rudolf. I ask you to please forward this letter to Meusebach.

San Augustine
10 January 1865
Rudolf to family

Still no letter has arrived from you. . . . It seems that they want to keep us here until they need us somewhere. We probably will be taken to another county soon where there is still supposed to be plenty of corn. They talk of Panola County and another county the name of which does not come to me now, that lies between here and Panola [Shelby]. There is supposed to be plenty of everything there that soldiers could possibly dream of. If letters for us should arrive here, they would surely be forwarded to us there, because it is only 40-50 miles from here. Our condition is not as good now as it was recently. Carl got an attack of malaria yesterday morning and had fever until this morning; now it has let up pretty thoroughly. He is living in town in a house with the [music] band, where I took him yesterday afternoon. He is well taken care of there and can sleep in a dry, warm room. There are a lot of people sick as a result of the bad weather we have had the last few days. Now (after noon) the sun is shining a little again, and I hope to still be able to dry the blankets and clothes. My rash is getting neither better nor worse. In the evening it keeps me from sleeping for a couple of hours. The rest of the time I only get good use out of it though, because I do not have any duties because of having it. Our hospital has no remedies for it, so I probably won't be healed for a long time yet. Carl's horse got a bad case of diarrhea the day before yesterday. We gave it tea made from oak bark. Now it seems to be rather well again, but it is very thin and doesn't eat the way it should either, but then it never does. I have asked a man who lives near Bratten to inquire about the horses and report to you.[11] It isn't very likely, to be sure, that they are there, but it is possible, after all. . . .

12 January [continued]

Yesterday a letter from Father from 27 November arrived. It put me in the same mood in which Father must have been when he wrote it. It just is completely unclear to me how the business can go on if Franz has to leave. I cannot imagine anything to do but repair the field fence as well as possible and let the pasture go. Things look a bit better here with us than a couple of days ago. The weather is clear again and Carl is better although not yet recovered. He had to take quinine to endure the fever. He came back to camp today. I think he will write you himself. This letter will leave here with a couple of people who have gotten a leave. . . . Today the clothes for the company got here at last. Had they come a couple of weeks earlier, they could have served the people well already and there would probably be fewer sick. There are so many clothes that we hardly know how to transport them. . . . Political reports have arrived, but they are not as good as they usually were last spring and summer. Beyond the Mississippi, it is said, we have had significant losses; and here, they say, the Yankees are coming up the River Road again. Whether this news is true I cannot say. It seems to be generally believed though; I am now rather indifferent to everything. I have made up my mind to wait a couple of months more, and the more pastime I have during that period, the more I'll like it. Do write me very soon whether Franz really has to leave and where he is going. Maybe something could be done to get us together. The news that he has to leave upset me very much. I cannot grasp how that will work out at all. Farewell for today. In the hope of getting news from you soon again, I remain as ever your Rudolf.

Camp San Augustine
12 January 1865
Carl to parents

Yesterday we finally got a letter from you; also I got three letters from Hedwig. The last is from 27 November. Unfortunately the news is not good. I can say that the news that Franz too has had to leave has depressed me monstrously.[12] I will stand for quite a lot, but that is practically a mortal blow. How is Father supposed to manage the farm, a man of his age. If only Franz had at least been able to come to us! The whole business is just too dreadful. I can say that soon it will be all the same to me how the war comes out, if only it would end soon. There is nothing but betrayal, robbery, and lies wherever one looks anyway, and the soldiers must give up their possessions, lives, or health for it, and the families at home too are deprived of whatever they have, or some-times, if possible, even of what they do not have. Today is Father's name day. But not a thing comes to me that I might congratulate him for. I can imagine too that he has no time for celebrating it either. Of politics one does not hear much that is good. In Virginia and elsewhere the Yankees are said to have gotten beat though. According to the *New York Herald,* they say, the same source reports that Hood's Army is shot to pieces and Sherman has moved to Savannah and taken monstrous loot. Even if in the end it turns out not to be that bad, it is definite anyway that Hood is thoroughly beaten. From Alexandria comes the report that the Yankees are coming up the river. Rudolf has probably already written you in greater detail. I am not quite well yet though. My head hurts too much for me to be able to write you a long letter. Actually there is nothing of importance anyway. So for today, farewell again. With a thousand warm regards as ever, your loyal son Carl.

Carl's letter is full of errors, which was quite uncharacteristic of him, and toward the end the penmanship is very unsteady. When he wrote it, he did not know that on 3 December, almost six weeks earlier, his wife Hedwig had once more given birth to a son. The child, who had arrived the day after its Grandfather Coreth's sixty-first birthday, she named Karl in honor of its absent father.

– – –

> H. Qrs. 32*nd* Regt. Texas Cavalry
> Camp above Richmond Tex.
> May 20th, 1865

(Extract)

> Died at San Augustine Texas on the Thirteenth day of January 1865 of congestion of the brain, Private Charles Coreth of Capt. Edgar Schramms Company "F" 32*d* Tex. Cav.

> I certify on Honor, that the above is a correct and true transcript of the Records of Company F. 32*nd* Tex Cav and that the fact stated above is true, to my personal knowledge

> > P. C. Bitter
> > 1*st* Lt. comdg Company F.
> > 32*d* T. C.

– – –

Carl's death almost coincided with his twenty-eighth birthday. Rudolf, just sixteen months his junior, once more buried a soldier brother, gathered together his possessions, and left for home, this time in the hope of having seen the last of soldiering. Carl's gravesite is apparently unknown.[13] Whether he lay with others or apart, he could have been no more alone than was Rudolf, who headed westward to carry the sad news home.

Dixitur

Rake Pocket[1]
5 February 1865
Rudolf from Hermann Kämmerling

Dear Rudolf! On 22 January, the day we left San Augustine, you did not leave my thoughts, because it must have been terribly hard for you, in your weak state of health, to ride in such gruesome cold. I had the norther directly in front of me, and although I am in good health after all and was warmly dressed, I was freezing quite awfully; indeed I had such dreadful pains in my feet from the cold that I could scarcely walk for a week. That Monday was even colder and it stayed unpleasantly cold here all that week actually; and so I pitied you and feared with all my heart that in the end you would get sick again and would have to interrupt your journey. I would have liked to be with you, which was made impossible by the curse that hangs over rabble the likes of us soldiers.[2] Meanwhile, I shall hope, you got to your people without hindrances. I found the regiment twelve miles west of Carthage in camp on the third day of my ride. The terrain is rolling land as at San Augustine, rather a lot of wood but bad water, and the ground sandy, so that the camp was rather clean and dry. Then it began to rain, with the temperature quite cold, the night of Sunday the twenty-ninth to Monday; and now just take note: it rained all night Monday, all night Tuesday, and Wednesday practically without stopping for even as much as a minute. Wednesday night it did not rain for a quarter of an hour from time to time. The bright moments became longer on Thursday, and at noon it stopped raining. Afternoon nice weather. On Friday very nice weather and very warm. Horses and men sank away in the sand at places where one least expected it. On Friday evening there came the order to go farther westward to Henderson. We broke up under a very overcast sky. Saturday morning we went five miles to Rake Pocket, and still had just enough time to pitch our tents before it began to rain. Now it is noon Sunday and it is still raining continuously with a rather strong, cold east wind, so that my fingers get cold and stiff as I write. Our going on today has been hindered by rain, and thus we are staying on here. Christian Pantermühl has the fever badly again, and Schimmel is drooping around so that I fear we shall be seeing him abed again soon. Schimmel has had especially bad luck, by the way, because his sick leave has still not arrived, while [Charles] Dambmann, whose application was sent three days later, already left camp about ten days ago. A week ago Schimmel's horse was condemned by [Lt. Col.] Hutchison and another application made for him, so that he could not fail to get home, and then there comes into camp an order on Friday (3 February), *stopping all leaves.* The sick are to submit to being cured in the hospital, etc. Meanwhile I have not yet completely given up hope, because I think that, if his leave gets here having been approved, it will not be withheld. Dambmann's leave was approved by [Gen. John Austin] Wharton, under whose command we are now, and therefore was back so much sooner.[3] . . . There is a lot of fantasizing in camp that we are going to Houston. In New Orleans, you see, a big expedition is being equipped, of which the destination is unknown. It is conjectured Houston. That is also supposed to be the reason that all leaves have been stopped.—Debray has been to Shreveport and is going to leave for there again one of the next days with the [music] band. *Dixitur* [L. = "It is said/Rumor has it"] that we are to have Sharpshooters,[4] sabers, sixshooters, which Debray is going to Shreveport to get now.—Now my fingers are so stiff though that I am going to stop for a while.

Camp two miles north of Bellevue, which is 8 [?; illegible] miles northwest of Henderson
10 February [continued]

Well, so it rained Sunday until evening and became very cold. The rain changed to snow and ice during the night, and on Monday morning everything was white. Then came the order to go on, since this region is said to be completely eaten out, and that neither men nor cattle could be sustained here any longer. So we had to thaw out our saddles and leather things by the fire, though it was raining and freezing merrily on all the while; meanwhile it did stop when we had been underway about two hours. Having put in at a wood-deficient camp at Henderson, we just had time enough to saddle up before receiving another cool rain. Schimmel had gotten a bad fever on the way and had stayed behind on a farm, Christian [Pantermühl] with him. They were treated exceptionally cordially and attentively there, the reason probably being that the owner is a lieutenant in Gould's regiment who was home because of a bad cold and walking on crutches.[5] In the evening it became clear, and it has been so since that time, with very cold nights and nice warm weather by day. Schimmel is well again—For the moment our destination is Leon County on the Brazos, to which we will slowly eat our way. Major General Polignac left the Confederate States two months ago and is supposed to make proposals to France as well as England that they recognize us. Polignac is a French prince and the last male heir from the house of Bourbon and this mission is supposed to have been turned over to him on that account.[6] I cannot tell you what truth there is to that; meanwhile everything in the army is revolving around an imminent peace. My nag is on the road to improvement again, and there is every hope that I can keep him alive. However, meanwhile it will be hard to get him as fat again as he was, since he is a miserably poor eater. Schimmel's leave arrived here yesterday disapproved by Wharton, since it was already of too late a date. Lt. Col. Hutchison did however send off another immediately and we have to wait to see what success it will have. His first leave had gone to [Gen. Simon Bolivar] Buckner [Gen. Kirby

Smith's subaltern, commanding CSA forces in La.]; he had already turned over the things to Wharton, and therefore the leave was on the road a very long time, whence the too-old date. Now I must still tell you of a nasty business that the government was in the process of conducting. Before this order that stopped all leaves, another had come into camp allowing a leave (staying at home for twenty days) to every soldier who would buy a gun from a civilian and give it to the government. Everybody had bought guns (Debray's regiment 180 [150?; unclear] and I think ours not many fewer) by the time this order came that stopped all leaves, so that now many soldiers have two guns and are not getting to go home— My gray trousers, dear Rudolf, just aren't going to make it after all, so it would be very agreeable for me if you could bring me down another light-weight pair of durable pants—Commend me to your parents and brothers and sisters most sincerely, and greetings to you from your H. Kämmerling. . . .

From San Antonio Rudolf meanwhile wrote to his family of the obstacles he was encountering in approaching the people in the best position to help him get detached service, or perhaps even a discharge because of his recurring illness. In great contrast to the letters from camp, the following is on very fine stationery decorated with an embossed "U.S." that indicates it is a relic of the pre-secession days. He had discovered that there was no longer a medical board in San Antonio and that if Dr. Kelley, who was away on leave though expected back momentarily, chose to act independently, he could supply him with a certificate that, though not worth as much as one from a board, would suffice. The other person from whom he most hoped to get assistance in his cause was the old family friend Gustav Schleicher, who was in a position to arrange for him to work in a shop in the city rather than return to camp. To act as intermediary between himself and this influential gentleman he called on his brother-in-law Meusebach, who was to have made contact with Rudolf in San Antonio but now lay sick somewhere in the city, his whereabouts unknown. Other family friends whom he encountered—Spiess, Rhodius, and Landa—did not offer any help and, indeed, were probably unable to provide him with anything beyond the sympathy and warm regards they asked him to convey to his family, having heard of the most recent bereavement that had befallen the Coreths. Only Alfred Kapp seemed to have specific suggestions.

San Antonio
8 February 1865
Rudolf from Alfred Kapp

Dear Rudolf! I did not get your letter of the third of the month until yesterday. I do not need to tell you how shattering the news is, for the misfortune is too great.—You yourself I would like to advise, if you have not already reached another decision, to come and try to get taken on here at the arsenal. You owe your parents that, since, it seems to me, things are bad with your health, because even if you may be feeling well at present, you have been sick too often and have been too violently medicated during the last year and a half not to be in constant danger of succumbing at the first recurrence. It is a remarkable fact that one never grows accustomed to camp life, but instead, the longer one is out there, the less one can endure. I hardly think that my letter in answer to Carl's outpouring to me, that you all wished to come here, still reached your hands. I mentioned in it that it is difficult to get out of the army, that one has trouble making his way here, etc. The former is made easier by the fact that you are now here, and the latter we shall see. You can probably get a paper from Dr. Kelley, who is hospital physician here, saying that you are "unfit for camp life," and will probably then be taken in here. It is not a certainty, but just come here in any case as soon as possible and make a try. I still have a little fodder for your horse, and after all, you know where I live. If then you want to carry out what you talked about the last time, you will have the easiest opportunity here.[7] Anyway, come soon. We can take the matter under consideration here.— I scarcely think, after the inquiries I have made, that one can sell a Sharps here [Carl's?; one Rudolf bought?]; somewhere in the countryside would probably provide a better chance. Many regards to your dear parents and my poor sister [Hedwig], to you and all of your people from your loyal friend Alfred Kapp.

An undated note from Rudolf to his parents appears to come from this period. It simply states that he and another person (or other persons) are working in a gunsmith's shop near Hummel's Store, which seems to have been located near Alfred Kapp's post-war place of business, if not at the same site.[8] What is certain is that his employment in San Antonio, if any, was very brief.

5 miles from Evergreen [San Jacinto County, Texas]
8 March 1865
Rudolf to family

. . . Actually I have nothing of importance to tell you; I only wanted to write you that our brigade is on the way to Fort Bend County. That is on the Brazos in the area of Richmond. I would probably already have encountered it in Washington [on the Brazos], if they had not been held back by the high waters of the Trinity. I am going from here to Union Hill, from there to Washington, then to Anderson, then to Madisonville, and from there to the Alabama crossing over the Trinity. On this route I am sure to meet the regiment. Up to now I have still made good progress and am looking forward to getting to the company, because we are going westward, after all. With many greetings, I remain as ever your loyal son and brother. Rudolf.

For almost a week Rudolf tried to close the distance between himself and his regiment, but at Madisonville his horse got sick, and he spent most of his energies on trying to restore it to a serviceable state, rubbing its joints, dosing it with Aconitum, and wrapping its legs with strips of wet blankets, the only rags he could get. At least he could stop worrying for the moment about what would happen when he did get back to the regiment, since Captain Schramm had sent him a message through a passing comrade, saying that there would be no difficulties.

Finally, on 15 March his regiment came through Madisonville, where he had been staying in a rooming house, and from there they moved to a camp about a mile and a half away. It is astonishing, even touching, to sense his relief at being back with the men, considering his determination to get away from them a few months earlier, when his spirits had reached their nadir. His report to the family exudes content in practical matters: his horse is almost well again; the mess is in rather good health, though a couple of the Pantermühls, as he puts it, still get an attack of fever every now and then; he was reported AWOL for four days, but Major Holmes excused him; others who came only a day late got a court martial, though they would not be punished either. The only specific reference to the men as individuals is the almost perfunctory "Kämmerling sends regards." What names do come in for mention are those of officers and officials who might advance or obstruct his cause—getting out of the army and going home. But there is also a visible lack of the old readiness to complain, resent, or lament, as he tells of Lt. Hoym's return, bringing with him "nothing but a lot of attestations from men who can't or don't want to return yet."[9] What mattered most to Rudolf was that, on 17 March, the regiment came through Anderson and camped four miles farther on, probably the last stop before reaching its destination in Fort Bend County. General Debray's headquarters were nearby, and soon Rudolf could go to see whether Dr. Koester had sent a certificate enabling him to go home to await the end of the war, an event that most were sure was fast approaching.

Camp on the Brazos
24 March 1865
Rudolf to family

Today I was at General Debray's to inquire about the leave that Dr. Koester requested for me. The general was very proper and friendly, but regretted not being able to give me a leave because he no longer has the right to do so [he said]. He said the application would have to be made to Kirby Smith, since we are not under Walker's command.[10] He advised me not to ask for a leave, because there would be a better chance of success if I am in the army and Dr. Koester and the governor pursue my cause on my behalf. He promises to do all he can for me and does not think there will be any difficulty in my getting the detail. Dr. Koester will probably have to make out a new application though. There is no news. My horse still has the glanders and will probably get very thin before it gets well. . . . I have to hurry in order to finish before dark and the letter has to be ready tomorrow morning because Lt. Bitter is going to New Braunfels. I wrote to Koester too. Adio for today . . . Rudolf. Kämmerling sends greetings.

Camp on the Brazos Bottom
28 March 1865
Rudolf to family

. . . We have no political news. [Lt. Granville H.] Sherwood, whom I saw
a couple of days ago, told me that they hardly get to hear anything about
the other side of the Mississippi and what one does hear is bad for us.
Likewise, here in the army things are happening that one cannot approve.
A lot of cavalry regiments are being dismounted, and because it is
thought the men will not put up with that in good humor, it is done by
force. Two days ago we had the unpleasant duty of helping to take the
horses from a regiment. The men were told that (by order of Gen. Wharton) they had to give up their horses. Then the horses were looked over
and those which could be used as artillery horses were appraised and
confiscated. The poor ones the men could send home. It is surely not to
be expected that this course of action will bear good fruit, and the generals should not become guilty of such treachery. If they cannot maintain
the cavalry anymore, they should discharge and then conscript them as
infantry. Then the people would not be betrayed anyway. The dismounting would probably not have happened without difficulties if they had
not set up other regiments behind several mounds, ready to shoot at
them if they refused to give up the horses. For the moment we are not
in danger of losing our horses. Gen. Debray told us on that occasion that
he has a letter from Gen. Wharton promising to leave our regiment and
Debray's old regiment as cavalry in reward for our good discipline and
behavior (?). In Louisiana and Arkansas a lot of regiments have had
their horses taken from them already in the same way as here. The state
of health in the regiment seems to be improving. Cases of fever do occur
even now, but seldomer than they used to anyway. I am trying to get the
men to drive out the fever with cooking salt. But there aren't many who
can overcome their revulsion against such large quantities of salt once
they have taken it. But all those who took it three or four times were
then free of fever. It has rained terribly here recently. All creeks are high
and the roads are almost impassable.

30 March 1865 [continued]
Rudolf to family

Since the twenty-eighth nothing has happened. The men have not even
so much as an inkling what is to become of us. We are living quite
tolerably well. The rations consist of bacon and flour. Both are usually
good and all are content with it. A couple of times we bought eggs and
chickens and lived quite fine then. The duties are not bad either. We
are supposed to drill an hour daily, to be sure, with the exception of
Saturday and Sunday, but there are still circumstances arising that make
it impossible on those five days. It rains every few moments, and then
the area is so submerged that one can't go out of the camp. Do be so
kind and inquire of Dr. Koester what he is considering doing on my
behalf, and whether he knows anything about the application that has
been sent to Gen. Walker. Adio. Rudolf Coreth.

Camp near Richmond
4 April 1865
Rudolf to family

... The day before yesterday the application from Koester to Gen. Walker got here, with the remark that the officers, one by one beginning with the captain, should give their evaluation of it and send it to Gen. Wharton. Whether it must then still go to Kirby Smith I do not know. [Capt. Edgar] Schramm approved and recommended my request. Major [Stokley] Holmes was against it; he said he had already disapproved many requests of that same sort and therefore could not do otherwise in this case either. Gen. Debray promised to support the request. What Gen. Wharton will say about it is very uncertain, but there is great likelihood that he will be against a favorable decision. It would have been significantly better if Koester had made the application to Kirby Smith. Now we will simply have to wait and see though what will become of the matter before doing any more. We moved the camp three miles in the direction of Richmond yesterday and got quite a good place. There is rather good water and grass here, wood in abundance and quite pretty trees under which we are situated. Yesterday, right after we arrived, we began to make troughs for the horses, work we did not finish until evening. We exerted ourselves for a change again, the way we used to do frequently, so that our clothes got really wet doing it, which, I think, did us all quite a lot of good. The condition of my horse seems to be improving. He is beginning to value my companionship again. . . . I don't perform duties on horseback. I accept only such details as I can do on foot. Naturally I cannot drill. Today we had a big inspection. The weapons were counted (for the how-manyeth time I do not know) and collected. They say we are to get short guns and maybe sixshooters too. Gen. Debray told Schramm they mean to see whether they can take the pistols from the regiment whose horses they took away. I am quite impatient for news of you and do not grasp the reason that no letter has come for so long. . . . With many regards to you all and Hedwig, I remain, as ever, your Rudolf.

New Braunfels
no date [postmarked 7 April 1865][11]
Rudolf from father

Dear Rudolf!

We already have two letters in our hands from you now. The first reported your fortunate arrival in camp; the second Lt. Bitter brought us. It got to us on 3 April. . . . Here things are going so-so. We always have work to do, and that is quite good; it deflects gloomy thoughts, and they will probably not depart as long as we are not all together in peace again. Franz has recovered and is working as he did before. How long that will continue though one cannot guess. What will happen to you and with you is completely obscured too, all the more so since I have not yet been in town to see Dr. Koester. The rain did not hurt our fields the way it did those of many other people. It washed the creek fence away for the most part, and since planting seemed more important to us for the moment, we had worked on it only a little, but sooner or later that too will probably come to pass. The cows have lots of calves now; I think there are now or are about to be ten, but they are very thin and the milk will come only very slowly, so we have to buy milk pans too, which are very high-priced now. Cathrin has a mare foal and Blondine a little stallion; Morette is not bearing young. Politically one hears nothing favorable. In the circle of our acquaintances nothing either. Wuppermann, Tips, Mrs. Schmitz and daughter, and lots of other people besides are going these next few days in a caravan to Matamoros or Camargo, partly to Mexico, partly to Europe.[12] Farewell, dear Rudolf. Mother, your brothers, sisters, and I embrace you in spirit and long to be able to do it soon in reality. As ever your loyal friend and father E. Coreth*

On the last day of March, General Magruder had returned to replace General Walker as commander of the District of Texas, New Mexico, and Arizona. A few days later on 3 April, Richmond, the Confederate capital, had been evacuated, but news of Lee's surrender at Appomattox, less than a week away, was not to reach Texas for a while. Not far from where Rudolf was encamped with his regiment, there occurred on 6 April an incident, reports of which covered the short distance very rapidly. The irrationality of that event is as revealing of the mental condition of the collapsing South as the lassitude of the father's and the son's letters.

Camp near Richmond [Texas]
9 April 1865
Rudolf to family

. . . That General Wharton was shot to death by Colonel [George Wythe] Baylor you will probably have discovered before getting this letter.[13] The more accurate circumstances have not reached our ears. Whether he forwarded or even received Koester's application before he was killed I have not yet heard. It is possible that his death is favorable to my cause. Some days ago an order was read to us that makes Gen. H. P. Bee our division general again. However, he will probably become corps commander now, because, as far as we know, he is the oldest general in the cavalry corps. If that were to be the case, there would be more probability of an approval of my detail than there was earlier, because Wharton was very stingy with the few men that he still had, and another can only be better than he was. The day before yesterday Colonel [Nat] Benton came back to us. He means to take over command of the regiment. The old man makes a really sad impression with his arm shot away.[14] The men all seem to be glad to see him again. The last two days we have had very bad weather. It rained almost without interruption day and night. Therefore we kept idle as much as possible. Our mess sat in the company tent all day and, in order not to be overcome with boredom, we whittled chess men, which turned out quite well. Today we dyed half of them black.

Now all we still lack is a board; we will get that soon too though, probably. What is to become of us nobody knows definitely. They say that when the Brazos has gone down enough that we can get across, we are to be transferred to the area around Independence in Washington County, because there is still supposed to be lots of corn and meat there. Yesterday for the first time in a long time we got beef again. They say that we are to get it from time to time now. The meat was hardly very good, but the grass is growing well, and so the cattle will soon be fat also, probably. . . . With the wish that I might at last get a letter from you again, I remain as ever your son and brother Rudolf.

In large ways and small, the Confederate military's disintegration was visible on every hand. Understandably, Rudolf Coreth, long since convinced that the war would end badly for the South, was preoccupied with how the developments would affect him. On 12 April Colonel Benton rode to Hempstead, where he promised to talk with General Bee about the fate of Private Coreth. Rudolf's hopes were pinned on Benton, who, he did not doubt, would persuade Bee for him. The change in officers, he thought, was to his advantage. His spirits were good, though the camp was so full of puddles the men could hardly go out. He had forgotten to bring a towel when leaving home. Would the family please send one by August Schimmelpfennig, if, as Dr. Koester had written, Rudolf's friend should be returning to camp soon?

New Braunfels
no date [16 April 1865]
Rudolf from father

Dear Rudolf!
Yesterday, the fifteenth, . . . I found your lines of the fourth, which put us at ease about your well-being. . . . I cannot conjure up a clear picture of your success, since General Wharton, the man who was responsible for making the decision about it, has died in the meantime, and Magruder is commander in Texas again, and he is said to be less in the governor's good graces than was the case with Walker. That is how Fate plays with our lot. I went to Koester immediately; he told me he had not received any report from the governor yet. As soon as he has one, he would immediately do what was necessary. So again it is wait, keep faith, hope, surrender to the supreme authority ["Also wieder warten harren hoffen sich in die Übermacht ergeben"]. In town I saw Hermann Runge, Grassmayer, Walter Tips, who is a lieutenant, and many soldiers who seem to be on leave.[15] There was an inquiry into the case of three Mexicans who are said to have robbed and murdered a fourth, their wagonmaster. Also I saw old [Hermann, Sr.] Conring. Miss Marie [Conring] is the betrothed of the Mr. [Hermann] Fischer at [Wilhelm] Wetzel's store. From Hermann Runge (Mrs. Julie Runge has a daughter), I discovered a rather interesting bit of news.[16] I said that even if France became involved in a war with the United States in order to maintain

its hold on Mexico, it would have a hard time delivering the necessary troops over the ocean, whereupon he responded that this would not cost France as much as a single man. All it would have to do was open its ports to the Southern freebooters, and allow the French to build new privateers for the South in their harbors. As soon as all the seas would be covered with Southern privateers, Northern trade would be totally ruined and the North would find it extremely hard to continue the war. This reasoning seems to me to make sense, but, come what may, once we have you back we will breathe easy again. A convoy [*"Condukt"*] from Mexico with $30,000 was attacked by robbers and the $15,000 that it had in gold was taken from it, while the rest, which was silver, they did not take along at all. Today is Easter Sunday and Ottilie's [seventh] birthday. Franz butchered a two-year-old beef yesterday. Ernst [Meusebach], who wanted to ride your mare, was bucked off, but without any harm being done. Franz then caught her and rode her. She did not do anything to him anymore. She is an infamous bitch. Adieux for today. Everyone sends greetings and embraces you. Mother, your brothers and sisters, and I. Hedwig sends greetings. She is to be fetched this week to be at home for a while. Your old man E. Coreth

Camp near Richmond
Sunday, 23 April 1865
Rudolf to family

. . . Benton, who came back from Houston, told me I should wait a bit more, that General Walker would probably take over Wharton's place soon and then it would work out. He assured me in so many words that he would do everything that he can to help me in the matter. . . . Yesterday the report of General Lee's capture arrived here. It caused great excitement. Many believe that will bring the war to an end. I was detailed for two days to work on a mill and just now got back into camp. . . .

Camp near Richmond
28 April 1865
Rudolf to family

I have not received another letter from you since I last wrote. Presumably the roads are in terrible shape, and that is probably the cause. . . . The last political reports came so unexpectedly that it is probable, I guess, that soon great developments will occur here too. We have the definite report that Lee has been captured. There have not yet been any confirmed reports about Johnston, but they say that he has likewise laid down his arms, and it is quite generally believed. Yesterday the rumor arrived that a fleet had appeared off Galveston and had demanded the surrender of Texas. I don't believe the report, but it seems probable to me that that will soon occur. It is remarkable what an impression these reports make on the soldiers. Many men express their undisguised joy about it quite overtly. We held a meeting a couple of days ago to reach decisions about what we would do in case of an invasion. The whole business, it seems to me, was instituted to give the civilians a false impression of our attitude. The decisions are empty phrases. The main thing about this was the orations by a few fire-eaters or charlatans who proposed not to give up until we either are dead or have achieved our independence. They say that Texas could carry on the war completely by itself for another twenty years; that, if a super force comes, we should scatter and begin a guerrilla war. These gentlemen are people I am convinced really would like quite a lot to give themselves up, if only they had the chance. It would go too far afield if I were to write you everything that proves the dissatisfaction of the men. I can assure you, however, there are daily proofs that the soldiers are tired of being handled like cattle by officers and civilians. I fear that the immediate future will bring terrible events, because the least that will happen is that the Negroes will be freed. But, since that would not be prevented anyway by a prolongation of the fight, I wish the whole thing might come to an end soon, because the prospect of personal freedom is really very nice, after all. What is to become of my detail is still not certain. Colonel Benton told me he would go to Hempstead to General Walker in a few days and would take up my cause at that time. He says . . . one can hardly know, after all, before Walker has expressed himself. In the end the war will be over before the detail arrives, which would be just as well. The day before yesterday we had heavy rain all day. The area is under water again, and the creeks are high. We probably will have to move our camp soon; the firewood is already becoming scarce here, the water dirty, and for some time the corn has had to be hauled from nine miles away. Where we will go is not yet known, but it seems probable to me that we will be taken to the Caney or the Bernard again, because the whole Brazos is occupied by troops that devour the corn. Walker's division and Polignac's division are staying at Hempstead. Of Walker's division they say many deserted every night on the way down from Shreveport.[17] . . . I still hoped some time ago that I would be spending my birthday this year at your place, but it does not seem to be turning out that way. I hope it will be the last one though that I spend in the army. Even if really hard times come, they are going to be more tolerable, if we can spend them together. Rudolf.

New Braunfels
5 May 1865
Rudolf from father [addressed to Richmond, Texas]

My dear Rudolf, Yesterday Mother brought along your letter of 20 April. . . . We assumed you were in Gonzales last week [to collect his horse, Ben] . . . but unfortunately still too far for us to hear one another's voices. The political reports agree about our not having very long to wait anymore for the conclusion of this four-act drama. I am prepared for anything and ready to surrender to patience, if only this one thing can be attained: that we can be reunited in order to embrace one another and close ranks, since our line is so full of vacancies [*"da unsere Reihe so sehr gelichtet ist"*]. Franz is generally well again, but still very weak; he coughs or becomes exhausted from every little bit of work or exertion. This time he managed to escape from their [the army authorities'] claws. They took thirty men, had to give up eleven again, since the District Court was meeting and the judge made that decision, but the decision costs these people $50 each in lawyers' fees, and, since, according to the judge's decision, the matter of arresting them is unjust, this seems rather high to me. The two Schimmelpfennigs [Hermann, the husband of Auguste Tolle, and his brother August of Co. F], [Conrad?] Kappmayer, [Franz?, Wenzel?] Novotny, Schulz [impossible to identify or limit], [Wilhelm] Bönig ["Pönig"] are among the ones released, of people known to me; but the vultures are still in the area in Jung's pasture, and they said that they would just have to let the trouble settle a while before coming back again. Actually it seems San Antonio is where they are intended to be. But there everyone is on the lookout too. How much essential work is being neglected is unbelievable. And Ø [= nothing] is achieved. Adieux, my dear Rudolf. We all send our best wishes, which we would so much have liked delivering in person. Your mother, brothers and sisters, and your old friend and father E. Coreth*

Gonzales
5 May 1865
Rudolf to family

. . . I am on the way back to camp from Bratten's ranch. I have Ben with me. Bratten took care that he didn't get ungovernable. He used him the way these people simply do use other people's horses. His neighbors told me that he or his Negroes had used the horse to chase cattle every day. Bratten was not home when I was there. Ben is in rather poor shape. . . . People say he is one of the strongest horses in the area. One could ride herd with him all day without straining him. . . . Münzenberger's bay was . . . at Bratten's, but bumped himself in the pen . . . when I wanted to catch him. He ran a fence rail into his belly and died. I feel very well; there is an entirely different atmosphere here in the west. It is somewhat hard for me to go back east, but I console myself with the hope that the war will end soon. . . . Best regards to you all from across a distance of fifty miles, and cherish me. Rudolf.

Camp near Richmond
12 May 1865
Rudolf to family

At noon on the eighth I got back to the regiment. I met it six miles from San Felipe. It was on the march up the Brazos. On the ninth we marched to within four miles of Hempstead. There in the evening we got orders to prepare for a forced march that would last a week. Nobody knew where we were to go. On the morning of the tenth all people who thought that their horses could take it left; the others stayed behind in camp. I rode Ben to give Jeff a rest. As we then saw and heard, the expedition was headed for Houston to catch up with a regiment that has broken up to go home. We went about 25 miles that day, then we got orders to give up the pursuit, since the regiment had not deserted, and were told to go back to our camp above Richmond. That is where we are now. . . . Something is certainly wrong, because otherwise Walker would not have received by telegraph the order that dispatched us. Also we still have to send out scouts to search for deserters. In the camp I found on my return two letters from Father awaiting me. . . . I do not want to see here in the army anybody whom I wish well, and that is the only place Franz could go, after all, if he has to leave where he is. On my birthday I was on the road. It just so happened that I got to the German settlement at Cat Spring in the evening, and I had looked forward all day to a pleasant evening. After I had inquired at several houses and was turned down, I got to a house belonging to well-off people named Amthor. They took me in, but I found my expectation unsatisfied. I often thought of you and am convinced that a stranger would be received quite differently at your place. The people were not exactly impolite, but though they are wealthy, they are terribly stingy. Two grown daughters were there too. I took great pains to get them to talk, but it was impossible. They always made their answers as brief as possible, until I finally gave up and kept quiet until we went to bed, when I was led into a little room that smelled very unpleasant and in which there stood a rather dirty bed.[18] So the day ended completely uneventfully. I shall hope that at that time next year I shall be with you. Otherwise I had quite a pleasant trip. I was received cordially everywhere and, since I knew quite well that I could not go to you after all because the time was too short, I traveled slowly and stopped over at good places as long as possible. I talked with Benton today about my detail at Koester's. He said he tried to get it for me at Walker's, but it is impossible. No soldiers are being detailed anymore for private enterprises, so we have to give that up. I don't care much about it. The war surely cannot last much longer now, and when it is over, then I shall be completely free at once. Be so kind and tell Koester about that. It seems to me that the war is now moving toward its end rapidly. It is generally believed that General Johnston's army is captured too, and if it should not be, then surely it soon will be, and it is not probable that there will long be fighting anymore on this side of the Mississippi. There is too poor a spirit in the troops and in the people. Men desert from the infantry daily, and most who stay there do it only because they hope and believe that they can leave honorably soon. The certificate for Carl I shall keep until I come myself.[19] Kämmerling sends regards. . . . Our regiment has been armed with sabers and carbines.

New Braunfels
19 May 1865
Rudolf from father

Dear Rudolf, As I hear it, Capt. [Edgar] Schramm is leaving tomorrow, and since I hope he will get to camp more directly than the postal service, I shall ask him to take this letter along. I hear from someone on leave that you mailed your last letter of 12 May, which brought us the happy news that you are well and relatively satisfied in the hope of soon getting your freedom. Your wish can scarcely be stronger than ours. One would think it cannot take long anymore, but it is nearly impossible to form a picture about when and how. The whole thing looks so nebulous. One blow after another fell so suddenly and unexpectedly that I suspect there is a secret behind them. Maybe time will clarify this for us. Here it is now relatively quiet. The troop that made the area so uncomfortable lately has orders, according to a man who came from Austin, to keep quiet and stay at their camp in San Marcos for now. The Seguin reserve recently made raids on the Santa Clara and Cibolo.[20] They caught several, among others a Schlather. Four deserters, among them two named Trebess, wanted to free him but when it got to that point, three ran away. The fourth, the younger Trebess, did not, however, and for that he got a shot in the forehead, which killed him. At his funeral twenty mounted deserters appeared at the cemetery, and are said to have had the intention too of seizing the other arrested men from the Seguiners; but on reconsidering, they decided not to do that, which was quite good; we could have gotten into a very distorted position very easily that way.[21] All in all, people are very daring now; they drive away horses and steal them along the Santa Clara by the bright light of day, etc. As if that were not enough, the New Braunfels reserve brought in five American deserters, who should have been delivered up in San Antonio but were taken away from them there again. I do not know if peace will put an end to all this for us, or whether it won't be as when a predatory animal is shot: the last convulsions are the most dangerous. We are not thinking about that as profoundly now as we are about the general joy at getting to see you again without having to begin counting from the first day you arrive how long it will be before you must leave again. When one has great worries, one feels only slightly the pressure of the small ones. But there is no shortage of the latter either. A couple of days ago Ernst [Meusebach] ran after the oxen to drive them home, and what does he do but stumble, fall on a rock, and break his collarbone, a rather painless, not very dangerous, but very annoying case for our good Ernst, who is a very good lad and has been helping me like an adult.[22] So Otto [his brother] came and substituted for him. Yesterday we chopped weeds among the imphee all day, which is full of grass. He worked very hard, could not be restrained, got sick in the evening, and is still not well. He overworked. All in all, the Meusebach boys are now quite well behaved and give *promise* of becoming not merely very strong but also quite industrious men. Joseph [the youngest Coreth son] does not work himself sick, but he is a good fellow too, for whom I have no fears. In the fields things are going so-so. The wheat in the entire region has been ruined by rust, but the rye, like the barley, is still good. We have corn of various sizes; whether there will be enough rain is questionable. I could not work in the bottom land this year; we will notice that in terms of fodder, just as on the big fence, on which no work has been done yet, and the field is naturally full of strange cattle, which we run off from time to time, of course. For now it doesn't matter yet; I will try to repair it in the summer. But before that time we will have to surmount many another hindrance from the elements, e.g. the Confiscation Law or the Loyalty Oath. Things seem to be going badly for poor Maximilian in Mexico. The pope played a trick on him, since he placed the wildest requirements on the clergy, and now the fall of the Confederacy [to which he was sympathetic, and it to him] too! The newspaper says that many Northerners released from service are going to Mexico and are putting themselves in a position of being placed at the disposal of the Liberalist recruiters.[23] I got a letter from Münzenberger recently. He is in Camargo in a rather bad position. He had losses when he departed from Texas. He had hoped to recoup or make them good through speculation that his brother involved him in. He lost not only what he had but also has debts for his trading house that he has to pay to creditors, who, by the way, are said not to be cruel ones.[24] Then too, I hear among other things, that the two Bremers [brothers-in-law of Anton Elsner] are said to be have been hiding here for quite some time. On Jakob Creek there are said to be a couple of camps of organized deserters that have been lying low up to now. Only people say that they have offered to attack the troops, if the latter were to bother the town again. Burn this letter when you have read it. It could perhaps get into the wrong hands. From Hedwig and young Karl we have good reports, but I think I have already written you since she last wrote, which was a letter to Mother. Adieux, dear Rudolf, for today. When you write give us news of how the rash is coming along. We are still itching quite a bit. From Meusebach Agnes gets lots of letters, and most of what she needs, money too. He himself, though, is in Fredericksburg. The store people are said to be having losses, because cotton prices are dropping very fast, they say two bits and 15¢ a yard. We have gotten unused to buying; it is a bad and boring habit anyway. Write us very soon, if you can; or better still, come yourself. Give our regards to Kämmerling. Mother, your sisters and brothers, and I embrace you in spirit. Your old friend and father E. Coreth. The telegraph poles are being set between here and San Antonio.

The telegraph did not come in time to speed up communications about the end of the war to isolated areas. Officially the war had ended on 26 April, but the last fighting of the war did not come until 12-14 May, when Confederate troops in the Brownsville area, unaware that the war had long since been concluded and their cause declared lost, won a battle over baffled Union soldiers. While Ernst Coreth sat writing his son about the happenings at home and abroad, Rudolf was writing the last complete and preserved letter he sent from camp.

Camp near Richmond
19 May 1865
Rudolf to family

I got Father's letter of the fourteenth yesterday. . . . My presence here does not bring any positive results, because our cause is as good as lost; but the time has not yet come when the army will dissolve, and if a man were to leave now, he would do himself and his relatives harm. It is horrifying that such great sacrifices have been made in the firm belief that something would be attained, and that it is now clear everything was in vain. Here among the soldiers a great embitterment against the generals and speculators prevails. Christian Pantermühl, who was in the hospital in Houston for several weeks and returned, said that Magruder had cannons set up in the streets of Houston to prevent the infantry from attacking and plundering the city. Other people also brought back the same report. Several regiments broke up and went home, and of those that still remain, 99 out of 100 men say that they are staying here only in order to be able to go home openly. Now the officers and rich civilians are trying to revive the troops' good morale again. The former give enthusiastic orations and the others take up collections for the benefit of the soldiers, but nothing has any effect anymore. The men know that will last only as long as the people are afraid. If I thought that there were still hope for us, I would be glad to hold out still longer in order to be paid for our sacrifice in lives and lost time. But I am of the firm conviction that everything is over. The citizenry of Texas has neither the means nor the will to defend itself longer, and all who know the conditions and contend that it is otherwise are speaking against their conviction. The money and the clothes you sent to my by Froboese I have not yet received, and I do not know either how Froboese can get them to me. We are encamped ten miles from Richmond, and there is no regular connection between here and there. If only Froboese has not turned over the things to a stranger, who will keep them for himself. There is a frightful lot of stealing now. In recent months more little things have been stolen from me than in all the previous time put together. I still have my two horses and don't intend to sell either one. I think I shall soon be able to make good use of them when I ride them alternately on the way home, and up to then they don't cause me any inconvenience. I collect corn for both and have no further trouble with them except to feed them. I was away from the camp the last three days. Kämmerling and I and two others went on Lt. Bitter's orders on a scouting expedition to San Felipe. We had quite a pleasant time doing it. We did not find any deserters and didn't make any effort to find any either. Our only efforts were expended toward having a pleasant time, and we achieved that. We were received quite cordially in a couple of houses, had good grass and as much corn for the horses as they wanted to eat. The blackberries are beginning to ripen and we found several quite good places, and almost everybody told us about joyful news. Some even claim to know that Kirby Smith has already surrendered the Trans-Mississippi

Department. The immediate future will be a very eventful time. In two weeks we will know what our top men intend doing, because the period during which they must reach a decision will be over in about nine or ten days; and should their decision not be in accord with the one generally held, the soldiers will find an opportunity to show what they want, because if such bad times are coming, it is better that they should come soon, for they are bound to come. Adio for now, in the hope of an imminent reunion with you, I am as ever your Rudolf.

When Co. F received orders to march for home, Rudolf left his horse Jeff with Christian Pantermühl, who was sick. Not knowing for sure that he would ever see this friend or his horse again, Rudolf headed westward. On the last day of May 1865, the regiment returned to New Braunfels,[25] but not until 2 June did General Kirby Smith surrender the Trans-Mississippi Department at Galveston. At last the cruel war was over, and the survivors straggled home, or else fled the country.

Spears into Pruning Hooks

Between 1860 and 1880 the typical German farm in Texas changed in highly visible ways, though it remained distinctive in some respects well into the twentieth century. From the purely economic standpoint, the lot of the average German Texan who made his living from the land improved after the Civil War. Records show that in Texas the German farmer on average had only about half as much land as the average slaveless Anglo-American during the decade preceding the war and that, furthermore, of his acreage only one fifth was improved, substantially less than of the Anglo-American's land. In addition the German farmer raised less corn and owned decidedly less livestock, of which the total cash value was much lower. By 1870 the German equalled the Anglo-American in farm production; and when yet another decade had ended, the improved acreage and cash value of his farm had also closed the previously existing gap.[1]

In part, the early state of affairs can be explained by the German farmer's habit of thinking in smaller terms because of the tradition from which he stemmed. Even more important, however, were purely financial considerations over which he had had little control. If, like most European immigrants, he had come to Texas after its annexation as a state, he had arrived too late to have the advantage of being awarded free land. Having had to spend very much more to make the trip to Texas than his Anglo-American neighbor, he also had less capital left to invest on arrival. Consequently he had a smaller farm, less equipment, fewer head of livestock, and frequently for years had a large indebtedness, since often he had to buy whatever he did acquire on credit, a situation that caused a delay in the improvement of his condition. The fact that he ordinarily bought his land from a German who had settled earlier than he made even more prevalent the pattern of the German as "small yeoman," a distinctive sub-class. Very few immigrants who had claims to land in the Fisher-Miller grant ever moved there, the majority instead selling this acreage for extremely low prices.[2]

The German Texan had always had a greater variety of crops than the Anglo-American in the state, who tended to specialize. The German almost from the first experimented with various small grains, partly in the hope of having bread more to his liking than corn pone, a central feature of the Southerner's diet. By 1880 the Texas German farmer on average raised as much corn as did others, even though he still had fewer cattle and hogs. He had come to enjoy cornbread but preferred to cut the meal with an equal part of wheat flour and used leavening in contrast to the Southern American.[3]

Haymaking, traditional in Europe, persisted among the Germans, who from the earliest possible time fenced their farms, generally with cedar rails where they were available but, especially in the Hill Country where sheep were raised on a large scale, with rock, which gave the terrain a truly distinctive appearance, particularly in Kendall County in the vicinity of Sisterdale. The Anglo-American showed a distinct inclination to raise his cattle on the open range. The first U.S. patent for a wire fence is said to have been issued in 1853 to William H. Merriwether, who also became the foremost slave owner of Comal County. This material did not prove particularly satisfactory, and by the time that barbed wire came into general use in the 1880's, the average German farm in western Texas was twice as big as, more valuable and better stocked than, the average Anglo-American's of the area. The German had gradually followed the developing trend away from farming and toward cattle ranching, at which many sons of immigrants were to excel.[4]

Almost simultaneously with the beginning of the war there was a general adoption of dry-farming methods occasioned by the devastating drought that began in 1859. These methods, absolutely counter to the Germans' experience, involved changing when and how plowing, planting, and cultivating were conducted. As a result there was a growing need for implements adapted to the new technology of farming and a corresponding increase in the use of the horse as the primary draft animal. The Anglo-American had always preferred the horse, while the German had used oxen because they were traditional in Europe and, more importantly, more economical in Texas. Not only was the initial investment lower, but also the cost of maintenance was smaller. Also, as the German soon discovered, the ox was less attractive to thieves than the horse because it was too ponderous to be readily whisked away. In the course of the war, however, the army had been a factor in the decline of the ox-drawn plow by offering very high prices in order to keep the soldiers supplied with meat. Post bellum, there was in addition a demand at the slaughterhouses for tallow to sell to England, so that, though the German still predominantly plowed his Texas fields with oxen in 1870, he had begun to buy mules for that purpose and, as time passed, increasingly used the horse as the American farmer customarily did.[5]

As late as 1850, there were no slave owners among the German farmers living in Comal and Guadalupe Counties, and ten years later this condition still prevailed in Gillespie, Mason, and Llano Counties, though a small percentage of Anglo-American farmers in these areas had begun to own slaves. In New Braunfels cotton was first planted in 1852 by slaveless Germans. That same year Merriwether, a Tennessean, built the first local gin on the Comal River, where he also operated flour, grist, and saw mills, all of which enterprises became the property of Joseph Landa in 1860, by which time the average German was raising as much cotton as the slaveless Anglo-American in the state. During the post-war period cotton became the dominant crop. Clearly cotton production and slave ownership bore little relationship in German Texas.[6]

In ante-bellum days it had actually been cheaper to provide room and board plus wages for a German than to own a slave who did the same work. The German and the Irish laborers had been willing to handle jobs that the Anglo-American considered appropriate only to a slave, a circumstance that frequently placed all three ethnic groups in positions of very low regard. After the war, the rare German who hired himself out was the most sought after of cotton pickers, along with the usually more recently arrived Czech, because these were found to be more thorough and careful than the freed slave. Thus the wage of the European cotton picker was relatively high compared with that of the Negro, who sank to the bottom of the scale, and a German without capital could sometimes in this way accumulate cash that enabled him to move into the land-owning class at just the time that the break-up of plantations made acreage of superior agricultural quality more available. However, most German laborers worked on farms belonging to their own families, and as late as 1870 a traveler was dismayed to see women plowing and children working draft animals in the vicinity of New Braunfels.[7]

The Anglo-American had always shown a willingness to pick up and move his domicile when conditions became too trying. The German, on the other hand, was little inclined toward the nomadic life, and was, in fact, conspicuous for his stability as a landowner. To improve his lot he was more receptive to re-education than to migration, and, judging from what is known of such men as Ervendberg and Lindheimer, horticulture and scientific farming experiments had long been conducted by a few of the Texas Germans. The German, always ready to form clubs for the sponsorship of balls, singing contests, athletic demonstrations, and theatrical performances for the enrichment of settlement life, now increasingly organized for practical gain, forming societies that fostered the sharing of knowledge about farming and sometimes conducted competitions for the design and forging of implements with improved features.[8]

Though by and large a sedentary farmer, the German was well represented among the freighters and teamsters serving south-central and western Texas during this period, demonstrating that he had no innate aversion to travel and adventure. Traffic between the German communities of central and western Texas and both Mexico and the Gulf Coast was lively, as many a young man who had come to Texas as a child saw a way to earn money for land of his own by satisfying his fellow-Germans' demands for creature comforts the frontier could not provide. Some found it difficult to settle down immediately after returning from army service; some had formed contacts in their supply areas while escaping Confederate induction.

As trail drivers, too, the Germans were to become active travelers. Until 1867, when Anglo-Americans started driving their herds to Kansas markets, Louisiana had been the destination; but as the frontier forts were re-activated and civilization pressed westward after the war, increasing numbers of Germans turned from farming to ranching and joined the northbound cattle drives to the middle-western railheads. The trend extended into the New Braunfels area also, as the town found

itself on a feeder route that at Austin joined the famous Chisholm Trail.
Consequently the Texas German, who had not been missing among the
prospectors of the 1849 Gold Rush, now also became a cowboy and
occasionally even a cattle baron in the best Western tradition. No longer
was the rural Texas German almost synonymous with the small yeoman
as he had been during the early years of colonization.

After Rudolf Coreth's first relief at being safely back home subsided,
his wanderlust returned as persistently and predictably as had his ma-
larial attacks during the war. He watched his Old World father continue
to struggle with New World conditions and marveled that there were
any harvests worth the reaping in this region where the rain was seldom
gentle, but rather fell without mercy or not at all. The seasons during
which the depleted land had been forced to produce under the care of
the frail, the tired, and the immature had taken their toll, so that now
only constant and backbreaking labor could keep the farm from losing
ground both literally and figuratively.

Sometimes during that summer of 1865 Rudolf must have envied his
friend Alfred Kapp, despite his complaints. Times were bad in his part
of San Antonio, where he continued to struggle with his business simply
for want of knowing a better course to take. Things suited him far worse
than at any time during the Confederacy, Alfred said, and his brother
Wolfgang and their father were leaving for Germany in a few days. At
least he was to be spared responsibility for the family farm, he was
relieved to report, because one of the Kapp sons-in-law, Christoph Flach,
was moving with his household and family to Sisterdale (7 Sept. 1865).

By winter a more optimistic Alfred wrote again from San Antonio,
enclosing a business card that announced his association with Mr. B.
Mauermann in a shop for the repair of small machinery, arms, sewing
machines, locks and keys. Proclaimed in bold-faced type was the legend:
"Depot for Colt Pistols and Agency for Singer's celebrated Sewing Machines." Their "lay-out" (sic) was in a little frame house between Hummel's and Richter's on Main Street, where for the moment their business
would consist of repairing; but once their order from New York had
arrived later in the month, they expected to add a regular weapon shop.
Adolph Münzenberger, purchasing agent for the firm, was away at the
time (5 Jan. 1866).

If Rudolf felt that Alfred's and Münzenberger's lives in San Antonio
were more interesting than his own on the farm, another wartime comrade wrote from Indianola on the coast, where he was in the employ of
the Runge firm, expressing nostalgia for life in New Braunfels—a "most
inviting little town" (*"ein urgemüthliches Nest"*) where there still
seemed to be "no shortage of balls and like pleasures," in contrast to
Indianola where "hardly anything but business is given any thought."
In one respect the two communities were alike, however: "a store in
almost every building" (Indianola, 18 Jan. 1866, Rudolf from G. W.
Froboese).

Despite the fact that New Braunfels was now under the surveillance of the occupying federal troops, in most respects the town went forward much as it had before the war. If one may judge from a list of business establishments of the time, life had actually improved for the average citizen. The population was only about 2,000, but there were thirty-two retail stores. For so comparatively small a community, there were also an uncommon number of provisions for entertainment, including three dance halls, three billiard halls, two bowling alleys, and one dramatic club, not to mention eleven taverns, two confectioneries, three bakeries, and one hotel. Industries, not counting the many shops of artisans, included three cotton gins, two brick and lime kilns, a cotton cloth mill with twenty-one looms, five flour and grist mills, two saw mills, a window factory, a brewery, and a distillery. Even the 59th Illinois Regiment stationed there found the community attractive, and two of its members ultimately returned to marry local girls and settle there permanently.[9]

Apparently Ernst Coreth and Rudolf debated the merits of the life of a merchant or shopkeeper, for in correspondence of this period their attitudes are clearly not in accord. Early in 1866, when his brother-in-law Meusebach wanted to spend time in New Braunfels with his wife and children, Rudolf had seized the opportunity to take over the store in Fredericksburg temporarily. Somewhat indignantly, his father wrote that he could not imagine what had led his son to think that he, Ernst Coreth, might consider running a store, he who "would rather retreat with wife and brood into a mousehole and live from roots and herbs" (12 Feb. 1866). (Regrettably, there are no post-war letters from Rudolf.) Actually, Ernst Coreth, who is said to have been a man held in high regard by those who knew him and who appears to have been a man of many personal gifts, might have been far better suited to the life of a merchant than to that of a farmer. That he could not see himself in that role may have been the result of a prejudice he brought with him from the land of his ancestors, where certain lines of work were closed to the nobility.[10] Clearly, Meusebach had no such objections to "pushing grocery sacks," as one of Rudolf's friends called it (Boerne, Texas; 14 Sept. 1866, Rudolf from G. A. Toepperwein).

Meusebach's residency in and around New Braunfels was temporary, and as the years went by he was increasingly to spend his time near the frontier. For many other people, the Hill Country had begun to lose its appeal, partly because of still-remembered wartime clashes between neighbors, partly because of the continuing danger from Indians. After the war's conclusion, some families retreated to the safer life of larger towns and cities in the state. Ernst Altgelt, for one, set up law practice in San Antonio, though even there life was not as safe as he expected initially. A cholera epidemic raging in the city delayed the immediate transfer of his family to their new home.

Meanwhile, Meusebach was arranging to purchase the place Hermann and Lina Spiess were vacating at Waco Springs on the Guadalupe above New Braunfels. Like most of the liberal intellectuals who had come to Texas from German universities during the revolutionary period, Spiess was preparing to leave for a more congenial area in the North. He was, actually, very late in following the trend. The more radical Dr. Douai had made the move many years earlier and in years to come was to continue his career as a journalist of some importance in New York. A rare exception was Eduard Degener, father of two of the victims of the Nueces Massacre and once involved in the liberal Frankfurt convention of 1848, who during the Reconstruction played a prominent part in the politics of Texas.[11] With the most radical of the intellectuals either flushed out or greatly moderated during and after the war, the politics of German Texas became more orderly if less colorful.

Among the Germans leaving Texas at this period were some who had been steadfast during the war and now returned to their former homes as they had been unable to do for some years. A few of those going to Europe for a visit did not contemplate a return; others found their visits stretching out until no end was in view. Herman Kämmerling proved to be of the latter kind.

Having departed on 28 June 1866 for a visit to his homeland, Kämmerling soon wrote about the limited size of the farms and the bulk of his clothing ("weather like February in Texas"), before turning to the fact that the beer was "not half as expensive delivered as in Texas, and a big mug at least twice as big. Grand!" Lest the Coreths had not kept abreast of how Prussia was taking the lead in German affairs, he courteously begged the indulgence of his Austrian friend who was on this occasion too far away to challenge him, then at considerable length extolled the excellence of the Prussian field hospitals, quartermaster department, and clever strategy in the recent combat. "The Austrian military," he continued, "well-behaved and courageous throughout, was however led by such incompetent officers and was so poorly taken care of that at first each captive was screaming for bread." His highest accolades were saved for the Prussian general, Count Moltke, whose superior intellect had brought about the successes. He concluded that the Main would in the future form the Prussian border. "Baden, Bavaria, Württemberg, South Germany, and Austria are to stand alone and independent"[12] (Jastrow in West Prussia, 7 August 1866, Rudolf from Hermann Kämmerling). Kämmerling's pride in the growing might of his native Prussia was unmistakable, but his nostalgia for the climate and the spaciousness of Texas was probably also quite sincere.

On 20 May 1866, little Karl, eighteen-month-old son of Carl and Hedwig Coreth, died. Hedwig, her responsibilities in Texas now at an end, almost immediately prepared to accompany her sister Elsbeth and their mother to Europe. Her father, Dr. Kapp, who had left the preceding autumn to consult German physicians about his health and to enroll his young son Wolfgang in a higher school, now decided to remain abroad. As Alfred Kapp packed up what things the Coreths had left at Sisterdale in more sanguine days and sent them to Rudolf at New Braunfels so that, should an acceptable offer be made, the Kapp place might be the more quickly sold, he wrote to Rudolf (San Antonio, 28 July 1866) that he was sending to their owner the tools with which the Coreth brothers had shaped the components of the house Carl was constructing for his bride at the start of the war and had fashioned parts of the sixshooters during the critical summer of 1862.

That fall Hedwig sailed with her mother and youngest sister to Bremen, and Rudolf, on one of his frequent trips between New Braunfels and Fredericksburg, stopped at Sisterdale to plant some native cacti on her infants' graves (Düsseldorf, 31 Jan. 1867, Rudolf from Hedwig). On the face of it, this seems an odd selection, but to those who know the spectacular blossom and the purple fruit of the spiny plant, it is the ideal and perennial decoration for a place too isolated for tending.

Arnsberg
4 November 1866
Rudolf from Hedwig

Dear Rudolf!

. . . If we could only take a walk together just once, I would have a lot more to tell you. This afternoon I went with Father to the so-called Oak Woods, where it is very lovely. The region here is very charming anyway. The little town is completely enclosed by wooded hills, only it is already a bit too autumnal. We picked the last plums from the trees in my uncle's garden today, but I am beginning with the most recent rather than with the most distant experiences. . . .

On the second of the month my last letter to you left here. . . . On the afternoon of 19 October Elsbeth and I were in Central Park with the four Kapp children. We walked and so I could really see and admire all the beauty of the magnificent facility. Nature significantly enhanced art by means of hills, boulders, and water there. The next morning at 10 o'clock we left from the Kapps'. Elsbeth still had time to get a cake with fifteen candles for her birthday, which is on the twentieth. We drove to Hoboken and from there got on the *America,* where we met [Adolph] Münzenberger. Friedrich Kapp remained with us until the ship embarked at 1 o'clock.[13] Soon the land disappeared behind us. We had a cabin in the middle of the ship . . . and a window so small that it was almost completely dark. . . . Elsbeth became seasick . . . and Mother lay down too, so I was the only one who went to dinner with Mr. Münzenberger at 5 o'clock, but . . . the meals were a matter of indifference to me every day of the trip. But I often had headaches and terribly cold feet. The heat was not on yet, and for some days the ocean was so restless that one could not get warm by strolling. . . . The last day on the North Sea was terrible. . . . Our company aboard ship was not at all pleasant, but fortunately it was very small. In addition to fourteen sometimes very naughty children there were forty passengers, of whom more than half left the ship at Southampton. . . . I could not keep from thinking of Carl and little Karl among strangers who keep asking questions constantly. I couldn't sleep much, and when I did fall asleep I would dream of Carl. I was not at all inclined to make new acquaintances, but toward the end of the trip I got to know a young man who offered me his arm for strolling, a wealthy farmer from Virginia, a native of Bremen, who was in the Southern army and is committed body and soul to our cause [?]. I enjoyed hearing him talk. Like so many he sacrificed his health to the war. On shipboard there was also a brother of [Charles] Dambmann. . . . In Bremen we went to the Ratskeller. . . . A little drop of wine from the barrels called "The Apostles" was worth 36.563 talers ten years go. 1,000 Troy drops go into a glass. In Bremen there is a magnificent statue of Gustav Adolph, which sank on the way to Sweden. The Bremen merchants had it brought up out of the ocean by skippers from Helgoland and set it up in their city for 12,000 talers. Even Bremen pleases me ten times better than any American city. We had to leave Bremen before six in the morning. Father immediately gave me Carl's watch, which works excellently, but the watchmaker who put it in good shape said he could just as easily have made a new one—

5 November [continued]

On the way here we came through several little hamlets, through Minden and the Porta Westphalica too, then through Hamm, where Mother lived; and in Soest, where Mother's father came from, we had to wait two hours in order to go from there by post-coach to Arnsberg. In Soest Wolfgang came to join us and accompanied us here. Tomorrow he will go back to Bochum. The traces of pockmarks are still visible on him, and I doubt they will ever disappear entirely. Nevertheless in my eyes he is a handsome young man. All in all he has changed little and is tired of being here. What he would like best is to leave here right away. Just think, our Wilhelm came in a charcoal brown suit to my uncle's to fetch money.[14] He aroused general amusement and attracted attention. Uncle had him dressed decently and cleaned up right away and then had him photographed. Since then he writes the most priceless letters, alternately to Father, Wolf, and Uncle Lücken. He tells in them repeatedly of his intentions toward a widow of forty-two, "naturally beautiful and of sweet temperament, with 500 talers and a little beer-and-brandy shop." . . . This afternoon we took a lovely stroll to a coffeehouse called the Potter's Hut. We saw in the *San Antonio Herald,* the only copy of it which is sent to Europe, that the cholera outbreak there is past. My worries about you all are not half over just the same. . . . My parents and brother and sister send their best regards. Father's health leaves a lot to be desired. Wolf contends that he himself is quite well here; I myself can unfortunately never eat as much as my uncle and aunt would like me to. People eat more here than in Texas. Farewell, and think sometimes of your loving sister-in-law Hedwig Coreth.

As Hedwig's letter was crossing the Atlantic, her brother Alfred wrote Rudolf a note from San Antonio, from which one may infer that Rudolf wished to sell what he had once designated as his entire estate, his horses, presumably the faithful Jeff and Ben.

Hedwig Coreth, née Kapp

San Antonio
13 November 1866
Rudolf from Alfred Kapp

As you have seen from newspaper notices, P. Murphy, Contractor, is now buying horses for the government, pays rather poorly, and most of the horses that have been offered are too fat or too thin, too small or too large, too old or too young, etc. It seems to me that they are looking for horses like your two, and I think that you would get $60 or $65 a piece. But you can demand more, because he bargains. Gachos and U.S. are not accepted.[15] I am going to Sisterdale again today. With best wishes and regards to you and yours, Your Alfred Kapp.

That Rudolf kept this note indicates that it had a deeper meaning for him, since in disposing of his horses he cut himself loose from one of the most tangible reminders of the war. He did this, no doubt, because he was preparing to take over for Meusebach in the store on a more permanent basis, since the latter was moving his family to New Braunfels. Meanwhile, Ernst Coreth also looked to the future.

New Braunfels
3 February [apparently 1867]
Rudolf from father

. . . The railroad affair gives considerable food for thought, e.g. that the
entrepreneurs don't have any choice about where to lay the track, if they
want it at all. The Guadalupe bottom ["Guadup Botton"] is the only
terrain [that is usable] from Gonzales to [New] Braunfels, and from
there the valley of the Comal Creek. In this [valley] it has to go through
on our side, at our place between the house and pond. That would make
our land here as well as in town worth doubly as much. Our farm provides
six good residential lots. . . . The County Road can be re-routed too in
Rückle's alley, then along the railroad till it leaves our land, by which
means our backland would get a much better division. I hear the wheel
of fortune spinning noisily in the distance already. Adieux, dear Rudolf.
Save us a warm little spot in your heart!

What, Rudolf probably wondered, would become of his father's pre-
cious privacy if these dreams about the railroad were to come to pass?
He need not have worried because more than ten years went by as the
International and Great Northern track crept up slowly on New Braunfels. Much later still, the Missouri-Kansas-Texas track was laid on the
opposite, or palisades, side of Comal Creek, so that, before the turn of
the century, the farm was hemmed in by the creek and one track to the
southeast and the old road and another track to the northwest, where
once Ernst Coreth had helped to hew a path through the wilderness.

⭐ Swords into Plowshares

The pleasures of peace-time existence were returning when, minding the store in the Hill Country, Rudolf received a letter at carnival time from his fifteen-year-old sister, along with a handful of tokens, possibly intended as a Valentine greeting and certainly conveying the affection in which the members of the family held one another.

New Braunfels
Thursday, 14 February 1867
Rudolf from Anna

Dear Rudolf:

You wish to know for what you can use the things, so I want to tell you. The foot, when your two are tired, so that you can brace yourself with a third, the way Fritz Vogt [a neighbor] uses his cane. The marble, when you and Meusebach are alone at night, so that you two have something to play with. The nut and the sugar I sent so that you won't get too thin. The button, for when one is missing from your trousers. The match, so you won't start any fireworks.[1] The feathers for cleaning your pipe. The bird for joy. The red beads as jewels for when you go to the ball. And the blue ring for eternal love. And the whistle because you don't have the violin just now. It was I who wrote the freight letter, and the invoice too. We are getting new hats; I hope they will be really pretty. On 2 March there is to be a theater performance and a dance, and I wish very much you might be here so that we could go there; nothing will come of it this way.

> The fun is now ended
> And I'm empty-handed.

Your loving sister. Anna Coreth.
Extend my best regards to my dear brother-in-law.

Ernst Coreth was obviously pleased to be able to provide simple delights for his remaining children and was himself attempting to recapture his former tranquility of spirit with reading, now that books and journals were more readily available again. But the pain of the family's losses, so carefully restrained in the existing letters, may be showing through as he ironically uses a standard German expression usually reserved for war memorials when he writes of his sacrifice of cash for the purchase of his daughters' finery.

New Braunfels
17 February 1867
Rudolf from father

. . . In our house there was great joy yesterday. The three new hats with
vines and flowers arrived. I do not know whether you know the story of
their life. A Mexican wagon train brought cotton frames for $10. I put
these $10 as a sacrifice on the altar of the fatherland. Mrs. [Rudolph]
Wipprecht took over the official duty of high priestess and bought the
said three hats shaped like Sancho Panza's barber bowl. They turned
out to be completely satisfactory, and one cannot see the true joy they
give without sharing in it. Mother is in good condition, bodily and spir-
itually, so too Amalia. Franz is studying really industriously. His teacher
is an old pedant, but for young Americans a bit of pedantry is not at all
a disadvantage. It is a little bridge into a wider extra-familial society.
Two of them are Europeans, Mr. Gies[s]en, Mr. Frikenhaus, a nephew
of Bechem, who wants to become an agricultural economist, and then
there are Lawrenz and [Julius?] Stein. It seems to me that things are
going quite respectably. Marie and Anna are in good spirits, Jos[ef] and
Ot[t]il[i]e quite all right also. The former has made quite a good pair of
shoes. One could not get better, nor even as good ones, from the shoemaker. All send you and Meusebach their most cordial greetings through
me. . . . Mother was in town for a couple of hours at Mrs. [Louise]
Benner's and her daughter's.[2] She [the daughter, Mrs. Edgar Schramm]
is recovering from her premature delivery quite well. Edgar Schramm
has been elected to the petty jury; he could easily have declined, since
he is the only man in the business, but he didn't, in order to be useful
to us perhaps. I am happy about his *bonhommie.* Two weeks from tomorrow the court convenes. . . . My reading is going very slowly. I have
very little time. I am beginning the third volume of *Pendennis.* I read
in the *Gartenlaube* from time to time. . . . What I saw in the [*New
York*] *Journal* I will still recount to you conscientiously. We are living
in an interesting era of technology. In Hamburg a man has invented an
artificial coal for the purpose of filtering. It is also suited for a thousand
other things, among others for pipes such as Philistines smoke, but also
for the preservation of meat, etc. Farewell, dear Rudolf. Have Faith,
Hope, and Love, even if not in the Catholic sense, but in that spirit
which is the result of your noble nature. Your old friend, E. Coreth*.

Rudolf was indeed at this time losing faith "in the Catholic sense,"
and in later years had little to do with his ancestral church. As pertains
to hope and love, the picture is somewhat more obscure at this period.
He was, it would seem, profoundly worried about his father, who, much
aged by the tragedies of the last years, was more inclined than ever to
chase will-o'-the-wisps that he felt might lead to added financial security
for his family or to intellectual stimulation for himself. Invariably, these
chimeras seemed to lead him to the conclusion that, for him at least, the
path to those goals was no longer clearly marked. Once, hearing that

Carl Gehren's brother had arrived, apparently from Germany, with fabulous accounts of what was being accomplished abroad in the world of chemistry, the old man had set about studying science books and even had had some materials sent him from Kalteyer's in San Antonio so that he might make simple experiments himself. For a while, his letters told excitedly of his having "discovered" certain chemical laws, and he was half serious when he chastised Franz—"What a Beotian!"—for showing little interest because he could see no immediate profits resulting from his father's activities[3] (Ernst to Rudolf, 12 Feb. and 15 Mar. [1867/68]).

Though Ernst Coreth did not pursue community involvement, he was soon to find that affairs nevertheless intruded themselves upon his life from the outside. Heretofore, the cold, deep pond called *"der Teich"* ("the dike") had simply been the place where the boys fished for black bass and swam and where all the family gathered the delicious watercress encircling the spring. Coreth and his remaining sons, especially Franz, however, had raised an embankment around the pond, making possible sufficient water storage during rainy spells so that some nearby fields could be irrigated during droughts. But in so doing, they disturbed the conditions desired by their neighbors, the Tolles, who operated a mill and a tannery downstream. Not long before the war, settlers living downstream from three Germans farming in the Fredericksburg area had instigated a restraining order when the farmers had attempted to irrigate with water they diverted from a creek.[4] What had seemed a solution to dry conditions there had created a legal problem that the Coreths were now to encounter at close range, as the Tolles brought suit against the Coreths. The progress of the suit from the local to the state level occupied both families for many months to come.

Life at the Coreths did not stand still while the case was hanging fire. The family played English canons for which Hedwig had sent the scores from Germany (Hedwig to Rudolf from Düsseldorf, 31 Jan. 1867), and sometimes Mrs. Wipprecht (Hedwig's sister) and Agnes Coreth would play *longuinne* (Ernst Coreth to Rudolf, 3 Feb. 1867; perhaps the card game called Patience). The Wipprechts were spending much of their time in New Braunfels at this period, since Mrs. Wipprecht was in delicate health and Dr. Wipprecht, who hoped to resume a professional life, was making plans to establish a school for boys. The Wipprecht farm, obviously not the ideal location for such an endeavor, was changing hands, like many another Sisterdale property.

New Braunfels
28 March 1867
Rudolf from father

Dear Rudolf: Franz brought us the pleasant assurance that you are getting along well. We are fine and working industriously. We have letters from Nany [Agnes Coreth's sister] . . . another from Sister Tony [Antonie, Ernst's sister]. She is well. The same old refrain: she would like to get a couple of girls into her hands [novices for the convent], whom

Meusebach should take along to Europe. I shall write her an answer of which you know the [negative] nature in advance. Another from Dr. Herff with a portrait of Ervendberg, who is Resident Minister of the Grand Duke of Hesse-Darmstadt in Paris, with a stipend of 30,000 francs.[5] Another from Hedwig, which includes nothing new, or I would send it on to you. *News from the town:* The day before yesterday the wool factory was incorporated. [Dr.] Koester sold for $9,000. He retains the apparatus for the furnace and the machinery.[6] [Wm.] Clemens has returned [from Germany] and the Tipses have bought the property of [their brother-in-law] Staehely. I had to assess my internal revenue tax [*"mein* Internal Revenue *assessen"*], but nothing had to be paid. Mr. Hetten, the assessor, is the bookkeeper at the new factory. . . . Bunsen has purchased the place in Sisterdale and Wipprecht will move off it in June.[7] I think now you have had quite a *dosis novitate* [Gr. and L. = "dose of news"]. Yesterday evening we had a marvelous rain. The creek is flowing hard but not causing any flooding. I think the rain did not come too late; in any case it did the grass a lot of good. The horse-pen has been cleared now, and the bushes burned, which was achieved in a six-hour-long afternoon with the help of Otto and Max [Meusebach]. Also one day we dug up stones, but we would need to do that for another week or four days more, and even then it would not be nice. So adieux, old friend. In anticipation of good news of you, as ever your old friend E. Coreth*.

New Braunfels
Sunday, 12 May 1867
Rudolf from father

Dear Rudolf. We got your letter and hope you have already washed off your Black Peter face and are as handsome as usual.[8] Everybody is well at home. Very little that is new this time, I think. Yesterday there was a railroad meeting in town. I was not there, because I preferred watering the [sweet] potatoes at home, and found out in plenty of time what was decided anyway. After much manipulating back and forth the purchase of Waco Springs was signed yesterday. Meusebach gave $4,000. It is a very lucrative business. There is 50 or perhaps 100% certain profit in it. Meusebach will write or tell you the details. Franz gets $15 a month as a sort of overseer for him, has to round up the cattle, and watch over the woods and the two Negroes, who lease there and are very respectable. . . . [Joseph] Landa is said to have sold out for $100,000 to a concern from the North and is to get $75,000 and keep $25,000 in stock in the business.[9] He dug a ditch in the cotton field behind the Mexican houses and can irrigate two acres of his field behind the blacksmith's with it. . . . Our corn is among the best in the area, not bad at all, on the whole. The field under the pecan trees we have let lie fallow and will plant it with cotton and a bit of corn this coming week.[10] The roses in the garden are blooming very nicely. . . . Spiess has written a book, and Meusebach has a printed copy. The title is *Das Ziel der Menschheit* [*The Goal of*

Mankind]. The point of it is supposed to be freedom and equality. There is no equality in Nature between two leaves, thus not between two human beings either. The same rights are based upon the same duties, consequently I think that there cannot be equal rights; and as far as freedom is concerned, there is no freedom anywhere in Nature, but rather only the necessary following of laws—chemical, physical, mechanical, logical freedom would thus be the negation of all these [laws]. Fate's irrationality enjoyed by means of what Meusebach calls melancholy [*"Wehmuth"*] is virtue [*"Tugend"*] and perception [*"Begriff"*]. I think that would be the appropriate motto. Now, dear friend, I am quite emptied out, and therefore don't know anymore what to write you except my best wishes for your welfare and that I remain your loyal friend E. C.

New Braunfels
8 and 9 June 1867
Rudolf from father

Dear Rudolf: Yesterday we got your dear letter with the news that you are well; we are all well and have not had time up to now to be sick either. The main jobs are finished too. The corn has been plowed and thinned; it is just developing tassels. Many people contend that our corn is among the nicest. Sugar barley, imphee and the black kind [of sorghum] are ready. The cotton likewise, except for the part under the pecan trees, which still needs cultivating. Half the [sweet] potato land is also set; the other half still has to be planted and staked, which Franz will do for me though. Franz is in Waco Springs five days a week, two with us. Agnes is in Waco Springs during the week too, as is Meusebach. Here, for the moment, are Amalia [Coreth] and Emma with Lucie [little Meusebach girls], and alternately a couple of children, until the masons will have made the house at Waco [Springs] livable. They have two Negroes up there. The association with them suits me quite well, and I would be much inclined to make a similar arrangement for next autumn, if I could find a couple of suitable individuals. They could quickly build themselves a log cabin at an appropriate place, e.g. in the pass, but it is very questionable whether one can find such people. *Vedremo,* says the blind man. That would be the means of keeping the farm for another three years, which I expect will have a mighty influence upon the price of the farms; and if we would make $6,000 from it now, we could aim at $9,000, that is to say with an expenditure of $1,000 for $3,000, through which a profit of 200% could be achieved, one which would fall to the advantage of the family. I know of nothing new to tell you. Your project for the holidays, I fear, will come to nothing because of the presence of Meusebach here. How much I would like to relieve you if I could! We are expecting several visits during the holidays; among others Dr. Bracht ["Pracht"] has announced himself.[11] He wants, I hear, to sell his house and move away. I cannot imagine to where. Hessler is putting up a store where Ferguson's tavern is located.[12] [Robt.] Bechem ["Böhem"] has moved into the house of the shoemaker [Heinrich] Voges. At Ludwig's in Wheeler's ["Whilers"] tavern things are very lively now. He has run the other places in town out of business. [Hermann] Kämmerling is said to have sent letters to Moureau and Koester and enclosed a portrait [photograph]. He is said to be thinking of returning again in the fall. . . . Tolle has asked the District Court for his bill (but has not paid it yet). [Hermann] Seele is said to see in this an indication he [Tolle] means to withdraw the charges. I only hear these things. I have not been in town since Easter. The rain damaged Tolle's dam very badly. . . . So Adio, dear old fellow, for today. Mother, your brothers and sisters, and I embrace you in spirit. . . . As always, your loyal friend and father E. Coreth*.

Shortly before the pony express ceased operating between Fredericksburg and New Braunfels (Ernst Coreth to Rudolf, 9 July 1867), Rudolf received news that during June the business that Adolph Münzenberger and Alfred Kapp operated together in San Antonio had been destroyed by fire. It was that summer also that the brother of the Coreths' former sovereign was executed by a firing squad at Querétaro. The death of Maximilian and the change in the political scene in Mexico resulting from that event were not unrelated to the futures of these Coreth friends, for soon Adolph Münzenberger established a stagecoach line between San Antonio and Monterrey with a partner, and Alfred Kapp transferred his business headquarters to Mexico for the brief remainder of his life. The stagecoach line was suspended after just two years, but Münzenberger continued to make Mexico his home thereafter.[13]

The changes in the Mexican regime brought about a general awareness that a confrontation between Napoleon III and Prussia was becoming inevitable, as a letter to Rudolf from Hermann Kämmerling suggested. "France keeps ordering 30,000 *chassepots* . . . from English and American factories, but keeps swearing the while *l'empire c'est la paix* [the (French) empire stands for peace]. . . . There was general sorrow about the fate of poor Max[imilian], even if people do say to themselves, what business did he have being there, and who gave him the right to have the captured Liberalists shot to death? The wife [Carlotta] insane and near her dissolution, the husband dead, and all this brought about through the greed of a bum such as this Louis [Napoleon] is. The French people are quite excited, and after the close of the big exposition, which at the moment is keeping all Paris busy, something might happen; indeed the French papers express quite openly that the death of Maximilian could easily become Louis's Moscow" (Jastrow in West Prussia, 9 July 1867). Kämmerling's impressions turned out to be quite accurate, for the close of the exposition signaled the acceleration of events that led to Germany's bringing about the collapse of the Second [French] Empire, soon followed by the unification of Germany under the Prussian aegis.

As always, Ernst Coreth was reading avidly that summer. The works he mentions late in the season are one Reichenbach's book on farm management, which Dr. Wipprecht had lent him, and a book that has become a part of many bibliographies dealing with the period, Friedrich Kapp's *Geschichte der Sklaverei in den Vereinigten Staaten (History of Slavery in the United States)*, that the family friend, Franz Moureau, had shared. The latter book Ernst Coreth found sufficiently interesting to give considerable space in a letter to Rudolf (18 Aug. 1867). The portions that most interested Ernst had to do with the inseparability of cause and effect and with the difference between the socio-political structures in Europe and America. Ernst Coreth preferred the American system because it was, in his (and Kapp's?) view, built on the importance of the individual, not upon the intervention of the state into every facet of life. He closes the letter somewhat cryptically with the words, "God outside the World. And Nature" (Ernst to Rudolf, 18 Aug. 1867). Friedrich Kapp, author of the book, returned to Germany in 1870 to stay and there became a Progressive legislator in the Reichstag of the new empire.

As Ernst Coreth was so much occupied with private pleasures and public problems, Agnes Coreth took responsibility for the pressing social needs of her girls by bridging the distance between the farm and the community, which might as well have been twenty, instead of two, miles away as far as her husband's involvement was concerned. When the time seemed to her to be proper, she and Franz took Amalia, Marie, and later sometimes Anna to Hartenstein's ballroom for entertainment (Franz Coreth to Rudolf, 16 Aug. 1867), or their friend Mrs. Moureau invited the ladies of the family to stay overnight and attend the theater that had resumed performances. Once the two older girls were fetched by their hostess but had to ride home on borrowed horses because rains had made the roads impassable for vehicles (Ernst Coreth to Rudolf, 16 June 1867). It was even more exciting to go to town than to have Mr. Wenzel come to the farm to play so the family might dance (Hedwig Coreth to Rudolf, 6 Jan. 1868), and the trips may have reawakened in the older members of the group some memories of the first winter they had spent in Texas, when their attendance at a ball given by Baron von Wedemeyer had filled some of the people of the town with eager anticipation.[14]

Fever raged through New Braunfels that summer of 1867, and in August the wind blew from the north almost constantly for three weeks, so rare an occurrence that Ernst Coreth commented upon it in several letters (e.g., 11 Aug. and 18 Aug. 1867). At Indianola, he had heard, the disease was a more deadly one, yellow fever, and carried away several Coreth acquaintances: Mrs. Runge's sister, Mrs. Pierce ("Pearce"), and her two children; Mrs. Iken; and one of the Frob(o)ese brothers.

The war was not forgotten, and the Reconstruction was much in the news. In his borrowed *New York Journal,* Ernst Coreth was shocked to read that, when Representative Stevens was explaining his Reconstruction Bill in the House of Representatives, Representative Eldridge proposed: 1) to set aside the First Amendment of the Constitution of the United States; and 2) to dissolve the Southern states! Some three weeks later he wrote: "I think the Negroes celebrated the second anniversary of their emancipation on Sunday. They appeared for a parade completely armed. A leading Negro from Comaltown [now part of New Braunfels] made a speech, in which he asked them not to go with the Loyal League, but rather to work hard and actively for themselves and on their own behalf. Then another Negro shot at him, and other Negroes chased him through Comaltown, where, however, his good horse succeeded in getting him away from his pursuers. . . . In *Frank Leslie's Illustrirte Zeitung* of 25 May 1867 there is a beautiful picture of the Paris Exposition.[15] Maybe somebody in Fredericksburg takes it. Try to see it; half of page 271 is the description of an electric gun, but I see I can cut it out without damaging the picture, so I am including it here. Adio" (Ernst to Rudolf, 25 Aug. 1867).

Economic matters occupied much of Ernst Coreth's attention that summer. His taxes amounted to $28 in silver, part of which he paid with the $5.00 he was given back when the jury decided, for the moment, that Tolle was loser in the matter of the Coreths' pond and as such had to pay the cost of the law suit. That August, Ernst Coreth posted the Houston land for $1.00 an acre but found no takers (25 Aug. 1867). Some years later he offered Rudolf the proceeds if he could sell it, even for a mere 50¢ an acre, in order that the latter might raise cash for a business venture (23 Dec. 1875). The Coreth children said in later years that their father had by then become philosophically opposed to holding land in excess of his family's needs and would not enlarge his farm even when he might have been able to do so.

At this juncture, Ernst Coreth found himself land poor but cannot have been entirely without funds because he had intended to bid for mules at an auction in New Braunfels following the break-up of Alfred Kapp's and Münzenberger's partnership. He was chagrinned that he had missed going as a result of mistakenly reasoning it would be called off because of rain. They sold at $19.50 currency a piece, though small and young, and, he thought, would soon bring a profit of $10-$12 each. "Ah well, it was not meant to be," he concluded, and returned to his reading. The letter ends on a happy note: "Mrs. Guinea Pig has three young; Ottil[i]e is in seventh heaven" (1 Sept. 1867).

In New Braunfels things were humming at the wool factory, where the machinist had arrived and the machines were being set up. The announced railroad meeting for the election of surveyors took place on 30 August, but two days later no contract had been signed. Groos and Bötsche (sic) wanted $2,400, and a Seguin surveyor wanted $2,100, but the prevailing preference seemed to be that the former do the job at the latter's price (Ernst Coreth to Rudolf, 1 Sept. 1867). In the end, the plans for the railroad were stalled for years to come insofar as New Braunfels was concerned. That summer, however, a bridge spanned the Comal. Meanwhile, Ernst Coreth, who had counted on the railroad to enhance the value of his New Braunfels property, saw the cotton in some fields grow quite black as it was eaten off by caterpillars and the corn become riddled with worms.

Once more Ernst Coreth's hopes were dashed as his 103 bushels of corn went for $.90 each, after deducting for the freight, while others sold theirs for $1.00 a bushel. Ernst Coreth was apparently coming to realize that, if profit were to be his motive in farming, as it had to be, he was not going about it in the right way. That fall, in an act that was a real departure for the family, he employed a helper. The hired hand, a Negro identified in the letters simply as Alan, proved even more efficient than Ernst Coreth had dared to hope.

New Braunfels
Sunday, 29 December [1867]
Rudolf from father

Your letter gave us great pleasure because of the news of your well-being. We all were well the entire [Christmas] time until Friday evening when Mother got sick . . . because of her great exertion, the usual effect of Christmas. . . . She was quite patient and thus encouraged us all to sympathize with her most warmly, which had the best effect. . . . The Christmas tree was very simple but cheerful. Josef had brought quite a nice cedarbush [juniper] and filled in a couple of thin spots very well with branches. On the second holiday [26 Dec.] Agnes came with the children and then everybody except me went to a circus that is said to have been very mediocre but gave a lot of pleasure to people who are unacquainted with such things. . . . A letter from Nany [Agnes's sister] arrived and brought pictures of the four Steinacher children, who are quite pretty. . . . The one of Cousin Hansell belongs to you and is enclosed. Quite a good-looking person; I see quite a resemblance to Franz. Hedwig was here for a visit with Mrs. Wipprecht and stayed over night. She sends regards to you. . . .

Sunday, 30 December [continued]

Barbaric norther with rain and snow. Mother is better but is still lying down. I am working with Alan and accumulating a supply of live oak that will protect us from the cold for a long time. Adieux, dear old fellow. Your mother, brothers and sisters, and I embrace you. Your old friend and father E. Coreth*.

Hedwig Kapp Coreth had returned to Texas for a visit and wrote Rudolf from New Braunfels on 6 January and 5 June, letters he received at Cold Spring in Mason County, later called Loyal Valley, where he seems to have been an advance guard for Meusebach, who ultimately established his family there in over-optimistic anticipation of the extension of the railroad to the area. From the changed tone of these letters, one senses clearly that Hedwig, though loquacious as ever, was consciously avoiding a tone of intimacy with her brother-in-law. The family on both sides has the impression that Rudolf wished to marry his widowed sister-in-law, of whom he had always been extremely fond, but that she, who never remarried throughout her long life, preferred the relationship to continue as it had always been. Her principal worry seems to have been her brother Alfred, who, she wrote, was in steadily deteriorating health while he insisted he was too busy to take care of himself.

For a time Dr. Wipprecht, his brother-in-law and a medical doctor, administered the Steinbacher cure. This consisted of his leaving off all liquids, particularly water, wine excepted, in order to lose ten pounds and ease his ailing foot. Alfred's illness was only one of Dr. Wipprecht's serious preoccupations, since his academy for boys was not succeeding as well as he had hoped. Wipprecht's ideas on pedagogy had to wait for their acceptance until later when he joined the faculty of Texas A&M College.[16] On at least one occasion Wipprecht took his twenty-five charges on a nature hike up the Guadalupe to spend the night in the open so that they might learn what books could not teach so effectively (Hedwig to Rudolf, from New Braunfels, 5 June 1868).

That spring had again brought illness to many. Josef recovered from "rheumatic fever" [poliomyelitis?], the same disease of which Dr. Koester's ten-year-old Annchen died (Ernst Coreth to Rudolf, June 1868). Ernst Meusebach was by then apprenticed to Mr. (Walter) Tips for $18 (a month?) with meals (Ernst Coreth to Rudolf, 1 Sept. 1867), but his brothers Otto and Max continued their lessons along with Ottilie and Josef Coreth under Ernst Coreth's direction. By June they had gone through twenty lessons in a text by Ollendosch, and soon all four could read German, though only Max, who his grandfather thought was making especially good progress, could write that language. They studied for six or seven days a week, also doing their other chores diligently, living very harmoniously together, the old man reported proudly. Meanwhile, Tony Meusebach, already a young lady, received instruction from Miss Jackerdal, one of the educated women tutoring young ladies of the town whose parents cared to pay the price. The little Meusebach girls stayed with their grandmother on the farm early that summer as their mother once more gave birth to twin girls (Ernst Coreth to Rudolf, 6 June 1868).

In the spring, Ernst Coreth had turned the low-lying patch by the creek into a rice field. He concentrated more heavily on the new vineyard, though his old reliable crop, sweet potatoes, was still being planted between the grapes and Neumann's fence. In these projects Alan proved invaluable. He was the first Negro with whom most of the family had ever had real contact, and Ernst Coreth was greatly impressed with the skill he showed in making 317 grape cuttings two feet long, based on his experience in planting a vineyard in Missouri. Characterized in the letters as "quite decent," "very respectable," and "a very good person," he is at last accorded the highest accolade of all when Ernst mentions him without any qualification simply as working alongside the family in the fields (Ernst Coreth to Rudolf; 15 March, 29 March, and 21 July 1868). Hedwig, on whom Alan made a good impression also, wrote of how he plowed, while Josef drove the oxen and the head of the family, with "the ladies," gathered up the sweet potatoes, which, though not large or very numerous, were of superior quality (6 Jan. 1868).

Turning from her report of the family to news of mutual friends, Hedwig tells of families who had spent the war years in Mexico. On one trip north, Alfred Kapp had brought back four Goldbeck children, the smallest a girl not yet two. Theodore Goldbeck, who had taken his family to Mexico because of his inability to support the Confederate cause in good conscience, was soon to return with at least one older child, but his wife, the former Bianca Nohl, remained in Mexico permanently after the divorce. Alice Nohl was in New Braunfels recovering from having nursed her father (Dr. Ludwig Nohl) and regretted not getting to talk to Rudolf before his return to Cold Spring. Miss Nohl hoped to take a trip to Germany the next year with Natalie Schenck and the Moureaus,[17] and she would like to take along all sorts of curios, things Rudolf might bring her from "up there in Indian territory: arrowheads, scalps, if not indeed a little Indian boy"! Miss Nohl seemed to think, Hedwig wrote ironically, that doing so would give Rudolf pleasure (5 June 1868).

The somewhat strained and flippant tone of these letters, the last in the preserved correspondence between Hedwig and Rudolf, tends to confirm that they may have had a misunderstanding. In any case, when Hedwig returned to her brothers in Mexico, it was Franz, and not Rudolf, Coreth who accompanied her on the Münzenberger-Santleben stagecoach.[18] Franz undoubtedly welcomed the opportunity for a prolonged visit with his friend Wolfgang Kapp, who later returned to Germany to live. The journey back from Mexico to Texas was so memorable for Franz that he committed the adventure to paper as a story entitled *"Eine Mondscheinnacht auf einer Hochebene in Mexico"* ("A Moonlight Night on a Plateau in Mexico"). With him, he brought back a wagonload of grapes (more logically grape cuttings), a fact that probably accounts for his inclusion among early teamsters of New Braunfels in a picture taken ceremoniously many years later, since it is thought that this was the only occasion on which he hauled freight for pay.[19]

As the 1860's drew to a close, several changes coalesced to influence Rudolf Coreth's decision to leave Texas, for a while at least. One was probably the fact that his father had long contemplated selling the farm, and the settlement of the Tolle case by the Supreme Court of Texas in October 1868 now made this seem possible. The decision in the case was precedent-setting and peculiarly Texan. Correth (sic), the defendant, was found to have been acting within his rights in using water for irrigation from a stream originating on his property, since he had not interfered with the stream's resuming its original channel before it entered plaintiff's (Tolle's) land. Citing as precedent the colonization law of Coahuila and Texas (1825) and legislative act of 10 February 1852 supporting the principles of Mexican law governing irrigation rights, the judge stressed that some western Texas land is essentially useless without irrigation. So different are conditions in Texas as compared with those in the northeastern United States, where the principle is, "The water runs and let it run," or, "Everyone has a right to have the advantage of a flow of water in his land without diminution or alteration," that he substituted in this case the dictum, "Water irrigates, and let it irrigate." He did not, however, pass judgment on the extent to which irrigation may tap a stream.[20]

Another factor which undoubtedly influenced Rudolf to consider leaving Texas was Meusebach's decision to take over the Loyal Valley business completely and expand his operations to include an extensive orchard. Had Meusebach needed an inducement to vacate Waco Springs, he found it in a tornado that destroyed his New Braunfels home on 12 September 1869, which, though it spared the family, killed Miss Jackerdal, daughter Tony's teacher (Hermann Kämmerling to Rudolf, 24 Feb. 1870). Meusebach's move to Loyal Valley left Rudolf unemployed for the moment, and certainly he was not needed at the parental farm now that his brothers Franz and Josef were both mature enough to help their father with the work there.

His friends Kapp and Münzenberger had long since left the country, and many another of his wartime companions had married. Hedwig's visits in Germany were gradually to become a permanent residency punctuated by rare trips to Texas, during only one of which, it is thought, they ever met again. Though Hermann Kämmerling continued to write occasionally even as late as 1881, it was not long before he informed Rudolf that his ailing father had dissuaded him from returning to Texas as he had hoped to do. Somewhat wistfully, after a recital of all the things that were going wrong in Prussia, he closed with the following words: "Countless times I give thanks to your old Papa, whom I so very much like to hear tell stories, since in the course of conversation every story became a scholarly lecture from which one was bound to learn something. Give my most cordial regards to all your relatives, also to Ottilie, who has probably become quite a young lady [she would soon be twelve] . . . and cherish in your good memories your loving friend" (Jastrow, 24 February 1870). Thereafter, his letters are increasingly full of vital statistics (his marriage, the birth of a son) and the sort of banalities (his business successes, his problems with weight) that one is forced to rely upon when reluctant to sever ties, while recognizing that a chapter of one's life has ended.

Ten years had passed since the North and the South had gone to war. Germany had unified at last—without Austria. In 1872, Ferdinand Lindheimer retired from journalism, and his erstwhile rival, Ferdinand Flake, died in New York.[21] As late as November 1873, the tone of a scorned inferior still underlay the editorial voice of Anselm Eiband, who had replaced Lindheimer at the *Zeitung,* as he wrote of the attempts of Democratic candidates for state office to woo the German voter with sweet overtures, only to snub "the German friend" when the election was won. Eiband's intent was evidently to prod his readership into being more analytical and voting with more enlightened self-interest.

Late the next spring, the press of the state took notice of the twentieth anniversary of the San Antonio convention that had divided the antebellum Texas Germans while attempting to make them politically more aware. Responding to hints in both the (Austin) *Statesman* and the (San Antonio) *Freie Presse* that a "German party" was in the making, Eiband described what he saw as the proper position for the contemporary German Texan in politics. It was ridiculous, he wrote, to say that those opposed to a specifically German party were simply cowardly toward Americans. "We well know that those who last did this assembling had selfish motives, but the *Freie Presse* is wrong to insinuate one who is against such is neither worthy to be called a free man nor has influence on his fellowman. The call should go out to all to enter into the discussion [of politics], not just Germans. One should talk of conditions in the state, immigration, temperance laws, in short of eveything that can contribute to the advantage and welfare of the state. If our American fellow-citizens do not participate then it is their own fault, and we are relieved of all responsibility toward them."[22]

Some of the self-confidence the German national had gained through victory in the Franco-Prussian War and the subsequent very tardy unification of his homeland had rubbed off on the German Texan without reducing his dedication to the land in which he had invested his future. Twenty-five years after the revolutions of 1848, the assimilation of the German immigrant into the public affairs of Texas was obviously well underway.

In 1870, the Coreth farm attained as high a cash value as it ever had during the lifetimes of Ernst and Agnes Coreth. This was also its highest cash value in relation to other farms in the county.[23] For whatever reason, the old people remained on the farm to the end. Not so Rudolf. That year, gathering together the pitiful residue of what he had accumulated during four years of bitter war and five years of meager peace, he set out, not for the tropics of the south, his wartime fantasy, but for the foundries of the North.

Epilog

Around 1870 many a young Texan was applying his efforts to the design of improved farm implements, sometimes with the encouragement of prizes offered by societies that had been formed among German landowners for the purpose of agricultural advancement.[1] Rudolf Coreth's background in farming and his wartime experience as a blacksmith prepared him admirably for implement design, and it was with the hope of marketing his new plow that he first set out for the North. Since the aspiration did not meet with immediate fulfillment, he spent six months of 1871 working for the Galveston City Railway, but apparently declined an invitation from that company to become its superintendent in 1874.[2]

During most of the 1870's Rudolf, or Rudolph, as it was now spelled, spent much time as Texas agent for both the South Bend (Indiana) Iron Works and for the Pump and Skein Co. of Belleville, Illinois. Thus, he became one of the managers of implement branch houses in Dallas, a group to whom Stanley Walker, a well-known journalist and Dallas historian, assigns the leading role in the development of Dallas as a major commercial center.[3] It was in Belleville, however, that he made his first attempt to put down permanent roots once more. In the fall of 1873 he joined a Masonic lodge there, and though he demitted after ten years, he never withdrew officially. It was also in about 1873 that the South Bend firm extended his territory to include Louisiana, so that for twelve years, until he became Mexico agent, he traveled in a commercial capacity the very territory he had traversed during the war.

In January 1875 at West Belleville, Rudolph joined Henry Lippert and the younger George Bunsen (George C. Bunsen, to distinguish him from his educator father) in an already existing business, now renamed Coreth, Lippert, and Bunsen, for the manufacture of Rudolph's "Texas Dumping Plow," originally patented in 1873 and repeatedly improved. That April a silent partner, John Brandenburger, was added. Though not a spectacular success, the firm succeeded brilliantly in comparison with the disastrous marriage Rudolph contracted in 1876. On 7 May 1877, a child was born to Rudolph Coreth's wife, ironically, considering how much the family had always made of birthdays, on the very day the ostensible father became thirty-nine years old. Exactly when he suffered the first agonizing and humiliating awareness that he had married a woman pregnant with another man's child is not known, but it led to a divorce a few months later, and he never remarried.[4]

Rudolph's territory changed several more times, so that before retiring to New Braunfels in December 1890, he was acquainted at first hand with Brazil, Argentina, Chile, and Peru, and had been to Mexico countless times. While living on the family farm, he served one term as county commissioner. During this period, he also became even more than before a surrogate grandfather to the three sons of his sister Ottilie and her husband, Hermann Altgelt, whose father Ernst Coreth had retained as his attorney when the Tolle suit went to the Supreme Court. Rudolph had persuaded the young Altgelt family to occupy his house almost as soon as he had bought the farm, and there the couple remained until 1925, when the place ceased to belong to any of the family. All three Altgelt brothers followed their uncle into the implement business, two remaining designers for their entire active lives.

The Coreth farm house in the 1890's

Devoted to music, books, and good cooking, Rudolph and Ottilie spent happy hours together trying to duplicate the unusual dishes he had sampled on the pampas, in some exotic hotel, or aboard ship. A frequent visitor from town was their sister Marie, who never married. To all the family, Rudolph represented a window looking out from their relatively circumscribed lives in a time when "exotic" and "gourmet" had not entered the average Texas vocabulary. He guided young visitors around the farm where he himself had romped as a boy, while holding mock-serious conversations with his devoted German shepherd, Kuhli, whose specialty was a game akin to drop-the-handkerchief.

No one seems to recall what induced Rudolph to travel again for the South Bend Iron Works between 1898 and 1900, but during those years he returned to Mexico, South America, and Cuba, went for the first time to Sweden and Russia, and made several trips to Germany. For each of these trips, he prepared intensively and thus became an accomplished polyglot. Though in the Belleville days he had learned phonography, an early-day shorthand, and may have kept journals of the trips, none of consequence have come to light.

During one of his longer intervals at home in New Braunfels, Rudolph became sick and so set out again, this time to consult doctors and to see his childhood home once more. He died at Vienna on 17 October 1901 and was buried in the Zentralkirchhof. The Coreths in America did not

Rudolph Coreth, taken in 1880's

realize one must pay a periodic fee to retain claim to a grave in many European cemeteries. Consequently, after World War II some of the Texas relatives discovered that his final resting place had become the grave of a stranger. Thus, the third of the Coreth brothers who wore the Confederate uniform lies in an unidentified grave, as do the other two. Unlike Carl and Johann, however, he lies in the Land of the Double Eagle, not in the Lone Star State.

Barely reconciled to the loss of two of his sons in the war, Ernst Coreth had never really recovered from the death of yet a third child within a decade. Amalia, wife of a German-born physician, Edmund Goldmann, died at Galveston in 1873 while trying to give birth to her first child.She lies buried in the old City (Episcopal) Cemetery between two family friends, both named Henry Runge.

After a tornado unroofed the Coreth home on 26 January 1879, destroying or mutilating many of the contents, including Ernst Coreth's valued books, the old man's health was irreparably damaged by a series of strokes that made his late letters almost illegible, though entirely coherent. Just the preceding summer (7 Aug. 1878), he had written Rudolph, "I have never been so *argent court* ["short of funds"] as I am now." On 10 July 1881 he died. The issue of the *Neu-Braunfelser Zeitung* carrying his obituary also notes that on the very same date the three bells in the tower of Ss. Peter & Paul's were dedicated. Meanwhile, the International and Great Northern Railroad had been providing service to San Antonio for five months.[5] The pealing of the new bells of the church from which he had become estranged and the whistle of the trains, the coming of which he had anticipated long and eagerly, must have been among the last sounds perceived by Ernst Coreth's dying ears.

Active almost to the end, Agnes Coreth died at the farm on 11 April 1888 and was buried beside her husband to whom she had always been such a willing helpmate. During the last months of her husband's life, she and her then still unmarried children, Mary and Franz, had begun raising strawberries, a modest cash crop that the new trains carried to market in San Antonio, then and later. In years to come, the Coreth place became primarily a dairy farm, with highly-prized butter its most lucrative product. It is now a mobile-home park, but the pond and especially beautiful live-oak tree that have distinguished it throughout living memory remain.

In 1882 Franz A. Coreth went to Austria to represent the heirs of Antonia Coreth, the children of her brother Ernst. The next year, the thirty-six-year-old Franz took a sixteen-year-old bride, Minna Zesch of Mason County.[6] Late in 1883 the Coreth heirs sold the land their father had purchased near Houston in 1846. Combining his share of the proceeds from the sale and of the inheritance, Franz purchased the Conring ranch west of New Braunfels, the nucleus of the present Coreth estate, which remains the home of Franz A. Coreth's only living grandson and the latter's wife and stepmother. Called Mission Hill because it includes the historic proposed site of Mission Nuestra Señora de Guadalupe, the portion of the ranch that still remains in family hands incorporates a promontory often used by the Coast and Geodetic Survey for its studies. After the death of Franz's son Rochette Coreth late in 1979, the ranch was taken into the corporate limits of the little city of New Braunfels. A part has subsequently been sold, permitting the expansion of the town toward the west at long last.

Around the turn of the century, Franz A. Coreth was elected to seven successive two-year terms as county tax assessor. In later years, as his son reached the age at which he was able to relieve his father of the more strenuous duties of a rancher, Franz Coreth, to a great extent aided by his son-in-law Max Altgelt, became a pioneer in the crushed stone industry that contributes substantially to the economy of the county.

Whereas Josef Coreth (later changed to Joseph) spent his active years as farmer and merchant, his namesake and only grandson, the son of another Rudolph (born just nine days after his uncle died), graduated from West Point and attained the rank of Major before resigning his commission during service in Southeast Asia. The younger Joseph's daughter (b. 1964) is the only Coreth of her generation in the Texas line.

This story is not without a phoenix. During World War II, an Austrian great-grandson of Antonia Dillon came to America as a prisoner of war. After serving in the United States Navy and marrying an American girl of German parentage, he settled in Richmond, Virginia. His two sons and grandson seem to have assured the survival of the Coreth name in America for some time to come, though the scene has shifted to the Old South, the futile determination of which to prevail cost the Texas Coreths so much. Thus, the fortunes of war might be said to have reunited a family they once divided when Franz Joseph Coreth fell at Austerlitz.

NOTES
From Tyrol to Texas

1. The Port of Galveston Ship Lists, on microfilm in the Genealogy Dept. of the State Archives in Austin, Texas, give the name of the Ship as *York*. The handwritten name on the contract is *Georg*.

2. See particularly R. L. Biesele, *The History of the German Settlements in Texas, 1831-1861,* for a complete discussion of the subject. For specific information about conditions in Texas as they presented themselves to German immigrants in late 1846, see Houston newspapers of the time and the memoir of Wilhelm Hermes in Oscar Haas, *History of New Braunfels and Comal County,* pp. 34-44.

3. *Texas in 1837: An Anonymous, Contemporary Narrative,* edited with an introduction by Andrew Forest Muir, note 8, p. 190, describes landmarks of Houston during the days of the Republic. A picture of the Capitol at Houston inserted between pages 98 and 99 of *Gustav Dresel's Houston Journal,* Max Freund, editor, is captioned with the information that the building was offered as a refuge for German immigrants after having ceased to function officially.

4. Deed Records of Harris County, Vol. L, pp. 137–138; Vol. O, p. 21. See also Vol. L, pp. 138–139; Vol. P, p. 704; Vol. XVIII, pp. 444–448, #2829.

5. According to a letter to me (9 Nov. 1978), the Rev. Msg. Anton J. Frank, Pastor Emeritus of the Annunciation Church in Houston (successor institution to the records of St. Vincent de Paul Church) certifies that the baptism of Franz Alcad Traugott (originally misspelled) Coreth, part of the original Saddle Bag Record Book of Bishop Jean Marie Odin, is recorded in Fr. Fitzgerald's handwriting as #104 of *Baptisms: 1841-1860.* Recopied as #102 in *Baptisms: St. Vincent de Paul Church 1841-1871,* the record retains the same misspelling, which is herewith corrected.

6. Franz Alcad Coreth some forty-six years later gave *his* only son the name Rochette. The Gillespie County census for 1850 (Fredericksburg) shows Alcad Rochette to have been the only French resident of the Mormon community of Zodiac, made up largely of Americans with English or Celtic names. An unmarried laborer, he died of cholera in July of 1850. The records of the General Land Office of the State of Texas show that one "Jeane Eckande Rochette" (an obvious misinterpretation of Gothic script) held a claim that was invalidated in 1855.

7. John O. Meusebach, *Answer to Interrogatories,* p. 16.

8. Most genealogical information in this book is taken from *Gothaisches Taschenbuch der Gräflichen Haüser*, editions of 1872, 1876, and 1902, and *Genealogisches Handbuch des Adels: Gräfliche Haüser*, edition of 1955. See also *Deutsche Grafen-Haeuser der Gegenwart*, Vol. I, pp. 166f.

9. A published death notice for Count Franz Coreth, giving details of his being slain at Austerlitz, is in the possession of this writer.

10. Stella Musulin, *Vienna in the Age of Metternich*, p. 98. The war of 1800 caught Austria in the midst of switching from voluntary enlistments for long service to a system of conscription. There was discord among the general officers, and the organization and supply services were antiquated. Both the merits and the weaknesses of the old system were abolished after the disastrous year of 1805.

11. The terms of this treaty that spelled the end of the Holy Roman Empire are easily found in a wide variety of sources.

12. Aldo Gorfer, "Castello di Coredo," in *Guida dei Castelli del Trentino*, pp. 562–67. See also "Castel Braghèr," pp. 518–32, and "Castel Valèr," pp. 619–34.

13. That Ernst Coreth moved with the family to Grasnitz in 1807 is recorded on an old picture in the family's possession, showing the city as it appeared at the time.

14. Musulin, p. 124.

15. Adam Wandruszka, *Das Haus Habsburg*, p. 180. Musulin, pp. 124–128.

16. Ernst Coreth's certificate of honorable discharge from the Austrian army is in the possession of Franz Ernst Coreth, his great-grandson. This writer has a photocopy of the original.

17. *Neu-Braunfelser Zeitung*, 15 July 1881.

18. Musulin, p. 300.

19. That Rudolf Coreth was born at Schloß Kahlsperg ["Karlsberg"] is recorded in the last will and testament of his aunt, Antonia Coreth, which is in the possession of this writer. Rudolf later gave his birthplace as Salzburg, which is located some 15 to 20 kilometers to the north. In the possession of this writer are the original baptismal certificates of Karl, Amalie, and Johann Coreth.

20. The original of the emigration contract dated 8 August 1846 is at the General Land Office in Austin, Texas.

21. For thorough discussions of the German immigration to America, see especially Friedrich Kapp, *Immigration and the Commissioners of Emigration*. For material about the immigration from German lands to Texas specifically see Biesele.

22. "Contemporary Austrian Views of American Independence," p. 4.

23. Friedrich Kapp, pp. 6, 12, 14. Moritz Tiling's *The German Element in Texas* is extensively quoted by Biesele in this connection also. See in addition Irene Marschall King, *John O. Meusebach*, and Meusebach's own *Answer to Interrogatories*. John A. Hawgood's *The Tragedy of German-America* supplies a somewhat different perspective.

24. King, pp. 82–83, 102–104; Biesele, pp. 126–127.

25. The contract made by Henry F. Fisher and Ernst Coreth on 22 January 1847 is at the General Land Office in Austin, Texas.

26. Biesele, passim pp. 139–190. King, pp. 111–136.

27. Viktor Bracht, *Texas in 1848,* translated by Charles Frank Schmidt, p. 176.

28. Bracht, p. 177.

29. Deed Records, Comal County, Bk. A, p. 198, #218. Cf. Bracht, p. 176.

30. Bracht, pp. 207–209.

31. Cappes to Castell, Galveston, 7 March 1848. Solms-Braunfels Archives, XLI, p. 321. Cappes considered Coreth to be one "who worships Texas." Cf. King, p. 150, which interprets the phrase inaccurately.

32. Records painted on the ceiling of the Schloβ Aschach dining room refer to the Coreth residency, as well as to that of other occupants in its history. Schloβ Kahlsperg also records Ernst Coreth as owner from 1836 to 1854.

33. Port of Galveston Ship Lists, second quarter 1850, on microfilm in Genealogy Dept., State Archives, Austin, Texas. In 1846 the Coreths were first on the list of *York* passengers, while in 1850 they were last on the list of *Colonist* passengers.

34. Biesele, pp. 154–157, 167–168. In the Spiess family papers there is an anonymous account of the life of Lina (Mrs. Hermann) Spiess. Oscar Haas of New Braunfels supplied me with a copy of the excerpt, entitled "The Exile." Other references to the story, but without mention of the Coreths, appear in Peter Herff, *The Doctors Herff* (p. 15), and in the bulletin of The Institute of Texan Cultures devoted to the Germans (n.p.). A fictionalized version, in which the girl is called Tina, is in Frances Alexander's *Orphans of the Guadalupe,* chapter 10. This book, intended for elementary school children, has recently been dramatized, and the play was performed by the Circle Arts Theater of New Braunfels.

35. For details see Bracht, Biesele, and Haas, *History of New Braunfels.* Of interest is the fact that in 1847 there were 51 slaves in Comal County; in 1850, ten more (Biesele, pp. 134–137). By 1854 there were 77, a number increased to 193 by 1860. The largest German slave-owner in Texas was the *Adelsverein,* which worked slaves on its Nassau Farm near present-day Roundtop.

36. King, pp. 145–156. Haas, *History of New Braunfels,* p. 74.

37. Biesele, pp. 203–204; Earl Wesley Fornell, *The Galveston Era,* pp. 270–273; Llerena B. Friend, *Sam Houston: The Great Designer,* p. 243.

38. Portions of the Kapp family papers were made available through Dr. Sam Woolvin, present owner and restorer of the Kapp farm at Sisterdale, who has copies of some official and private sources. For biographical information and, in some instances, photographs, see Biesele, King, Olmsted, Ragsdale, Flach, Ransleben, and numerous other sources. Friedrich Kapp, a nephew of Ernst Kapp, visited Texas in order to maintain family contacts. An ardent abolitionist, he may have helped rekindle Ernst Kapp's involvement in political matters. The Friedrich

Kapp family is mentioned in Hedwig Kapp Coreth's letter to Rudolf immediately following her return to Germany. The Wolfgang Kapp who led the right-wing Kapp Putsch in the Germany of 1919 was an American-born son of Friedrich and not the like-named son of Ernst Kapp.

39. The priest's handwritten Latin baptismal records of Ss. Peter & Paul's Church, New Braunfels, Vol. I, p. 46, Nos. 4, 5, 6, and 7; see also p. 143, no. 15.

40. Biesele, pp. 204–205; Friend, pp. 243, 316–320; Fornell, passim pp. 131–139, also p. 288.

41. A letter from Carl to Rudolf (from Sisterdale, 10 April 1860) tells of a thrashing in Comfort a few days earlier, for which E(rnst Hermann). Altgelt, U. N. (?) Riske, Faltin and possibly Faltin's uncle were "hauled in (to court)." Carl thought Altgelt had to pay the fine. That such incidents were taking place at the time is confirmed by Hermann Seele. See "The Cypress" and Other Writings of a German Pioneer in Texas for various references. Altgelt is credited with founding Comfort in 1854, as well as with developing the King William Street district in San Antonio, where he later practiced law. Listed in the Texas State Archives muster rolls as having enlisted as a private in a Kendall County cavalry squadron under Sgt. J. B. Doering, Altgelt never served, since not even 50% of the number called could be raised in the pro-Union county. Concerned about Altgelt's frail health and ardent Southern sympathies, his wife, the former Emma Murck, persuaded him to return to Düsseldorf to stay with his father for the duration of the hostilities. When trying to get back to his family in Texas, Altgelt was caught up in the last fighting of the war near Brownsville.

The "Woolentier"

1. See *The Dresel Family*, Clyde H. Porter, compiler (available at the main San Antonio Public Library). Also, Theodore Huebener, *The Germans in America*, p. 124; Max Freund, *Gustav Dresel's Houston Journal;* A. B. Faust, *The German Element in the United States*, vol. 2, p. 48.

2. On 10 August 1855 Carl Coreth had acquired 320 acres on the south bank of the north fork of the Llano River from Meusebach. By 1865 he also owned 480 acres on the Blanco River in Comal County (17½ miles northwest 12 degrees from New Braunfels) and one horse. At the time of his death, his total estate was appraised at $325 by his erstwhile fellow-soldiers Christian Pantermühl and Anton(io) Elsner and endorsed by a former lieutenant of his army company, Deputy County Clerk P. C. Bitter. Handwritten partly in German and partly in English, the record will soon be too faded to read. Carl probably received the first parcel by means of some trading within the family, for Ernst Coreth, like the others who had contracted with the German Emigration Company, received 640 acres after the claims were validated 8 Oct. 1854. See Book in Probate Matters, Comal County, Texas, vol. 1, pp. 335-336, no. 592. Also Certificate no. 987, Letter Patent no. 195, and field notes as recorded in bk. G, no. 2, pp. 527-528, in Bexar District files. The contract and the original claim are available at the General Land Office.

3. *New York Times* Index: A Book of Record, Sept. 1861-Dec. 1862.

4. Haas, *History of New Braunfels and Comal County*, p. 186.

5. Ernest Wallace, *Texas in Turmoil*, pp. 87-88.

6. This may have been the home of Christian Schuhart on the San Geronimo Creek just east of Seguin. See August Santleben, *A Texas Pioneer*, pp. 5-6.

7. Probably L. E. Neuhaus, founder (1847) of the village of Hackberry in the northeastern part of Lavaca County, about 11 miles from the county seat on the old Hallettsville-Schulenberg Road. In 1862 the settlement acquired its official name and post office. See Paul C. Boethel, *A History of Lavaca County*, rev. ed., p. 10 and p. 121.

8. This is presumably William Edgar, whose First Texas Battery was part of Scurry's Third Brigade. The men were later taken prisoner at Fort Russy, Louisiana, then exchanged and rearmed with weapons taken at Pleasant Hill. A Wm. A. Edgar, probably the same man, was quartermaster sergeant at the Alamo when the base was surrounded and captured by the Knights of the Golden Circle on 18 February 1861 (Mary Olivia Handy, *History of Fort Sam Houston*, p. 15).

9. According to Egon Tausch, "Southern Sentiment Among the Texas Germans During the Civil War," p. 41, Flake was the only influential editor in Texas supporting Douglas. Lindheimer helped develop the anti-Flake bias among many Texans, says Ella Lonn, *Foreigners in the Con-*

federacy, pp. 47-48. Flake's post-war English-language *Bulletin* was for a while the area's official Republican organ (Tausch, pp. 101-102). Flake died in New York in 1872.

10. Franz Moureau, originally from Nassau, was a merchant, prominent citizen, and consul in New Braunfels. See many references in Haas.

11. Perhaps *Captain* Theodor Oswald of Co. B, Eighth Texas Infantry, a unit reputedly raised in New Braunfels and developing a bad record for desertion (Lonn, *Foreigners in the Confederacy,* p. 126). After 1854, Oswald had been editor of the *Texas Staats-Zeitung,* which his brother had purchased from the abolitionist Dr. Adolf Douai. In 1858 Gustav Schleicher acquired the paper, and his editor, Rudolf Dresel (see n. 1, this chapter), conducted it as a Democratic paper (Frederick C. Chabot, *Genealogies of Early San Antonio Families,* p. 373). The publisher Oswald (H. Fr. or F. H.) had been vice-president of the San Antonio convention of 1854 (Biesele, p. 198).

12. A mistake on Rudolf's part, this undoubtedly ought to read "Harrisburg." When the war stopped construction, the Buffalo Bayou, Brazos and Colorado Railroad reached northwestward 80 miles from Harrisburg to Alleyton, and passengers bound for Galveston switched at Harrisburg to the Galveston, Houston and Henderson Railroad. No railroad seems to have served Hallettsville. See map with legend based on conditions of 1 June 1861 in Robert C. Black, III, *The Railroads of the Confederacy.*

13. ". . . the finest, best, and most partonized hotel that I have ever visited" (Bracht, p. 153).

14. Fornell (p. 134) identifies I. E. Rump (listed elsewhere as J. E. Rump) as a Justice of the Peace and close friend of Flake's with much political power in Galveston.

15. B. (or E.) Kauffman(n) & Co. of Galveston, sometime *Adelsverein* agent at Carlshafen (Indianola). See Bracht, p. 194; Biesele, p. 144. In 1856 one Kauffman of Galveston, along with a man named Klocker and others, saw the *Iris,* a 700-ton ship they had had built in Bremen, bring 240 emigrants to Texas on its maiden voyage (Fornell, p. 128). Later Julius Kauffman was the business partner of Henry Runge (see *The Handbook of Texas,* vol. 2, p. 515 for biography), a close friend of the Coreths.

16. Immigrant Irish stevedores composed the bulk of Dick Dowling's force that achieved a brilliant victory at Sabine Pass. It should be remembered that Rudolf Coreth was himself a great-grandson of a Dubliner.

17. *Apis mellifera* Linné, clarified honey, used as a flavoring agent, especially in gargles and in the preparation of Blue Mass, according to the *The Dispensatory of the United States of America,* 23rd ed., pp. 674-675. Hereinafter this source will be identified simply as *DUSA.*

18. The Galveston City Directory for 1859-1860 lists only one Wagner, Theodor, a commission merchant. Miss Nohl remained single and conducted a ladies' college, first in New Braunfels and then in Austin with her friend Natalie von Schenck and others. Both women were daughters of well-educated settlers of New Braunfels.

19. Henry J. Huck (or Huch) for many years was a commission and forwarding agent in Port Lavaca, Indianola, and later in Victoria and other inland towns. He was also in the lumber business and raised vegetables and fruits, including grapes, for market, according to Port Lavaca historian, Paul H. Freier, to whom I am indebted for this information. See also Roy Grimes, *300 Years in Victoria County*, p. 283.

20. The USS *Sam Houston* (which Rudolf consistently spells "Huston" while calling the city "Houston") had captured the *Reindeer* off San Luis Pass on 3 October 1861, according to *Texas in the War 1861-1865*, second edition, p. 201. This valuable source will hereinafter be referred to as *Wright/Simpson*, the names of the compiler and the editor.

21. Calomel (*Hydrargyri Chloridum Mite* or mild mercurous chloride), a heavy white or yellowish powder, is a powerful diuretic and was long applied in treating eye infections, venereal ulcers, and ulcerated nasal or mucous membranes, often as an ointment. It is thought helpful in some cases of enteritis or dysentery and has an anti-syphilitic effect (*DUSA,*, pp. 521-522). Superseded by ipecac early in the nineteenth century, it was in demand again, particularly for treating dysentery, during the war, when it was available as a powder, fluid extract, or in combination with opium (George Winston, "Medicines for the Union Army," pp. 16-17). Blue Mass (*Massa Hydrargyri* or Blue Pill) tends, like arsenic, to increase the patient's weight by inhibiting destructive metabolism. It stimulates the blood-making organs and increases the number of red cells while reducing the fibrin content in blood. Toxic doses may cause anemia. Sometimes used in the past to treat syphilis, pleurisy, iritis, and peritonitis, it is usually less likely to cause griping than calomel if employed now as a cathartic (*DUSA*, p. 259). Oil of cinnamon (which Rudolf calls "Cassiaöl") is sometimes applied to the gums. A highly irritating germicide and fungicide, it is used as an "adjuvant to stomachic or carminative medicines" (*DUSA*, pp. 754-756). Spanish flies (dried *Cantharis vesicatoria* Linné or *Catharides*) have been medically in use from at least the time of Pliny. The commonest native species in the United States, *Cantharis vittata* Latreille, was officially recognized here in 1850. Its favorite habitat is the potato vine. Usually a yellowish brown to moderate olive brown powder with an unpleasant odor and acrid aftertaste, it often contains iridescent wing particles. Taken internally it is an especially powerful and very dangerous uro-genital irritant and remedy for impotency. Similar or identical insects were used for dropsy and amenorrhea as early as the time of Hippocrates. Sometimes useful in neuralgias, it is the best blistering agent for reddening the skin preparatory to application of a flax-seed poultice. The results of excessive doses are truly grotesque and frequently fatal (*DUSA*, pp. 252-254).

22. The company in which Rudolf and Münzenberger were volunteers was stationed at a place called Hardeman in Matagorda County. The "Caney Mounted Rifles" had as their captain Edward ("Ned") S. Rugeley. The two muster rolls for the group list among the privates

Saml. W. Hardeman; D. Hardeman, Jr.; and Dickinson D. Hardeman (Texas State Archives, no. 325). Both muster rolls are for the summer of 1861, before Rudolf and Münzenberger joined.

23. "Cleuner" is how Rudolf adapts the spelling of this name to his own speech and spelling idiosyncrasies. D. H. Klaener was the *Adelsverein's* agent at Galveston and was responsible for the earliest publicity in European newspapers concerning its incapacities. See Biesele, p. 144, p. 127, and p. 210.

24. William Walker, the American filibuster who had died before a Honduran firing squad scarcely a year earlier, had close connections with Galveston. This article, unfortunately not available to me, seems to have been written to attract more peaceable emigrants to Nicaragua.

Ebb and Flow

1. James Murray Mason and John Slidell, Confederate envoys, were taken off the British steamer *Trent* by a United States naval officer while on their way from one neutral port to another. They were soon released, but the incident was not forgotten.

2. Herman(n) and Henry Runge were among the first trades and merchants at Indian Point, the "Old Town" of Indianola (Grimes, pp. 238-239). Henry Runge was one of several men who on 21 January 1858 received a charter for the Indianola Railroad Company (ibid., p. 520). During the Civil War the Runges had a mercantile business in New Braunfels. In 1863 the firm of (Henry) Runge and (John) Torrey was granted a charter by the State of Texas to import cotton-weaving machines from Mexico (Haas, p. 140). See also entries in *The Handbook of Texas*, v. 2, p. 515.

3. Theodor Butz was a member of an immigrant Prussian family living in New Braunfels. In the 1860 census he was a sixteen-year-old apprentice to David Wheeler, a native of Maine, who had a mercantile business in New Braunfels. The Butz mentioned as serving with Capt. Julius Bose's company in Louisiana late in 1864 was probably Theodor. See Haas, p. 169. After the war, Butz performed in at least one amateur theatrical, *"Prinz und Nachtwächter."* See *Deutsch-texanische Monatshefte* for 1900, p. 20, one of a retrospective series about amateur theatre in Texas German communities.

4. Ernst Coreth sometimes used an abbreviation or symbol after his signature. It appears to be "mia" and is connected to the name and at a downward angle to it. No definite interpretation has been found, but it has been suggested this may be an unconventional abbreviation of *"manu propria"* (m. ia.), Latin for "by his own hand." Hereinafter this symbol will be represented by an asterisk.

5. Ernst Coreth seems to have written "Bakfong" or "Baktong," logically his adaptation of "paktong," which Webster's *New International Dictionary*, 2nd unabridged ed., hereinafter called simply Webster's, defines as: "A Chinese alloy of nickel, zinc, and copper, resembling German silver." The term is not used in German.

6. The original reads "Dura," obviously durra, which Webster's defines as: "A grain sorghum derived from *Sorghum vulgare,* having medium-sized, dry, pithy stalks and narrow leaves. It is widely grown for food etc. in southern Asia and northern Africa, and was introduced into the United States in 1874." The Coreths, it would appear, were raising it at least twelve years before that date. They never mention kaffir, which Webster's states is the other principal variety of non-saccharine sorghum. On the agricultural schedules no distinction was made between various kinds of sorghum grown at this period.

7. According to the appraisal of Carl Coreth's estate, he received 480 acres in Comal County on the Blanco River by patent of 18 January 1862 (see n. 2 in "The Woolentier"). The reference to another house is puzzling.

8. It appears Rudolf and Carl lived on or near Carl's future property at some earlier date. Conceivably this could have been while camping with the company they later joined, for this group is known to have trained on the George family farm during the summer of 1861, in an area not far from where Carl meant to settle with his bride-to-be, Hedwig Kapp. No records show the Coreths as having participated in this training, however.

9. Otto and Hermann Kämmerling, brothers, later returned to their native Jastrow (West Prussia) to live out their lives. R. H(ermann?). Kämmerling purchased 160 acres in Comal County in July of 1860. He paid $400 for the place described as on the east bank of the Guadalupe River about 21 miles north of New Braunfels and having belonged to a family named Bishop for the five years preceding (Comal County Deed Records, bk. G, p. 150, no. 514).

10. Major General P. O. Hébert was appointed commander of all Confederate troops in Texas on 14 August 1861. On 10 October 1862 General J. B. Magruder arrived to take over this command, which he assumed on 29 November (*Texas in the Civil War: A Résumé History*, pp. 47-50; hereinafter to be called simply *Résumé*. See also Ernest Wallace, *Texas in Turmoil*, p. 89.

11. "Communists" is used here pejoratively but without political connotation.

12. "South" here means the tropics or the southern hemisphere.

13. Rudolf compiled many preserved vocabulary lists, paradigms, and such, in which the languages used are German, not English, and Spanish. He became completely proficient in these three languages and used several others with relative ease, it is said, because of his later work and travels.

14. In December all debt collecting, except from enemy aliens, had been suspended until 1 January 1864, or six months after the war. The New Braunfels assessor for the tax was a Scot, hotelier Mathew Taylor. To be declared were real estate, slaves, merchandise, stocks, money drawing interest, livestock, gold and silverware, pianos, and wagons, but not CSA bonds nor estates worth less than $500. The tax was 50¢ on $100 assessed valuation (Haas, p. 188).

15. It is not the specific customary wording that is at issue here. The customary German "Nichts Neues" used here was translated as "All Quiet" in the title of the Rémarque novel about World War I.

16. No dates listed by Don H. Biggers, *German Pioneers in Texas*, Gillespie County ed., check with this Indian trouble. In January 1862, James Billings, who had formerly lived in Lavaca County, was scalped and killed by Indians twelve miles north of Fredericksburg; his son John, who had been left for dead, managed to survive. The family moved to Kerr County (Paul C. Boethel, *On the Headwaters of the Lavaca and Navidad*, p. 6).

17. The Federal navy was patrolling Aransas Pass at this time, particularly on 11-13 January. On 22 February 1862 it attacked Aransas Pass (*Résumé*, pp. 48-49).

18. *Aconitum* was introduced into modern pharmacopoeia by Störck of Vienna in 1763. The very first U. S. Pharmacopoeia admitted it officially. Of the numerous European and the American varieties, only the root is now in official use, whereas the leaves and flowers were formerly accepted. It irritates and paralyzes the peripheral sensory nerves and is unreliable because of its variable potency. Used internally the drug slows the pulse, lowers the blood pressure, and retards respiration, making the extremities and lips tingle and feel numb. It was used in the past for fevers, neuralgias, and as a local anaesthetic for the stomach (*DUSA*, pp. 56-61).

19. "Hepa." is probably *Hepar Sulfuris*, which was sometimes used for asthma. See *DUSA*, pp. 882-83.

20. On 21 February, General H. H. Sibley's brigade defeated Federal forces at Val Verde in New Mexico and captured Albuquerque and Santa Fe. On 28 March the Federal troops defeated the Confederates under Sibley at Glorietta, N. M. The brigade contained many Texas Germans whose paths crossed with the unit in which the Coreths served.

21. When the Caney Mounted Rifles unit formed in the summer of 1861, it elected the following officers: E. S. Rugeley, captain; G. J. Bowie, first lieutenant; A(lex?). J. Rugeley, second lieutenant; and Wm. F. Davis, third lieutenant (Texas State Archives, no. 961).

22. This illegible name could be any of the following: Ruiz, Rug. (abbreviation of Rugeley), Buiy (misspelling of Bowie), or even Reuss (misspelled), the last-mentioned name associated with military affairs in the Indianola area.

23. George Friedrich Tolle and his oldest son, Christoph, were tanners from Hanover. The family were neighbors of the Coreths, apparently the only ones with whom the family clashed on occasion. The Tolles also included the druggist August, who lived with his sister Sophie and her husband, Dr. Theodor Koester, the Coreths' family physician; Fritz, a miller; Harry, later in Co. F with the Coreths; and Auguste, whose wedding is mentioned in the letters.

24. The Navarro County Historical Society professes to know of no such unit. The only unit specifically listed as from Navarro County by *Wright/Simpson* was the "Navarro Rifles," which became Co. I of Hood's brigade (Fourth Texas Infantry; *Wright/Simpson*, pp. 64 and 211). This company, commanded by C. M. Winkler, is represented by three muster rolls in the Texas Archives (no. 1149). It had been organized as a cavalry (or mounted rifles) unit. Two muster rolls have been preserved for a company of active mounted riflemen in the Nineteenth Brigade organized at Springhill in Navarro County and commanded by R. H. Matthews (no. 422).

25. *Hep. mercurium* is not listed as such in the USP or British or National formulary. It is probably *Mercuric sulfide*, which was dropped, but was formerly official (*DUSA*, pp. 1441-42).

Roll Call

1. Oscar Haas, *History of New Braunfels and Comal County*, p. 188, lists the counties of which Comal is the easternmost.

2. Ibid., p. 158, quoting the *Neu-Braunfelser Zeitung* of 13 September 1861.

3. For documentation of the marriage of Carl and Hedwig see Marriage Records of Comal County, Texas, vol. C. p. 238, no. 238.

4. Haas, p. 162, quoting *Neu-Braunfelser Zeitung* of 4 April 1862, muster rolls, and records of the General Services Administration, Washington, D.C. Lester N. Fitzhugh, *Texas Batteries, Battalions, Regiments, Commanders and Field Officers in the Confederate Army 1861-1865*, p. 21. Carl L. Duaine, *The Dead Men Wore Boots*, pp. 98 and 104. Carl and Johann appear in the files at the Texas State Archives in which individuals listed on Confederate muster rolls are to be found. Rudolf and Münzenberger do not.

5. The original expression *"schwemmte den Jux weg"* may have resulted from an etymological mingling of Latin *iocus* (related to English "jocund") and *iuxta* (related to English "juxtapose").

6. According to Ella Lonn, *Foreigners in the Confederacy*, p. 328, this uniform was designed by one Nicola Marschall, a Prussian musician-painter in Alabama, who based his drawing upon memories of Austrian sharpshooters' clothes he had seen in passing through Verona.

7. Perhaps Brown's battalion, which Rudolf at this point intended joining, was temporarily in Austin.

8. In April of 1862, Indians killed Heinrich Grobe where he was working on Landrum's Creek and drove off all the victim's stock. On the same day, some eight miles away, Indians also killed a Mr. Berg, who was taking whiskey to town; possibly because of some taboo, they left the whiskey untouched. See Don H. Biggers, *German Pioneers in Texas*, Gillespie County ed., pp. 169 and 171-72.

9. "Zarwash" is an attempt at phonetic spelling of Hungarian *"Szarvas"* (stag). This had also been the name of Ernst Coreth's army mount.

10. On 10 April Rudolf was in Bates's regiment. On 25 March, Capt. E. S. Rugeley had asked for volunteers to form a battalion, implicitly under Reuben R. Brown. *Wright/Simpson* gives support to the theory that the shuffling of membership between Brown's Twelfth Texas Cavalry Battalion, Bates's Texas Infantry Battalion, and Rountree's Texas Cavalry Battalion may have also included the First Texas (Heavy) Artillery Regiment, which was organized in Galveston at about the same time as Rudolf's (Rugeley's) unit. See notes #118 and #119, p. 106; also n. #304, p. 130. A certain Capt. Jordan W. Bennett signed as "Commanding Company B, 1st (Texas) Artillery (Regiment)" (ibid., p. 44). This man took over command of Teel's (or Bennett's) Texas Battery in

the spring of 1862 (ibid., n. 367, p. 137). Possibly, therefore, "L. T." Bennet(t) was "Capt. *Lt.*" Jordan W. Bennett. Cf. Rudolf's letter of 25 March, in which "Maj. Col. Brown" is mentioned. Bennett became a captain 21 Feb. 1862.

11. "Tunkan" should read "Duncan." Paul C. Boethel, *On the Head-waters of the Lavaca and Navidad,* p. 38, refers to a place called Duncan Prairie, which is evidently within the area Rudolf was traversing.

12. The former lieutenant governor, before succeeding Henderson as governor of Texas, had built a two-story log house which was called "Sycamore Grove" on the banks of Caney Creek (Fannie M. B. Hughs, *Legends of Texas Rivers,* p. 79).

13. Col. Joseph N. Bates's Thirteenth Texas Infantry Regiment, of which Col. Reuben R. Brown was second in command, underwent repeated reorganization during the war, but was almost always on the Galveston-Matagorda section of the Texas coast, which it helped to guard (*Wright/Simpson,* pp. 21 and 106).

14. Mary Olivia Handy, *History of Fort Sam Houston,* p. 17.

15. Duaine does not list Major Gray with Woods's regiment in *The Dead Men Wore Boots.* This was probably Major Edward F. Gray (later lieutenant colonel), who served the Third Texas Infantry, which Lt. Col. Augustus Buchel commanded before organizing the First Texas Cavalry Regiment. Buchel's and Woods's regiments, both under the command of Brig. Gen. Hamilton P. Bee, were in frequent contact and contained many Germans. Gray served on Bee's staff, and on 1 May 1862 was serving as assistant adjutant general (*Wright/Simpson,* p. 3).

16. Auguste Tolle married 31 May 1862. The bridegroom, Hermann Schimmelpfennig, seems to have been a brother of August Schimmelpfennig, a close friend of the Coreth boys. See Comal County Marriage Records, vol. C, no. 265.

17. A reference to W. G. M. Samuel, Capt. & P., C. S. A. Ordnance Officer, appears in the *San Antonio Semi-Weekly News* of Monday, 9 February 1863 (vol. 2, #127). There is much praise for the depot and for Capt. Samuel: "In every portion of this department we witnessed the greatest activity, which proved to us conclusively, that Capt. Samuels [sic] permitted no idlers about him." An advertisement calling for brown paper cartridges at the Texas Arsenal (ibid., issue of 21 June 1862, p. 2, c. 2) is signed by this man. In addition, the San Antonio Museum of Art displays paintings by William G. M. Samuel, notably one of a man on horseback and a large oil copy of a famous photograph that the New York photographer Frederick made of Sam Houston in 1856. In the last-named of these, Samuel (1815-1902), described as a lawman by profession, replaced the shawl of the original with a Mexican serape. Among the skirmishes and minor incidents listed in *Wright/Simpson* is one that sounds more like a running feud, occurring 28 May-21 June 1862 at the San Antonio Arsenal and Barracks.

18. Lt. Col. Nathaniel Benton, second in command to Woods. A veteran of Mexican and Indian wars, Benton joined the regiment at forty-six. Later, as Rudolf recounts, Benton lost his (right) arm at Blair's Landing.

19. Theodor Koester was married to the oldest daughter of the Coreth neighbor, George Friedrich Tolle. A physician for the *Adelsverein* during the early days, Koester was a delegate to the Secession Convention, where this native of Frankfurt (am Main, probably) voted to leave the Union.

20. Duaine, p. 27.

21. Ibid.

22. Louis (Ludwig) Kessler was a New Braunfels saddler according to the 1860 census. In 1865-1866 he served as county clerk. "Kreuz" was evidently Florenz Kreuz, one of the most enterprising New Braunfels residents of the time. Kreuz operated a ferry at the confluence of the Guadalupe and Comal Rivers, made and sold soap, candles, and other by-products of his tannery, manufactured horse-collars, and had charge of a brickyard. Oscar Haas, *History of New Braunfels,* refers to him many times. Kreuz was among those calling for a political meeting in 1860 (Rudolf L. Biesele, *German Settlements in Texas,* p. 205).

23. Co. F included three Schulzes, a father and two sons, all blacksmiths. The elder Friedrich Schulze, aged sixty-five when he joined, was company farrier (Haas, p. 163; Duaine, p. 24). August Schulze, twenty-eight when he enlisted, was the first lieutenant and later the captain of the company. His older brother Friedrich was second lieutenant. They were natives of Brunswick.

24. A native of New York, Granville H. Sherwood is listed in the 1850 census as an attorney living in a New Braunfels hotel. When he joined Co. B of Woods's regiment, Sherwood was thirty-eight and living in Guadalupe County.

25. Edgar Schramm rose from third lieutenant to captain of Co. F. He later married a daughter (Antonie) of Louis Benner, reputed to have been the first postmistress (Haas, pp. 131 and 198). He is mentioned in several Coreth letters. For some years in the late 1880's and early 1890's, Schramm published the *Texas Staats Zeitung* in San Antonio, after which he sold the newspaper to his son-in-law (Frederick C. Chabot, *Genealogies of Early San Antonio Families,* p. 373).

26. Capt. Eugene B. Millett from Seguin, who enlisted in Co. B. of Woods's regiment, was apparently the son of Samuel Millett from Maine, a New Braunfels hotel-keeper according to the 1850 census. Young Millett himself was born in Texas. See Stanley D. Casto's *Settlement of the Cibolo-Nueces Strip.* In latter years, Eugene Millett was frequently called the "Cattle King of Northwest Texas" (ibid., p. 33). He had succeeded to the command of Co. B, when Nat Benton became lieutenant colonel under Woods.

27. See Theophilus Noel, *A Campaign From Santa Fe To the Mississippi,* Martin Hall and Edwin Adams Davis, eds., for a history of Sibley's New Mexico campaign.

28. Much of the material in Guido E. Ransleben's *One Hundred Years of Comfort in Texas* concerns the Neuces massacre. None of the accounts anywhere make much of the near-identity of the names Degener and Tegener. Eduard Degener had bought the Nicolaus Zink place at Sis-

terdale. Of all the German liberals who settled in central Texas in the years right after the 1848 revolutions, he is considered to have been the most dedicated and powerful. Even one historian who labeled Degener a radical felt impelled to concede that he was "possibly the ablest" of these in the Reconstruction Convention that opened its session at Austin on 7 February 1866. That historian also points out that Degener, who represented San Antonio, was the only foreign-born member and the only candidate campaigning for such office who openly advocated Negro suffrage (Ernest Wallace, *Texas in Turmoil*, pp. 167 and 172).

29. The tragic affair to which Rudolf refers actually occurred near, but not at, Fort Clark.

30. John M. Carolan of San Antonio was thirty-nine when he became commander of Co. H of Woods's regiment in the spring of 1862. He, or one of the same name, was mayor of San Antonio in 1853-54 (August Santleben, *A Texas Pioneer*, facs. ed., p. 316). He died at Ringgold Barracks on 2 May 1863 and was succeeded as company commander by Samuel Lytle (Duaine, p. 37).

31. Near Comfort, Texas, this was the site of Jeff Davis's "great camel experiment."

32. Duaine, p. 31.

33. Rudolph Wipprecht, a Kapp descendant, makes these assertions in *The Texas Gun Collector* (no. 20; March 1952). This issue is devoted to the so-called "Kapp Sixshooter." The gun, long on display at the Sophienburg Museum in New Braunfels, no longer belongs to members of the Coreth family.

34. Either Rudolf had not known the Kapps well before, or else he is referring to other people at Sisterdale, which is more likely.

35. Also called *Potassa Sulfurate* (or, in German, *"Schwefelleber"*), this substance was in the past used internally. The USP has long since discontinued the process for making this preparation. Usually applied in the form of lotion or ointment, it is a valuable external treatment for some skin diseases. Sometimes mixed with oil of anise to counteract the odor, this antiparasitic is useful in giving tone to blood vessels that have become dilated (*DUSA*, pp. 882-83).

36. Also called Dogs-bane, this powder is made from *Apocynum cannabinum* Linné or *Apocynum androsoemifolium* Linné, the roots or rhyzomes of plants that are found in many parts of North America. A vasomotor stimulant and diuretic, it often causes nausea and catharsis. Used to treat dropsy, it works similarly to digitalis but proves too powerful for many patients. The medical profession first came to know it through M. L. Knapp in 1836 (*DUSA*, pp. 142-43). The Coreth letter calls this starchy powder *"Hundegagel,"* a fairly obvious variation of *Hundskohl*, which Cassell's *New German and English Dictionary* (1939) gives as the German for "dogbane."

37. Letters in my possession (not from the Coreth collection) indicate that Degener was a teamster between San Antonio and Comfort right after the war. Obviously, he fared well during Reconstruction.

Grains of Sand

1. According to Paul C. Boethel, *A History of Lavaca County,* rev. ed., pp. 1-2 and 11, Kent's Place was about nine or ten miles south of present-day Hallettsville, across the Mustang Creek from and just south of the Zumwalt settlement, directly north of the old Victoria-Gonzales County line on the west bank of the Lavaca. Rudolf and his companions would seem to have been somewhat west of this location, however.

2. Roy Grimes, *300 Years in Victoria County* mentions three Victoria hotels for 1860 (pp. 198 and 245). The war could have spawned additional ones.

3. This 5′ 6″ gauge track served the 14-15 mile stretch from Indianola via Port Lavaca to Victoria. Chartered in 1858 by Henry Runge and others, the railroad served this section by the start of the war. It is thought that Gen. Magruder used the materials to construct additional coastal fortifications after having torn up the railroad early in 1863 with scant opposition from CSA headquarters in Richmond (Robert C. Black III, *The Railroads of the Confederacy,* p. 299). Soon after hostilities ended, the federal government restored the portion from Indianola to Port Lavaca (Grimes, p. 272). The Indianola Railroad connected with the San Antonio and Mexico Railroad just west of Port Lavaca (ibid., p. 204).

4. Evidently Woods received one of the Sisterdale sixshooters.

5. In an earlier letter, Carl refers to Mexican helpers named José María and Felix whom he and Rudolf obviously knew. The extent of the earlier studies is uncertain.

6. Port Lavaca historian Paul H. Freier is certain this was John Frizzie (originally Frizzi?), who owned property facing the bay. Calhoun County court records, Freier says, indicate he came from Switzerland in 1857 and was unmarried. Frizzie dealt in real estate and shipped livestock by sea on a large scale.

7. Woods, himself a physician, is said to have been liberal with leaves and lax in keeping records, even medical ones. See Carl L. Duaine, *The Dead Men Wore Boots,* pp. 17 (unnumbered), 24, 28, 46, 50, 55, 63, and 64.

8. Surely William Frob(o)ese, and probably the same as G. W. Frobese (see letter to Rudolf of 18 Jan. 1866). The artillery mentioned was J. M. Reuss's Indianola Artillery Guards, which late in 1863 joined what had been Shea's battalion to become Shea's Texas Artillery Battalion in Hobby's regiment, the Eighth Texas Infantry. See Texas State Archives, Civil War muster rolls and related documents, no. 95, pp. 30, 34, 73, and 79, for the names of Rudolf's friends in Hobby's regiment. See also *Wright/Simpson,* notes #35, #106, #308, #341, and others. Hobby's regiment saw out-of-state action at Mansfield and Pleasant Hill. William

Frobese and Emil Reiffert bought out Henry Runge at Indianola and continued to do business under his firm's name. See *Indianola Scrap Book,* facs. repr., p. 25. Indianola historian P. H. Freier, in a letter to me, states that William Frobese was later a prominent citizen of Cuero.

9. See n. 8 above. Daniel D. Shea later was next in command under John Ireland in Hobby's regiment.

10. Ferdinand Dietz is thirteenth on a list of the members of Ireland's company from Guadalupe County appearing in the *Seguin Enterprise* for 7 Feb. 1889 (copy in Texas State Archives, no. 306). Accompanying the archives copy is a statement (initialed WMW; probably Willie Mae Weinert) that indicates Dietz is buried in Seguin. Houston historian Bill Winsor has told me in a letter (6 May 1977) that he believes Ferdinand Dietz to be the "Captain Deitz" mentioned by Lt. Col. O. Steele and Maj. Gen. J. B. Magruder in correspondence of May 1864 (*The War of the Rebellion: Official Records,* vol. 34, pt. 3, pp. 804-5 and pp. 833-34). Deitz (a misspelling that does not disturb many non-Germans), an engineer, deserted just before the Louisiana campaign and joined the staff of (Federal) Gen. McClernand, Gen. N. P. Banks's second in command, taking with him fortification plans for Galveston and topographical drawings of the Texas coastal region. Capt. John Ireland (later governor of Texas) led a company of infantry in the Twenty-Fifth Brigade from Seguin. The formerly independent company became Co. K of Hobby's regiment (Texas State Archives no. 95 and no. 306).

11. The British and Spanish, who had a coalition with the French, withdrew their troops from Mexico completely by April 1862. The French, on the other hand, sent more troops, whose advance was thwarted by Zaragoza and Diaz forces on 5 May, a date since celebrated by Mexicans. That year also, the Pan-Slavic movement gained momentum in Turkey, where several fortresses were turned over to Serbians.

12. *"Brennsuppe,"* a dish for the frugal, is made in various ways. Often it is simply the water in which vegetables were cooked, thickened by a roux.

13. The *San Antonio Semi-Weekly News* of 11 May 1863 carried the following item from the *Fort Brown Flag* of 1 May 1863: "Col. Woods' Rgt. marched into town on Friday last, and elicited general remark that the boys looked like a fighting set."

14. For other mention of Theodor Butz, see also note no. 3 in "Ebb and Flow." Gepart appears as simply "Daniel Gephart [sic]" on p. 34 of Texas State Archives, no. 95, devoted to the Hobby regiment. Gep(h)art was apparently a private in Co. A. Major John H. Kampmann was normally third in command of Buchel's regiment, the Third Texas Infantry Regiment (*Wright/Simpson,* p. 19). When commanding this regiment in August 1863, Kampmann was unable to prevent a mutiny among his men, who refused to drill (ibid., note #406, p. 143).

15. August and Valentine Heick (or Heicke), brothers, were commission merchants at Indianola after the war (August Santleben, *A Texas Pioneer,* p. 153). Heicke and Helfri(s)ch was a similar firm in Galveston.

The German Texans, published by The University of Texas Institute of Texas Cultures (pages unnumbered), refers to a certain J. Valentine Hecke (Heicke?) who had traveled in Texas in 1818-19 and had shortly thereafter published a book in which he urged the Prussian government to buy territory from Spain for colonization.

16. The merchant Jordan may well have been William Jordan, Sr., who, Lonn states, came to Fredericksburg in 1854, and who was the maker of the first specifically Confederate suits used in Texas (*Foreigners in the Confederacy,* p. 334).

17. Capt. Julius Bose's Comal County Volunteer Infantry is discussed in Oscar Haas, *History of New Braunfels,* pp. 164-70. According to Bose himself (ibid., p. 167), the unit was assigned to Scurry's brigade and together with Waul's brigade formed Walker's division. In the spring of 1864 it served in Arkansas against the Union general Frederick Steele, who was trying to rendezvous with Banks's forces advancing up the Red River.

Drops of Water

1. At least for a while the official name of this camp was Post Gonzales. Located near the town of Gonzales, the camp existed as early as 1842, when the Somervell Expedition assembled there. It acquired the name of Camp Rocky from facetious comments about the site (Gerald S. Pierce, *Texas Under Arms*, p. 63).

2. The rocky creek on the Johann Heinrich Merz place in the Comal Creek community became part of Servtex Materials Company, now a subsidiary of Brown & Root.

3. The original term, *"eine Triste,"* Wahrig's *Deutsches Wörterbuch* (s.v. *"Triste"*) defines as a roofed shelter for piles of hay or straw, in which the material is piled around a pole. The term is identified as Bavarian, Austrian, and Swiss (Upper German).

4. Vicksburg fell the very next day. This event and the Battle of Gettysburg are viewed by most scholars as the turning points of the war.

5. The image of the soldiers bringing back a wagonload of melons along with a coffin they had made for their dead comrade is haunting. Haas, *History of New Braunfels*, lists the war dead of Co. F as Johann Coreth and Henry Puls only (p. 190), but indicates elsewhere that the war dead were First Sgt. Ernst Schwantes and Rudolph (sic) Coreth (p. 163), in the latter case giving his source as a photostatic copy of eight rolls acquired from the General Services Administration in Washington, D. C., in 1956.

6. Sweet Home is said to have been named about 1854 or 1855 when Mary B. West, a settler from Tennessee, said on seeing the site, "Oh, Pa, this would make a sweet home" (Paul C. Boethel, *On the Headwaters*, p. 159).

7. Perhaps the "Canadian" horse came from around the Canadian River in North Texas.

8. A false but recurrent rumor.

9. Otto von Roeder, who had a fine home near Victoria in the Guadalupe Valley at Mission Valley, joined Co. A of Victoria's County Reserve Troops, which in 1863 entered the Twenty-fourth Brigade of Texas State Troops. He and other members were taken prisoner in November 1863, while trying to defend Mustang Island. Roeder was released in June 1864. His oldest son, Ludwig Joachim, was in Sibley's forces. The young man's mother was a Donop, a family name associated with Sisterdale. The women were evidently Otto von Roeder's daughters by a second marriage, Caroline and Henrietta, and his stepdaughter, Ottilie Sack. Most of this information was graciously provided me by Flora von Roeder in a letter dated 23 Oct. 1975.

10. Emil Reif(f)ert and G. W(illiam?). Frob(o)ese were in (J. M. Reuss's) Co. B of what became Hobby's Eighth Texas Infantry. They

later bought out the Runge firm at Indianola. In Co. G of this regiment there was a Pvt. J. Runge. See Texas State Archives, no. 95, pp. 30, 73, and 79. This cannot have been the Julius Runge (b. 1851 at New Braunfels) who became a very important banker and cotton speculator at Galveston later in the century, but he was probably a relative.

11. H(enry?). Iken was a commission merchant at Indianola when his wife and at least one child died in a yellow fever epidemic at that town in the summer of 1867 (*Indianola Scrap Book,* facs. repr., p. 117).

12. Undoubtedly the reference is to Philip N. Luckett's Third Texas Infantry Regiment. *Wright/Simpson* states that Maj. Kampmann, not Col. Luckett, was in command when this mutiny took place (p. 19 and p. 143, n. #406).

13. This may be the same newspaper as the *Fort Brown Flag,* since both came from Brownsville.

14. Kemper's Bluff was 48 miles below Victoria on the banks of the Guadalupe River. John Frederick Kemper had a trading post there by November 1845, when it was the terminal point of steamship lines and for a while threatened to overshadow Victoria. Kemper was the last white man killed by Indians in Victoria County. The Karankawas shot him with an arrow and then branded his chest. By 1859 extensive warehouses were located there and a good road led to Goliad (Victor M. Rose, *Some Historical Facts in Regard to the Settlements of Victoria, Texas,* p. 28; and Roy Grimes, *300 Years in Victoria County,* pp. 216-18 and 513-14).

15. Viktor Bracht, *Texas in 1848,* p. 137, also stresses that the "weesache" and the bois d'arc (which Texans generally call the "bo-dark") will in the future make serviceable fences.

16. Here the father had copied several pages describing in detail various similar ways of rendering and using indigo, information he says he took from three sources: Steckhard, Krapf, and Benjamin Scholz.

17. Jacob Schmitz, a Prussian, operated quite a luxurious hotel on the town square of New Braunfels. The building has been preserved. After the war the Schmitz family were in the Düsseldorf area and visited with the Kapps there. Jacob Schimitz had become a colonel in the Thirty-first Brigade TST, of which Robert Bechem was brigadier general.

18. Though Rudolf may well have had cholera, the symptoms he describes sound suspiciously like those given for overdoses of Aconitum and Arnica (*DUSA,* pp. 56-61 and 164-65). Both were favorite home remedies of the Coreths.

19. Haas, *History of New Braunfels,* p. 193, says Capt. William Seekatz was in charge of the plant but does not give the names of the associates. Haas also refers there to statements in the *Neu-Braunfelser Zeitung* (issues of 17 July 1863 and 29 April 1864) to the effect that guano from a cave on the Cibolo was being used in this connection, with the government furnishing kettles for the operation.

20. Ernst Coreth evidently did his banking primarily through Franz Moureau and Jacob Schmitz.

21. The War Meeting took place at San Pedro Springs in San Antonio on Saturday, 26 Sept. 1863 (*San Antonio Semi-Weekly* of 1 Oct. 1863, vol. 2, no. 185, p. 1, col. 5).

22. Major (later Lt. Col.) W. O. Hutchison, a Virginian, practiced law in San Marcos after the war and became widely known throughout the state before his death in 1900. See Duaine for photograph and this information (page unnumbered). *Wright/Simpson* misspells the name in the index, but spells it correctly elsewhere (p. 29).

23. Sgt. Ernst Schwantes of Guadalupe County was killed at Blair's Landing (Duaine, p. 109). His widow married August Schulze of Co. F, whose first wife's death is mentioned in the Coreth letters.

24. The original reads *"Kelleresel,"* the Texas German term for pill bugs, which the Blue Mass pill evidently resembled. The *Armadillidium vulgare* (pill bug or wood-louse) is normally called *"Holzlaus"* in German, but Wahrig also gives *"die Kellerassel,"* saying the possible source for the second portion of the compound is Latin *asellus* ("little ass," i.e., donkey; NHG *"der Esel"*).

25. Oddly enough, Münzenberger himself here omits the last syllable of his name. I have chosen to use the form of his name which is the only one I found in legal or official sources. In the Coreth letters he is often simply "M." and at least once "Münzberg."

The Ponds and the Pines

1. At Sabine Pass Lt. Dick Dowling and his men had in forty-five minutes achieved a spectacular victory over the Yankees attempting to launch Banks's attack there on 8 September 1863 (*Résumé*, pp. 21 and 50).

2. Burchard Miller's partner in dealings with the *Adelsverein*.

3. Col. Henry M. Elmore ("Elmor" to Rudolf) headed the Twentieth Texas Infantry Regiment, made up largely of prominent, middle-aged men. Its principal function was to guard the coast between the mouth of the Sabine and Galveston, which city it helped to retake on 1 January 1863, after it had been under Union control for a few months (*Wright/Simpson*, p. 22; n. #525 on p. 164; and plate no. 42).

4. P. N. Luckett, a Corpus Christi physician, had represented Nueces and Webb Counties in the Secession Convention. In February 1861 he was a member of the commission representing the state and co-signer of correspondence directed to Col. Ben McCulloch and Brev. Maj. Gen D. E. Twiggs with regard to the Federal evacuation of Texas. Col. Luckett at times headed the Third Texas Infantry Regiment (*Wright/Simpson*, pp. 177 and 189-96). Born in France, Xavier Blanchard Debray was an honor graduate of the St. Cyr military school. After a brief diplomatic career with the government of Napoleon III, Debray resigned and came to America because of his republican sentiments. Three years after first arriving in Texas, he settled at San Antonio, where he published the Spanish newspaper *El Bejareno* from 1855 until the war. After a short period as aide-de-camp to Gov. Edward Clark, Debray held major commands in the Houston-Galveston area, which latter city he helped to recapture. He played a major role in the Red River Campaign in Louisiana. Once the war was over, he lived in Houston, then Galveston, and finally at Austin, where he resumed his work as a General Land Office translator. See especially *Wright/Simpson*, p. 76, n. #26, and Ella Lonn, *Foreigners in the Confederacy*, pp. 20 and 136-37.

5. Perhaps Major Waldemar Hyllested of the Zouave Battalion, Louisiana Cavalry, who could have been on Trans-Mississippi business in Houston at the time. Hyllested's unit was first under the command of Lt. Col. M. A. Coppens (Stephen B. Oates, *Confederate Cavalry West of the River*, p. 170).

6. The Beaumont depot had been burned 2 October 1862 (*Résumé*, p. 50). The only railroad to serve the city was the Texas and New Orleans (4' 8½" in gauge), that ran between Orange and Houston. The Eastern Texas Railroad (of uncertain gauge) stopped short of Beaumont by a few miles and thus did not quite connect the city with Sabine Pass, the other terminus. See map with legend in Robert C. Black III, *The Railroads of the Confederacy*.

7. Woods's regiment is described in Oscar Haas, *History of New Braunfels* (p. 162), as having had a sixteen-member band. Checking the roster of the regiment in Carl L. Duaine, *The Dead Men Wore Boots* (pp. 96-109), one discovers that only two men from New Braunfels, both from Co. F, were among the members: Edward Eberhard, evidently the chief musician, and Emil Mergele.

8. During the first week of November the Federal army and navy units along the coast and the Mexican Border occupied Brazos Island and Brownsville.

9. By the end of 1863 there were Federal forces at several locations from Corpus Christi to Port Lavaca and some on St. Joseph's Island, Mustang Island, and at Pass Cavallo (*Résumé*, p. 22).

10. Capt. Podewils ostensibly resigned because rheumatism, resulting from an old war injury in Europe, made him a burden to his men. The always generous Woods placed him on extended furlough rather than drop him from the rolls, "since he is one of my most efficient captains," but accepted his resignation on 7 November 1863 (Duaine, pp. 24 and 105). The term Rudolf applied to Philip Bitter is *"Erz-kaffer."* Many dictionaries do not give the word *"Kaffer"* at all, but the Coreths used it rather frequently. It means something like "country bumpkin." The Coreths would no doubt have been startled to learn that it is said to have entered the German language via the gypsies and the criminal class (Wahrig, s. v. *"Kaff"*).

11. Alex Rugeley, a brother of Rudolf's erstwhile captain, E. S. Rugeley, was the oldest son of John Rugeley, who was married twice and fathered twenty-one children. Alex Rugeley visited a sister of his, a Mrs. Blair (Blair's Landing?) living on Bayou Pierre in April of 1864 (Duaine, p. 54). Arda Talbot Allen has described him as having been very well educated in the eastern states and being "most austere and stern" but "brilliant in conversation" (*Miss Ella of the Deep South of Texas*, pp. 80-82).

12. Charles L. Pyron, who rose to the rank of colonel, commanded the Second Texas Cavalry Regiment (or Mounted Rifles). See *Wright/Simpson*, p. 23; also p. 111, n. #152. In December of 1863 Woods was commanding the First Brigade, which was made up of Pyron's nine companies and Woods's own ten. In January of 1864 Pyron was commanding Luckett's old regiment. Pyron's men are said to have called Woods's men "Racoon Roughs" (Duaine, pp. 48-49).

13. The Enfield, made by Barnett of London, was the best foreign-made military rifle available. Actually its ammunition was of .577 calibre, while American ammunition of the closest calibre was .58, but this presented no problem (Waldo E. Rosebush, *American Firearms and the Changing Frontier*, pp. 59-60).

14. To Rudolf, *"der Westen"* evidently meant anything west of the Brazos.

15. This *"Sturranfall"* could indicate a slight convulsion.

16. Approximately twenty of E. S. Rugeley's company perished at Matagorda Bay in a sudden norther which drove their boats from the

shore. Sources differ as to the date, saying either 30-31 Dec. 1863 or New Year's night 1864.

17. See n. 2 in "Drops of Water."

18. At the time of this letter, Otto von Roeder's son and two˙ of his nephews, Franz Joachim and Ludwig August, cousins, were serving in the army. Both nephews were in Co. G of the Thirty-second Cavalry under Capt. Josiah Taylor. A third nephew later joined the same outfit. All were named von Roeder. Information from Flora von Roeder, letter dated 23 Oct. 1975.

19. Capt. Franz Vander Stucken (or van der Stucken or simply Stucken) was from Fredericksburg and commanded Co. E in the First Texas Cavalry, which Lt. Col. Augustus Buchel (or Buechel) formed and then commanded after leaving Luckett's Third Texas Infantry Regiment. *Wright/ Simpson* evidently does not list Stucken or his company separately.

20. Duaine (p. 48) calls this plantation simply "Hawkins," but it should not be confused with the northeast Texas town of Hawkins. For a picture of the Hawkins Ranch House, see E. M. Schiwetz, *Buck Schiwetz's Texas* (p. 43). Located 10-15 miles below Caney (Duaine, p. 48), the house was begun in 1852 by a Dr. Pierson and became the property of Col. J. B. Hawkins, a cotton and cane planter (Junann J. Stieghorst, *Bay City and Matagorda County,* p. 23).

21. Twenty-sixth Texas Cavalry.

22. Kirby Smith, the general in charge of the Trans-Mississippi Department, was made a full general in February 1864. He was the last Confederate general to surrender (26 May 1865) and was one of the prominent figures to leave for Mexico thereafter. The literature on the Mexico exiles is extensive.

23. August Schulze later married the widow of Ernst Schwantes (Co. F; died at Blair's Landing). Among their descendants are two great-great-grandchildren of Ernst and Agnes Coreth.

24. According to Duaine, Carl Mergele, like his older brother Emil, divided his time between service with Co. F and with the regimental band (p. 103). The 1860 census shows the family to be from France, a rarity in New Braunfels. The original name is thought to have been germanized.

25. Henry Weil, a Comal County farmer from Nassau, may have owned the farm of which Ernst Coreth writes in connection with the saltpeter operations (letter of 20 Nov. 1864). Haas does not list Weil with Co. F (p. 163). See Duaine, p. 108.

26. Including this information evidently did not speed later correspondence to its destination, possibly because of spelling errors. The *San Antonio Semi-Weekly News* of 10 April 1862 (and others) carried a notice dated 13 March 1862, in which a Lt. J(illegible). Clute of Houston (Co. A, Fifth Regt.) was "detailed, empowered, and requisitioned" by the Adjutant General's Office in Austin to accept enlistments. A small town near present-day Freeport (old Velasco) bears this man's surname.

27. The regiment had two men named Stevens, both captains. This is probably Edward Stevens of Co. I, whom Duaine shows as having been in pursuit of deserters in February 1864 (p. 107).

28. Probably George Lueders, who was made prisoner of war on 21 November 1864 and transferred to Ship Island, Miss. (Duaine, p. 102). Oscar Haas's *History of New Braunfels* (p. 163) appears to have listed one Henry Luerson by mistake as Henry Lueders.

29. Stokely M. Holmes, a Mississippian who had come to Texas as a youth, had served in Nicaragua, South America, and Mexico. He led Co. K, made up mostly of Caldwell County residents, which may have been an organized militia troop before. Duaine says he ultimately became a lieutenant colonel (p. 101), while *Wright/Simpson* (p. 29) gives his top rank as major.

30. According to Max Krueger's *Pioneer Life in Texas* (p. 35), the majority of horses in Texas prior to 1870 had descended from animals introduced into the area by Spanish *conquistadores*. Krueger describes the animal as "short and stout, with well-formed head, intelligent eyes and long mane and tail nearly touching the ground." Unequalled for use in herding cattle, the Spanish horse had hoofs so tough no shoes were required.

31. Co. F had both a Frederick and a William Huebotter, both of Guadalupe County (*Neu-Braunfelser Zeitung* "Pionierdenkmal" issue of 18 Aug. 1938, pp. 20-21). On 23 April 1864 William Huebotter was under sentence at General Headquarters in Galveston (Duaine, p. 101). Both Huebotters and Adam Daum deserted from Co. F at Camp Hardeman on 1 February 1864 (ibid., pp. 98 and 101).

32. William D. Kelley, surgeon to the Thirty-second Texas Volunteer Cavalry whom Rudolf mentions several times, had played a prominent role in public health at Indianola as early as 1855, when he persuaded the aldermen to establish a permanent hospital for the city. "He reminded council members that, in the previous year, yellow fever had decimated the population of the city by a total equal to the increase through birth and immigration" (Brownson Malsch, *Indianola: The Mother of Western Texas,* pp. 93-94). See also p. 97 and p. 292 in Malsch for Kelley references.

33. An undated note, evidently written by Rudolf, indicates Fritz Pantermühl lost this rank after overstaying a leave. Other sources list him as a private.

34. Dr. Collier, surgeon with Woods's regiment, was wounded in the thumb at Blair's Landing (Duaine, pp. 109 and 118).

Battles and Bayous

1. John D. Winters, *The Civil War in Louisiana,* p. 358.

2. Gen. Tom Green, a Virginian, had served Texas in the revolution, in Indian campaigns, as inspector general of the Somervell Expedition, in the Mexican War, and had represented Fayette County in the legislature, as well as having held the position of clerk of the Supreme Court of the state. In the Civil War he had been with Sibley in New Mexico, had commanded ground forces at the recapture of Galveston, and had led the old Sibley unit in various engagements in Louisiana. When he was killed, he had only recently returned from a brief assignment on the Rio Grande against Gen. Banks (*Wright/ Simpson,* pp. 78f.).

3. Col. Nicholas C. Gould commanded the Twenty-third Texas Cavalry Regiment. Col. William H. Parsons commanded the Twelfth Texas Cavalry Regiment and, late in the war, a brigade that bore his name. A native of Alabama, Parsons published a newspaper, *The Southwest,* at Waco just before the war. He organized his regiment at Waxahachie and in 1883 wrote a history of the brigade he had led. After the war, he spent much of his time in practicing law at Washington, D. C. (*Wright/Simpson,* p. 25, and n. #181, p. 115).

4. This is evidently not a standard expression but a personal memory of Rudolf's from 1846, when his family had embarked from Antwerp. The noise-makers may have been the sort that Jewish children clatter whenever the name of Haman comes up as the Book of Esther is read on certain religious holidays.

5. Winters (p. 358) quotes Theophilus Noel's *Autobiography and Reminiscences of Theophilus Noel* (pp. 100 and 143) and David D. Porter's *Private Journal* (p. 763).

6. Bose's company was assigned to Scurry's brigade, which, along with Waul's brigade, formed Walker's division (Oscar Haas, *History of New Braunfels,* p. 167). Bose's unit was Co. K of the Third Texas Infantry Regiment (ibid., p. 164). Camille Arnaud Jules Marie, Prince de Polignac, attained the rank of major general in the Confederate army. Before coming to America from Europe, he had been awarded the Crimean medal. The end of the Civil War found him on a mission to Louis Napoleon's court. Thereafter he retired to the family lands in Austria. See, for example, Ella Lonn, *Foreigners in the Confederacy,* pp. 38-9, 88, 168, 170, and 213, as well as Chester Alwyn Barr, *Polignac's Texas Brigade.*

7. Noel states that from 1 Oct. 1863 to 26 April 1864 Arthur Bagby of the Seventh Regiment led Sibley's Brigade, but bad health soon forced him to relinquish command to Col. William P. Hardeman. See Paul C. Boethel, *A History of Lavaca County,* rev. ed., pp. 75-76.

8. Winters, pp. 365f.

9. Ibid., p. 373. Also, George Purwell Whittington, *Rapides Parish, Louisiana,* p. 192.

10. Winters pp. 375-76.

11. Ibid., passim, pp. 383-87.

12. The common blackberry was one of the many native remedies for dysentery. See H. H. Cunningham, *Doctors in Gray,* pp. 186-87.

13. This British version of the proverb comes nearer the feeling of the original than does the more familiar "necessity is the mother of invention."

14. The Duff and Waldrip gangs, often called *"die Hängebande"* ("the hanging gang"), supposedly murdered twice as many people as the number killed by Indians in the Gillespie County area between 1846 and 1870. Actually, most of these gangsters were never indicted. Some disguised themselves as Indians. See Don H. Biggers, *German Pioneers in Texas,* Gillespie County ed., especially pp. 175-90.

15. The Fayette County Historical Commission (La Grange) says it knows nothing about the existence of such a factory (letter of 19 Oct. 1976). However, Ragsdale (p. 65) mentions that Wilhelm Fuchs worked there during the Civil War also. The factory, Ragsdale states, made wool hats.

16. Since Ernst Coreth states that the local newspaper was not coming out at that time, details are almost impossible to come by in the usual ways. The name "Alsens" should perhaps read "Alsenz," and the man bearing it may have been the son of the local midwife (Haas, p. 262). The only adult male named Bodemann in the 1860 census for Comal County was Gustav. The other persons mentioned are even harder to identify. In any case, the challenger of the incumbent mayor Hermann Seele lost. Seele served until 1866 (Haas, p. 299).

17. "Pabieco" is a corrupted spelling of *babieca,* in line with Rudolf's system of phonetics. *El babieca* means "a stupid, ignorant fellow," according to F. Corona Bustamante, *Dictionary of the Spanish and English Languages.* With a cedilla, Babieca becomes the name of El Cid's mount. It is another instance of the quaint names the Coreths gave their horses.

18. Perhaps the Battle of Cold Harbor (3 June 1863), part of the Wilderness campaign. In a few hours the Union lost an estimated 7,000 men in what has been called "the most horrible slaughter of the war" (*Columbia Encyclopedia,* second ed., p. 2146, s.v. "Wilderness campaign").

19. John D. Winters has supplied the information that this would have had to be a grist mill, since the state had no flour mills. For references to the Osborne plantation, see *The War of the Rebellion: Official Records,* Series 1, vol. 34, pt. 1, pp. 425, 428, and 441. Evidently the plantation was approximately twelve miles downriver from Alexandria, though some references indicate it was several miles farther away from the town then.

20. See n. 18, "The Ponds and the Pines."

21. The letters are on a wide variety of types of paper. The poorest in quality by far was used for letters between February and May of 1862. During much of 1863, the letters are on pages obviously torn from a

daybook or ledger, with blue numbers in the upper right-hand corner. The paper is relatively good in the case of letters from 1864.

22. In German, malaria is called *Wechselfieber,* literally, "alternating fever," because of the characteristic of causing fever on alternate days.

23. At this stage, William P. Hardeman was commanding the old Sibley brigade. See n. 7, this chapter. A veteran of many campaigns beginning with the Texas Revolution, Hardeman, a native of Tennessee and resident of the Caney Creek area in Matagorda, was made a brigadier general by Kirby Smith on 17 March 1865. After the war, Hardeman was a surveyor of lands in Mexico. When he returned to Texas to farm, he soon was chosen for important state offices. See *Wright/Simpson,* p. 80, for example.

24. This was probably Ernestine Schimmelpfennig, a Prussian widow, the mother of August and H[ermann]. Schimmelpfennig. She was only about two years older than Ernst Coreth, actually. Goethe's dying words, usually given as "Mehr Licht!" and interpreted as profoundly symbolic, here appear in a much less esoteric form. Clearly Ernst Coreth, like many liberals of present-day Germany, did not feel unqualified admiration for the great poet.

25. Steel(e?) and Gordon may be impossible to identify. Far fewer copies of San Antonio newspapers were being printed at this period because of paper shortages.

26. It is unclear whether three or four men are involved. These names do not appear in the 1860 Comal County census. "Bringmann" should probably read Brinkmann. The connection with the name Schramm strongly suggests the men may have lived in Guadalupe or Bexar County.

27. Many patients reacted so badly to quinine that it was better to omit it in such cases. This may have been true of Carl Coreth. Men from less settled areas and higher terrain were sicker oftener than urban men from low-lying regions. Charles Theodore Mohr, a highly-respected German pharmacist at Mobile who was responsible for checking the content of drugs smuggled into the South after the outbreak of the war, stated that hospitals frequently confused quinine sulphate and morphine sulphate with terrible results. Much of the French quinine was thought to be badly adulterated, and in the spring of 1862 the Union was charged with deliberately permitting smugglers to bring poisoned quinine into the Confederacy.

The Slough of Despond

1. Walter F. Preston, a Virginian, came to Texas in 1859 and bought the very large Merriwether farm on the Guadalupe downstream from New Braunfels. He and Dr. Koester represented Comal County at the Secession Convention in Austin (Oscar Haas, *History of New Braunfels,* p. 154). When he purchased the 1003-acre "Riverside Farm" for $1.00 an acre, Preston gave his residence as New Orleans. His widow lost possession of the place during Reconstruction (ibid., p. 184). Ernst Scherff was already a merchant, as was Gustav Conrads (ibid., pp. 265 and 284). No Tischler appears in the 1860 Comal County census. Daniel Wheeler, a merchant in New Braunfels as early as 1860 at least, was a native of Maine, but had evidently come by way of Louisiana (ibid., p. 291). Hermann Spiess was Meusebach's successor as commissioner general of the *Adelsverein* (see n. 34, "From Tyrol to Texas").

2. Emil Dittmar was a son of a prominent jurist from Darmstadt and was the husband of the former Bertha Moller (Chabot, p. 388). Allowing for possible errors in spelling, Dittmar's companion may have been his wife's brother. Dittmar's sisters were married to John Torrey, the mill owner, and the merchant Gustav Conrads (see n. 1 above).

3. Cf. n. 26 in "The Ponds and the Pines."

4. Originally from Connecticut, John Torrey and his brothers in Houston were associated with New Braunfels as teamsters from the earliest times. The Torrey mill was repeatedly destroyed by the elements and rebuilt, until the persistent owner finally gave up and moved away. See the many references in Haas; also Chabot, p. 389. Joseph Landa came from Poland by way of England. Some nine years later he owned much of the Merriwether property, which included facilities for ginning cotton, as well as a saw mill and a flour and grist mill. Part of this property is now the famous Landa Park (Haas, pp. 252, 151-52, and 184f.). Landa seems to have been the only Jew of prominence in early New Braunfels. Much like Merriwether, who had earlier played a leading role in New Braunfels as the principal slave owner and the first person to hold a U. S. patent for a wire fence, Landa became increasingly prominent in the post-war years. Samuel Mather ("Matters" to Ernst Coreth), who came from Williamson County, in 1863 joined David Richardson of Travis County and Dr. Koester (Comal County) in acquiring a charter for establishing the Texas Paper Manufacturing Company at New Braunfels. The corporation bought land by the Comal River, on which site an older mill, once the property of the Holekamp family, already stood. A list of New Braunfels industries for the year 1866 does not include a paper mill. See Haas, pp. 192 and 197.

5. Standard, and even medical, dictionaries give no translations for the several terms of illnesses that Ernst Coreth uses in this letter. A native Austrian who has practiced gynecology and obstetrics in Texas

for some years was also consulted, but was unable to translate what are probably regional and also archaic words for common sicknesses. Similarly difficult terms appear in later letters.

6. Ernst Coreth evidently meant that Hermann Runge's departure gave hope for imminent peace. See, for example, his observation in an undated letter, immediately preceding Rudolf's of 11 Nov. 1862.

7. Haas (p. 195) quotes the *Neu-Braunfelser Zeitung* of 18 Nov. 1864 as reporting that there were twenty such camels, all born at Camp Verde, delivering corn to San Antonio.

8. See n. 7 in "Battles and Bayous." Arthur Bagby, a West Point graduate, had resigned his commission to practice law at Mobile before settling in Gonzales, Texas, in 1858. When the war began, Bagby recruited a company in Victoria. After several important assignments with units that saw considerable fighting, he headed a battalion composed of (Alexander) Terrell's and (Xavier B.) Debray's Brigadiers with the Second Louisiana Cavalry. Promoted by Gen. Kirby Smith to the rank of major general, Bagby remained in command of all cavalry forces in Louisiana for the rest of the war. Thereafter, he practiced law at Hallettsville. See Paul C. Boethel, *A History of Lavaca County*, rev. ed., pp. 75-76.

9. All names on Haas's roster of Co. F (p. 163) are German ones. Carl Duaine, *The Dead Men Wore Boots*, p. 106, gives almost no information about Henry Smith, except that he was a lieutenant and was sick in camp near Pottsville in March 1865. James Calhoun, a Comal County resident of long standing, was a native of Ireland and had been a member of Jack Hays's Rangers before becoming overseer of Merriwether's plantation. At some time before he died on 17 April 1866, he had acquired a ranch west of New Braunfels.

10. Which twelve states are meant is baffling. The Confederacy consisted of eleven states, some of which by this time had been largely defeated and restored to Union control.

11. The Gonzales County Historical Commission states that Jonathan T. Bratten owned a large place between Gonzales and present-day Nixon, around the Bebe community (letter of 13 October 1976).

12. According to Franz A. Coreth's younger daughter Lina (Mrs. C. V. Windwehen), her father was assigned to patrol the block between the town square or plaza and Mill Street, property now largely occupied by the Doeppenschmidt Funeral Home. He did not have to leave New Braunfels because he became sick with a congestion of the lungs that weakened him greatly. He had grown from an undersized youngster to a man well over six feet tall, but he was very thin during the war years.

13. The family always thought Carl was buried in "the Confederate cemetery at San Augustine," but several historians of the area assure me that no such designation ever existed. J. B. Sanders's *Index to the Cemeteries of San Augustine County, Texas 1836-1964* does not list Carl Coreth or more than a few other Confederate soldiers.

Dixitur

1. Located in Rusk County, the little community of Pine Hill (now spelled Pinehill) acquired the nickname "Rake Pocket" early. During the days when the Timpson and Henderson Railroad was thriving, the town had a bank, post office, depot, school, and several businesses and churches. It is said to have been founded unintentionally when Henderson Hillin ran out of feed for his oxen there about 1844 and was joined shortly afterward by relatives and friends from Alabama, Georgia, and Mississippi (Garland R. Farmer, Sr., *The Realm of Rusk County*, p. 42).

2. The word in the original, *"Soldateska,"* comes from the Italian and is pejorative in German. Wahrig says it was introduced into German by Schiller in 1792 (s.v. *"Soldateska"*), while another scholar attributes its use in German to the publicist Ignaz Kuranda, writing in the *Stuttgarter Morgenblatt* of 15 Nov. 1848, saying it was applied especially by radicals to the Prussian soldiers with their close adherence to tradition and their antipathy to civilians and the cause of liberty (Georg Buchmann, *Geflügelte Worte*, 31st ed., p. 694). Kämmerling was Prussian and returned to live in Prussia.

3. A native of Tennessee, Wharton came to Galveston as a child with his family. He married a daughter of the governor of South Carolina, the state where he received his higher education. He practiced law in Brazoria and served that county as representative to the Secession Convention of Texas. After having raised a company of cavalry that became part of Terry's Texas Rangers, he commanded the Eighth Texas Cavalry Regiment with distinction at Shiloh. By November of 1863 he was a major general, and the next year he took a position of leadership in the Red River campaign. Still with the Trans-Mississippi Department, he was shot and killed at Houston by Col. George Wythe Baylor just three days before Lee surrendered (*Wright/Simpson*, n. #75, p. 95).

4. Here "Sharpshooters" means the Sharps guns. Christian Sharps was issued two patents, in 1848 and 1852, for a "breech-loading percussion gun with downward sliding block operated by an underlever." The Sharps, unlike earlier breechloaders, utilized a metallic cartridge (Waldo E. Rosebush, *American Firearms and the Changing Frontier*, pp. 48 and 56).

5. See n. 3 in "Battles and Bayous."

6. Polignac's service to the Confederacy is remembered especially in connection with the victory at Mansfield. His unsuccessful mission to France, begun when the Confederate cause was already all but lost, was thwarted because the Duc de Morny, who was to have acted as intermediary between him and Louis Napoleon, died before Polignac reached his destination. Polignac was facetiously known as "General Polecat" by his sometimes mutinous men.

7. This strongly suggests that Rudolf had expressed the desire to escape to Mexico. Münzenberger was already there.

8. Hummel's Store was located where the Stower's Furniture Store stood in the 1930's. At various times the family dealt in stationery, paint and art supplies, hunting and fishing equipment, munitions, and weapons. The old Hummel Building housed the first meetings of the famous Casino Club of San Antonio, which was a predominantly German society. The Hummels spent the war years in Mexico, but returned later and operated a store at 270 W. Commerce St. until at least 1900. Its advertisements in the *Deutsch-texanische Monatschefte* of the turn of the century state the firm was established in 1847. See especially Frederick C. Chabot, *Genealogies of Early San Antonio Families*, pp. 283-84.

9. Nowhere else have I found any indication that Hoym rose above the rank of private.

10. Gen. John A. Walker at the close of the war commanded a cavalry division composed of Steele's, Bee's, and Bagby's men and of the brigades of Cooper and Slaughter. Walker had been a regular officer of the U.S. Army during the Mexican War, but resigned his commission. He distinguished himself with the Army of Northern Virginia. He took prominent part also at Mansfield and Pleasant Hill (*Wright/Simpson*, n. #527, p. 164).

11. Of all the letters in the correspondence only this one has both envelope and stamp in good condition.

12. "Wuppermann" is probably George Wuppermann who lived in the Upper Blanco community (Rudolph L. Biesele, *German Settlements in Texas*, p. 168). Wuppermann is mentioned repeatedly, as are his wife and children, in Hedwig Coreth's letter to Rudolf from Düsseldorf, 31 Jan. 1867, because the family was also in that area, as were Mrs. Staehely, her brother and sister, Walter and Helene Tips, and the Jacob Schmitz family.

13. George Wythe Baylor was born in the Indian Territory but at thirteen (1845) came to Fayette County, Texas, with his family. After living for some years in California, he settled at Weatherford, Texas. An ardent secessionist, he is said to have been the first man to raise a Confederate flag in Austin. Having served on Albert Sidney Johnston's staff and commanded a regiment of the Arizona Brigade, Baylor was singled out for gallantry at Mansfield and Pleasant Hill. On 6 April 1865, just before Lee's surrender at Appomattox, Colonel Baylor shot Major General John Austin Wharton to death in General J. B. Magruder's Headquarters (Fannin Hotel, Houston), the motive having been related to Confederate reorganization in the Trans-Mississippi Command a few months earlier. "General Wharton was supposed to have slapped Baylor's face and called him a liar, whereupon Colonel Baylor drew his pistol and shot Wharton, who was unarmed at the time" (*Wright/Simpson*, n. #75, p. 95). After the war, Baylor served as a Texas Ranger until 1885, then represented El Paso County in the legislature and was clerk in district and circuit courts. He died in San Antonio in 1916 and is buried in the Confederate Cemetery there (*Wright/Simpson*, n. #51, pp. 84-85). See also n. 3 in *"Dixitur."*

14. See Rudolf's letter of 17 April 1864.

15. Hermann Runge seems to have been a brother of Henry Runge, but information about him is scant, beyond the fact that he did business in New Braunfels. F. W. Grassmeyer had a ferry on the Colorado below Bastrop as early as 1835 (Hermann Seele, *Die Cypresse und Gesammelte Schriften*, p. 101). Biesele, quoting Tiling, lists him among one hundred German settlers who took active part in the Texas Revolution (pp. 191-92). See n. 12 above for reference to Walter Tips. Tips became a prominent Austin businessman.

16. This cannot have been Mrs. Julius Runge, since Julius was only fourteen at the time. It appears to have been Hermann Runge's wife.

17. Known as the Greyhound Division because they moved with such extraordinary speed and efficiency (*Wright/Simpson*, n. #527, p. 164), these men of Walker's division apparently could also run fast *from* the army.

18. This family had certainly seen better days. In September 1842, Henry Amthor was among thirty-eight residents of Austin County petitioning to create Hermann's University, which unfortunately never developed. In 1859, Mrs. Amthor accompanied Adolphus Fuchs of Cypress Mill on the piano when he, a guest of the household, sang "arias from Haydn's *Creation* and Beethoven's 'Adelaide' " (Biesele, pp. 215-16, and p. 222). The graciousness of the cultivated ménage undoubtedly had been undermined by the war, and Rudolf is perhaps making an unfair comparison with nostalgic memories of home. Not too surprisingly these strangers were less than eager to invite a soldier into a home where several young ladies lived. The Cat Spring area had been decidedly unenthusiastic about the Southern cause early in the war, and Rudolf was presumably still in Confederate uniform. In later generations, some Amthor, Fuchs, and Coreth descendants became the closest of friends.

19. See the end of "The Slough of Despond."

20. Streams in the San Antonio/New Braunfels area.

21. Ernst Trebess, a wagoner, and August Trebess, a saddler, were sons of a Prussian farmer in Comal County in 1860 (Oscar Haas, *History of New Braunfels*, p. 289). At thirty Ernst enlisted in Co. F of Woods's regiment (31 March 1862), and shortly afterward (12 May 1862) his younger brother August, about twenty-two, enlisted in the same unit. August had become a corporal before both brothers deserted from Camp Hardeman on 1 Feb. 1864 (Carl L. Duaine, *The Dead Men Wore Boots*, p. 107).

22. Ernst, the oldest of the Meusebach children, was not yet twelve. Otto was ten, as was Josef Coreth. Ernst in later years married Lina Nimitz; their only child, a son, was first cousin of Fleet Admiral Chester Nimitz. Ernst Meusebach was buried in Torreon, Mexico, about the time of the overthrow of Porfirio Diaz.

23. Throughout the war, the Union tended to ally itself with the Juaristas (Liberalists) while the Confederacy was essentially on the side of the Imperialists. Many former leaders of the Confederacy, political as well as military, crossed the border at the end of the war, some offering

their services to Maximilian. See especially Andrew F. Rolle, *The Lost Cause,* and A. W. Terrell, *From Texas to Mexico and the Court of Maximilian in 1865.*

24. According to the *San Antonio Semi-Weekly News* (e. g., issue of 24 March 1865, vol. 5, no. 269, p. 2, c. 1), Carl Münzenberger, not a citizen of Texas or of the C. S. A., was being sued by creditors and had fled the country. Issues shortly before this time carry advertisements for his fine wines and liquors.

25. Haas, p. 196.

Spears into Pruning Hooks

1. Terry Jordan, *German Seed in Texas Soil,* pp. 97-101.
2. Ibid.
3. Ibid., pp. 101, 130, and 156.
4. Ibid., pp. 163-65, 168-69, and 197. Also, Patsy Miller, "Collectors help chronicle development of the West," *Fort Worth Star-Telegram,* 5 Aug. 1978, section C, p. 1.
5. Jordan, pp. 83-86, 115, 143, and 176.
6. Ibid., pp. 101 and 180; Oscar Haas, *History of New Braunfels and Comal County,* pp. 149 and 184.
7. Jordan, pp. 111-12 and 185.
8. Ibid., pp. 114, 178, and 190; Samuel Wood Geiser, *Naturalists of the Frontier,* pp. 137-38.
9. Haas, p. 197.
10. Hugo Klein, *Alt-Innsbrucker Gaststätten,* p. 122.
11. See Guido Ransleben, *A Hundred Years of Comfort in Texas,* pp. 80-81, 113, and 124-25.
12. Frankfurt am Main, like Hanover, Hesse-Kassel, and Nassau, was annexed by Prussia after the Austro-Prussian War. Austria lost Venetia to Italy by the terms of the treaty and remained outside the gradually unifying Germany.
13. Friedrich Kapp, Ernst Kapp's nephew, was U. S. Commissioner of Emigration and later was a member of the Reichstag as a Progressive. One of his American-born children, named Wolfgang like Ernst Kapp's younger son, became the leader of the right-wing Kapp Putsch in Germany in 1920 (La Vern J. Rippley, *The German Americans,* pp. 70, 82, and 83). Kapp returned permanently to Germany in 1870. Frederick Law Olmsted, one of the designers of Central Park, had visited Comal County in 1855.
14. "Schmidt Wilhelm," who had helped forge the sixshooters at Sisterdale in 1862, committed suicide, as Hedwig reported to Rudolf in a letter not long after this one.
15. A "gacho" is a broken-down or swaybacked horse (Sp. *gacho*=curvated or slumping). A "U. S." was surely a horse with federal brand.

Swords into Plowshares

1. Flints, tinder, and steel were still in common use, though the safety match had been invented in 1855.

2. See n. 25, "Roll Call."

3. Hermann Wilhelm August Gehren, Ph.D., came to Texas for a visit in 1867 and returned to Germany in 1868. Educated at Heidelberg, Marburg, and Berlin, he wrote his dissertation on fluorine (Robert Robinson-Zwahr, *The Bremers and Their Kin in Germany and in Texas*, vol. 2, p. 1045). Ernst Coreth used the French term when he wrote, "Welch ein Beotier!" ("What a Beotian!") The term "Beotian" never acquired currency in German or English, but means essentially "dunce." A Greek agricultural people, the Beotians were considered by the Athenians to be provincial and slow.

4. Terry Jordan, *German Seed in Texas Soil*, p. 176.

5. This can be no other than Louis Cachand Ervendberg, whom *The Handbook of Texas* and Samuel Wood Geiser's *Naturalists of the Frontier* (p. 148) describe as having been killed by bandits in February 1863 at Pachuca, Mexico, where he had resettled. Ervendberg's origins—and obviously his end—are very cloudy.

6. See Oscar Haas, *History of New Braunfels and Comal County*, p. 148, for a picture of the woolen mills, with detailed caption. In 1882 the factory produced the cloth for A & M College to use in making cadets' uniforms (Haas, p. 199).

7. The official records of this transaction have not surfaced. It is thought that the new owner of the Kapp farm at Sisterdale was the youngest son of the elder George Bunsen, the Illinois educator who had come to America in the early 1830's after the liberal uprisings in Germany. Since the Bunsen family was intimately and intricately connected with both the Münzenbergers and the Lindheimers by marriage, the newcomer inevitably came into contact almost immediately with the Coreth family. A Mr. Bunsen ("a very natural man, interested mainly in hunting and farming") is mentioned as having gone with Franz to hunt and to look at area caves (Rudolf from Ernst Coreth, 3 Feb. [1866 or 1867]). Albert W. Bunsen, who owned property in Llano County and lived in Travis County (see Transcript from Bexar County Records, which replace some of the burned records of Llano County, pp. 605-06), accidentally shot and killed himself while surveying. Gustav Bunsen, brother of the elder George Bunsen, had in 1835 gathered a company of soldiers in Louisville, Kentucky, and led them to Texas to fight for independence. On 27 February 1836, he was killed with a group of other volunteers near San Patricio and is among those named on a monument commemorating the event. See *Monuments Erected to Commemorate the Centenary of Texas Independence*.

8. Black Peter is a children's card game in which the loser (whoever holds the joker when the game ends) is penalized by having his face painted with burnt cork.

9. See also n. 4 in "The Slough of Despond." Joseph Landa's son Harry and Franz Coreth, along with the latter's son-in-law Max A. Altgelt, were pioneers in the crushed stone industry at New Braunfels in later years. See Harry Landa, *As I Remember,* pp. 86-87.

10. It is said that the Coreths frequently had two harvests of corn annually.

11. Dr. Felix Bracht, a physician brother of Viktor Bracht (see bibliography and "From Tyrol to Texas"), served as president of a convention held to determine how Comal County stood on secession (New Braunfels, 9 December 1860). He had been a strong supporter of Breckinridge. He and Gustav Dreiss lost to Dr. Koester and W. F. Preston, more conservative candidates, when delegates to the state convention were chosen (Rudolf L. Biesele, *German Settlements in Texas,* pp. 204-206). See also Haas, pp. 185 and 264.

12. Henry Hessler and James Ferguson (a Scot) were business partners at New Braunfels from very early times. The firm had transferred there from St. Thomas Island, it is said. Hessler is in neither the 1850 nor the 1860 censuses as these appear in Haas. Ferguson died in 1860.

13. Adolph Münzenberger and his second wife, Sophie Bunsen, a daughter of George Bunsen, Sr., of Belleville, Illinois, lived in Coahuila, Mexico, until at least 1878 (see Deed Records of Bexar County, v. 11, p. 275). He died at El Paso (August Santleben, *A Texas Pioneer,* p. 214). His widow, who outlived him by twenty-nine years, died at San Antonio in 1930 (W. P. A. files of local news items at Belleville, Illinois, Public Library).

14. See n. 28, "From Tyrol to Texas."

15. The German edition of *Frank Leslie's Illustrated Newspaper,* an historically invaluable newspaper originating in New York in 1855, ran from August 1857 until March 1889. (The title was retained by another publisher who continued the paper until 1894.) From 1870 until 1874, three other German-language periodicals appeared at various times under Frank Leslie's aegis, and in 1870-71 he brought out the *Pictorial History of the Franco-German War,* also in German (Madeleine B. Stern, *Purple Passage: The Life of Mrs. Frank Leslie*).

16. Rudolf Wipprecht, later the first teacher of foreign languages at Texas A & M College, had a medical degree.

17. Misses Natalie and Antoinette (von) Schenck and Miss Alice Nohl were later principal faculty members of the German American Ladies' College at Austin, a school said to have begun at New Braunfels (Mary Starr Barkley, *History of Travis County and Austin, 1839-1899,* p. 172). Bianca Nohl (Mrs. Theodore Goldbeck) was Alice's sister. Mrs. Franz Moureau (née Alwine vom Stein) was a stepsister of Dr. Ludwig Nohl. See Robert Robinson-Zwahr, *The Bremers and Their Kin in Germany and in Texas,* especially vol. 2, p. 1031.

18. Among passengers that Santleben recalls as having traveled on his San Antonio-Monterrey stage line, which lasted only two years, were "Frank [Franz Alcad] Coreth and Mrs. [Hedwig] Coreth," as well as many other people mentioned in the Coreth letters. See Santleben, pp. 96-97.

19. Haas, pp. 312-13.

20. Tolle v. Correth, 31 Tex. 362 (1868).

21. See "From Tyrol to Texas."

22. "Noch einmal eine deutsche Convention" in *Neu-Braunsfelser Zeitung,* issue of Friday, 3 July 1874, p. 2.

23. See Agricultural Schedules for 1860, 1870, and 1880 accompanying census, available on microfilm in Genealogical Department, Texas State Archives. The Coreths are not on the 1850 records, and the 1890 records were destroyed.

Epilog

1. Terry Jordan's *German Seed in Texas Soil* (p. 114) mentions, for example, that in 1873 the agricultural society of Cat Spring published its intention of awarding a cash prize to artisans of the area who might demonstrate skill in implement design. The next year, blacksmiths of the area were given a monopoly for the production of cotton and corn planting machinery, which exclusive right was to be theirs thenceforth.

2. That Rudolf Coreth did work for the company in Galveston for only six months is stated in his obituary (*Neu-Braunfelser Zeitung,* issue of 24 October 1901). The invitation to superintendency is in the possession of this author (Rudolf from D. The. Ayers, wholesale grocer, 176 and 178 Strand, Galveston, president of the organization; 16 May 1874).

3. Stanley Walker, *The Dallas Story,* pp. 11-12.

4. Bill in Chancery, Divorce Decree, Circuit Court, 20th Judicial Circuit; Belleville, St. Clair County, Illinois: Rudolph Coreth vs. Jane Coreth.

5. *Neu-Braunfelser Zeitung,* issue of 15 July 1881; Oscar Haas, *History of New Braunfels and Comal County,* p. 204.

6. Already married were Minna's brother Leo Zesch to Franz's niece "Betty" (Elizabeth) Meusebach, Franz's sister Anna Coreth to Hans Marschall, and Hans's brother Otto Marschall to Betty's sister "Tony" Meusebach. Ultimately, the two other Marschall brothers, Ernst and Willie, became the husbands of the two other Meusebach sisters, Lucie and Emmy. Helen, the daughter of Otto and Tony Marschall and first great-grandchild of Ernst and Agnes Coreth, married August Altgelt, a younger brother of Ottilie Coreth's husband. In 1903, two grandchildren of Ernst and Agnes Coreth, Agnes Coreth (daughter of Franz and Minna) and Max Axel Altgelt (son of Hermann and Ottilie), were married to one another, the only marriage among these in which blood relatives were involved. Since none of the Meusebach sons was survived by grandchildren, the Meusebach family may be said to have been absorbed by the Marschall and Zesch families.

Bibliography

Books/Theses/Scholarly Articles

Alexander, Frances. *Orphans on the Guadalupe.* Wichita Falls, Texas: Nortex, 1971.

Allen, Arda Talbot. *Miss Ella of The Deep South of Texas.* San Antonio: Naylor, 1941.

Allers, Ulrich Stephan. *The Concept of Empire of German Romanticism and its Influence on the National Assembly at Frankfort 1848-1849.* Washington, D. C.: North Washington Press, 1948.

Altgelt, Emma Murck. *Beobachtungen und Erinnerungen.* New Braunfels, Texas: *Neu-Braunfelser Zeitung,* 1930.

Andrews, Rena Mazyck. "German Pioneers in Texas: Civil War Period." Master's degree thesis, University of Chicago, 1929.

Barkley, Mary Starr. *History of Travis County and Austin.* Waco: Texian, 1963.

Barr, Chester Alwyn. *Polignac's Texas Brigade.* Texas Gulf Coast Historical Association, November 1964.

Barraclough, Geoffrey. *The Origins of Modern Germany.* 1946; rpt. New York: Capricorn, 1963.

Bauschinger, Sigrid, Horst Denkler, and Wilfried Malsch, eds. *Amerika in der deutschen Literatur: Neue Welt-Nordamerika-USA.* Stuttgart: Philipp Reclam jun., 1975.

Beals, Carleton. *Porfirio Diaz, Dictator of Mexico.* Philadelphia: Lippincott, 1932.

Benjamin, Gilbert Giddings. *The Germans in Texas: A Study in Immigration.* 1910; rpt. Austin: Jenkins, 1974.

Bennett, Bob. *Kerr County, Texas: 1856-1956.* San Antonio: Naylor, 1956.

Bernard, Paul P. *Jesuits and Jacobins: Enlightenment and Enlightened Despotism in Austria.* Urbana: University of Illinois Press, 1967.

Berwanger, Eugene H. *The Frontier Against Slavery: Western Anti-Negro Prejudice and the Slavery Extension Controversy.* Urbana: University of Illinois Press, 1967.

Biesele, Rudolph L. *The History of the German Settlements in Texas, 1831-1861.* Austin: privately printed, 1930.

Biggers, Don H. *German Pioneers in Texas.* Gillespie County ed. Fredericksburg, Texas: Fredericksburg Publishing Co., 1925.

Black, Robert C., III. *The Railroads of the Confederacy.* Chapel Hill: University of North Carolina Press, 1952.

Blasio, José Luis. *Maximilian, Emperor of Mexico: Memoirs of his Private Secretary.* Trans. and ed. Robert Hammond Maury. New Haven: Yale University Press, 1934.

Boethel, Paul C. *A History of Lavaca County.* Rev. ed. Austin: privately printed through Von Boeckmann-Jones, 1959.

_____. *On the Headwaters of the Lavaca and Navidad.* Austin: privately printed through Von Boeckmann-Jones, 1967.

Bracht, Viktor. *Texas in 1848.* Trans. Charles Frank Schmidt. San Antonio: Naylor, 1931.

Bramsted, Ernest K. *Aristocracy and the Middle Classes in Germany: Social Types in German Literature, 1830-1900.* Rev. ed. Chicago: University of Chicago Press, 1964.

Bridges, C. A. "The Knights of the Golden Circle: A Filibustering Fantasy." *Southwestern Historical Quarterly* 44 (January 1941), 287-302.

Bruford, W. H. *Germany in the Eighteenth Century: The Social Background of the Literary Revival.* 1935; rpt. Cambridge: Cambridge University Press, 1965.

Bruncken, Ernest. *German Political Refugees in the United States During the Period From 1815-1860.* Special print from *Deutsch-Amerikanische Geschichtsblätter* of 1904. San Francisco: R & E Research Associates, 1970.

Burkholder, Mary V. *The King William Area: A History and Guide to the Houses.* Photographs by Graham B. Knight. San Antonio: The King William Association, 1973.

Carpenter, Jesse T. *The South as a Conscious Minority 1789-1861: A Study in Political Thought.* New York: New York University Press, 1930.

Casto, Stanley D. *Settlement of the Cibolo-Nueces Strip: A Partial History of La Salle County.* No. 2 of Hill Junior College Monographs in Texas and Confederate History. Waco: Texian, 1969.

Chabot, Frederick C. *Genealogies of Early San Antonio Families: With the Makers of San Antonio.* San Antonio: privately published through Artes Graficas, 1937.

"Contemporary Austrian Views of American Independence: A Documentary on the Occasion of the Bicentennial." *Austrian Information,* 29. Austrian Information Service, April 1976.

Coulter, E. Merton. *The Confederate States of America.* Baton Rouge: Louisiana State University Press, 1950.

Crews, Litha. "The Know Nothing Party in Texas." Master's degree thesis, University of Texas at Austin, 1925.

Cunningham, H. H. *Doctors in Gray: The Confederate Medical Service.* Baton Rouge: Louisiana State University Press, 1958.

Curlee, Abigail. "The History of a Texas Slave Plantation 1831-1863." In *Plantation, Town, and Country.* Ed. Elinor Miller and Eugene D. Genovese. Urbana: University of Illinois Press, 1974.

Dick, Everett. *The Dixie Frontier.* New York: Capricorn, 1964.

Dielmann, Henry B. "Emma Altgelt's Sketches of Life in Texas." *Southwestern Historical Quarterly* 63 (1959-1960), 363-384.

Duaine, Carl. L. *The Dead Men Wore Boots: An Account of the 32nd Texas Volunteer Cavalry C S A 1862-1865.* Austin: San Felipe Press, 1966.

Durzak, Manfred. "Nach Amerika. Gerstäckers Widerlegung der Lenau-Legende." In *Amerika in der deutschen Literatur: Neue Welt-Nordamerika-USA*. Ed. Sigrid Bauschinger, et. al. Stuttgart: Philipp Reclam jun., 1975.

Ehrenberg, H(ermann). *Der Freiheitskampf in Texas im Jahre 1836*. 4 vols. in 1. Leipzig: Otto Weigand, 1844.

Emmel, Hildegard. "Recht oder Unrecht in der Neuen Welt. Zu Charles Sealsfields Roman *Der Legitime und die Republikaner*." In *Amerika in der deutschen Literatur: Neue Welt-Nordamerika-USA*. Ed. Sigrid Bauschinger, et al. Stuttgart: Philipp Reclam jun., 1975.

Farber, James. *Texas C. S. A. : A Spotlight on Disaster*. New York and Texas: Jackson, 1947.

Farmer, Garland R., Sr. *The Realm of Rusk County*. Henderson, Texas: *Henderson Times*, 1951.

Faust, Albert Bernhardt. *The German Element in the United States: With Specific Reference to its Political, Moral, Social, and Educational Influence*. 2 vols. Boston and New York: Houghton Mifflin, 1909.

Fisher, O. C. *The Story of a Texas County: It Occurred in Kimble and How*. Houston: Anson Jones, 1937.

Fitzhugh, Lester N. *Texas Batteries, Battalions, Regiments, Commanders and Field Officers, Confederate States Army 1861-1865*. Midlothian, Texas: Mirror, 1959.

Flach, Vera. *A Yankee in German-America: Texas Hill Country*. San Antonio: Naylor, 1973.

Foik, Paul J. *Early Plans for the German Catholic Colonization in Texas*. 1934; rpt. Preliminary Studies of the Texas Catholic Historical Society, vol. 2, no. 6.

Fornell, Earl Wesley. *The Galveston Era: The Texas Crescent on the Eve of Secession*. Austin: University of Texas Press, 1961.

Freund, Max, ed. *Gustav Dresel's Houston Journal: Adventures in North America and Texas, 1837-1841*. Austin: University of Texas Press, 1954.

Friend, Llerena B. *Sam Houston: The Great Designer*. 1954; rpt. Austin: University of Texas Press, 1969.

Gardner, Robert E. *American Arms and Arms Makers*. Columbus, Ohio: College Book Co., 1944.

Geiser, Samuel Wood. *Naturalists of the Frontier*. Dallas: Southern Methodist University Press, 1937.

George, J. N. *English Pistols and Revolvers*. Onslow County, N. C.: Smallarms Technical Publishing Co., 1938.

The German Texans. The Texians and the Texans series. San Antonio: The University of Texas Institute of Texan Cultures, 1970.

Gorfer, Aldo. *Guida dei Castelli del Trentino*. Trent: Arti Grafica "Saturnia," 1965.

Graves, John. *Texas Heartland: A Hill Country Year*. Photographs by Jim Bones, Jr. College Station, Texas: Texas A & M University Press, 1975.

Grimes, Roy. *300 Years in Victoria County.* Victoria, Texas: *Victoria Advocate,* 1968.

Haas, Oscar. *The First Protestant Church: Its History and Its People 1845-1955.* New Braunfels, Texas: *New Braunfels Zeitung,* 1955.

_____. *History of New Braunfels and Comal County, Texas 1844-1946.* Austin: Steck, 1968.

Hall, Ada Maria. "The Texas Germans in State and National Politics 1850-1865." Master's degree thesis, University of Texas at Austin, 1938.

The Handbook of Texas. Vols. 1 and 2. Ed. Walter Prescott Webb and H. Bailey Carroll. Vol. 3 (supplement). Ed. Eldon Stephen Branda. Austin: Texas State Historical Association, 1952, 1976.

Handy, Mary Olivia. *History of Fort Sam Houston.* San Antonio: Naylor, 1951.

Haslip, Joan. *The Crown of Mexico: Maximilian and His Empress Carlotta.* New York: Holt Rinehart and Winston, 1971.

Hawgood, John A. *The Tragedy of German-America.* New York: Putnam, 1940.

Henderson, Harry McCorry. *Texas in the Confederacy.* San Antonio: Naylor, 1955.

Herff, Ferdinand Peter. *The Doctors Herff: A Three-Generation Memoir.* Ed. Laura L. Barber. San Antonio: Trinity University Press, 1973.

Hering, Julia Lee. "The Secession Movement in Texas." Master's degree thesis, University of Texas at Austin, 1933.

Historical Landmarks in and Around New Braunfels, Texas: A Bicentennial Guidebook. Spirit of '76 Committee, Mrs. Charles Ritter, Chairman. New Braunfels, 1976.

Hollon, W. Eugene, and Ruth Lapham Butler, eds. *William Bollaert's Texas.* No. 21 in The American Exploration & Travel series. Norman, Okla.: University of Oklahoma Press in co-operation with The Newberry Library, 1956.

"Horace M. Hall's Letters from Gillespie County, Texas, 1871-1873." Ed. Joseph S. Hall. *Southwestern Historical Quarterly* 62 (January 1959), 336-355.

Huebener, Theodore. *The Germans in America.* Philadelphia: Chilton, 1962.

Hughs, Fannie M. B. *Legends of Texas Rivers.* Dallas: Mathis, Von Nort, 1937.

Hyer, Julien. *The Land of Beginning Again: The Romance of the Brazos.* Atlanta: Tupper & Love, 1952.

Indianola Scrap Book. 1936; facs., with added index. Austin: San Felipe Press, 1974.

Jordan, Terry. *German Seed in Texas Soil: Immigrant Farmers in Nineteenth Century Texas.* Austin: University of Texas Press, 1966.

Justman, Dorothy Eckel. *German Colonists and Their Descendants in Houston Including Usener and Allied Families.* Quanah and Wichita Falls, Texas: Nortex, 1974.

Kapp, Friedrich. *Immigration and the Commissioners of Emigration.* 1870; rpt. New York: Arno Press and *New York Times,* 1969.

Kapp, Ida Cappel. "Briefe aus der Comalstadt 1850." Ed. Alex Brinkmann. *Neu-Braunfelser Zeitung Jahrbuch* 31 (1936), 15-38.

King, Irene Marschall. *John O. Meusebach: German Colonizer in Texas.* Austin: University of Texas Press, 1967.

Klein, Hugo. *Alt-Innsbrucker Gaststätten: Historische Plaudereien.* No. 222 in *Schlern-Schriften* series Innsbruck: Universitäts-verlag Wagner, 1962.

Klotzbach, W. and W. *Deutsche Pioniere in Texas.* Göttingen: W. Fischer, 1974.

Knapp, David. *The Confederate Horseman.* New York: Vantage, 1966.

Kneipp, Sebastian. *My Will: A Legacy to the Healthy and the Sick.* ["Only copyrighted and complete English edition, translated from the 12th German edition."] Kempten, Bavaria: Jos. Koesel, 1897.

Koerner, Gustav. *Das deutsche Element in den Vereinigten Staaten von Nordamerika 1818-1848.* Cincinnati: Wilde, 1880.

_____. *Ein Lebensbild.* Cincinnati: H. A. Rattermann, 1902.

_____. *Memoirs of Gustav Koerner (1809-1896).* 2 vols. Ed. Thomas McCormack. Cedar Rapids: Torch, 1909.

Kotler, Norman, ed. *Texas: A Picture Tour.* Intro. Lon Tinkle. New York: Scribner's Sons.

Krueger, M(ax). *Pioneer Life in Texas: An Autobiography.* Privately printed; 1925.

Kunert, Günter. Foreword to *Nikolaus Lenau: Gedichte.* Frankfurt a. M.: Fischer, 1969.

Landa, Harry. *As I Remember.* San Antonio: Carleton Printing Co., 1945.

Lea, Tom. *The King Ranch.* 2 vols. Boston: Little, Brown & Co., 1957.

Lich, Glen E. and Dona B. Reeves, eds. *German Culture in Texas: A Free Earth; Essays from the 1978 Southwest Symposium.* Boston: Twayne, 1980.

Löher, Franz von. *Geschichte and Zustände der Deutschen in Amerika.* Cincinnati: Eggers and Wulkop, 1847.

Lonn, Ella. *Desertion During the Civil War.* New York and London: Century, 1928.

_____. *Foreigners in the Confederacy.* Gloucester, Mass.: P. Smith, 1965.

McComb, David G. *Houston, the Bayou City.* Austin: University of Texas Press, 1969.

McGuire, James Patrick. *Iwonski in Texas: Painter and Citizen.* San Antonio: San Antonio Museum Association with the co-operation of the University of Texas at San Antonio Institute of Texan Cultures, 1976.

Malsch, Brownson. *Indianola: The Mother of Western Texas.* Austin: Shoal Creek, 1977.

Meusebach, John O. *Answer to Interrogatories in Case No. 396.* 1894; rpt. Austin: Pemberton, 1964.

Moore, Albert Burton. *Conscription and Conflict in the Confederacy.* New York: Hillary House, 1924.

Monuments Erected to Commemorate the Centenary of Texas Independence: The Report of the Commission of Control For Texas Centennial Celebrations. Compiled by Harold Schoen. Austin, 1938.

Muir, Andrew Forest, ed. *Texas in 1837: An Anonymous, Contemporary Narrative.* Austin: University of Texas Press, 1958.

Musulin, Stella. *Vienna in the Age of Metternich: From Napoleon to Revolution 1805-1848.* Boulder, Colo.: Westview Press, 1975.

Neale, William, and William A Neale. *A Century of Conflict 1821-1913: Incidents in the Lives of William Neale and William A. Neale, Early Settlers of South Texas.* Ed. John C. Rayburn and Virginia Kemp Rayburn, assisted by Ethel Neale Fry. Waco: Texian, 1966.

Newcomb, William W., Jr., and Mary S. Carnahan. *German Artist on the Texas Frontier: Friedrich Richard Petri.* Austin & London: University of Texas Press in collaboration with Texas Memorial Museum, 1978.

Noel, Theophilus. *A Campaign From Santa Fe To the Mississippi: Being a History of the Old Sibley Brigade.* 1865; rpt. Ed. Martin Hall and Edwin Adams Davis. Houston, Stagecoach, 1961.

Oates, Stephen B. *Confederate Cavalry West of the River.* Austin: University of Texas Press, 1961.

Olmsted, Frederick Law. *A Journey Through Texas: A Saddle-Trip on the Southwestern Frontier.* 1857; rpt., rev. by James Howard. Austin: Von Boeckmann-Jones, 1962.

Pickrell, Annie Doom. *Pioneer Women in Texas.* Austin: Pemberton Press, 1970.

Pierce, Gerald S. *Texas Under Arms.* Austin: Encino, 1969.

Pioneers in God's Hills. Gillespie County Historical Society. Austin: Von Boeckmann-Jones, 1960.

Polk, Stella Gipson. *Mason and Mason County.* Austin: Pemberton, 1966.

Pollard, E. A. *Southern History of the War.* 2 vols. in 1. New York: Charles B. Richardson, 1866.

Ragsdale, Crystal Sasse. *The Golden Free Land.* Austin: Landmark, 1976.

Ransleben, Guido E. *One Hundred Years of Comfort in Texas: A Centennial History.* San Antonio: Naylor, 1954.

Reinhardt, Louis. "The Communistic Colony of Bettina." *The Quarterly of the Texas State Historical Association* 3 (July 1899), 33-40.

Rippley, La Vern J. *The German-Americans.* Boston: Twayne, 1976.

Robinson-Zwahr, Robert. *The Bremers and Their Kin in Germany and in Texas (Die Bremerverwandtschaft in Deutschland und in Texas).* Vol. 1. Wichita Falls, Texas: Nortex, 1977. Vol. 2. Burnet, Texas: Nortex, 1979.

Roeder, Ralph. *Juarez and his Mexico.* New York: Viking, 1947.

Roemer, Ferdinand. *Roemer's Texas 1845 to 1847.* Trans. and ed. Oswald Mueller. 1935; rpt. Waco: Texian, 1967.

Rolle, Andrew F. *The Lost Cause: The Confederate Exodus to Mexico.* Norman, Okla.: University of Oklahoma Press, 1965.

Rose, Victor M. *Some Historical Facts in Regard to the Settlements of Victoria, Texas: Its Progress and Present Status.* Laredo: *Daily Times,* 1883.

Rosebush, Waldo E. *American Firearms and the Changing Frontier.* Spokane: Eastern Washington Historical Society, 1963.

Rosenberg, W. von. *Kritik der Geschichte des Vereins zum Schutze der Deutschen Auswanderer nach Texas (The German Emigration Company) wie sie im "Auswanderer" Jahrgang 1894 (#127 und #129) vorgetragen ist. Mit dem ausgesprochenen Zwecke, die Beschuldigung, der Verein habe im Interesse der englischen Regierung die Auswanderer nach Texas gelenkt, und sei dafür von derselben bezahlt worden, also unwahr aufzudecken.* Austin: Dec. 1894.

Rosengarten, J. G. *The German Soldier in the Wars of the United States.* 2nd ed. Philadelphia: Lippincott, 1890.

Ross, Colin. *Unser Amerika: Der Deutsche Anteil an den Vereinigten Staaten.* Leipzig: Brockhaus, 1936.

Santleben, August. *A Texas Pioneer: Early Staging and Overland Freighting Days on the Frontier of Texas and Mexico.* Ed I. D. Affleck. 1910; facs. Waco: W. M. Morrison, 1967.

Schiwetz, E. M. *Buck Schiwetz's Texas.* Intro. Walter Prescott Webb. Austin: University of Texas Press, 1960.

Seele, Hermann. *Die Cypresse und Gesammelte Schriften.* New Braunfels, Texas: *Neu-Braunfelser Zeitung,* 1936.

_____. *The Cypress and Other Writings of a German Pioneer in Texas.* Trans. Edward C. Breitenkamp. No. 9 in the Elma Dill Russell Spencer Foundation series. Austin and London: University of Texas Press, 1979.

Siemering, August. "Die lateinische Ansiedlung in Texas." Trans. C. W. Geue. *Texana* 5 (September 1967), 126-131.

Smith, Cole Vernon. "New Braunfels, Texas, 1845-1965: A Sociological Study." Master's degree thesis, Trinity University, San Antonio, 1963.

Smyrl, Frank H. "Unionism in Texas, 1856-1861." *Southwestern Historical Quarterly* 68 (October 1964), 172-195.

Solms-Braunfels, Prince Carl von. *Texas 1844-1845.* Anon. trans. Houston: Anson Jones, 1936.

Sowell, A. J. *History of Fort Bend County.* 1904; facs. Waco: W. M. Morrison, 1964.

Speer, John W. *A History of Blanco County.* Ed. Henry C. Armbruster. Austin: Pemberton, 1965.

Spiel, Hilde, ed. *The Congress of Vienna: An Eyewitness Account,* with introduction. Philadelphia: Chilton, 1968.

Stambaugh, J. Lee and Lillian J. Stambaugh. *The Lower Rio Grande Valley of Texas.* San Antonio: Naylor, 1954.

Stampp, Kenneth M. *The Era of Reconstruction 1865-1877.* New York: Vintage, 1965.

Stern, Madeleine B. *Purple Passage: The Life of Mrs. Frank Leslie.* Norman, Oklahoma: University of Oklahoma Press, 1953.

Stieghorst, Junann J. *Bay City and Matagorda County: A History.* Austin: Pemberton, 1965.

Tausch, Egon Richard. "Southern Sentiment Among the Texas Germans During the Civil War." Master's degree thesis, University of Texas at Austin, 1965.

Terrell, Alexander Watkins. *From Texas to Mexico and the Court of Maximilian in 1865.* Dallas: The Book Club of Texas, 1933.

Tiling, Moritz. *The German Element in Texas, 1820-1850, and Historical Sketches of the German Texas Singers League and Houston Turnverein, 1853-1913.* Houston: n. p., 1913.

Urbantke, Carl. *Texas Is the Place For Me.* Austin: Pemberton, 1970.

Walker, Stanley. *The Dallas Story.* Reprint of *Times Herald* Dallas Centennial Edition of 5 February 1956. Dallas: *Times Herald,* 1956.

Wallace, Ernest. *Texas in Turmoil.* No. 4 in The Saga of Texas 1849-1875 series. Austin: Steck-Vaughn, 1965.

Wandruszka, Adam. *Das Haus Habsburg: Die Geschichte einer europäischen Dynastie.* 2nd ed. Vienna: Verlag für Geschichte und Politik, 1956.

Weber, Adolf Paul. *Deutsche Pioniere: Zur Geschichte des Deutschtums in Texas.* San Antonio: n. p., 1894.

Wharton, Clarence. *Wharton's History of Fort Bend County.* Houston: Anson Jones, 1950.

Whittington, George Purwell. *Rapides Parish Louisiana: A History.* 1932; rpt. Baton Rouge: Franklin, n.d.

Wight, Levi Lamoni. *The Reminiscences and Civil War Letters of Levi Lamoni Wight: Life in a Mormon Splinter Colony of the Texas Frontier.* Ed. David Bitton. Salt Lake City: University of Utah Press, 1970.

Winfrey, Dorman H. *A History of Rusk County, Texas.* Special ed. Waco: Texian, 1961.

Winston, George. "Medicines for the Union Army." Madison, Wisconsin: American Institute of the History of Pharmacy, 1962.

Winters, John D. *The Civil War in Louisiana.* Baton Rouge: Louisiana State University Press, 1963.

Wipprecht, Rudolph. *The Texas Gun Collector* 20 (March 1952).

Wittke, Carl. *Refugees of Revolution: The German Forty-Eighters in America.* Philadelphia: University of Pennsylvania Press, 1952.

Woodman, David, Jr. *Guide to Texas Emigrants.* 1835; rpt., with preface by Dorman H. Winfrey. Waco: Texian, 1974.

Woodward, Joseph Janvier. *Outlines of Chief Camp Diseases of the U. S. Armies as Observed During the Present War.* Philadelphia: Lippincott, 1863.

Wurzbach, Emil Frederick. *Life and Memoirs of Emil Frederick Wurzbach to which is appended some Papers of John Meusebach.* Trans. Franz J. Dohmen, with preface by Frederick C. Chabot. San Antonio: Yanaguana Society, 1937.

Young, S. O. *A Thumb-Nail History of the City of Houston Texas from its founding in 1836 to the year 1912.* Houston: Rein & Sons Press, 1912.

Atlases/Encyclopedias/Indexes/Lists

An Illustrated Historical Atlas of St. Clair County, Illinois. Compiled, drawn and published from personal examinations and surveys by Warner & Beers. Chicago: n. p., 1874.

Arndt, Karl J., and May E. Olson. *German-American Newspapers and Periodicals 1732-1955: History and Bibliography.* Heidelberg: Quelle & Meyer, 1961.

Büchman, Georg. *Geflügelte Worte: Zitatenschatz des Deutschen Volkes.* 31st ed. Berlin: Haude & Spener, 1964.

"Coreth." In *Deutsche Grafen-Haeuser der Gegenwart in heraldischer, historischer und genealogischer Beziehung.* Vol. 1. Ed. Ernst Heinrich Kneschke. Leipzig: Weigel, 1852.

"Coreth." In *Genealogisches Handbuch des Adels: Gräfliche Häuser.* Limburg a. d. Lahn: Starcke, 1955, 1967.

"Coreth." In *Gothaisches Taschenbuch der Gräflichen Haüser.* Gotha: Justus Perthes, 1872, 1876, 1902.

"Frank Leslie." In *The Columbia Encyclopedia.* Ed. W. Bridgwater and E. J. Sherwood. 2nd ed. New York: Columbia University Press, 1950.

Friedrich, Wolf. *Moderne Deutsche Idiomatik.* Munich: Max Hueber, 1966.

Geue, Chester W. and Ethel Hander Geue, eds. and compilers. *A New Land Beckoned: German Immigration to Texas, 1844-1847.* Waco: Texian, 1966.

Geue, Ethel Hander, ed. and compiler. *New Homes in a New Land: German Immigration to Texas 1847-1861.* Waco: Texian, 1970.

Gilbert, Glenn G. *Linguistic Atlas of Texas German.* No. 5 in *Deutscher Sprachatlas: Regionale Sprachatlanten* series. Austin: University of Texas Press, 1972.

"Hungary." In *The Encyclopedia Britannica.* Chicago: Encyclopedia Britannica, 1951.

Index to the Cemeteries of San Augustine County, Texas 1863-1964. J. B. Sanders, compiler. Center, Texas: privately published through *The Champion,* 1964.

The Laws of Texas, 1822-1897. 10 vols. H. P. N. Gammel, compiler. Austin; n. p., 1898.

Miller, Thomas Lloyd. *Bounty and Donation Land Grants of Texas 1836-1888.* Austin: University of Texas Press, 1967.

Schultz, Arthur R., ed. *Bibliography of German Culture in America to 1940.* Henry A. Pochmann, compiler. Madison: University of Wisconsin, 1953.

Simpson, Harold B., ed. *Texas in the War 1861-1865.* Marcus Wright, compiler. Waco: Texian, 1965.

Texas in the Civil War: A Résumé History. Austin: Texas Civil War Centennial Commission, 1961.

Tiroler Adelsmatrikel: Nachtragsheft zum Mitgliederverzeichnis 1950.
Innsbruck: printed by "Tyrolia" for the Matrikel-kollegium, 1952.
"Wilderness campaign." In *The Columbia Encyclopedia.* Ed. W. Bridg-
water and E. J. Sherwood. 2nd ed. New York: Columbia University
Press, 1950.
Wood, Horatio C., et al., eds. *The Dispensatory of the United States of
America.* 23rd ed. Philadelphia: Lippincott, 1943.
Works Progress Administration index to newspapers of Belleville, Illi-
nois. Public Library, Belleville, Illinois.
City Directories of Belleville and West Belleville, Illinois; Galveston and
San Antonio, Texas.
Texas State Archives Indexes/Lists:
  Index to Applications for Texas Confederate Pensions.
  Index of Personnel on Confederate Muster Rolls; especially regarding
  Ernst Hermann Altgelt, Carl Coreth, Johann Coreth, Hermann
  Kämmerling.
  Index of Military Units formed in Texas during the War Between the
  States: Caney Mounted Rifles election of officers, no. 961; Caney
  Mounted Rifles muster rolls, no. 325; Hobby's Regiment, no. 95 and
  no. 306; Hood's Fourth Texas Infantry Brigade, no. 1149. Ireland's
  Co. (Guadalupe County), no. 306; R. H. Mathews's Co. Active Ri-
  flemen (Navarro County), no. 422.
  Ships' passenger lists, Port of Galveston, second quarter 1850; Genea-
  logical Department; on microfilm.
  Agricultural Schedules, Comal County, for 1860, 1870, and 1880; Ge-
  nealogical Department; on microfilm.

Dictionaries/Lexica

Brockhaus Illustrated German-English/English-German Dictionary.
New York: McGraw-Hill, 1960.
Bustamante, F. Corona. *Spanish-English Dictionary.* Paris: Garnier
Bros., 1905.
Cassell's Italian Dictionary: Italian-English/English-Italian. New
York: Funk & Wagnalls, 1967.
Cassell's New French-English/English-French Dictionary. New York:
Funk & Wagnalls, 1930.
Cassell's New German and English Dictionary. New York: Funk &
Wagnalls, 1939.
Merino-Rodriguez, Manuel. *Elsevier's Lexicon of Parasites and Dis-
eases in Livestock: Latin/English/French/Italian/Spanish/German.*
Amsterdam: Elsevier, 1964.
The Oxford Classical Dictionary. 2nd ed. Oxford: Clarendon Press, 1970.
Servotte, J. V. *Wörterbuch Für Handel und Finanzwesen: French/Ger-
man/English.* 3rd ed. Offenburg, Baden: Dokumente, 1964.
Traupmann, John C. *The New College Latin & English Dictionary.* New
York: Grosset & Dunlap, 1966.

Wahrig, Gerhard. *Deutsches Wörterbuch.* Gütersloh: Bertelsmann, 1968.
Webster's New International Dictionary. 2nd unabr. ed. Springfield, Mass.: G. & C. Merriam, 1934.
Weiman, Ralph. *Common Usage Dictionary: French-English/English-French.* Rev. ed. New York: Crown, 1955.

Newspapers/Popular Periodicals

Deutsch-texanische Monatschefte (publ. San Antonio 1895-1908?), as available in Special Collections, Library of The University of Texas at Arlington.
Galveston Tri-Weekly, on microfilm, as available at Rosenberg Library, Galveston; especially issue of 28 March 1873 (death notice of Amalia Coreth Goldmann).
Galveston Union, as available in Archives Dept., Rosenberg Library, Galveston.
Democratic Telegraph and Texas Register (publ. Houston), as available at main Houston Public Library; especially issues of 2 Sept., 16 Sept., 23 Sept., 30 Sept., 7 Oct., 21 Oct., 26 Oct., 2 Nov., 23 Nov., 30 Nov., and 7 Dec. 1846; 4 Jan. 1847; 21 Dec. 1848.
Fort Worth Star-Telegram, issue of 5 Aug. 1978 (Patsy Miller, "Collectors help chronicle development of the West," Section C, p. 1).
Neu-Braunfelser Zeitung and its successor, *New Braunfels Zeitung,* as available at Emmy Seele Faust Library (archives), New Braunfels; especially issues of 21 Nov. 1873 (politics in Texas), 3 July 1874 (Anselm Eiband, "Noch einmal eine deutsche Convention," p. 2), 15 July 1881 (obituary of Ernst Coreth), 19 April 1888 obituary of Agnes Erler Coreth), 24 October 1901 (obituary of Rudolph Coreth), 24 November 1904 (destruction by fire of Franz A. Coreth home at Mission Hill), and 27 January 1921 (obituary of Franz A. Coreth). Also special edition commemorating end of 80th year of publication, 15 December 1931; and "DeLuxe Edition" commemorating 100th anniversary of publication, 21 August 1952.
Neu-Braunfelser Zeitung Jahrbuch (1936), for Ida Cappel Kapp, "Briefe aus der Comalstadt," pp. 15-38.
Neu-Braunfelser Zeitung Jahrbuch (1938), for list of members of Podewils's Co. F and their home counties, pp. 20-21, and for passenger lists of some immigrant ships. See p. 31 for Coreths.
San Antonio Express, on microfilm at main San Antonio Public Library; especially issues of 4 March 1928 (article on German-English School) and 28 January 1932 (obituary of Anna Coreth Marschall).
San Antonio Semi-Weekly News, as available on microfilm at main San Antonio Public Library; especially issues of 10 April 1862 (notice from Adj. Gen. Off. mentioning Lt. Clute of Houston), 21 June 1862 (Texas Arsenal advertisement for brown paper), 9 February 1863 (column on Capt. W. G. M. Samuel), 11 May 1863 (Woods's men entered Brownsville), 1 October 1863 (War Meeting at San Pedro Springs), and 24 March 1865 (notice of Carl Münzenberger's creditors).

San Jose (California) *Mercury-News,* issue of 14 October 1973 (Majorie Pierce, "Their Own Private World," regarding Dr. Ed. Goldmann and "Villa Bergstedt").

Unpublished papers

Douai, Adolf. "Autobiography," unpublished typescript. Translated and edited by Richard H. Douai Boerker. Main San Antonio Public Library.

"The Dresel Family," unpublished typescript with photographs. Complied by Clyde H. Porter. Main San Antonio Public Library.

"The Exile," unpublished (?) typescript. Anonymous. From private files of Oscar Haas; New Braunfels, Texas. Spiess family papers.

Selected records, articles, etc. concerning Ernst Kapp family and Sisterdale. From private files of Samuel Woolvin; Sisterdale, Texas.

Official Records

Certificate of "especially satisfactory" discharge from Austrian army, First Uhlan Regiment of the Duke of Sachsen-Coburg, issued to Ernst Graf Correth von Corredo (sic); confirmed 27 Jan. 1831, effective 1 Jan. 1832 (original held by Franz Ernst Coreth).

The War of the Rebellion: A Compilation of the Official Records of the Union and Confederate Armies. Washington, D.C.: Govt. Printing Off. Series 1, vol. 34 (1891), pt. 1, pp. 425, 428, and 441; and pt. 3, pp. 192, 725, 755-6, 804-5, and 833-4.

Court Records:

District Court Minutes, New Braunfels

Records C, p. 7 (Ernst Coreth granted citizenship); p. 110 (Charles H. Coreth granted citizenship); p. 239 (Rudolf Coreth granted citizenship). Records D, p. 22, Continuation of Records C, p. 692, which concern the proceedings in Case No. 369, *Tolle vs. Coreth,* and which are missing. Grand jury list of March 1858 (Ernst Coreth a juror). General election returns for 6 November 1888, 4 November 1890, 8 November 1892, 6 November 1894, 3 November 1896, 8 November 1898, 6 November 1900, and 4 November 1902. In all but the last, Franz A. Coreth was the successful candidate for tax assessor of the county. In 1894 Rudolf Coreth was also the successful candidate for county commissioner of precinct #1, his only candidacy for public office.

Supreme Court of Texas: *Tolle v. Correth,* 31 Tex. 362 (1868).

Circuit Court, 20th Judicial Circuit; Belleville, St. Clair County, Illinois. Bill in Chancery, Divorce Decree. *Rudolph Coreth vs. Jane Coreth.*

Deed Records:

Bexar County, Texas

Vol. 1, p. 459. Vol. T3, pp. 203 and 380. Vol. 11, p. 275.

Comal County, Texas

Bk. A, pp. 166, 197, 198, and 602. Bk. C, p. 416. Bk. E, p. 206. Bk. F,

p. 311. Bk. G, p. 150. Bk. O, pp. 97-98. Bk. P, pp. 347-348. Bk. R, pp. 288-290. Bk. T, pp. 450-451, 454-456. Bk. U, pp. 11-12. Bk. 51, pp. 542-543, pp. 631-632.
Gillespie County, Texas
Vol. F, pp. 33-34.
Harris County, Texas
Vol. L, pp. 137-139. Vol. O, p. 21. Vol. P, p. 704. Vol. 28, pp. 444-448.
St. Clair County, Illinois
Bk. 133, p. 167 (Agreement of Copartnership between Rudolph Coreth, Henry Lippert, George C. Bunsen, and John Brandenburger [silent partner]).
General Land Office Records:
Certificate no. 987, claiming title to 640 acres, for Ernst Correth (sic). Claim no. 143 as signed 22 Jan. 1847 and no. 217 as validated 8 Oct. 1854.
Letter Patent no. 195 and Field Notes, surveys no. 47 and no. 48, dist. 6; vol. 10, no. 195, and as recorded bk. G, no. 2, pp. 527-528 in Bexar District files.
Immigrant Contract (*Einwanderervertrag*) between Ernst Graf Coreth and *Verein zum Schutze deutscher Einwanderer in Texas*; signed at Antwerp, 8 August 1846.
Marriage Records; Comal County, Texas:
Bk. C, no. 226 (Adolph Münzenberger and Hedwig Boehme); no. 238 (Carl Coreth and Hedwig Kapp); and no. 265 (Hermann Schimmelpfennig and Auguste Tolle).
Book in Probate Matters; Comal County, Texas:
Vol. 1, pp. 335-336 (Hedwig Coreth's petition for deceased husband's estate with inventory and appraisal thereof).
Bk. G, pp. 149-151 (Ernst Coreth's last will and testament).
Bk. L, p. 420 (Rudolph Coreth's last will and testament; also copy of Report of the Death of an American Citizen, from Consul General of the United States).
City Records:
Records of Interments in Galveston, Texas; p. 157 (March 1873; death of Amalia Goldmann). Available at Archives Dept., Rosenberg Library, Galveston.
Church Records:
Filialkirche Oberalm/Decanat und Stadtpfarr Hallein (near Salzburg, Austria; record books lost; handwritten and officially stamped copies of certificates held by Minetta A. Goyne). Folio (?) 80, "Haus" (house) 121: Karl (sic) Coreth; copied October 1837 (day missing). Amalia; copied from book of baptisms 19 October 1841. Johann de Deo Ernest Ignatz Coreth; copied 7 July 1846.
Annunciation Church, Houston, Texas; depository for records of first Catholic church in Houston. Saddle Bag Record Book of Bishop Jean Marie Odin, Baptisms 1841-1860: #104 Franz Alcad Traugott (?) Coreth. Copied into Baptisms, St. Vincent de Paul Church as #102.
St. Peter & Paul's Church; New Braunfels, Texas. Baptismal Records,

vol. 1, p. 46: #4 Josephus Ernestus Graf Coreth; #5 Anna Gräfin Coreth; #6 Ernestus Otfridus O. Meusebach; #7 Otto Carolus O. Meusebach; and p. 143, #15 Ottilie Francisca Emmane Coreth.

For the convenience of the reader, acceptable English translations that are known to exist are listed in the bibliography rather than the German originals.

INDEX

Military ranks and affiliations, particularly among officers, changed frequently at this period. Those interested in the activities of a particular unit should see references given with the name of the commanding officer or officers.

Prairie Point, in south central Tex.:
105
Preston, Walter P.: 145, 239 (n. 1),
248 (n. 11)
Price, Sterling: 84, 129, 131
Prose: 141
Puls, Henry: 92, 227 (n. 5)
Pyron, Charles L.: 112, 118-20, 232
(n. 12)

Quintana, Tex.: 22, 44, 56

Railways: 19, 20, 75, 109-10, 179, 186,
194-95,, 201, 203-04, 212 (n. 12),
215 (n. 2), 223 (n. 3), 231 (n. 6), 241
(n. 1), 251 (n. 2)
Rake Pocket, Tex.: 159, 241 (n. 1)
Reif[f]ert, Emil: 99, 223-24 (n. 8),
227-28 (n. 10)
Rhenhaus family murder: 134
R[h]odius, Christoph: 69, 161
Richmond, Tex. (camp above): 158,
162, 165-66, 168-71, 174-75
Richter store in San Antonio: 180
Rio Grande River: 38, 67, 81, 84-5,
115, 141, 232 (n. 8)
River Road (La.): 157
(Camp on the) Rocky/Post Gonzales:
89, 92, 94, 96, 227 (n. 1)
Rochette, Jean Alcad: 2, 207 (n. 6)
von Roeder family: 98, 103, 115, 129,
139, 227 (n. 9), 233 (n. 18)
Rose, Jacob: 61
Rossly, Alex: iii
Rueckert, Carl: 59
Rugeley, Alex: 112, 232 (n. 11)
Rugeley, Edward S. ("Ned"): 22, 26,
28, 31, 33, 35, 38, 42-5, 49-51, 113,
213 (n. 22), 217 (n. 21, 22), 219 (n.
10), 232-33 (n. 16)
Rump[f], J. E./I. E.: 20, 22, 212 (n.
14)
Runge family: 33, 71, 84, 99, 147, 149,
167, 180, 193, 203, 212 (n. 15), 215
(n. 2), 223 (n. 3), 223-24 (n. 8), 227-
28 (n. 40), 240 (n. 6), 243 (n. 16)
Russia: 78, 202

Sabine Crossroads, Battle of: see
Mansfield, La.
Sabine Pass, Tex.: 18, 107-09, 151,
231 (n. 3)
Camp Salado: 18, 53-4, 57-8

Saltpeter factory, vicinity of New
Braunfels: 104, 150, 228 (n. 19)
Saluria, Tex.: 112-13
Salzburg, Austria: 8
Samuel, W. G. M.: 60, 220 (n. 17)
San Antonio, Tex.: 1, 10-11, 13, 15,
18-9, 54, 58, 60, 66-8, 70, 92, 94, 97,
104, 114, 126, 134, 145, 161, 203-04,
224 (n. 13), 229 (n. 21), 233 (n. 26),
239 (n. 4), 244 (n. 24)
San Augustine, Tex.: 127, 130, 155-57,
159, 240 (n. 13)
Sandy/Sandies/Sandis Creek, Tex.:
55-6
San Felipe, Tex.: 123, 170, 174
San Fernando, Tex. (camp on): 87, 92
San Marcos, Tex.: 61, 64, 172, 229 (n.
22); see also Hutchison and Woods.
San Patricio, Tex.: 80, 247 (n. 7)
Santa Clara Creek (Tex.): 172, 243 (n.
20)
Santleben stagecoach: 197
Scheel[e] family: 54
v. Schenck sisters, Natalie and
Antoinette: 197, 212 (n. 18), 248 (n.
17)
Scherff family: 92, 94, 97, 145
Schimmelpfennig family: 67, 71-2, 75,
79, 98, 101, 107, 116, 125-26, 141,
153, 159-60, 167, 170, 220 (n. 16),
237 (n. 24)
Schleicher, Gustav: 13, 135, 212 (n.
11)
Schloß Aschach, near Innsbruck: 12,
209 (n. 32)
Schloß Coredo, in the southern
Tyrol: 5
Schloß Friedberg, near Innsbruck: 7
Schloß Kahlsperg, near Hallein: 8,
208 (n. 19), 209 (n. 32)
Schmidt, Wilhelm/Willem: 67-8, 71,
184, 245 (n. 14)
Schmitz family: 73, 103-04, 166, 228
(n. 17, 20)
Schmuck family: 69, 100
Schramm, Edgar: 64, 84, 90, 97, 124,
141, 147, 153, 158, 163, 165, 172,
188, 221 (n. 25)
Schuhard/Schuhart, vicinity of
Seguin, Tex.: 19, 75, 211 (n. 6)
Schulz: 170
Schulze family: 64, 76, 79-81, 83-4, 87,
97, 105, 111, 118-20, 122, 124, 127,